P9-DGU-376

WORLD

THE BATTLE FOR EVANGELISM

Arthur P. Johnston

Tyndale House
Publishers, Inc.
Wheaton, Illinois

Library of Congress Catalog
Card Number 78-51419.
ISBN 0-8423-0109-7, cloth;
0-8423-0101-1, paper.
Copyright © 1978
by Arthur P. Johnston.
All rights reserved.
First printing, March 1978.
Printed in the United States
of America

CONTENTS

CHAPTER ONE / THE DECLINE OF EVANGELISM / 21

FOREWORD

by Peter Beyerhaus

Arthur P. Johnston's study of the unfolding of two competitive theologies of evangelization—ecumenical versus evangelical—is more than a pioneering adventure in ideohistorical research It is a couragcous buuk written out of holy unrest that gives it a prophetic sound. It was not written primarily for academic purposes, although it bears the marks of sound scholarship. Its main objective is to provide a diagnosis of the causes for the fatal development in the ecumenical theology of missions from Edinburgh 1910 to New Delhi 1961, viz., Bangkok 1973, which necessitated the formation of a new evangelical counterpart by the two World Congresses on Evangelism in Berlin 1966 and Lausanne 1974.

Johnston's analysis is as succinct as sobering: Having departed from the unexchangeable reformation principles ("Scripture alone, Christ alone, grace alone, faith alone"), the IMC and its successor, the WCC's Commission on World Mission and Evangelism, allured themselves by fancy concepts like "Larger Evangelism" and "Cosmic Christ" and cnded up with "another Gospel" (Galatians 1:6, 9). The ecumenicals replaced lost mankind's eternal salvation from sin by tackling its sociopolitical needs and

proposing an earthly utopia as realization of God's coming
Kingdom. Thus the need for Berlin 1966 and Lausanne
1974 is established beyond doubt.

But this apologetic treatise expresses only the chief
aspect of Johnston's concern, which in fact he shares with
other evangelical spokesmen who have pointed out the
same fallacies. Even more exciting, however, is the other
aspect of his thrust, articulated in the latter part of his book
in the form of this question: Can we be assured that the
new "Fourth Evangelical Awakening," which gave birth to
Berlin, Lausanne, and its continuing International
Committee of World Evangelism, will not finally tumble
into the same pit? And here Johnston is far from becoming
a self-asserting evangelical triumphalist. On the contrary,
he makes us tremble by painstakingly drawing our
attention to seemingly small, highly significant indications
that at Lausanne and in its follow-up development, not all
points were reshifted to the original evangelical direction:
"Although no one can legitimately question the evangelical
theology of Lausanne, evangelism lost its earlier centrality.
Evangelism was blurred."

This verdict will provoke many evangelicals passionately
to object. Personally I must confess that my own constant
endeavors to scrutinize the theology of Lausanne and the
Guidelines of the Lausanne Committee, of which I am still
a member, have led me to rather similar conclusions. It is
particularly one new element, widely hailed by others as a
sign that the new Evangelicals have come of age, about
which I—like my friend Arthur Johnston—have argued
with my other beloved friend John Stott. For, unlike some
of our Latin American colleagues, I consider this element
as incompatible with the concept of evangelism as
normatively laid down in God's inspired Word, and as
expounded by both the Fathers of the Reformation and of
the Evangelical Awakening. I am referring to the *theological
coordination of evangelism and sociopolitical involvement* as
equally constitutive elements of our Christian duty, or
even—which is not the same—of the mission which Christ
gave to His Church.

If, in spite of urgent warnings, such concept of mission

(the semantic distinction beteeen "evangelism" and "mission" as allegedly comprising both evangelism and sociopolitical involvement is irrelevant here!) is adopted as the "Mandate of Lausanne," if the ideas of "holistic salvation" and of "radical discipleship" as necessary for authenticating the proclamation of the biblical Gospel (which, in reality, is self-authenticating), become integral for our new evangelical mission theology, then we might one day wake up to the shocking realization that we have broken down our doctrinal walls for importing ecumenical ideology in the belly of the Trojan horse!

This book of Arthur Johnston's will, no doubt, stir up a vital controversy within our evangelical ranks. It cannot and must not be bypassed by any responsible mission leader. Some may even deplore it as being divisive. But an imminent new division among evangelicals can and will be avoided if we heed the voice of this evangelical watchman.

FOREWORD
by Robert P. Evans

In this volume Arthur P. Johnston continues the study of the theology of evangelism begun in his earlier work, *World Evangelism and the Word of God.* To that task he brings both historical and theological tools. The documents of the ecumenical gatherings of this century are carefully examined. Similar scrutiny is given to the more recent, clearly evangelical congresses on evangelism beginning with the World Congress on Evangelism at Berlin in 1966. Both historic streams are contrasted with each other and considered in the light of the Bible's teachings on world evangelization.

The reader would do well to heed the author's advice to read the last four chapters only after weighing the historic antecedents outlined in the first four. He often cites precedents to warn evangelicals of compromises they made earlier in the century with deviations from biblical theology, to the detriment of their fulfillment of the Great Commission. Such compromises have been joined with extrabiblical concepts since the first century, and continued in our day.

Obviously the most controversial parts of the book are the discussions about the Berlin and Lausanne congresses and the post-Lausanne developments. Some evangelicals may not agree with Dr. Johnston's interpretation of the strengths and weaknesses of the Lausanne Covenant. Others may applaud emphasis on the inerrancy of Scripture as the central plank of a sound biblical theology of evangelism. Whatever the reader's reactions, he can be grateful for the viewpoints so sincerely and lucidly expressed.

As one who served on the organizing committees for the congresses at Berlin, Amsterdam, and Lausanne I am thankful for the continuing discussion of the issues raised in these gatherings, and of their theological implications in particular. A strong biblical doctrine of the theology of evangelism is essential to our evangelization of the world. It must be constantly restated in the light of contemporary events and attitudes. Dr. Johnston rightly insists that Jesus Christ is the only Savior, and the Word of God the inerrant revelation of His saving grace. As Christian believers and as members of His body, the church, we are individually and corporately responsible to finish the work He has committed to us. Sometimes the process involves conflict, as reflected in the title of this book.

FOREWORD
by Philip Teng

It is a general consensus that the Berlin Congress on Evangelism was the beginning of a revival of a sense of urgency in evangelism among Evangelicals throughout the world while the Lausanne Congress on World Evangelization has proved to be a great incentive to a general deep sense of responsibility for worldwide evangelization with a clarified direction. Both Congresses have awakened and strengthened a new consciousness of emphasis on biblical orientation in evangelism; a new understanding of the biblical nature of mission; a new emphasis on methodology in evangelism which is a meaningful combination of biblical principles, spiritual dynamics and modern technology; a new realization of their own missionary responsibility on the part of Third World church leaders; a new sense of identity among Bible-believing Christians and church leaders which has generated new vigor and optimism in evangelism and missions.

As chairman of Asian Missions Association and of The Association of Christian Missions in Hong Kong, I unreservedly acknowledge the decisive influence of Berlin and Lausanne on the formation of these organizations. Then, as chairman of The Chinese Congress on World Evangelization, held in 1976—attended by some 1600 participants from twenty-four countries including bishops, pastors, and lay leaders from both the major denominations and independent groups—I again testify gratefully to the undeniable fact that this Congress had its inspiration and origin in Lausanne as mentioned clearly in its declaration. We sensed a new interest and burden for evangelism and missions in all these new ventures.

While we remember Berlin and Lausanne with appreciation and gratitude, we are in need of a historical and theological analysis of these two Congresses against the background of major movements and developments in Christendom during the last decades. The timely appearance of Dr. Arthur P. Johnston's book provides a deeper and fuller understanding of these epoch-making events. We Christians in Asia will be much indebted to this book.

**CONTEMPORARY
EVANGELICAL AND
ECUMENICAL
CONFERENCES**

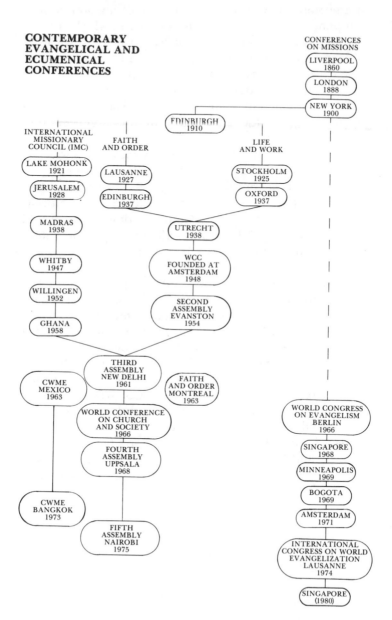

ACKNOWLEDGMENTS

I want to express sincere appreciation: to Billy Graham for the encouragement given to complete research on the theology of evangelism begun under the direction of the University of Strasbourg in 1968 and partially accomplished in my doctoral dissertation; to Dr. Victor Nelson of the Billy Graham Evangelistic Association, who provided resource material, wise counsel, and help over the past eighteen months of preparation.

I am also very grateful to scholarly colleagues who are friends and critics for their evaluations, corrections, and discernment: Drs. Kenneth Kantzer, Donald Hoke, George Marsden, and David Wells. However, failures in organization, style, structure, and content are mine. At certain points of disagreement, I have had to be true to myself and to the facts as I see them.

LIST OF ABBREVIATIONS

AEAM   Association of Evangelicals in Africa and Madagascar
BGEA   Billy Graham Evangelistic Association
CLADE   Latin American Congress on Evangelism
CWME   Commission of World Mission and Evangelism
DWME   Division of World Mission and Evangelism
EFAC   Evangelical Fellowship in the Anglican Communion
EID   Evangelism-in-Depth
ICOWE   International Congress on World Evangelization
IMC   International Missionary Council
LCWE   Lausanne Congress on World Evangelization
LTEG   Lausanne Theological Education Group
NCCC/DOM   National Council of Churches of Christ/Division of Overseas Ministries
SCM   Student Christian Movement
SVM   Student Volunteer Movement
WCC   World Council of Churches
WEF   World Evangelical Fellowship
WSCF   World Student Christian Federation
Y.M.C.A.   Young Men's Christian Association
Y.W.C.A.   Young Women's Christian Association

INTRODUCTION

The battles for world evangelism today represent a continuing world war that has been waged in one way or another throughout the centuries. Many in this generation are unaware of the theological battles in this century and their effect upon evangelism. Consequently they are inclined to think that the present battles are either Western in origin or irrelevant. It is difficult—if not impossible—to evaluate the present theological and practical issues of evangelism without an in-depth knowledge of what has transpired in this century.

This book focuses upon three main subjects. First, it attempts to show what is the evangelical message of the Gospel in contrast to the "social gospel" of the earlier decades of this century, to the "larger evangelism" of Madras (Tambaram) 1938 and to the "holistic evangelism" of this decade. This has been done by showing how evangelism declined when the message of the Gospel lost its source in a fully authoritative and infallible Bible. While many great servants of the Lord have proclaimed the Gospel in past decades, the messages and writings of Billy Graham have been liberally quoted as representative of an historical evangelicalism that can be traced back beyond American revivalism or the Reformation of the sixteenth century to the pages of the New Testament era. The international character of this message should be apparent. The Word of God is living and powerful in every nation of the world (Hebrews 4:12).

Second, the World Congress on Evangelism of 1966 held in Berlin represents a continuity in evangelism that has its roots in the New Testament as well. The great evangelistic and missionary movement of the last century was concluded by missionary conferences held in London 1888 and in New York 1900. The Edinburgh 1910 World Missionary Conference was no longer evangelical: the infallibility of Scripture was sacrificed for the principle of organizational unity. World evangelism would be accomplished, they thought, through an ecumenical movement. The drift of theological pluralism and progressive theology has led to the contemporary evangelistic sterility in the WCC. Berlin 1966 was a necessary result of a growing evangelical movement in the world and, consequently, can trace its immediate roots to New York 1900. When the Gospel is proclaimed in the power of the Spirit there will always be opposition, but God will bless His Word (Isaiah 55:10, 11).

Finally, the entire study culminates in the 1974 International Congress on World Evangelization held at Lausanne, Switzerland. Its evangelical impact upon world evangelization is most encouraging and the Lausanne Covenant has caught the attention of the major bodies of Christendom. By a study of the regional conferences between Berlin 1966 and Lausanne 1974 certain trends in evangelism and in evangelicalism itself may be discerned. Some of these theological trends are incorporated in the continuation committee of Lausanne 1974. Of special concern is the new understanding of the mission of the church. Historically the mission of the church is evangelism alone. The resultant trend from Lausanne seems to be a synthesis with the "holistic evangelism" of the WCC. In this the mission of the church is broadened beyond evangelism alone to evangelism and sociopolitical action. The final words of the resurrected Lord commanded world evangelism until He returns (Matthew 28:19, 20; 24:14).

A careful reading of the entire book is necessary to understand the historic progression of thought and the present trends in evangelicalism. The author is concerned that the redefinition of the mission of the church will distract from historic evangelical evangelism and, thereby, diminish *both* world evangelism and the by-products of evangelism in social and the political spheres of life in this world.

God has blessed world evangelization in this generation because His servants have been faithful to the evangelistic message of past generations. We are simply building upon that which we have received by the Holy Spirit from the Scriptures. The rising tide of evangelical evangelism will only continue through Evangelicals if we are faithful (Galatians 6:9).

Arthur P. Johnston
Trinity Evangelical Divinity School
Deerfield, Illinois

1
The
Decline of
Evangelism

The Berlin 1966 and Lausanne

1974 congresses were historical and theological
necessities. Conferences on evangelism and missions
seem to have solid biblical precedents. They have roots
not only in the past century-and-a-half, but also in earlier
church history. Certain periods have been marked by
intense evangelistic and missionary zeal, others by
apathy. This century has experienced a decline of
evangelism associated with the modernism and liberalism
introduced into Western Christianity during the
nineteenth century.

MISSIONARY CONFERENCES IN WORLD EVANGELIZATION

For well over one hundred years the missionary
conference has made a great contribution to world
evangelism. Christian missionaries have crossed
denominational and national lines in every continent to
seek inspiration and instruction, in order to better
accomplish the task the Lord of the Harvest committed

to them. Whether at home or abroad, Christians have gathered together in local churches, as denominations or as individuals concerned with the advance of the Gospel. These conferences have not only provided missionary manpower and financial support on the home front, but missionaries and national leaders of evangelism have also acquired deeper insights into the will and continuing work of the resurrected Lord (Acts 1:1).

Berlin 1966 and Lausanne 1974 stand among the great missionary and world evangelization conferences that reach back into the apostolic age. They were a revival of the missionary conferences in the last century. In Edinburgh 1910, there was a change in the character and pupose of the ecumenical missionary conferences. Contemporary evangelical and interdenominational conferences have renewed the former vision of the missionary conference because the leaders of these efforts are soundly anchored to the inspiration and authority of the Holy Scriptures. Without this sound foundation, these conferences become sterile—and biblical evangelism slowly diminishes.

IN THE NEW
TESTAMENT ERA

The entire ministry of Christ may be considered an evangelistic or missionary conference. Nevertheless, several occasions deserve particular attention: Jesus ordained the Twelve, sending them out to preach (Mark 3:14); the parable of the sower expressed the concern of Jesus for a fruitful evangelistic ministry by the proclamation of the Word (Mark 4:1-20); Jesus explained the worldwide responsibility of the disciples in terms of His second coming (Matt. 24); in the hours before His death, Jesus prepared the disciples for the adversities to be encountered in their mission to the world (John 14–16); Jesus' last resurrection appearances were conferences with a few, or many, concerning evangelism and world mission (John 20:19-29; Luke 24:36-49; Matt. 28:16-20; Mark 16:14-18; Acts 1:3-11).

The days of prayer before Pentecost may also be considered as a great prayer conference on evangelism that resulted in the first gathering of converts into the Church (Acts 2). The ministry of the Holy Spirit to the apostles and to the crowds of new believers stimulated a bold proclamation of the Word and a generosity to the cause of Christ that added further multitudes to the Lord (Acts 4:31; 5:14). The sending out of Barnabas and Paul and their report of the Gentile receptivity to the Antioch church were missionary conferences (Acts 13:1-3; 14:26-28).

While it may be difficult to conclude how many attended these "apostolic conferences," it easily may be seen that missionary and evangelism conferences have their roots in the life of Christ and the apostolic age.

IN THE POSTAPOSTOLIC ERA AND THE MIDDLE AGES

The evangelistic and missionary work of the first three centuries resulted in the spread of the Gospel throughout the Roman Empire. In the midst of frequent severe persecution, each assembly of believers appears to have become an evangelistic "conference"! Countless individuals zealously committed themselves to the evangelistic work as the well-known passage from Eusebius of Caesarea's *Ecclesiastical History* describes:

> They (the converts) began by following the Saviour's advice and distributing their goods to the poor. Then, leaving their country behind them, they went forth to fulfil their mission as evangelists, their ambition to preach the word of faith to those who had as yet heard nothing of it, and to hand on the books of the divine Gospel. They were content to lay the foundations of the faith among foreign peoples and then establish other pastors there, and to these they gave the task of nourishing those they

had brought to the faith. Having done so, they went
on to other lands and other nations by the grace
and with the help of God.

Without a doubt, the centers of Christianity that sprang
up during the first five hundred years at Rome,
Alexandria, Constantinople, North Africa, Lyon, and
Ireland were also outposts of evangelistic endeavor and
sources of information and inspiration. Growing
monasteries also contributed to the spread and stability
of the Gospel. In many nations of Europe, it seems that
"conversions" were imposed on the people by a ruler.
Nevertheless, evangelism retained its distinctly apostolic
character in the missionary efforts to reach all of Europe,
Russia, and even the Mongols and China by the
fourteenth century! In a later period, South American,
Dominican, Augustinian, Mercedarian, and Jesuit
missionaries met together for their first conference at
Lima, Peru, in 1552. They discussed the problems
among these orders, the teaching of the catechism, public
worship, language, study methods, and a national
priesthood. These questions also were considered at the
nineteenth-century evangelical interdenominational
missionary conferences.[1]

The division of the organized church in 1054 A.D. into
Eastern Orthodoxy and Western Roman Catholicism
ended the monarchical coordination and strategy of
world evangelism program centered at Rome. By the end
of the eighteenth century, missionary efforts in the
Western Church were reduced by colonial competition
between the Protestant European powers and Rome, and
also among Roman Catholic France, Spain, and
Portugal.[2]
The growth of Protestant missionary vigor in the
decades after William Carey entered India in 1793
revived the need for national interdenominational
conferences in mission lands. The missionary spirit that
for centuries spearheaded the growth of apostolic
Christianity within a united Christendom was again
released in the Evangelical and Pietist movements of the

nineteenth century. Evangelical missions greatly contributed to the "Great New Fact" of the twentieth century: the implantation of the Gospel in all continents of the world, and in almost every country. The missionary conference became a means in the modern age to advance the Gospel that cannot be restrained or contained by ecclesiological structures or harassed by organizational restrictions.

IN MODERN MISSIONARY HISTORY

Contemporary evangelical conferences on world evangelization, such as Lausanne 1974, owe much of their interdenominational character to the missionary conferences of the nineteenth century. One of the earliest brought together missionaries of various mission agencies at Bombay in 1825. Subsequent conferences in India 1872, China 1877, and Japan, each attracted representatives from the entire country.

The growing strength and importance of these conferences may be seen by comparing two conferences held in Shanghai. In 1877 there were 473 missionaries present from twenty different Protestant missionary societies; and in 1890, thirteen years later, there were 1,295 present—an increase of more than 270 percent. Subsequently, conferences of missions and evangelism took place in Africa, South America, and even the Middle East.

One might expect that the national conferences would grow to acquire a world dimension, and they did. National conferences were characterized by much prayer and provided spiritual refreshment, exchange of information, reports of growth, and an enlarged perspective of methods and objectives.

One of the first international missionary conferences of the sending countries was held in New York City, November 4 and 5, 1854, when the great English missionary statesman Alexander Duff inspired a cooperative effort to promote missions. The questions proposed by a committee reflected the continuing concerns of evangelistic missions:

1. "To what extent are we authorized by the Word of God to expect the conversion of the world to Christ?" (eschatology)

2. "What are the divinely appointed and most efficient means of extending the Gospel of salvation to all men?" (methods of evangelism)

3. "Is it best to concentrate laborers in the foreign field or to scatter them?" (field strategy)

4. "In view of the great extent of the heathen world, and the degree to which it is opened, is it expedient for different missionary boards to plant stations on the same ground?" (comity)

5. "How may the number of qualified laborers for the evangelization of the world be multiplied and best prepared?" (missionary recruitment and education) .

6. "How may the cooperation of all our congregations be best secured to aid in the spread of the Gospel?" (missionary support)

7. "How can missionary intelligence be most extensively circulated among the churches?" (communications with sending churches)

8. "Is it expedient to hold such a meeting as this annually?" (continuation committees)[3]

The Centenary Conference on Foreign Missions, held in London, June 1, 1888, brought together 1,576 missionaries and missionary representatives of 140 mission agencies. The impact of this conference upon the public of Great Britain was so great that missionary giving increased by 40 percent between 1888 and 1890. On that occasion, Gustav Warneck of Germany proposed a Standing Central International Committee composed of representatives elected by the National Missionary Conference of each land.[4]

The primary object of London 1888 was neither to stir up mass excitement nor to legislate for the churches, but

to encourage the churches to press forward in obedience to the last command of Christ, by setting

forth the experience of evangelical missions during
the last hundred years, and to confer together on
those numerous questions which the large
expansion of the work had brought to the
foreground. . . .the kingdom of truth advances by
the spread of information concerning the principles
of that kingdom and the facts connected with its
progress in the past.[5]

In the light of the international structuring of missionary
work in the twentieth century, beginning at Edinburgh
1910, Evangelicals during that century of evangelistic
progress (later to become known as The Great Century,
because of its evangelistic expansion into all continents of
the world) sought inspiration through information and
instruction rather than through missionary or
ecclesiological organization. Edinburgh 1910 began a new
type of conference to coordinate and organize Protestant
missions. The fifty years following Edinburgh 1910 point
toward the steadily diminishing evangelistic spirit among
many of the missionary agencies represented at
Edinburgh 1910. Organization, leadership, and
missiology, while good and necessary, could not *replace*
the dynamic of the Holy Spirit working through
dedicated servants committed to inspired Scriptures.

After the more limited international participation at
conferences in Liverpool 1860 and in London 1888, the
first call to a world conference came from a Bible
conference sponsored by D. L. Moody in 1885 at
Northfield, Massachusetts. On August 11, a day given to
prayer for worldwide missions, Arthur T. Pierson
addressed the conference:

What is needed. . .is a world missionary conference.
Let witnesses come from all parts of the world to
tell what the Lord is doing, so that we may light
upon the altars of our hearts new consecrated
fires. . . Let us have. . .an ecumenical council,
representative of all evangelical churches, solely to
plan this world-wide campaign and proclaim the
good tidings to every living soul in the shortest
time.[6]

Moody responded enthusiastically and this call led to
broader North American and continental participation in
London 1888.

A. T. Pierson was again invited by Moody to
Northfield in July 1886, to assist in the ministry to 250
students from 90 colleges. Pierson appealed to those who
would later become leaders in the Student Volunteer
Movement for Foreign Missions. He challenged them to
give their lives for "the evangelization of the world in
this generation." From that time to the present, student
missionary movements began to increase the momentum
of world evangelization. The contribution of youth
movements attracted considerable attention in the New
York 1900 Ecumenical Missionary Conference, for in less
than fourteen years, the Student Volunteer Movement
for Foreign Missions had received 5,000 volunteers of
which 1,550—almost one-third—had already gone to the
mission field!

The first outstanding evangelical missionary
conference of the twentieth century was held in April
1900, at Carnegie Hall in New York City. Approximately
200,000 people attended the various sessions of the
ten-day conference. It proved to be a great
demonstration of united Western missionary effort.
Because of its world concern, New York was called
"ecumenical"—for the term had not yet received the
technical significance it now represents.[7]

By 1900, many of the strong evangelistic voices of the
nineteenth century had passed away. Moody died in
1899, but Hudson Taylor, founder of the China Inland
Mission, was present and spoke to the 1,666 participants
representing some 400 mission agencies. Taylor
reminded the conference of the supernatural power
given by God to those who trust in Him, pray, and
sacrifice. He warned them: "We have given too much
attention to methods, and to machinery, and to
resources, and too little to the Source of Power, the
filling with the Holy Ghost." This concern was echoed at
Lausanne 1974 by many Third World representatives,
who have seen a spontaneous and unusual movement of
mission and evangelism in their lands.

New York 1900 had its attention focused upon the
person of Jesus Christ by the first paper presented.
Augustus H. Strong affirmed that both the authority and
the purpose of foreign missions is Christ:

> Christianity alone gives to me a proper authority in
> matters of religion, because it presents to me a God
> made known, partially in reason and conscience,
> most fully in incarnation, atonement, and
> resurrection. Because Christ is a person, the highest
> person, and that person made known to me, He can
> truly say: "All authority hath been given unto me,
> in heaven and on earth."[8]

Strong saw the command of Christ and the publication
of God's redemption as:

> Christ's method for the re-establishment of God's
> authority over an apostate and revolted humanity.
> Without any uttered command of Christ they would
> have claims upon us, for they are founded in right
> reason and in the best instincts of our nature. But
> that uttered command has been added, and today
> derives the authority for foreign missions from
> Christ's express direction, from His single word,
> "Go." His one injunction to the unbelieving world
> is, "Come"—"Come unto me." But His one
> injunction to all His believing followers is, "Go."
> . . .It is the sublimest order ever given upon earth.

Strong related these commands to the Christian Church
as not only "the body of Christ where Christ is the soul,"
but that "the body is Christ." The Church is "the fullness
of Him that filleth all in all."

> The Church is the expanded Christ, and the
> purpose of foreign missions is the purpose of the
> universe, to multiply Christ, to reincarnate the Son
> of God, to enthrone Christ in the hearts of men, to
> make all men the temples for His personal
> indwelling that He may be the first-born among
> many brethren, and may fill the world with
> Himself.[9]

Strong's address was a reaffirmation of the convictions of the great missionaries throughout the centuries who saw the biblical necessity of a personal individual relationship with God through the indwelling of the resurrected Christ. The future of the world depended upon the incorporation of believers into the visible Church, as God's means of ultimately establishing His authority over the world.

Even in the last century, missions were confused over sociopolitical responsibilities. Robert Speer saw "The Supreme and Determining Aim" of foreign missions as religious.

> We can not state too strongly in an age when the thought of men is full of things, and the body has crept up on the throne of the soul, that our work is not immediately and in itself a philanthropic work, a political work, a secular work of any sort whatsoever; it is a spiritual and a religious work. Of course, religion must express itself in life, but religion is spiritual life. I had rather plant one seed of the life of Christ under the crust of heathen life than cover that whole crust over with the veneer of our social habits on the vesture of Western civilization.[10]

Speer echoed the words of the apostles as he defined the distinction between the *aim* of missions, "to make Jesus known to the world," and the *results* of foreign missions:

> There is no force in the world so powerful to accomplish accessory results as the work of missions. Wherever it goes it plants in the hearts of men forces that produce new lives; it plants among communities of men forces that create new social combinations. It is impossible that any human tyranny should live where Jesus Christ is King. All these things the foreign mission movement accomplishes; it does not aim to accomplish them. I read in a missionary paper a little while ago that the foreign mission that was to accomplish results of

permanent value must aim at the total
reorganization of the whole social fabric. This is a
mischievous doctrine. We learn nothing from
human history, from the experience of the
Christian Church, from the example of our Lord
and His apostles to justify it. They did not aim
directly at such an end. They were content to aim at
implanting the life of Christ in the hearts of men,
and were willing to leave the consequences to the
care of God. It is a dangerous thing to charge
ourselves openly before the world with the aim of
reorganizing States and reconstructing society.[11]

At the turn of the century there were "modernistic"
theologians, who began to influence the rising leaders of
the missionary movement by discrediting the infallibility
(verbal inerrancy) of the Scripture and limiting the
authority of Scripture to the ethical teachings of Jesus.
Those in the youth movements with little training in
evangelical theology were especially vulnerable to a more
social approach to the Bible and missions. The SVMFM,
they felt, should no longer be identified with "one
particular school of thought" but be enlarged beyond the
evangelical elements to include all those who consider
themselves Christian.[12] In less than ten years, this youth
leadership gained control of the missionary movement
and dramatically changed the purpose and character of
the World Missionary Conference at Edinburgh 1910.

THE DEMISE OF EVANGELICALISM AT EDINBURGH 1910

No one questions seriously the evangelical stance of the
missionary movement of the nineteenth century. It was
known to be biblical in doctrine, godly in conduct,
emphasizing personal reconciliation with God, and
concerned for human and national welfare. While the
Church in some countries was adversely influenced by

Socinianism, rationalism, Darwin evolutionism, and,
finally, modernism and humanism, the forces allied with
the cause of world evangelization had their moorings in
the authority of the infallible Holy Scriptures. The result
was The Great Century (1800-1914) of world missions.

What, then, were the forces at work during the present
century which have undermined this phenomenal
movement of world evangelization and blunted the
thrust of these world-renowned evangelistic agencies?
Edinburgh 1910 seemed to capture and commend all the
outstanding lessons and qualities of the previous century.
Yet history has revealed a marked digression from the
spirit represented first by Gustav Warneck, D. L. Moody,
Robert Wilder, and then by Robert Speer and John R.
Mott.

What seem to be the root causes of the contemporary
deadlock between those who are committed to a
nineteenth-century revivalism and personal evangelism,
and those who place greatest emphasis upon the
temporal "salvation" of man in society? Where was the
point of departure? A careful study of the theology of
evangelism in the Edinburgh 1910 World Missionary
Council and in the International Missionary Council
reveals a number of areas meriting careful consideration.

THE HEART OF THE QUESTION: THE INSPIRATION AND AUTHORITY OF SCRIPTURE

The implicit trust in the Bible as God's full and final
revelation of Himself in Christ to mankind and to the
individual has been the wellspring of evangelism since
the first century. The Holy Spirit who gave the
Scriptures "is at all time in, with, and by the Word," said
Spener in the seventeenth century. The Holy Spirit bears
witness that these writings are from God and true. This
was the issue to which James Orr spoke in 1907 at the
Eleventh International Conference and Diamond Jubilee
Celebration of the Evangelical Alliance in London. He

sternly reproved the "New Theology" for its departure
from biblical authority and reaffirmed the "Evangelical
Principles in the Bible":

> . . .the Bible is an Evangelical book. To say that,
> again, is to say that the Bible contains a Gospel for
> the world, that this Gospel is of God, that it is a
> Gospel which the world needs, and without which it
> must perish, and furthermore, that this Gospel is
> the essence of the book—it is the very thing that
> makes it what it is. . . It is the Bible itself, I will be
> reminded, that in these days is being discredited,
> and I ought to begin by establishing its authority.
> First prove that the Bible is God's Book, then go on
> to speak of its authority. But I take the liberty
> tonight to turn the matter about, and say—it is the
> fact that the Bible has this Gospel in the heart of it
> which proves to me that it is God's Book.[13]

The heart of the question at Edinburgh 1910 goes
back to the ambiguous nature of the Paris Basis, adopted
in Paris at the first World Conference of the Y.M.C.A.
August 19, 1855.

> The Young Men's Christian Associations seek to
> unite those young men, who regarding Jesus Christ
> as their God and Saviour, according to the Holy
> Scriptures, desire to be his disciples in their
> doctrine and in their life, and to associate their
> efforts for the extension of his kingdom among
> young men.

Because of their struggles with heresy in the churches,
the American evangelical pastors of the nineteenth
century refused to support the newly formed Y.M.C.A.
until the word "evangelical" was defined. The
"Evangelical test" was adopted in the Portland Y.M.C.A.
convention of 1869. To be allowed to vote or hold office,
a person had to testify of his biblical faith by becoming
and remaining a member of an evangelical church, and
affirming the basic creeds of Christendom concerning
the person and work of Jesus Christ:

> We hold these churches to be evangelical which,
> maintaining the Holy Scriptures to be the only
> infallible rule of faith and practice, do believe in the
> Lord Jesus Christ (the only-begotten of the Father,
> King of Kings, and Lord of Lords, in whom
> dwelleth the fullness of the Godhead bodily, and
> who was made sin for us, though knowing no sin,
> bearing our sins in his own body on the tree), as the
> only name under heaven given among men
> whereby we must be saved from everlasting
> punishment.[14]

The Basis, adequate for the early years of the Y.M.C.A.,
did not respond to the needs of Evangelicals in their
confrontations with theological deviation within the
historical churches of Christianity, with non-Christian
religions, and with secularism. The Paris Basis alone,
however, guided the inclusively-minded leadership of the
International Missionary Council.

Historians agree that, to a marked degree, the
leadership of the World Student Christian Federation,
the Y.M.C.A., and the Y.W.C.A. were interrelated. As
parachurch organizations, they possessed an ecumenical
spirit that minimized doctrine. Until his death in 1899,
D. L. Moody's moral and spiritual influence seemed to
sustain the evangelical position of these movements.
After that, there seemed to be a slow but steady erosion
of the theological stance of the leadership of these
movements as they approached Edinburgh 1910.[15]

While some look back toward Edinburgh 1910 as the
last great evangelical expression of nineteenth-century
missionary movement, others would have to refer back to
the Ecumenical Missionary Conference of New York in
1900. Edinburgh 1910 was an epoch-making conference,
but its inclusive nature sowed the seeds of a progressive
theology so evident later on in Life and Work, Faith and
Order, and especially in the International Missionary
Council. It was the young leadership of Edinburgh 1910
who exerted great influence in these later world
movements, which resulted in the WCC and its inclusive
doctrinal basis.[16]

THE PRE-EDINBURGH
THEOLOGICAL
ATMOSPHERE

The great changes became evident in the period between 1900 and 1910. Franklin H. Little believes that the decades preceding Edinburgh 1910 "were far more critical in shaping the Christian Church than those decades which culminated in the Peace of Augsburg (1555) and the Treaty of Westphalia (1648)."[17]

Liberalism's introduction and influence. Although the outward *visage* was evangelical, nineteenth-century evangelicalism by 1910 no longer represented the decisive and directing voice of the missionary movement. Evangelical influence remained in the popular church program and in the national councils, but the brilliant, maturing leadership of the youth missionary movements had clearly cut their ties with their nineteenth-century beginnings.

The social gospel. Yoder contends that since 1890 the major churches of the United States "have had a strong intinction of biblical criticism and the Social Gospel."[18] In his doctoral thesis, Wilhelm Visser 't Hooft concluded that the revivalist movements unwittingly contributed to the social gospel by the synergistic principles of Methodism whereby man cooperates with God both in salvation and in the outworking of the Christian life.[19] The liberal view of Albrecht Ritschl, consequently, easily synthesized with a revivalism weakened by the "higher criticism" of the Bible. This compromise eroded the theological foundations of the nineteenth-century missionary movement and produced a "social gospel": the Kingdom was on earth (community) and Christ sought to establish an ethical reign on earth as the final objective of the Gospel. As a God of love, the object of His redemptive love is His own created community, and it is in the Christian community that all things are fulfilled. The Kingdom, consequently, is broader than the Church; and man's responsibility, consequently, is to

work together with God as His instrument to establish
God's reign in the social order.

A low view of the inspiration of the Bible led to this
"modernist" position in which the high ethic taught by
Jesus should be applied to society even if one could not
be certain of the historicity of the miracles and of other
events in the life of Christ. This "modernism" became
more popular in the two decades preceding the 1928
Jerusalem Conference of the International Missionary
Council. The "supernatural" of the Bible was often
rejected in a "scientific" world. Evangelical evangelism
that brought individuals supernaturally into a personal
relation with Jesus Christ was disdained as
"old-fashioned." When Billy Graham began his ministry,
many churches considered evangelism a relic of the
nineteenth century practiced only by "obscurantists" of
the "fundamentalist sect"!

*Literary criticism of the Bible destroyed or diminished confidence
in it.* Literary criticism, it was contended, had exploded
the myth of an infallible Bible. Many Evangelicals were
so influenced by the weakened authority of Scripture
that Edinburgh 1910 referred instead to the authority of
Christ or to the Christian faith.[20]

*Experience substituted for the historicity of the apostolic
testimonies as the ground of faith.* The scientific method
adopted by theologians led those of the "new theology"
toward confidence in experience. Consequently, the
authority of the Scripture was replaced by the authority
of an experience with Christ. The Bible became a means
toward this experience. Ritschl spoke of "the immediate
impression made on us by Christ, and the experimental
knowledge we have of His power to give us spiritual
deliverance and moral freedom."[21]

A revived authority of the Church. A diminishing emphasis
upon the authority of Scripture also resulted in an
undue importance given to the authority of the Church
and church membership. Adherence to the Church, as

the corporate identity of Christ, came to have greater
importance for the liberal than a personal faith and
commitment to Jesus Christ, proposed by a revivalism
which to the liberal was based upon the weak authority
of a fallible Bible. Personal lay evangelism, so evident
and fruitful in the nineteenth century, became a clerical
and church responsibility.

Theological uncertainty. Stephen Neill observes that "the
liberal was not by any means sure that Jesus Christ was
the *last* Word of God to man."[22] The result was that
uncertainty began to replace the authoritative Bible and
its evangelistic message. Troeltsch went even further—to
suggest that among religions, Christianity should be
considered the highest up to the present time.[23]

The search for truth. Another parallel consequence of note
was the development of "the search for truth." The
earlier constituency of the Student Movement had
accepted the authority of the Scriptures; they had been
committed to the teaching of the Bible and to evangelism
at home through Bible studies and abroad through
foreign missionary service. By 1910, the theory of
evolution had cut the vital roots of Christianity; the
constituency of the SCM struggled with intellectual
doubts concerning miracles, the incarnation, and the
atonement. The Bible, Tatlow records, had become a
source of difficulty for those in the Movement who
considered themselves Christian.[24]

YOUTH MOVEMENTS BECAME THE STRUCTURES LAUNCHING THE CONTINUATION COMMITTEE OF THE IMC

The Student Christian Movement in England gave
significant leadership to the World Student Christian

Federation, which in turn provided the international
structures adopted by the Continuation Committee of
Edinburgh 1910 and the resulting International
Missionary Committee.

Verbal inspiration of the Bible is replaced by a "modern view."
Tissington Tatlow records how the SCM adopted "the
modern position" about the Bible between 1900 and
1910. As early as 1900, the leadership of the Movement
had a different attitude toward the doctrine of
inspiration and toward eschatology than those of the
college constituency.[25] By 1901, the future Bible study
method of the Movement was established: "Bible
scholarship" had triumphed. Christian Unions in places
like Edinburgh and Cambridge, Tatlow said, were the
result of the evangelical revival of the previous two
centuries and possessed the theology of the day that had
passed.[26] Cambridge continued, for example, to hold
strongly to the doctrine of verbal inspiration, a
theological view that dominated the Movement from
1890 to 1900.[27] In 1901

> the movement gave consideration to the relation of
> the Bible and its authority of modern Biblical
> scholarship. For a number of years the views of
> those who had been trained in the verbal
> inspiration school of thought, and in the school of
> thought which is the outcome of modern Biblical
> scholarship, existed side by side. Then the modern
> view gained ground, and the day rapidly
> approached when the Movement would take its
> stand definitely and clearly for the modern view of
> the Bible.[28]

This new theological development within the movement
led the Cambridge group to withdraw its membership
from the SCM in March 1910[29]—the same year that the
SCM leaders exercised a predominant role in the World
Mission Conference at Edinburgh. J. H. Oldham, for
example, was secretary of the Executive Committee. The

great facts of Christianity "do not alter," Oldham said,
yet theology is "dynamic and not static"—theology
changes.[30] Since Edinburgh 1910, the ecumenical
movement has been characterized by a progressive
theology—a changing, developing theology leading it to
the frequent and radical changes only possible when one
is able to interpret a fallible Bible more freely.

Inclusivism. Almost immediately the movement also
became more inclusivist. First, the nonevangelical,
church-related schools were invited to enter the
movement. By the 1909 Oxford meeting of the WSCF
General Committee, John R. Mott, the chairman, asked
the committee, "What is the policy, as to the basis of
active membership, in Roman Catholic countries of
movements now in the Federation?"[31] While no decision
was reached, it became clear to the Committee that the
basis of membership could be interpreted to include all
those that considered themselves to be Christian. From
that time on, one of the most crucial questions facing the
ecumenical movement has been, "What is a Christian?"

A social emphasis. This same year revealed a change in its
social emphasis—introduced first at the Soro, Denmark,
Conference of the WSCF in 1902. At the Matlock
Conference 1909, a commission chaired by J. H. Oldham
called the Student Movement to consider the social
conditions which deny to "our fellow men . . . their share
in the Fatherhood of God."[32] At Oxford 1909, Mott
encouraged a study of social needs by saying, "It is
believed by discerning leaders that one of the most
distinctive features of the next decade in the life of the
Student Movement is to be a larger recognition and
realization by students of their social responsibility."[33]
Ruth Rouse observes,

> From the Oxford Conference onwards, there was in
> most Movements a continuous and developing
> concern for social questions. . . . It was a happy
> feature that the little conflict arose, at least in the

leadership of the Movements between the claims of
"foreign missions" and "home missions," and the
ministry of social service in the homeland. The task
of winning the world for Christ is seen as one.[34]

Rouse could hardly foresee that this conflict between
world evangelization and social responsibility would
culminate in the demise of evangelism and eventually the
death of the movement.

Roots of a "new theology." The theological climate of the
period between 1900 and 1910 strongly influenced the
leadership of the youth movements. In general, these
leaders had changed from the course of the original
evangelical movements they represented. The Student
Volunteer Movement for Foreign Missions developed a
new attitude toward the inspiration of the Scriptures. A
departure from verbal inspiration in the WSCF decidedly
influenced the doctrine of the authority of the
Scriptures, the question of social responsibility, and the
policy of inclusivism.

The WSCF and the Y.M.C.A. came to Edinburgh 1910
represented by their national and international leaders,
Mott,[35] Oldham, Tatlow, and Gairdner. While Edinburgh
1910 was prompted and promoted by the evangelistic
and evangelical dynamic of the nineteenth century, these
leaders introduced a "new" theology. Evangelism already
included social and political action in the youth
movement. Their viewpoints found expression after
Edinburgh 1910 in the powerful organ *The International
Review of Missions,* edited by Oldham. By the Jerusalem
Conference in 1928, "new theology" produced a major
crisis in missions.

THE THEOLOGICAL
PROBLEMS
OF EDINBURGH 1910
IN RETROSPECT

The historian must give due credit to the great amount
of good done by John R. Mott as an outstanding

missionary statesman, by J. H. Oldham as a brilliant editor and theoretician, and to the IMC for its insights and lasting contributions to world evangelization. Nevertheless, Edinburgh 1910 did have problems which became apparent in the International Missionary Council (1921-61) and which have been resolved to this date. A potentially great instrument of God for world evangelization became the subject of a controversy that led missions such as the China Inland Mission to withdraw from its ranks in 1916 during World War I —and others, such as the Christian and Missionary Alliance, to withdraw after the controversial 1932 Hocking Report. Edinburgh 1910 hoped to harness the global forces of Christianity, to complete world evangelization, and to introduce the coming Kingdom of God upon the earth. It served rather to hinder evangelism by what it did *not* say concerning the authority of Scripture, and what it did through the agencies which grew out of it.

A broader inclusive theology. It has long been believed by the non-theologically-oriented youth leadership that doctrinal statements hindered their interdenominational programs. Liberal scholarship tended to confirm the tradition of a minimum doctrinal statement. Harnack contended, for example, that Christianity changed as soon as it codified its doctrines:

> Whatever finds expression in doctrines, regulations, ordinances and forms of public worship comes to be treated as the thing in itself. This, then, is the first force at work in the transformation: the original enthusiasm, in the large sense of the word, *evaporated,* and the religion of law and form at once arises.[36]

The International Committee of the World Missionary Conference 1910 decided that "no resolution shall be allowed which involves questions of doctrine or church policy with regard to which the Churches or Societies taking part in the conference differ among

themselves."[37] The conference was thereby limited in its
doctrinal position and pronouncements to the breadth of
the theologies represented by the various delegates.

In practice, the consensus of the individual study
commissions became the real and invisible authority of
the WMC. The Bishop of Birmingham (The Right Rev.
C. Gore, D.D.) in the introduction to his Commission
Report said that "documents like the Thirty-Nine Articles
or the Westminster Confession are documents full of
controversies, which are partial, which do not belong to
the universal substance of our religion."[38]

A broader, more inclusive, conference. Previous missionary
conferences had enlisted the support of Evangelicals
from a wide spectrum of evangelistic efforts throughout
the world. The desire of the Edinburgh leadership to
include even more Christian communities was evident.
Gustave Thils, a Roman Catholic historian, notes that
"even though missionary meetings were characteristically
evangelical, Edinburgh enlarged its constituency and the
Anglo-Catholics participated actively there."[39] Gairdner,
under Oldham's guidance, seems to express the desire of
the leadership to extend the representation even further.
He notes,

> The communions whose absence at once strikes the
> observer are of course the great Greek and Roman
> churches . . . with foreign missions all over the
> world. But who on this ridge of memories and
> hopes, can say what the future may bring forth?[40]

The Eastern Orthodox churches joined the WCC in 1961
and it was hoped that the Nairobi Assembly 1975 would
include full participation of the Roman Catholic church.

A limited mission field. In harmony with the more
inclusivistic atmosphere, the Roman Catholic and Greek
Orthodox countries were not considered to be mission
fields, and the missions of these large churches were
included in the Conference considerations. The original

title of Commission I at Edinburgh, as proposed by Dr.
George Robson and John R. Mott, was "Carrying the
Gospel to All the World."[41] This was changed to add
"Non-Christian," "in order to remove misconception."[42]
The *Statistical Atlas* published for the Conference
excluded the Roman Catholic and Orthodox lands, and
both Europe and South America were omitted from
missionary consideration. L. S. Albright observes,

> It is significant that there was no representation
> whatever of Latin America, reflecting current
> opposition in certain quarters to Protestant missions
> in Roman Catholic countries.[43]

John A. Mackay, a former missionary to South
America, wrote that in the pre-Edinburgh preparations
the High Church Party of the Church of England not
only objected to the word "ecumenical" as applicable to
the Conference,[44] but said,

> . . .they would refuse to attend the conference at all
> if the Hispanic world were to be regarded as a
> legitimate field for Protestant missionary effort, and
> if Protestant missionaries and church men from
> Latin American countries were admitted to
> membership.[43]

The admission of representatives of the High Church
Party was negotiated by Tissington Tatlow and J. H.
Oldham.[46] This admission changed the character and
theology of missions at the Conference, gave the
Continuation Committee and the IMC a broader, more
inclusive mandate, and limited the number of "mission
fields." Madras 1938 modified this decision and Mexico
1963 considered all six continents as "mission fields."

Wider theological presentations. Among the Edinburgh
Conference speakers and the members of the
Commission, the names of more socially-conscious men
than those of New York 1900 were readily recognized:
Henry Sloan Coffin spoke on "Christianity the Final and

Universal Religion as the Ethical Ideal."[47] D. S. Cairns, well known by the WSCF for his broader outlook on Bible study, was appointed to the strategic position of Chairman of the Commission on the Missionary Message. A comparison of the New York 1900 address of A. H. Strong with the basic theological addresses of W. P. Paterson and Henry Sloan Coffin reveals a very distinct theological retreat from evangelicalism during the ten-year period. In those theological foundations of the conference, the laws of positivism, pragmatism, and historical research were exposed as presuppositions that to some extent diminished the former and full authority of Christ and the Scriptures.

An opening to progressive theology and syncretism. In spite of the multiple references to historic evangelical evangelism, this emphasis of Edinburgh did not prevail and predominate for many years in the IMC sphere of influence.[48] Perhaps it was because of the cataclysmic and destructive effect of World War I upon the optimistic eschatological outlook for a Christianized world; perhaps it was the nontheological atmosphere of Edinburgh that influenced its leadership.

Commission III, chaired by D. S. Cairns, endeavored to discover the realities of the Christian message by sending a series of questionnaires to missionary correspondents in non-Christian lands, in order to make an appraisal of the religions in that country and of the missionary message which had met with most success. By a scientific study of each major religion, the "points of contact" with Christianity would be discerned. The missionary could then emphasize the elements of the Christian message which would be most readily grasped by that particular non-Christian religion. In effect, the study of non-Christian religions would enable the missionary to preach the appropriate message and, thereby, speed world evangelization.[49]

Christianity was seen as the final and absolute religion in this section. The replies from the mission fields, however, brought to the conference a "mass of evidence" concerning the "latent elements of Christianity" brought to light by the non-Christian religions. A study of comparative religions, Robert Speer concedes, would bring new insights into what had been as yet undiscovered in traditional Christianity.[50]

The Commission did not give a definition of the content of the Gospel. Gustav Warneck, in a letter to Mott, expressed concern that the missionary dynamic would be damaged—either by an alteration of the apostolic message in the attempt to find points of contact with the non-Christian religions, or by outright syncretism:

> The New Testament contains no regulative prescriptions concerning missionary methods, but it does contain a regulative definition of the content of the Gospel which is our commission to bring to the non-Christian world. . . Yet by this endeavor to draw close to the hearts of the non Christian peoples, we dare not allow ourselves to be betrayed into the mistake of altering the content of the Gospel message as it was proclaimed by the apostles.[51]

The Commission did express concern over the dangers of syncretism in India, but the methodology of evangelism research was not buttressed by the definition of the Christian message. What the Gospel is, is intimately related to our convictions in propagating it. Consideration was given to those who held other theological convictions. This entire theological debate was crystallized at Jerusalem 1928 and received extensive treatment at Madras 1938.[52]

THE EXPLODED MYTH OF A CHRISTIANIZED WORLD

Edinburgh 1910 generated a tremendous spirit of optimism toward the Christianization of the world. Each of the Christian colonial powers, whether Anglican, Protestant, or Roman Catholic, would assume responsibility for the evangelization of their colonial interests. Thus the world would be evangelized and the "coming Kingdom of God" would be ushered in. The organizational ability of the keenest minds applied to this endeavor would accomplish this goal perhaps during the lifetime of Edinburgh 1910 delegates. For some, this meant that the benefits of Western civilization would be shared with the entire world. For the leaders of Edinburgh 1910, it meant the formation of National Christian Councils in each country so that the missionaries and national church leaders would participate in this effort as a united body. The unity of the Church would become the mightiest apologetic for world evangelism. And the evangelization of the world by foreign missions would hasten the visible unit of the one united Church of Christ in every non-Christian nation.[53]

It is difficult to imagine the disillusionment and the discouragement the outbreak of World War I brought to Christianity. Protestant Germany and Roman Catholic Italy were united in war against Anglican England, Roman Catholic France and Belgium, and Orthodox Russia. This un-Christian demonstration not only reduced the supply of Western missionaries but also discredited the missionary cause and Christian unity.

Another generation at Jerusalem 1928 began to look toward a "Christlike" world based upon the ethic of Jesus, as the ideal of a Christianized world faded. This social and political optimism has remained to dominate its thinking and action in the post-Uppsala 1968 period. Without denying Christian responsibilities, Evangelicals in this century have been considered pessimistic because of their general prophetic view that political and social life will deteriorate until the return of Jesus Christ, who said, "My kingdom is not of this world."

CONCLUSION

A review of Edinburgh 1910 is of great significance, because it reveals principles of theology and methodology that have characterized the ecumenical movement up until the present time. Some important lessons can be learned from the pre-Edinburgh 1910 era and the studies of the World Missionary Conference. First, the reports and studies were essentially made on the foundations of nineteenth-century evangelism, church planting, and church growth. It would be difficult not to commend the vast amount of good that was said and preserved for future generations. Nevertheless, the pluralistic atmosphere created by concessions made for the inclusion of the Anglican communion brought not only a restriction on what areas of the "Christian" world could be considered as mission fields (i.e., Europe and South America were eliminated), but also created a "spirit of catholicity" that went beyond an evangelical ecumenicity, which insisted upon the "new birth" as prerequisite for eternal life. The evangelical doctrine of an infallible Bible as the only source of revelation and object of faith was implicitly denied when the Roman Catholic and Eastern Orthodox communions, holding to a sacramental means of salvation, were invited; and Christian "tradition" upstaged the Bible. Edinburgh 1910 was no longer evangelical, but ecumenical in the present understanding of the word. It denied implicitly those essential apostolic teachings the postsixteenth century Reformation so vigorously and sacrificially reaffirmed.[54] The expected conquest of Christianity over the non-Christian religions before the return of Jesus Christ manifested a "triumphalism" exceeding that of which Evangelicals are accused today.

Second, the verbal inspiration and infallibility of Scripture in the original manuscripts is essential and fundamental to sound exegesis and interpretation of Scripture. A hermeneutics based upon anything less than an infallible Bible opens the door to exegetical conclusions foreign to the purposes and intent of the prophets of the Old Testament and the New Testament authors. Since Edinburgh 1910, the principle of "progressive theology" has governed the theological and methodological studies in the ecumenical movement.[55] As the authority of the Word of God was questioned at the end of the nineteenth century, theologians turned either implicitly or explicitly to other sources of authority in natural theology—the Church, the creeds of Christendom, Church "tradition" or traditions, Church history, preaching, secular history, personal experience, and a Bible which contains a word from God. During each period in these last seventy years one special source or a combination of authorities has been emphasized. The resulting conference or assembly consensus report, then, is canonized and quoted as authoritative.

The modern theologian of the West has produced a *new* or different view of man, sin, the world, the Church, salvation and eschatology—leaving both the churches and their members in confusion. When equivocal conference language is used to satisfy the divergent theologies represented, the results are even more complicated. For example, before the Fourth Assembly of the WCC at Uppsala in 1968, the ecumenical theology of evangelism was stated in terms to satisfy liberals and Evangelicals, but it could not be both. If unity in evangelism is difficult at times among Evangelicals, cooperation is nearly impossible in the WCC. There is little or no common ground of authority to determine what the message really is!

Third, the doctrine of scriptural inspiration and authority cannot be avoided because of its divisive nature, for it is the lifeblood of evangelism. The evangelist must be able to say—under the direction of the same Spirit who inspired the Scriptures—"God says," "Jesus said," "the apostle says." The authority is not that of the evangelist, of *the* Church, or of *a* church, but that of God's Word which He has revealed to us through His servants, the prophets. An evangelist committed to the verbal infallibility and full authority of the Scriptures possesses the theological foundation necessary to clearly discern the message and to declare it simply with the power and persuasion given by the Holy Spirit (Acts 1:8).

Fourth, Edinburgh 1910 attempted to be nontheological by recognizing the various participating societies as "Christian" and by charitably tolerating the differences among themselves. This had been possible among Evangelicals in the previous century who had established broad guidelines governing their limits of Christian brotherhood according to the Basis of 1847.[56] But Edinburgh 1910 made a serious mistake.

At the formation of the International Missionary Council in 1921, it was decided that the IMC would adopt a nontheological position, which left the movement in a measure defenseless against any theological error or even heresy:

> Recognizing that the IMC has been brought into being as representing the national missionary organization of the various countries, for the purpose of investigation and cooperation within the appropriate sphere of these organizations, and, therefore, is not to be considered as representing churches or ecclesiastical organizations as such, we adopt the following declaration as governing our own deliberations and as conditioning our relation to conferences of a missionary character:

> No decision shall be sought from the Council and no statement shall be issued by it on any matter involving an ecclesiastical or doctrinal question on which the members of the Council or the bodies constituting the Council may differ among themselves.[57]

In practice, however, this is not "no theology" but a "new theology" which opened a door to winds of theological extremes. This weakness became apparent in the following decade by the publication of the Hocking Report 1932, and greatly embarrassed the IMC. The image of the IMC was tarnished and some groups disassociated themselves from it.[58] The greatest weakness, however, was its inability to unite or to promote a generally accepted theology of evangelism such as Berlin 1966 and Lausanne 1974 did. Evangelism became a problem for both the IMC and the WCC rather than the means for world evangelization.

Fifth, there can be no question that the proclamation of the Gospel and the planting of churches has socially uplifted individuals, families, and societies. Evangelism is the mission of Christians. The Scriptures have not promised to make a man or a society perfect in this present age, yet nothing contributes more to the ultimate needs of the world than evangelism. Nevertheless, the goal of biblical evangelism is not a Christianized world or a Christlike world but a world evangelization that will bring back the King. New York 1900 was evangelical in the historical sense of the word. Edinburgh 1910 was no longer evangelical but ecumenical, upholding a pluralistic, progressive theology. After Edinburgh 1910, evangelism hesitated, then faltered and almost died in the IMC.

2

The "Larger Evangelism" of the International Missionary Council 1921-1961

Contemporary questions

concerning social action and evangelism have their origins in the pre-Edinburgh era and their particular expression in the Jerusalem 1928 and the Madras 1938 conferences of the IMC. Evangelical missions have always been "holistic" in the biblical sense and they have always sought the welfare of the "whole man" not just his soul. The distortion of these issues is found in this period when evangelicalism was at its lowest ebb in this century and, perhaps, in world Protestantism as well. Jerusalem 1928 was the first world conference of the International Missionary Council, which was organized in 1921 as a result of Edinburgh 1910. The IMC merged with the WCC in 1961 to become the Division of World Missions and Evangelism. This chapter recalls the elimination of "old" evangelism at Jerusalem 1928 and the efforts to restore evangelical evangelism in combination with an "errant" Bible at Madras (Tambaram) 1938. This "Larger Evangelism" in turn contributed to the present ecumenical theology of mission and evangelism and has exerted considerable influence upon some contemporary Evangelicals.

THE ELIMINATION OF "OLD" EVANGELISM

Social issues received their first major attention in the Stockholm 1925 Life and Work Conference led by Nathan Soderblom. In the International Missionary Council organized in 1921, J. H. Oldham took an active role in social issues and was subsequently asked to lead the Oxford 1937 conference of Life and Work. The primary architect of the WCC and the first general secretary, W. A. Visser 't Hooft, wrote his doctoral thesis on *The Background of the Social Gospel in America*.[1] His theology has done much to establish the social and political priorities of the WCC built upon the defective view of biblical inspiration and the tendency toward universalism inherent in the theology of Karl Barth. In our day, many Evangelicals have been confused and adversely influenced by the nonevangelical "holistic" evangelism of the WCC. They have been led to believe that Evangelicals have only been interested in souls. The post-Nairobi 1975 air will be clouded again by the rising importance of "spirituality," an emphasis which represents an implicit denial of "holistic" evangelism by a revival of mystical experiences transcending human privations! This may signal a new asceticism in the ecumenical evangelistic pilgrimage.

THE FUNDAMENTALIST-MODERNIST CONTROVERSY

The older liberalism and modernism were characterized by a strong shift of activity away from evangelical evangelism, involved in winning individual souls to Christ, to a "social gospel." It was not that evangelism had not inspired or encouraged social reforms or responsibilities, but that the message of the Gospel had become confused in some cases and distorted in others. The evangelical churches reacted against this trend in American Protestantism,[2] but Handy believes that they were still united in their common desire to "Christianize a nation"—the United States.[3] The concerns of the Evangelicals,.who became known as "Fundamentalists" through the publications of their convictions in a series of pamphlets entitled "The Fundamentals," reacted and focused their attention primarily upon that which the Modernists omitted in their social gospel:

    1. The infallibility of Scripture was rejected and its authority weakened and vitiated.

    2. The deity of Jesus Christ and His supernatural birth were questioned or rejected.

    3. The atonement of Christ, if upheld at all, was more collective than individual and personal.[4]

    4. The necessity of personal salvation by faith in Christ was considered "old-fashioned."

    5. The Kingdom of God found its reality more in this world than in the heart of the believer, in the Church, or in the world to come at the second coming of Jesus Christ. Evangelicalism, then known as "fundamentalism," became unpopular in the decade preceding Jerusalem 1928.

JERUSALEM 1928

At Edinburgh 1910, authority shifted perceptibly from that of the infallible Scriptures to an undefined "authority of Christ." The Scriptures were to receive the same scientific, critical treatment as any other ancient book. Modern scientific methods were also applied to the study of missions. Lack of consensus on the Christian message resulted in a request for further study of the question of the authority of Christ.

By Jerusalem 1928, the right to evangelize non-Christian lands was no longer taken as self-evident. Missionary optimism and enthusiasm had vanished. For the first time since the Reformation, the very content of the Christian Gospel required redefinition by the missionary movement.[5] The united front of evangelical missions—so characteristic of the nineteenth century—had been broken. Ecumenical leadership in the post-Edinburgh 1910 era hoped to unite both Evangelicals and "Modernists" around an undefined "authority of Christ," instead of the "divisive" authority of an infallible Bible. Evangelicals maintained that the Bible was God's infallible revelation of Himself to men. Those who advocated the "higher critical" view in general considered the Bible to require scientific examination in the same way as any ancient book.[6] A nonsupernatural source of authority had detracted from the historicity of the biblical events that stimulated and enabled evangelism.

Several major political events and theological conferences exerted a strong influence upon the fledgling International Missionary Council organized at Lake Mohonk, New York, in 1921. First, the involvement of "Christian" nations in World War II demonstrated the practical impossibility of obtaining a Christianized world by evangelism. The League of Nations was cited as an example of political unity in sharp contrast to a divided Christendom.

Second, the Life and Work Conference at Stockholm in 1925, inspired by the social gospel, assumed responsibility for some areas of social work anticipated by the IMC; new goals for the IMC were difficult to define.

Third, increased responsibilities toward the "older" churches of the West, with their evangelistic inertia, weighed down the new Council.

Fourth, Evangelicals hesitated to support the IMC because of its theological inclusivism, and because the IMC had excluded missions to the Hispanic world and Latin America.

Fifth, new problems of proselytism arose in the face of rising nationalism.

Sixth, Faith and Order met for the first time in Lausanne in 1927 and spoke of unity as necessary for the missionary enterprise of the Church. Increased attention

THE "LARGER EVANGELISM" OF THE
INTERNATIONAL MISSIONARY COUNCIL
59

was given to the authority of an organized united
Church and its responsibility for evangelism. It was
decided that the studies of Faith and Order should
become the unofficial IMC theological position.

DEEDS MUST PRECEDE PROCLAMATION

The Jerusalem Conference 1928 stood at mid-point
between two world wars—in the midst of rapid social
change, political turmoil, and world financial crisis.
Consequently, the application of the Gospel received
greater attention than its proclamation. The Gospel was
seen as a way of life, not only a subject for belief. Deeds,
they said, must precede proclamation. This new
emphasis, however, was not only pragmatic but also a
result of the triumph of "modernism" and liberal
theology. It was the consequence resulting from a lower
view of the Bible. The Scriptures were no longer living,
and able in and of themselves to transform man (Heb.
4:12); the witness of social action was necessary in order
to give evangelistic credibility.

SOUL WINNING IS REJECTED

Jerusalem 1928 was strongly influenced by the "modern
theology" of German universities imported into the
United States by Walter Rauschenbusch, an American,
who "took a leave from his parish in 1891 for a study of
social movements in England and of the New Testament
in Germany. Thereafter his theology grew more and
more distinctly liberal; he adopted critical approaches to
the Bible and to the history of Christianity, and
identified himself with the names of Schleiermacher,
Bushnell, Ritschl, Wellhausen, and Harnack. His work
reflected the romantic, monistic idealism that pervaded
much of liberal theology."[7] Rauschenbusch's adaptation
of more liberal views of the Scriptures brought him to
question the authenticity of the biblical records and our
understanding of them.

Most Evangelicals would respond warmly to Walter
Rauschenbusch's eloquent pleas for social and political
reforms in an unjust economic system, for there are few
who are concerned only about the soul of man to the
exclusion of the needs of society. Rauschenbusch, in
earlier years, possessed a deep pietist and evangelical
faith that surfaced occasionally, but he strongly
denounced its individualism and futuristic viewpoints.

> To concentrate our efforts on personal salvation, as
> orthodoxy had done, or on soul culture, as
> liberalism has done, comes close to refined
> selfishness. . . . Seek ye first the Kingdom of God
> and God's righteousness, and the salvation of your
> souls will be added to you. Our personality is of
> divine and eternal value, but we see it aright only
> when we see it as part of mankind. Our religious
> individuality must get its interpretation from the
> supreme fact of social solidarity. . . . A religion
> which realizes in God the bond that binds all men
> together can create the men who will knit social
> order together as an organized brotherhood.[8]

Historians concur that Rauschenbusch was strongly
influenced by Ritschl, Schleiermacher, Dilthey, and
Harnack.[9]

THE SOCIAL GOSPEL
AND SIN

Several contemporary social theologies have roots in the
theological presuppositions of sin and evil adopted by
Rauschenbusch, for it was liberalism that provided the
content of his theology, making it ethical rather than
metaphysical. Sin is interpreted by Schleiermacher as
"produced in every individual through the sinful acts
and conditions of others. . . ."[10] Sin is social solidarity
rather than an individual responsibility before God. He
dismisses the attributing of evil to Satan and his angels as
"a fading religious entity" and the belief in a demonic
kingdom of evil as incompatible with modern life.

> The social gospel is the only influence which can renew the idea of the kingdom of evil in modern minds, because it alone has the adequate sense of solidarity and a sufficient grasp of the historical and social realities of sin.[11]

Rauschenbusch's remedy for sin is to teach the social ethic of Jesus as the solution to world needs. He wrote little concerning the atonement, one of the first evangelical doctrines to be distorted or discredited after questioning the infallibility of Scripture.

THE "NEW" EVANGELISM

Evangelism suffered because of the social gospel, for Rauschenbusch vigorously criticized it as insufficient to lift man up and make him truly man:

> The substitutions of personal salvation for the establishment of the Kingdom of God (on earth) in the teaching of the church is the cause of false asceticism everywhere. It has twisted the words of Christ out of their natural meaning. It has diverted the energy of religious men from public affairs and concentrated it on themselves. It has produced a false type of godliness. Not until the doctrine of the Kingdom of God shall have entered once more into the consciousness of the church, and Christianity shall become a revolutionary movement, will Christian morality lose its worldly pallor and become once more the sublimest type of civic virtue.[12]

Shortly after the death of D. L. Moody, a "new evangelism" was sought by the church leaders who were scanning the horizons for some sign of a new awakening. Rauschenbusch wrote an article entitled "The New Evangelism" and recognized the dissatisfaction with the "old evangelism" characteristic of Moody. His approach is apparent in nonevangelical theology today, for a sense

of man's eternal lostness is missing. The appeal of the
Gospel has changed from the concern for personal
salvation to love for our fellow man; the "old 'scheme of
salvation' seems mechanical and remote."[13]
Between 1900 and World War I, the major
denominations of the United States turned from their
preoccupation with evangelism to become advocates of
social justice, and to proclaim the obligation of the
Christians to fashion Christ's Kingdom on earth.[14]
Evangelism in youth movements continued, but slowly
became unpopular as the theology and methodology of
the movements shifted toward social concerns.
Nevertheless, the fifteen years following 1890 proved to
be years of great spiritual awakening in many places of
the world.[15]
Shortly before Jerusalem 1928, evangelicalism and its
evangelism suffered another major blow. The Scopes
Trial of 1925 received such damaging news coverage that
evangelicalism became the laughing stock of the
American public as well as in the "modernist" and liberal
circles.[16] Evangelists of that day, such as Paul Rader and
Billy Sunday, spoke to minority groups—or to those that
had splintered from the large denominations.

RAYS OF LIGHT IN NON-CHRISTIAN RELIGIONS

Continental theologians and missionaries were
uncomfortable about the socially oriented Jerusalem
1928 Message influenced by modernism. The Message,
written for the conference by William Temple, found
some rays of Gospel light in non-Christian religions:

To non-Christians also we make our call. We rejoice
to think that just because in Jesus Christ the light
that lighteth every man shone forth in its full
splendor, we find rays of that same light where He
is unknown or even is rejected. We welcome every
noble quality in non-Christian persons or systems as

further proof that the Father, who sent His son into
the world, has nowhere left Himself without a
witness.[17]

Some wondered if this implicit syncretism was leading
the IMC toward a future world-religion. The "values"
from general revelation found in the non-Christian
religions eliminated to a marked degree the evangelistic
obligation. The Jerusalem message proved unsatisfactory
to many non-Evangelicals as well as to Evangelicals, yet it
seems to be a foundation of much nonevangelical social
theology today.

Jerusalem saw the mission field as the secular world of
men rather than that of the non-Christian religions.
Efforts should be made to enlist the labors of scientists,
artists, and the noble elements of patriotic movements in
securing a new world of social justice freed from every
occasion for war or threat of war.

EVANGELISM AS
PERMEATING OTHER
SYSTEMS

The earlier erosion of the doctrine of inspiration and
authority of the Bible resulted in the deterioration of
biblical evangelism, and produced the most controversial
of all conferences in the history of the International
Missionary Council. The road from Edinburgh 1910 and
its doctrinal inclusivism led the entire missionary
program of world evangelization toward syncretism.
Canon Quick, writing his evaluation of the Conference,
noted the distinction between the older and newer
schools of evangelism. The newer school no longer
depended upon the uniqueness of the Gospel, because
the study of comparative religion had found moral and
spiritual values in the non-Christian systems. The newer
school, "may be inclined to summon to its aid the parable
of the leaven, and to suggest that Christianity may best

spread itself by permeating other systems rather than by demanding the immediate and overt conversion of individuals."[18] The older school, Quick recognized, preached

> . . .that by Christ's death, and by that alone, is human sin really and fully forgiven, and its call to the non-Christian has been simply that he should pass from death into life, by accepting through faith Christ's atonement, and by renouncing once and for all the whole system of religious belief and practice in which he had hitherto vainly striven to make himself right with God.[19]

It is evident that the very heart of the biblical message was eliminated by modernism at Jerusalem 1928. Ten years later, Madras 1938 would attempt to find a mediating position, one which would allow for a social gospel, a fallible Bible, and an historical evangelism.

THE NEO-ORTHODOX EVANGELISM

At the Madras, India 1938 Conference, the International Missionary Council both revived and redefined evangelism. After a decade of reaction to the Jerusalem 1928 Conference and its "social gospel," Madras 1938 attempted to return to a more moderate position, one which would include both an evangelical and a modernist synthesis of evangelism. This conference is of great importance, because it reflects the evangelistic viewpoint of Philip Potter, the present general secretary of the WCC. John R. Mott, the great leader of Edinburgh 1910 who chaired his last conference, called the new theology of evangelism "The Larger Evangelism." Currently, this kind of evangelism is called "holistic," an effort to restate an evangelism concerned with the total needs of man.

MADRAS LOOKS
TOWARD A
SYNTHESIS OF
EVANGELICALISM
AND MODERNISM

Madras 1938 represents an attempt to end the
polarization between historical evangelicalism and the
modernism-liberalism as expressed in the social gospel.
Mott, an astute layman, believed that good will could
reconcile the two, for he did not seem to recognize the
basic theological incompatibility between evangelicalism
and liberalism. J. H. Oldham, architect of Edinburgh
1910, editor of the IRM, and a brilliant theologian,
recognized the difference and committed himself to a
social priority by resigning from the International
Missionary Council and becoming chairman of the
Oxford 1937 Life and Work Conference. He pointed out
the fundamental difference between the two theological
positions in a letter to Mott:

> The divergencies go very deep and can be
> transcended not merely by goodwill but by very
> fundamental and prolonged rethinking of the
> existing position. The difference between
> fundamentalists and modernists is almost a
> difference between two quite distinct religions. I do
> not think the problems can be resolved purely as a
> matter of cooperation.[20]

It became evident in the years before Madras 1938
that the dichotomy was not a superficial one. Dr. Helen
Kim of Korea, a delegate at Jerusalem 1928, had asked
the question, "What is the central thing in Christianity,
the heart of the message?"[21] The committee members
who attended the Williamstown, Massachusetts, 1929
meeting of the IMC, believed that evangelistic
movements lacked educational depth and substance, and
that religious-educational movements lacked the power
of the Gospel. Traditional evangelism had been rejected
because of its failure to include a social element.
Evangelism, some believed, could best be accomplished

by Christian education. Others believed that a
demonstration of social concern was necessary in order
to prove the relevancy of Christianity.

Alfred Wasson saw the root problem to be the
Christian view of society as represented by the Korean
Christians. In his case study of Korea, Wasson concluded
that "one view held, in effect, that the church has no
concern with social conditions; the other was that the
church is a saviour of society."[22] The issues were by no
means Western. The IMC conferences and the
propagation of these Western theological innovations by
liberal missionaries had begun to touch the life of the
entire Church.

Evangelical mission leaders in Germany reacted to this
deviation in world evangelism. Karl Hartenstein pleaded
for a return to the centrality of the Scriptures, as the
basis and content of missionary preaching. The Scripture
is the instrument of God in evangelism for the one who
speaks "in Christ's stead." It is this Word of God which
enables the extension of the Gospel.[23]

It is difficult to understand how one can evaluate the
controversy by suggesting that the Evangelicals failed to
recognize and implement the social implications of the
Gospel, while the modernist was weak on the authority of
Scripture—a sort of balancing act that implies that one
complemented the other.[24] It should be recognized that
historical biblical Christianity was engaged in an
energy-consuming struggle for survival with a deadly
theological heresy. Furthermore, careful historians attest
to the social impact of the awakenings of evangelical
Christianity throughout the world.

REDEFINED
EVANGELISTIC
DOCTRINE

Since 1938, the concept of the Larger Evangelism has
not increased ecumenically-oriented evangelism. The
reasons for this may be more readily understood when

the differences between evangelicalism and
liberalism-modernism are explained. First, the liberal
questioned the historicity of the Genesis accounts of
creation and sin because of the influence of Darwin's
evolution, Kant's epistemology, and the "higher criticism"
biblical interpretation. Theology became progressive, its
message changeable. This general outlook prevails even
today, and will be discussed later.

Sin, for example, became relational and
relative—rather than vertical and absolute. Sin became
wrong relationship with the community of mankind that
found its solution in the individual's salvation through
the Christian community. Sin is no longer the
transgression of the moral law of God, but rather those
acts which hinder the attainment of the Kingdom of God
on earth. The death of Christ became an example of
love, rather than the basis of divine forgiveness of that
transgression which separated man from God.[25]

Since the historical authenticity of the Scripture was
seriously questioned and truth could no longer be stated
in propositional forms, the validity of the confessional
creeds and the authority of the biblical text were also
brought into disrepute. Could an evangelist make more
than descriptive statements concerning the acts of God in
history? Could an evangelist do more than share his
subjective experience with God? Were not the fruits of
Christianity's good works necessary to validate the
message? Were not the power and life of historical
evangelism vitiated because the evangelist could no
longer quote with certainty, "God says," "Jesus says,"
"Paul said"? Evangelistic appeal could only be made on
the basis of the pragmatic values of Christianity, and not
with the certainty of forgiveness of sin against God and
peace with God.

MADRAS 1938 AND
THE CHURCH

The Madras 1938 meeting was preceded by the Oxford
1937 meeting of the Life and Work, that found the

Church to be the responsible instrument of evangelization. Attention was still focused upon the individual need for repentance and conversion as the starting point of the Christian life, for it is evangelism that strikes at the root of social evil. Evangelism should hold a central and preeminent place in the life of the Church. But it was the Church, which was established "to proclaim the message of salvation to all nations."[26]

Oxford 1937 "spoke" to Madras 1938 and strongly suggested that the International Missionary Conference belonged within the ranks of the yet unofficial WCC. The conference also looked forward to the coming Kingdom of God to which the Church bears witness.

Further theological preparation for Madras 1938 came from the Faith and Order meeting at Edinburgh 1937. While there was a strong place given to the Bible, it was a Bible with human limitations. This Bible, therefore, is recognized as a valid source of revelation because the Bible is within the stream of the Church's life, in its tradition. Edinburgh 1937 said that it is "the Church, enlightened by the Holy Spirit (that) has been instrumental in the formation of the Bible."[27]

Oxford 1937 and Edinburgh 1937 established several trends which dominate the entire ecumenical movement to this day:

1. The utilitarian value of evangelism in the social scene of the world, in contrast to an eternal importance because of the eternal value of the soul.

2. The prominence of the Church visible and organized in evangelism, in contrast to the responsibility of individual Christians to evangelize.

3. The authority of the Church as an institution in evangelism, in contrast to the authority of Scripture. The Bible has human limitations, but has validity because it is in the tradition of the Church.

4. The testimony of the Church in society becomes fundamental for evangelism, in contrast to the inner witness of the Holy Spirit accompanying and commending the proclamation of the Scripture. If the testimony of the Church is defective because of disunity,

or is unaccompanied by social concern or action, the
authority of the Church in its witness to the world is lost,
and evangelism is either hindered or impossible.

THE MESSAGE OF THE
LARGER EVANGELISM

The Jerusalem 1928 meeting expected a new and better
world, but the world situation resulting from the world
economic crisis of 1929 and the rise of European
totalitarianism prior to World War II destroyed any
optimism that remained. Madras 1938 could only look to
the Church as a source of hope.

It was the composition of Madras that influenced the
Message. Jerusalem 1928 had been the first conference
to invite the younger national churches to participate,
and Madras 1938 included more "Third World"
churches through their national councils than ever
before. Schmidt records this development,

> The prior divisions had been Continental
> traditionalism, American liberalism, with the British
> near the center mediating the debate. Now,
> according to Van Dusen, Continental thinkers
> composed a "small rather extreme right wing." The
> Americans had moved closer to the center than
> usual, while a "liberal evangelicalism" formed the
> major group represented by the Younger
> Churches.[28]

It appears that Evangelicals in the Western churches had
largely withdrawn from the IMC and that another form
of evangelicalism reentered through the younger church
founded by nineteenth-century evangelical missions.

The utter bankruptcy of the modernism of the 1920s
was manifested by the publication of the Hocking Report
in 1932. At the same time, there was a biblical renewal in
the IMC due to Karl Barth and Emil Brunner. It was
upon the superstructure of an errant, fallible
Bible—nevertheless, taken seriously—that the Message of
the Larger Evangelism was built. It was neo-orthodoxy,

the acceptance of higher critical "findings" and of
modern scientism, that were foundational in this earlier
expression of what is now "holistic" evangelism.

Attention is focused upon the incarnation. The continuing
influence of liberalism caused Madras 1938 to hesitate in
making a clear statement about the person of Jesus
Christ and His atonement. Greater agreement could be
found concerning the incarnation, as well as the Church.
Madras did not make clear in what sense Jesus Christ
was the revelation of God. Barth believed the incarnation
of Jesus Christ to be the revelation of the Word of God,
"God with us."[29] Kraemer viewed the incarnation as the
essential feature of the Christian faith.[30] Madras asserted
in bold letters: "GOD IN HIS INFINITE LOVE HAS
ACTED FOR MEN'S SALVATION. HE HAS COME
AMONG THEM IN JESUS OF NAZARETH, HIS
WORD MADE FLESH."[31] Contemporary "holistic"
evangelism in ecumenical thought has strong roots in the
Larger Evangelism—in its uncertainty regarding the
inspiration and authority of the Scripture, in its greater
emphasis upon the place of the incarnation than upon
the work of the Cross, and in its concern for the present
world almost to the exclusion of the destiny of man in
the world to come.

At Madras 1938 the "acts" of God—and especially the
incarnation—began to be viewed with greater confidence
than the "Word" of God, the Bible. The mystical
presence of Christ in the world since the incarnation
became the foundation of incarnational theology. Christ
present in His Church led to Christ present in the world,
and in all world events. The providence of a
transcendent God became the presence of an immanent
God. These pantheistic tendencies made it difficult to see
where God is and where He is not, in whom He dwells
and in whom He does not dwell.

The Mandate of Madras 1938. The German minority at
Madras disagreed with the preoccupation of Madras with
the Church and the temporal world: they looked forward

to a new heaven and a new earth through a creative act
of God, the appearance of Christ Himself to transform
this present world structure. Christians have a dual
citizenship:

> The Church of Christ, being an interim-body
> between the times of God who has sent the Saviour
> and will send Him again, is moving forward into
> this world to proclaim the redeeming message, that
> our sins are forgiven in Christ and we are saved by
> faith in hope.[32]

This minority reiterated the importance of proclamation,
the forgiveness of sins, and the return of Christ as the
promised hope for the world. Salvation at Madras 1938,
however, meant a fulfillment in Christ of both society
and the individual. In some undetermined way, there
would be an ultimate fulfillment of all things in Christ
because the Christian community was an instrument of
world reconciliation. There were two views: one
pessimistic concerning the future of society without the
return of Christ; the other optimistic of what the Church
can accomplish for the totality of mankind.

The Madras means of evangelization. Edinburgh 1910 saw
evangelism in terms of the individual and missions;
Jerusalem 1928 established a partnership between
missions and the younger churches. Madras focused
upon the Church universal, as the divine answer to the
needs of men:

> World evangelism is the God-given task of the
> Church. . . This conception of the Church as the
> missionary to the world is given in the New
> Testament. The Church's evangelism is the
> expression of its loving devotion to Christ and of
> the insight given to it by the Holy Spirit that Christ
> is the Answer to the needs of man.[33]

The entire Church should participate in evangelism.

> Every part of the Christian enterprise must be
> saturated with and controlled by the conscious
> evangelistic purpose, and this should be true of the
> whole range of the church's practical activities.[34]

It was the corporate witness of the Church that would be
"a powerful factor in determining the measure of
response men make to the message of the Gospel."[35]
This means of evangelism—the Church—was no longer a
"soul-winning" Church that supposedly concerned itself
with the inward part of man, to the exclusion of his
physical needs. It was the Church, rather than the
individual as a disciple of Jesus Christ, which brought
others to the life of the Christian community. "Personal
evangelism" by the Church replaced "soul-winning" by
the individual believer.

A Madras method of evangelism. In the Protestant
evangelism of the nineteenth century, the individual
approach prevailed. Latourette, however, in his
preparatory historical research for Madras concluded
that individualism was not characteristic of either the
early Church or that of the Middle Ages. Individual
conversions tended to separate one from one's culture, to
place an emphasis upon a conscious experience of the
new birth, and to demand a high standard for church
membership. Mass conversions of previous centuries
avoided alien and unnatural expressions of Christianity.
Furthermore, political, economic, and cultural influences
mold the religious life of a people and can result in mass
conversions capable of the Christianization of the society,
as well as speeding the evangelization of the
non-Christian world.[36]
   Madras, however, had clearly repudiated the growing
trend toward syncretism of Jerusalem 1928 and now
spoke cautiously and concernedly regarding

> the tendency to preserve group institutions and
> patterns of behaviour inconsistent with the
> obligations of Christian discipleship, and the

disposition to be satisfied with the group aspects of religion to the neglect of personal devotion and purity.[37]

There was a place given to a piety distinct from that of the non-Christian aspects of culture.

THE CONSEQUENCES OF THE LARGER EVANGELISM

The mission and evangelism aspect of the WCC seemed to indicate a dramatic reversal from the social gospel direction of previous decades. The outbreak of World War II in the following year, in 1939, hindered the first attempts to evangelize as an ecumenical movement. During World War II, the men who had been involved in the IMC from the very beginning passed from the scene through retirement or death. The Larger Evangelism was never successfully implemented.

Evangelism in the Third World churches. Traditional evangelism in the Western churches was not popular and almost died out, except in the then-small separatist movements and churches. It was the younger Third World churches from nearly fifty lands that were primarily responsible for the evangelistic conclusion of Madras. Hogg says that they

> were concerned with evangelism—intensive and extensive evangelism. They rejected that view which made it a "missionary" or departmental task and offered rather the Church, the whole community of believers, as the supreme instrument of total evangelism.[38]

Evangelism in evangelicalism. Campaign evangelism in North America was no longer generally acceptable to the denominational churches. The status of evangelicalism was illustrated by the name that Charles E. Fuller gave to his Sunday evening radio broadcast, "The Old-Fashioned

Revival Hour," in 1933. Local church evangelism
continued in new movements and "tabernacles."
"Storefront" and frame church buildings of Evangelicals
and Pentecostals sprang up as a result of these
campaigns in the 1930s. Bible schools began to replace
the liberal seminaries as a source of pastors, and
evangelicalism began to regain its former vigor, especially
during the World War II years, as youth movements
such as Youth for Christ introduced new evangelistic
leadership to the national scene. Nevertheless,
evangelism in general, and mass evangelism in particular,
was far from popular. Theological confusion concerning
the place of evangelism reigned in the denominations,
and God called new voices such as Billy Graham.

The twenty-eight year period between Edinburgh 1910
and Madras 1938 had seen evangelism slip to its lowest
level of theological acceptance by the Church. Popular
opinion held religion and evangelism in disdain. About
five years before Madras 1938, however, the IMC led by
John R. Mott brought evangelism back into a measure of
theological respectability. This evangelism was not
evangelical, but rather a compromise based on a
synthesis of modernism and fundamentalism in the
neo-orthodoxy theology of Karl Barth. Yet this Larger
Evangelism had its advocates in the nineteenth century
among the missions that had lost their evangelical
evangelistic zeal.[39] Yet evangelical missions involved in
soul winning built schools, hospitals, orphanages, fought
the opium trade and slavery, sought the moral and social
welfare of young men and young women, and spread
their salvationist efforts from the slums of England to
the ends of the earth.

The basic issues of inspiration and authority. The theological
nuance, the inspiration and authority of the Bible,
seemed trite and divisive, yet this was the basic question.
God the Holy Spirit uses the proclamation of His Word,
the Bible, to regenerate the heart of the sinner and lead
him to faith in Jesus Christ (Rom. 10:17). The errant
Bible of the nonevangelical led to the evangelistic
"hesitancy" within the historic churches of the West.

The Larger Evangelism most aptly characterized the post-World War II mainline churches of the West. Their sterility in Europe, making it one of the most needy mission fields in the world today,[40] and their decline in North America[41] are widely recognized. On the other hand, evangelical churches—whether in Africa, South America, Indonesia, or North America—possess vitality and are growing. Admittedly, many factors are involved, but the patient sowing of the written Word of God has brought about the transformation of the heart and soul and then abundant improvements of family and civic conditions, as new believers turn from idols to serve the living God (Mark 4; 1 Thess. 1).

If ecumenical evangelism was unable to implement the evangelism which Madras 1938 restored, God was able to do so through those who remained committed and faithful to the Scripture. The post-Madras 1938 decade began to see a resurgence of evangelical evangelism in many nations of the world. In the United States, Billy Graham became one of the most prominent mass evangelists, and led evangelism to a new level of acceptance and respect in this country.

The authority of the Scripture provides the dynamic of biblical evangelism. The apostles accurately recorded what Jesus Christ said and did. Their interpretation of His message provided the instruments for evangelism since the first century. Madras 1938 mistakenly substituted the authority of the Church in evangelism and, because of its low view of the Bible, required the authenticity of the works of the Church, or organizational unity, to commend the Gospel to the hearts of men. But the earthly limitations of this institution between the times will never possess or replace the power that God has put within His Word. The Bible is the living and energizing dynamic of evangelism.

Modernism and liberalism nearly destroyed the sense of need for evangelism rooted in the sinful nature of man and his eternal lostness without personal faith in Christ Jesus. The neo-orthodoxy of the Larger Evangelism hindered effective proclamation, by either depreciating the Bible as Brunner did by calling it a "paper pope," or by sharing the authority of the apostolic message given once for all with the authority of the pastor who speaks "the Word of God," or the authority of a personal experience.[42]

The authority of the Church—whether expressed in preaching, proclamation, or personal experience—is not that final and necessary instrument used by the Holy Spirit to regenerate the sinner. The evangelist is to preach the Word, the Word written (2 Tim. 3:13–4:5). Madras 1938 said that the Church and individuals had to win the right to be heard. The Bible says that the works of Jesus in His life and His death have already won for Him the right to be heard. The believer is to witness and evangelize, to spread the message, to preach and proclaim who Christ is, and what He has done for sinners.

3
Developments in Evangelism Before Berlin 1966

The post-World War II era was
marked by three principal developments in the theology
and practice of evangelism. First, the International
Missionary Council emerged from Madras 1938 with the
"Larger Evangelism" that would represent a step forward
from the evangelical evangelism characteristic of the "old
school" of evangelism. Plans for the intensive
implementation of this new kind of evangelism were
decimated by both the turmoil of World War II and by
the death or retirement of the IMC leaders who were
involved in formulating this evangelistic program.
Another factor that made the IMC more of a holding
operation was the drive toward the integration of the
IMC with the newly-created WCC at Amsterdam 1948.
Since Madras 1938, it appeared that evangelism and
mission belonged within the WCC and not outside of the
"Church." The rejection of the evangelicalism by the
IMC provoked the withdrawal of most of them from the
ecumenical movement and left the IMC with little
apparent evangelistic enthusiasm. The IMC continued to
be moved steadily toward integration with the WCC at

New Delhi 1961 and also developed an even more liberal
and radical attitude toward evangelism.

Second, the WCC at their first Assembly at Amsterdam
1948 gave promise of having both a traditional view of
evangelism and a far more receptive attitude toward
evangelical evangelists and evangelism. The pluralistic
theological basis of the WCC, however, did not seem to
be able to retain the historical views of sin, redemption,
and reconciliation through personal faith in Christ. The
theological pilgrimage toward the integration of the IMC
records their implicit rejection of even the "Larger
Evangelism" concept of the Madras 1938 meeting of the
IMC. The WCC established a Department of Evangelism
at Amsterdam 1948, but demonstrated no ability to fulfill
the promises of church renewal in evangelism either
before the New Delhi 1961 Third Assembly or after the
integration with the IMC. One primary post-Amsterdam
1948 concern was upon a decision on "proselytism" so
that New Delhi 1961 could assure the Eastern Orthodox
churches that the remaining Evangelicals in the IMC
would not threaten their churches by evangelism in the
Eastern Orthodox parts of the world. Evangelism in the
WCC at New Delhi 1961, integrated with the IMC,
became the Division of World Mission and Evangelism
(DWME). *Proclaiming* the biblical message began to be
totally eclipsed by an emphasis upon the importance of
the nonverbal presence of united Christendom. Because
of this evangelistic vacuum, the Berlin 1966 Congress on
Evangelism became necessary.

Third, struggling evangelicalism, separated from the
ecumenical movement, began to recover the numerical
strength lost in the earlier years of this century. The
post-World War II era was a time of rebuilding the
churches in North America, and a surge of evangelical
national churches emerged with the rise of nationalism.
This rise was led by the Bible institute, Bible college, and
Christian liberal arts movements that supplied evangelical
pastors, missionaries, and evangelists. Billy Graham
became the most acknowledged representative of
evangelical Christianity around the world.

HESITANT EVANGELISM DEVELOPS IN THE IMC
EVANGELISM FACES INTEGRATION

The last three post-World War II conferences of the IMC leading to New Delhi 1961 were dominated by four considerations influencing evangelism. First, the call to evangelism endorsed at Madras 1938 continued as a persistent missionary responsibility. World War II disrupted the plans for a World Mission prepared by the National Christian Mission Committee of the Federal Council of Churches of Christ of America and reported to the Provisional Meeting of the WCC meeting at St. Germain-en-Laye in January 1939,

> . . .as many churches as possible should join in a World Mission to be held from October, 1940, to April, 1941. Each church or country would carry on the Mission in its own way, but the simultaneity of effort, the interchange of plans and possibly in some cases missionaries might be helpful.[1]

The first and only worldwide simultaneous evangelistic effort of the WCC was welcomed and recommended for circulation among the churches. In spite of the theological problems of the IMC, it is significant to note that in the earlier years of the WCC there was a place for evangelical evangelism.[2] Few within or without the ecumenical movement would have had time to absorb or implement the Larger Evangelism concepts of Madras 1938. The word "evangelism" still maintained its traditional significance. It was not until the New Delhi 1961 Assembly and the Uppsala 1968 Assembly that evangelical evangelism was almost totally excluded and "evangelism" was redefined.

Second, the WCC was officially inaugurated in 1948 at

Amsterdam. The IMC, now church-oriented instead of
missions-oriented since Madras 1938, could not ignore
the existence of this new ecclesiastical organization
grouping "Faith and Order" and "Life and Work" but in
existence without the missionary enterprise.

Third, the Madras 1938 emphasis upon the
evangelistic mission of the Church continued to insist
upon a growing theological and practical relationship
between missions and churches. Finally, the two world
wars, a major world financial crisis in 1929, and the
rapid rise of secularism and communism forced first
historians and then theologians to rethink and to restate
the Christian philosophy of history and the biblical view
of eschatology: Toward what goals is history directed?
What is the goal of missions and evangelism? Is the
Kingdom of God a Christianized world, the Church, the
utopian millennium, or the return of Christ?

PARTNERSHIP IN
EVANGELISM:
WHITBY 1947

After the interruption of the Madras 1938 program by
World War II, Whitby 1947 incorporated into the
organizational structure of the IMC the theological
conclusions of Madras on evangelism. The Larger
Evangelism was to be accomplished by the full
partnership of missions with the younger churches.

Preparations for Whitby attempted to restudy
fundamental missionary principles in relation to the
Amsterdam 1948 assembly of the WCC the following
year, "The Order of God and the Disorder of Man." The
biblical theology of C. H. Dodd predominated, built
upon views of revelation expressed by Karl Barth and
William Temple. Each Christian is to proclaim the
kerygma, that essential kernel of truth concerning Christ
given within the Bible. But that "Word" was understood

by some to be articulate and understood only through a living community of Christians. Evangelism is valid only within the framework of the visible church. By others, the "Word" is incarnate in human lives; the Scripture by itself is insufficient for evangelism. While the Bible was once again recognized as *an* instrument of evangelism, it remained a fallible Bible, not the authoritative apostolic Scripture. Nor does God reveal Himself in propositions: Truth may be described but not defined in doctrinal creeds or statements. Nor is revelation confined to the Bible. Christ may also be incarnate in history, in events, and in individuals—in much the same way as the "Word" is given to us in the Bible. No clear limits are placed upon the revelations of the "Word." Theology became open-ended, yet it was the Bible, Whitby concluded, that was necessary for Church renewal and evangelism.[3]

As at Madras 1938, Whitby also declared that evangelism should include the "entry of the risen Christ into every part of the life of the world."[4] This was "total evangelization" whereby the revived Church would, in a passionate concern, give leadership in "true social revolution—the fight against ignorance, want, disease, oppression, and sin."[5] The results of this kind of evangelism would show that the Kingdom of God is "far more satisfying than the kingdom of man believed in and proclaimed by the communists."[6] The Christian way of life, consequently, was seen as in social competition with secularism. The social superiority of Christianity became a motive for evangelism! Good works are not only individual, but corporate, community, collective, and, possibly, national. Can the collective good works of a united Church result in world evangelization? If they can, what will it lead to? This raised the question of the relationship of eschatology to evangelism which Willingen 1952 and the Evanston 1954 WCC Assembly would strive unsuccessfully to resolve. Whitby was a return to Jerusalem 1928, for a concern for the "souls" of men and their eternal destiny was not apparent.

REALIZED
EVANGELISM:
WILLINGEN 1952

Willingen was influenced strongly by the 1948
Amsterdam Assembly of the WCC and the continued
expressions of these views by the presence of the WCC
leadership in the IMC committee meetings. Amsterdam
insisted that there could be no separation between
church and missions. Evangelism is an ecumenical task of
the spiritually renewed community. The Church should
not depend upon "the devotion and initiative of a gifted
individual."[7] Evangelism was seen both as a solution to
the problem that the Church is losing ground, and as a
source for promoting unity. Every individual in the
Church is responsible to win others to Christ, and the
Church is to have a redemptive influence in society.

Biblical renewal should be the true bond of
ecumenicity. Toward achieving this goal, the WCC
sought agreement on adopting a common "biblical
theology" rather than the divisive systematic theologies of
the denominations. This adoption of "biblical theology,"
however, did not mean a return to a precritical
(nineteenth-century) attitude toward the Bible, yet it did
recognize that the Word of God spoke through the Bible.
As within the WCC, the dialectical Christocentric
theology of Karl Barth seemed best suited to establish a
"new consensus" with the missionary movement, in
preparation for its integration with the WCC.
Barthianism was especially compatible because it directed
attention toward the *kerygma* within the Bible, rather than
toward the high authority of the text, toward the *discovery*
of the "Word," and away from intensive Bible study, and
toward God's message to the Church, nations, and
communities, rather than toward individual souls alone.

The post-World War II era before Evanston
represented a period of strong biblical renewal in the
WCC and in the IMC. W. A. Visser 't Hooft, then
General Secretary of the WCC, optimistically recalls the
surprising measure of agreement among the

WCC-related scholars concerning the judgment of Scripture.[8] Two observations, however, must be made: 1. Few, if any, scholars invited by the WCC would hold to a non-higher-critical view of the Bible. Consequently, they generally consider the Bible to be fallible, errant, and containing the introduction of human viewpoints that are non-revelational in nature; the interpretation of the Bible, therefore, can never give definitive results, for if the exegesis was conclusive and crystallized, it is said, God would cease to speak in a fresh and new way to us.[9] It is conceded that Bible study in the WCC is difficult because of the differing views concerning the Bible as revelation, its inspiration, and determining just what the *kerygma* is—those essential doctrines of the New Testament proclamation.[10] Ecumenists generally insist that Evangelicals have too closely identified the Bible and the Word of God, and therefore, Evangelicals have limited their understanding of the Word of God (not the Bible) to its apostolic "form" (the Bible), and have not been able to listen to the "Word" which God is now speaking to His Church.
2. Some in the early years were deeply distressed by the disunity concerning the Bible. Suzanne de Dietrich, prominent in the WCC biblical renewal found that,

> many would say that there is no more controversial subject in the ecumenical exchange of thought than our interpretation of the Bible, and they would add perhaps that, the Bible being such a factor of disunity, we had better evade the subject.[11]

Why did this biblical renewal not produce revival and evangelism in Europe and wherever it was adopted and taught? It was because Barthian theology adopted by the WCC leadership believed the Bible to be a witness to revelation recorded in the Bible rather than a revelation itself. That is, the Bible is an inspired record of the revelation given to the prophets and apostles, but the Bible per se is not revelation. The Bible is only a witness to God's revelation of Himself in Jesus Christ. The

believer, it is said, is not in direct contact with the
"Word" in the Bible, but the Bible can only lead to a
personal experience of revelation of the "Word." The
evangelist, therefore, cannot speak with any biblical
authority except to say that Paul, for example, had an
experience of revelation with God, but you must have
yours. There is a qualitative distinction between the
evangelical and neo-orthodox Bible. The evangelist of
the Larger Evangelism cannot say, "Jesus says," "God
says." Consequently, neo-evangelical evangelists cannot
present a definitive plan of salvation to the seeker, so
that he may commit himself to Jesus Christ as Savior and
Lord. The "acts" of God in biblical and secular history
become necessary to substantiate the individual
experience of God's Word, but not the totality of the
biblical records. To the neo-orthodox, the Spirit of God
does not work in, with, and by the Word.[12]
    This low view of Scripture would influence evangelistic
methods. In a paper prepared for Willingen 1954, W.
Lillie logically concluded that the *kerygma*, the "Word of
God," would give "a message not only to individual souls,
but to nations and communities of all kinds, and
especially to the fellowship of the Church."[13] Puritan
individualism and great evangelists, he wrote, "caused an
emphasis upon individual conversions and a neglect of
the Church."[14] In the Barthian view of Scripture, the
Word of authority is discovered. Lillie implies that the
interest of Evangelicals in intensive Bible study would
decrease as the extreme verbalism characteristic of
individual evangelism diminished. The Barthian view of
Scripture and theology led away from modernism, but it
also led away from "soul winning" toward a salvation
found in the Christian community and toward the
salvation of society.
    Willingen resulted in the first theological deadlock in
the life of the IMC. As it sought an eschatology, the wide
divergencies of opinions concerning the sources of divine
revelation became more evident. Even among those who
accepted the biblical text, there were strikingly different
methods of interpretation. There was a basic

disagreement with the mediating theological work of
Oscar Cullmann concerning the philosophy of history.
Was the death and resurrection of Christ, for example, a
redemptive historical event of the past, or was it a
symbolic expression of man's total present life, or was it a
message to the apostles—one of many redemptive events
of Christ in history—a Kingdom realized at the present
time in the life of the Church? The literal hell of
old-fashioned orthodoxy was rejected, and a real heaven
received little attention.

In the Second Report to the WCC Evanston Assembly
1954, the apocalyptic return of Christ to establish a
millennial reign in a restored political Israel was
considered an unsatisfactory eschatological
interpretation.[15] Evanston and Willingen seem to have
attempted to resolve eschatological questions by using
biblical theology as a common source of theology,
between natural theology and existential theology. No
consensus on the missionary obligation was obtained
because of the theological extremes. The question as to
"from what and to what" man is saved was never
resolved but had to await the "horizontal" solution
supplied by the 1973 DWME Bangkok meeting.

The "realized evangelism" declared at Willingen 1952
produced a more decisive dichotomy between
Evangelicals and ecumenists than any other doctrinal
issue. Realized evangelism is understood as the
recognition that the "full and perfect atonement" of
Christ has already saved Christians and non-Christians
alike. This universalism goes beyond the true biblical
teaching that the God of Israel included the entire world
in His redemptive purposes, and erroneously adds to this
that the death of Christ is not only adequate (sufficient)
for all but efficative (efficient) for all. William Schmidt
outlined the rise of this ecumenical universalism in the
period between Amsterdam 1948 and Evanston 1954.[16]

Evangelism was disassociated from the damnation of
souls, and it was associated with the proclamation of
Christ's present reign "in every moment and in every
situation."[17] The reign of Christ was not seen as

futuristic—for man is *already* reconciled and part of the new humanity resulting from the death of Christ. Willingen said,

> God has sent forth one Savior, one Shepherd to seek and save all the lost, one Redeemer who by His death, resurrection and ascension has broken down the barrier between man and God, accomplished a full and perfect atonement, and created in Himself one new humanity, the Body of which Christ is the exalted and regnant Head.[18]

GHANA 1958: THE MISSION IS GOD'S, NOT MAN'S

The future theology of evangelism and mission of the ecumenical movement would be greatly influenced by universalism, for the implied rejection of the eternal damnation of the unbelieving soul redirected the purpose of evangelism toward the realization of the reign of Christ upon the earth. As David Jenkins expressed this purpose a few years later, in preparation for the 1958 Ghana conference that introduced the mission as God's (missio dei), and not man's,

> . . .the mission is the activity of God, not the conversion of men to belief or the recruiting of men to the ranks of the saved (and incidentally to our side!), but the living out in the world of the life of God which is the life of love and in which the Church lives.[19]

Since God has saved all men from sin, the mission of the Church is to gather men into the *fullness* of Christ which is to be found in the life of the Church. The Church is already eschatological "in the sense that it partakes in the End and not merely that it waits for it or works toward it."[20] Through this erroneous view of the atonement, universalism led the IMC even further away from an

evangelical evangelism, which was anchored in the
immortality of the soul and in the eternal lostness and
damnation of those without a personal faith in Christ.
Realized evangelism intensified the IMC preoccupation
with the present reign of Christ upon the earth. For the
Evangelical, Christ is Lord in the Church, but Satan is
the prince of this world and its system, until Christ
returns the second time to reign.

The preparatory paper for Willingen 1952 by Bengt
Sundkler was accurate:

> The missionary motive and outlook have . . .
> changed radically in the last decades. . . .in our
> thinking the corporate category of the large-scale
> organisms of church has replaced the individualistic
> outlook of 19th-century pietism and revivalism.[21]

Does the Church exist as a demonstration of what the
world will be, or is the world the field where the seed is
sown and the harvest is gathered in for the day when the
redeemed will reign in the world? The problem is
eschatological and ecclesiological as well as soteriological.
The fusion of God's plan for the Church with God's plan
for the present world has brought continual confusion in
evangelistic methods.

Ever since Edinburgh 1910, integration was believed to
be necessary for evangelism as well as for the Church.
Evangelism belonged to the Church and was essential for
its spiritual health.[22] Not all were convinced that the
reasons for integration were historically true,
theologically sound, or practically feasible. Nevertheless,
Ghana 1958 decided upon integration. Mission became
part of the Church.

Evangelism between Ghana 1958 and the New Delhi
Assembly was described by Bishop Lesslie Newbigin as
"hesitant." Evangelism had lost its momentum by the end
of the 1950s.

> The sense of direction, the feeling of urgency, and
> the depth of conviction which underlay the slogan
> "The Evangelization of the World in this

Generation" are not present today in anything like
the same measure in most of the bodies represented
in the IMC and the WCC. . . We are in a period of
hesitancy.[23]

AMSTERDAM 1948 ACCEPTS EVANGELICAL EVANGELISM

The momentum of evangelism launched at the IMC
meeting at Madras 1938 continued in the WCC.
Evangelism was to be practiced in the lands of the older
as well as the younger churches. Philip Potter, now
general secretary of the WCC, saw the Larger
Evangelism of Madras 1938 as the beginning and center
of the IMC-DWME understanding of evangelism.[24] It
was normal and necessary, therefore, for ecumenical
unity to incorporate and integrate the IMC evangelistic
work into the WCC program.

Because of the conservative definition of evangelism
given at Madras 1938 and because of the pluralistic
theological atmosphere which prevailed at the first
Assembly in Amsterdam 1948, evangelical evangelism
retained a place in the ecumenical movement. This place,
however, was sustained only by the weak inclusivist Basis
adopted by the WCC.

THE BASIS OF THE WORLD COUNCIL OF CHURCHES

An evaluation of the 1948 Basis adopted by the WCC is
fundamental to an understanding of the pluralistic views
and theologies of evangelism expressed within the WCC:

> The World Council of Churches is a fellowship of
> churches which accept our Lord Jesus Christ as God
> and Saviour.[25]

This brief statement said nothing about the authority of the Scripture, and nothing about the Trinity. Since it had been affirmed consistently that this Basis is not intended to be a creed or a full statement of the Christian faith, it had not provided adequate theological guidelines to maintain even a stable ecumenical theology.[26] This first Basis was expanded at New Delhi in 1961 to include a declaration on the Scripture, the Trinity, the "confessing" nature of the Church and its unity of purpose:

> The World Council of Churches is a fellowship of churches which confess the Lord Jesus Christ as God and Saviour according to the Scriptures and therefore seek to fulfill together their common calling to the glory of the one God, Father, Son and Holy Spirit.[27]

The continuous insistence by the Church of Norway and by the Orthodox churches who joined the WCC in 1961[28] prompted the adoption of these amendments. In spite of the pluralistic theological atmosphere, less and less consideration was given to an evangelical theology of evangelism. The expanded Basis of New Delhi 1961 did not impede the strong "horizontalism" so evident in future WCC conferences and assemblies. The Basis was intended only "to say what holds us together in the World Council, what is the starting-point of our conversation and the foundation of our collaboration."[29] The addition was seen as an expansion of what was already implicitly contained in the Amsterdam 1948 Basis. It was not meant to exclude error or discipline heresy. For Evangelicals its weakness is not in what it said but what it did *not* say about the inspiration of Scripture, sin, the person of Christ, the atonement and eternal punishment.

CHURCH RENEWAL
INSTEAD OF REVIVAL

Over the past decades, nonevangelical pluralistic theology has consistently discouraged evangelical evangelism and qualified its acceptance. Nor has it resulted in the church renewal so needful in Western Europe. Visser 't Hooft has admitted that the WCC's return to the Bible and to biblical theology as a unifying force has not resulted in the renewal of the older churches in the ecumenical movement.[30] As has been shown, the return to "biblical theology" was a theological effort to promote unity built upon an errant Bible and depending upon the ultimate authority of the Church.

The increased authority of the Church restricted the ecumenical "evangelist" to saying, "Thus saith the Church." Ecumenical unity is not conceived as the unity of individuals brought into a saving relationship with Christ by the "new birth," but rather upon the visible unity of the Church.[31] Its focus has been upon the churches as institutions in need of *structural* renewal rather than gatherings of individuals in need of spiritual revival.

Ecumenical renewal blurred distinctions between the Church and the world. Visser 't Hooft saw the WCC as bringing the Church and the world back together! They had been separated by the pietist theology of the nineteenth century. The approaching social unity of the world and the necessity of molding a world civilization require a world stature for Christianity, which will replace the postion of privilege formerly held by traditionally Christian countries of the West. The growing estrangement between the Church and the world must be bridged by "the new sense of the integrity of the Church and the refusal on the part of Christians to accept a coexistence with the world in which Christianity loses its identity."[32] After recognizing the "debate" between conservative Evangelicals and the ecumenical movement over this concentration of ecumenical energies on social and international problems, Visser 't Hooft asks "the great question,"

> What is evangelism? Is the Church evangelistic only if it preaches the Gospel to individuals? Or is it also

> evangelistic if it throws the light of the Gospel on
> the great human problems of our time?[33]

His view of evangelism extended to interaction with
sociopolitical problems.

EVANGELICAL
EVANGELISM AT
AMSTERDAM 1948

The first WCC Conference on Evangelism was held at
Geneva February 11-19, 1947, under the auspices of the
Reconstruction and Inter-Church Aid Department
directed by Dr. J. Huckinson Cockburn. In addition to
five staff members, including the general secretary, W.
A. Visser 't Hooft, there were twenty-four representatives
from Western Europe, Austria, Hungary, and
Czechoslovakia. The United States was represented by E.
G. Homrighausen of Princeton Seminary and chairman
of the Department of Evangelism of the Federal Council
of Churches in America.

This conference is significant because of the
predominant evangelical atmosphere and statements.
Visser 't Hooft, in addressing the conference,
emphasized the ecumenical aspects of evangelism and
related its conclusions on evangelism to the forthcoming
1948 Amsterdam Assembly and, specifically, to the
second Assembly Commission, "God's Design and Man's
Witness." The conference adopted a definition of
evangelism closely resembling that of the Federal Council
of Churches in America which was proposed by
Homrighausen. The finding report indicates the
thoroughly evangelical nature of this post-World War II
conference of primarily European evangelists. The
report was entitled "Definition and Description of the
Concept of Evangelism."

> The basis of Evangelism is the outgoing and
> redeeming Love of God, made known and made
> effective in Jesus Christ. . . .

> Evangelism is the proclamation and presentation of
> the good news of God in Jesus Christ so that men
> are brought, through the power of the Holy Spirit,
> to put their trust in God; to accept Jesus Christ as
> their Savior from the guilt and power of sin; and to
> follow and serve Him as their Lord, within the
> fellowship of the Church, in the vocations of the
> common life. . . .
> We are convinced that the present situation in
> Europe and in the world constitutes an urgent call
> to the Church and to its members to realize that
> everyone who has been called by the living Christ is
> sent to be a joyful witness to God's love and grace
> and to proclaim the good news of Christ's lordship
> and salvation to his neighbor, that is to all with
> whom he is brought into relationship by the
> circumstances of daily life. . . .
> Evangelism must proceed from the Church and
> must gather into the fellowship of the Church those
> who are evangelized. It is the work of the whole
> Church, but at the present time there is urgent
> need to recognize and to develop the special gifts of
> those to whom God has given the call to be
> evangelists as their particular vocation within the
> Church. We should pray for the awakening of these
> special gifts, as well as for the awakening of the
> whole Church by the Spirit to its evangelistic
> responsibilities.[34]

Few Evangelicals would take exception to the above
statements.

The Reports from the Commissions dealt with:

> I. The Spiritual Status of the Church in the
> Post-War World
> II. Methods of Evangelism
> III. Report 1. Evangelism and the Ecumenical
> Approach
> IV. Report 2. In What Way Can the World Council
> Make Its Best Contribution in the Interest of
> Evangelism

V. Evangelism in the Current Program of the
Church
VI. Evangelism among Youth
VII. Press, Cinema, and Radio

In Report 2 of Commission III, a Commission on
Evangelism in the WCC was proposed that "will not
impose any particular theology upon the churches, but it
cannot be indifferent to the evangelistic message of the
Bible."[35] Of particular interest are the functions of the
proposed Commission:

> The functions of such a Commission may be to
> serve the constituent churches in their evangelistic
> tasks, to study ways and means by which evangelism
> can be more effectively done, to investigate some of
> the problems involved in evangelistic efforts, to
> conduct and finance Conferences on Evangelism for
> pastors and laymen as the churches may desire, in
> Geneva or elsewhere, to recruit and train
> evangelists for special types of work, to exchange
> information among the churches regarding
> evangelistic projects now in progress, to assist the
> churches in the training of laymen for evangelistic
> work, to keep before the churches the urgency and
> ecumenical nature of evangelism, to provide
> opportunities for the creation of an evangelistic
> fellowship of prayer and study for representatives
> of the churches, to finance and publish evangelistic
> literature, to circulate books and pamphlets, to
> discover ways of making Christian Education
> evangelistic, to provide ecumenical evangelistic
> teams where they may be desired by the churches,
> and to coordinate various evangelistic activities of
> the Council.[36]

The Report of Commission III, chaired by
Homrighausen, introduced one of the most ambiguous
elements for Evangelicals into the reports. The overtones
of universalism are apparent, "The Son of God
incarnate. . .has reconciled the world to God through his

Cross, and reigns as Lord of the Church and of the
world."[37] It implied that all have already been reconciled
by the Cross, and it recognized the Lordship of Christ in
the Church as also reigning similarly in the present
world system.

Other Reports, such as Commission IV, leave little for
Evangelicals to desire:

> The Christian Church as the body of Christ is called
> to express the love and mind of her Master. Her
> primary task is to proclaim the glorious Gospel of
> God's redeeming love to those who do not know
> God, as well as to work for the mutual edification of
> those who have been saved from their sins through
> humble repentance and surrender to Jesus Christ as
> Redeemer and Lord. This task of the Church is
> inherent in her calling and is never finished because
> of the multitudes of individuals who must be called
> to make a surrender to Him who alone saves.[38]

The initial theological position of the first conference on
evangelism, with the exception of Commission III, was
far more evangelical than that of the International
Missionary Council. Homrighausen, however, reported
several different impressions to the Federal Council of
Churches in America:

1. The responsibility of the churches to be involved in
a "total salvation" when totalitarianism, humanism, and
nihilism arose in a country.

2. Evangelism was becoming less "individualistic" by
the rediscovery of the Christian community.

3. The churches are becoming more conscious of their
task to evangelize a "de-Christianized world."[39]
Nevertheless, the conference looked forward to
evangelism as a continued ecumenical force to unite the
churches and to solve the post-World War II problems.
In some places people would hear Christ, but were
embarrassed by the Church.[40]

The Amsterdam 1948 Assembly spoke to many aspects
of evangelism. Section I revealed a basic agreement, "We
all believe that the Church is God's gift to men for the

salvation of the world. . . ." There were deep differences expressed, however, regarding the atonement, "The relation, in the saving acts of God in Christ, between objective redemption and personal salvation, between Scripture and tradition. . . ."[41] This division concerning the authority of Scripture would make it difficult or impossible to arrive at a biblical soteriology, essential for a unified and evangelical theology of evangelism.

Section II, "The Church's Witness to God's Design," reflects the post-World War II pessimism concerning the future of the world system and the unquestionable priority of personal reconciliation.

> The purpose of God is to reconcile all men to Himself and to one another in Jesus Christ. . .It continues in the gift of the Holy Spirit, in the command to make disciples of all nations, and in the abiding presence of Christ with His Church. . . .To the Church, then, is given the privilege of so making Christ known to men that each is confronted with the necessity of a personal decision, Yes or No. . .Those who obey are delivered from the power of the world in which sin reigns, and already, in the fellowship of the children of God, have experienced eternal life. Those who reject the love of God remain under His judgment and are in danger of sharing the impending doom of the world that is passing away.[42]

This statement was essentially evangelical as well.

Amsterdam committed itself to the salvation purposes of God for all men and to the responsibility of the churches to the "prayer, service and sacrificial missionary enterprise involved in that acceptance."[43] Cooperative evangelism and comity were recognized as important, even though most evangelism is carried out on a denominational level.[44] The Assembly rejoiced in the program of evangelism within the WCC and, aware of the urgency of the need, declared that "it is our earnest hope and prayer that He will do a mighty work in our

day, giving the Church again wisdom and power rightly
to proclaim the good news of Jesus Christ to men."[45]

This evangelistic appeal by the major Protestant
denominations of the world was heard by a Youth for
Christ International observer, Billy Graham.

THE PILGRIMAGE TOWARD AN ECUMENICAL THEOLOGY OF EVANGELISM, 1949 TO 1961

The theologies of evangelism of the IMC and of the
WCC at Amsterdam 1948 were far apart. Amsterdam
1948 reflected the pietistic elements of evangelism
inherent within some of the older denominations, State
churches, and Third World churches. The IMC at
Jerusalem 1928, by the Hocking report and by Madras
1938, had witnessed the domination of the evangelicals
who had either withdrawn from the IMC or had
surrendered to the Larger Evangelism. Even in 1959,
there was strong mutual opposition to integration with
the WCC. Ecumenical historians attribute this to the
Orthodox churches, concerned over proselytism, and to
the "fundamentalist" or evangelical churches.

The period between Amsterdam 1948 and New Delhi
1961 represents a slow synthesis of the evangelical WCC
theology of evangelism with that of the more liberal IMC
theology of mission. In addition, the Eastern Orthodox
churches were reassured that the WCC would restrain
evangelical evangelism within their ranks by the New
Delhi 1961 document defining and opposing
proselytism.[46] Although the IMC had been "in
association with" the WCC since Amsterdam 1948, by
1959 only forty-five of the 171 member churches of the
WCC had approved the integration and only twenty-two
of the thirty-eight IMC councils had responded favorably

to it. Three national councils were opposed to integration and the large, strongly evangelical Belgian Congo (now Zaire) council even withdrew from the IMC over this issue!

By New Delhi 1961, the WCC theology of evangelism became acceptable and most of the strongly committed evangelical elements in the IMC had withdrawn. The IMC and the DWME became one. This theological pilgrimage—that of the IMC from an evangelical *visage* at Edinburgh 1910 and that of the WCC from Amsterdam 1948—can only be understood by considering the open, undefined position on the inspiration and authority of Scripture. This ambiguity permits a "progressive" theology only possible with theological guidelines that extend beyond the interpretations of an infallible Bible. The present ecumenical theology of evangelism was adopted by the 1959 Central Committee at Rhodes and was published as *A Theological Reflection on the Work of Evangelism.*[47]

It had long been recognized that evangelism promoted and produced unity. Amsterdam 1948 not only had recognized this unifying force but also sought to unite the churches in this common task: Evangelism "transcends the traditional distinction between the so-called Christian and so-called non-Christian lands."[48] Visser 't Hooft interpreted Amsterdam 1948 as introducing a new epoch of missionary enterprise by breaking down the distinction between "mission" and "evangelism."[49] Prior to Amsterdam 1948, the distinction was primarily *geographical;* evangelism was local, while missions were primarily foreign. The elimination of the distinction between "mission" and "evangelism" not only led to *Witness in Six Continents,* as the Mexico 1963 DWME meeting was described, but also to a redefinition of mission and its relationship to evangelism. The existence of the Church in every continent of the world as the "great new fact" of this generation led to a debate which continues among Evangelicals even today: Is social action to be viewed as a partner of evangelism? Does mission describe "everything the church is sent in the

world to do"?[50] A deepening understanding of the
Scripture always proved to be stimulating and
constructive, but other views of evangelism resulting
from a theological bias, or based upon a low view of
Scripture, resulted in disunity and a neglect of traditional
evangelism. Following Amsterdam 1948, these opposing
positions on evangelism became increasingly polarized.

DIVERGENCY IN EVANGELISM APPEARS IN THE WCC

From March 2-8, 1949, a Study Conference on
Evangelism was held at the newly acquired Ecumenical
Institute at Bossey, near Geneva. It devoted its study to
the work and methods of evangelism in a post-Christian
era. The Study Conference report observed that the
evangelical-nonevangelical theological divergencies in the
Conference went very deep. "Probably for the first time,
it came out so clearly in an 'ecumenical' meeting on
Evangelism, and the significance of the conference
resides mainly in this fact."[51] The division was so
"insistent" that the conclusions were inconclusive and,
consequently, the discussions were described
prophetically as "in the beginning stage of the journey of
the Church into the world."[52]
    The first approach represented that of the first 1947
meeting and contained strong elements of the evangelical
position:

> On one side stood the spokesman for the
> evangelistic approach, that may be called the
> spontaneous form of Christian witness as it has
> happened through all the ages, calling individuals
> to surrender their lives to Christ as the Redeemer
> of sin and the Bringer of Salvation and of a new
> life in God through Him. The urge is
> straightforwardly missionary, an urge born from
> grateful obedience and a passion for souls. Also

with this approach, various "methods" are possible and actually practiced, according to gifts and circumstances, but the motivation is always the same: to witness for Christ, to confront man with the call to conversion. Much evangelism of this kind has been in the past, and partly in the present, too spiritualistic in the sense that it was concerned mainly with Christian faith as an other-worldly affair. However, this cannot be said of many of the present individualist forms of Evangelism. There is often great church-consciousness and also knowledge of the modern mood behind it. However, the *structure* of the world, socially, politically, culturally, does not really enter into the way of approaching the world. The Church is criticized, often severely, but never in the sense that in her encounter with the world she is not only the Giver, but also has to be the Receiver. It is not denied that the Church has also a social task, but this has to be distinguished clearly from the misisonary task of unambiguous and direct witness to Christ.[53]

It was primarily the Anglican members of the conference that introduced the second approach to evangelism based on "an incarnational conception of the Church" in contrast to those who saw the Church "as 'Ecclesia,' those called out of the world."[54]

The other approach was concerned with the problem of a real encounter between the Church and the world, in which concern the challenge to conversion is the last step after a long-drawn dialogue between the Church and the world. In this encounter the Church remains as it were incognito. What is envisaged is a real encounter with the cultural and social structure and situation of the world, in give, but certainly also in take, evolving in this encounter a new idiom for expressing the Christian faith, a prophetic witness of the biblical interpretation of history, of the meaning of human life, and of the Church as community. In this long-drawn dialogue the Church must find the right way to express what is God's plan with the world and humanity, and that men are called to take as individuals and community their responsible place in this plan. The aim has to be more to win men for the 'obedience in the world' than to win them for the Church. The Church has to enter in such a way in the life of the world that it becomes incarnated in it. Those advocating this approach find it difficult to understand the individual evangelistic approach, because they are convinced that the old evangelistic phrases that were rich in biblical content, are not meaningful to the modern world. The great concern must be that the Church gives the answer to the burning questions of the world. This is not proper evangelism, but preparation for the Gospel, trying to make the Church and its Message relevant. It was, therefore, even suggested that for this approach the word "evangelism" should be dropped and replaced by "strategy of the Church" or "plan of the Church."[55]

The debate was ecclesiological in that it sustained the role and responsibility of a European "State church" in a world to be Christianized. This was, as Latourette pointed out, the continuing struggle of the European medieval churches in their efforts to evangelize a "world" already declared politically to be "Christian." The volunteerism and pluralism of North America and the Third World was more responsive to this evangelical approach. But the division also persisted in the area of biblical authority. The report of Commission I stated that "the task of evangelism is not only the salvation of the individual but the translation into modern society of that new way of life found in Jesus Christ."[56] This equivocal language attempted to satisfy both points of view.

A September 1949 pamphlet entitled "The Evangelization of Man in Modern Mass Society" reviewed the program of evangelism in the WCC and called for a revolution that will lead to "a recovery of the sense of the true nature of the Church and of the real meaning of evangelism."[57] It recommends "a reconsideration of the real meaning of *evangelization* as a call 'to the obedience of the faith'. . ."[58] It confesses that there is

> an almost chaotic confusion about the essence and aims of evangelization. On the one hand, there is a continuous temptation to interpret evangelization as propaganda or proselytism, in which man is treated as an object or victim, to be molded by our work, in our own image and likeness. On the other hand evangelization is likely to degenerate into merely taking church members.[59]

A marked effort to change the Amsterdam 1948 theology of evangelism was evident.

DIVISION IN ECUMENICAL EVANGELISM

The WCC Study Department, chaired by H. P. Van Dusen, isolated the problem as the meaning of "conversion." He avoided the deeper issue of the Bible, even though he was involved in the WCC study of "The Bible and the Church's Message to the World," a continuing debate even today on the very nature of Scripture and its interpretation.[60] In the study, the various views of E. Stauffer, K. Barth, E. Brunner, and R. Bultmann present conflicting opinions regarding the historicity of biblical events, such as the resurrection. However, the pamphlet reporting the WCC study of evangelism avoided the question of biblical authority and requested a study of the whole subject of "conversion."

> According to one school of thought all evangelistic activity should be focused on conversion in a particular sense; according to another school, it should be detached from all attempts to convert individuals.[61]

In 1951, two years later, J. C. Hoekendijk, then secretary for evangelism in the Study Department of the WCC, reported that "there was a great confusion in the churches about the character of evangelism."[62] The churches were disinterested in the study, and evangelistic movements showed little disposition to change their present methods. The radical movements, however, were welcomed by the Study Department as important pioneers, "but there was danger of undermining their efforts by making ecumenical headlines of them."[63] The WCC had to be cautious in its development of a new theology of evangelism, lest it be subverted by publicity in the churches.

THE ESCHATOLOGY DIMENSION OF EVANGELISM

In recent years, it has become increasingly difficult to appreciate how the subject of evangelism permeated ecumenical thought. The post-World War II era brought a resurgence of evangelical strength and a growing apocalyptic atmosphere, due to the rising fears of nuclear warfare and the "midnight" of the destruction of humanity. Eschatology also became a very divisive force in the ecumenical movement.

Before his resignation from the Department of Evangelism in 1952, Hoekendijk reported that the main obstacle to the development of national study groups on evangelism seemed to be different conceptions of evangelism.[64] The division over eschatology at the IMC Willingen 1951 conference must have been known at this meeting but the unacceptability in the churches of the main theme on "The Christian Hope" for Evanston 1954 was unexpected. Visser 't Hooft concluded that it was necessary to push forward in obedience on this theme despite the difficulties. "The World Council will—humanly speaking—be finished if in 1954 we produce nothing but a host of generalities."[65] The WCC found that the question of the Christian hope was

divided between the temporal view of the Kingdom in
North America and the futuristic view in Europe. In
general, the former looked forward to the building up of
the Kingdom on earth through evangelism, while the
latter—disillusioned by World War II—looked to the
future reign of Christ. An eschatological position greatly
influences the theology, methodology,[66] and urgency of
evangelism.

The first draft of the Second Assembly at Evanston
1954 united "evangelism" and "mission" and rightly
placed evangelism in its historical priority as "the
ultimate orientation of all the Church's activities."[67] It
noted several trends:

1. An increase in concern for evangelism
2. An increase in the sense of urgency because of the
eschatological character of evangelism
3. A mood of sober self-criticism regarding the life of
the Church and traditional methods of evangelism
4. The need to consider evangelism in terms of its
total impact upon the Christian community and its
environment, i.e., lay communication rather than
ecclesiastical communication alone
5. The decline of verbalism in the evangelistic
approach, for "witness can never be reduced to a *verbal*
proclamation"[68]
The life of the community was introduced as a major
means of evangelism in contrast to a verbal witness.

> Biblical witness is at least three dimensional: it
> happens through proclamation (kerygma),
> fellowship (koinonia), and service (diaconia). This
> forbids us to think of evangelism in purely, or even
> primarily, verbal categories.[69]

The ministry of Billy Graham in the Greensboro, United
States, campaign was classified as "an old form of
evangelism."[70] Latin American evangelism was described
as using the Bible and possessing a "rather emotionalized
faith with a deep sense of fellowship and a strong
missionary zeal." It declared that

the Church is an evangelistic agency first and last and all the way through and does not deviate from its course.[71]

Another pre-Evanston 1954 publication expressed concern for the evangelistic spirit in the churches, that

> something must have gone wrong when a vocation which should be the characteristic mark of the Church as a whole, and of every individual Christian, is looked upon as a rare, intermittent, and sometimes even queer specialty.[72]

Mission and evangelism were to be reincorporated into the activities of the Church because there is no longer a "Christendom." Younger churches should discover ways of presenting the Gospel to the unconverted.[73]

The Report on Section II at Evanston, U.S.A., 1954, was entitled "Evangelism: The Mission of the Church to Those Outside Her Life." The discussion, debate, and dissension concerning the Assembly theme, "Christ—The Hope of the World," also influenced the theology of evangelism:

> God's purpose and the meaning of His revelation in Christ, were fundamental starting- and finishing-points in the entire discussion, and these in turn raised questions concerning the nature of His Kingdom on earth and the place of the Church in relation to it.[74]

This theological issue was of practical significance in relation to hope for the six-year-old nation of Israel. After three discussion sessions, the references "to the New Testament concepts of the ultimate fulfillment of God's promises to the people of Ancient Israel" were eliminated by a 195 to 150 vote.[75] A minority report signed by twenty-four delegates anticipated the conversion of the Jewish people as a hope inseparable from the evangelization of the Gentiles under the New Covenant:

The New Testament, however, speaks also of the
"fulness" of Israel, when God will manifest His
glory by bringing back His "eldest son" into the one
fold of His grace (Rom. 11:12-36; Matt. 23:39).
This belief is an indispensable element of our one
united hope for Jew and Gentile in Jesus Christ.
Our hope in Christ's coming victory includes our
hope for Israel in Christ, in His victory over the
blindness of His own people. To expect Jesus Christ
means to hope for the conversion of the Jewish
people, and to love Him means to love the people
of God's promise.

In view of the grievous guilt of Christian people
toward the Jews throughout the history of the
Church, we are certain that: the Church cannot rest
until the title of Christ to the Kingdom is
recognized by His own people according to the
flesh.[76]

If the statement on Israel had been accepted, it would
have revealed a far different attitude toward the
evangelization of both Jew and Gentile in the WCC.
    The Statement on the Report of the Advisory
Commission on the Main Theme openly admitted sharp
differences in theological viewpoints. The Message
blandly stated that, "we affirm faith in Jesus Christ as the
hope of the world, and desire to share that faith with all
men."[77] The Church is the new community
"commissioned to make Him known throughout the
world. He will come again as Judge and King to bring all
things to their consummation."[78]
    The Report of Section II first emphasized "The
Evangelizing Church," by whose ministry the Holy Spirit
"changes the lives of sinful men and they, forgiven and
restored to their true heritage as God's children, are
being gathered together against the day of Christ's
return in power."[79] This section also appeals to those
concerned primarily with social issues:

> One is surely so to proclaim the gospel that it will
> transform the groupings and patterns of society in
> which men and women are involved, to the end that
> human institutions and structures may more nearly
> conform to the divine intention, and respect the
> limiting prerogative of God.[80]

Nevertheless, the individual, personal, and eternal issues
of evangelism remain at Evanston:

> But underlying these concerns of evangelism is the
> bringing of persons to Christ as Saviour and Lord
> that they may share in His eternal life. Here is the
> heart of the matter. There must be personal
> encounter with Christ. It is not enough to present
> Him merely as an example to follow. The Gospel
> proclaims a living Christ. Just as to remain with
> Him is the mark of Christian experience, so to
> bring men to meet Him is the purpose of all
> evangelism. For on his relationship to God in Christ
> depends the eternal destiny of every man.[81]

This statement concerning the nature of evangelism most
clearly rejects the social gospel and universalism. But this
evangelical statement is qualified by a syncretistic
paragraph referring to "light" that is found in
non-Christian faiths wherein God has "left not Himself
without witness."[82] Then the human aspect of the
Christian witness to non-Christian religions is so stressed
that the value of a verbal testimony seems negligible.
Would the ecumenical evangelist or missionary be able to
proclaim without great difficulty, "Thus saith the Lord"?
   Evanston 1954 gave continued evidence of conservative
theology within the WCC, for the subject of eschatology
did not create as great a division within the WCC as it
had in the more liberal IMC at Willingen 1952. Yet the
eschatological question was not settled, and future
decades would ultimately witness the triumph of those
seeking to evangelize by straddling contradictory
theologies: a manifestation of the Kingdom of God on
earth by the reconstruction of society, and an earthly

Kingdom to come when Christ returns. The next seven
years would prove to be more decisive.

AN ECUMENICAL
THEOLOGY OF
EVANGELISM

"A Theological Reflection on the Work of Evangelism"
was "adopted" in 1959 after final revision by the Central
Committee at Rhodes. The republication of this first text
without any alterations in 1963 indicates the "consensus"
acceptance of this document and its basic theology of
evangelism. The reprinting also affirms its acceptance
after study by the Section on "Witness" at New Delhi
1961. Philip Potter, general secretary of the WCC,
identifies this pamphlet as the most fully expressed
conception of the dimensions of evangelism. It has
become a critical element in the understanding of the
entire WCC program.[83]

The responsibility for developing this theology rested
upon Canon T. O. Wedel as committee chairman
(vice-chairman of the Evangelism Section at Evanston),
but the main theological work was done under the leadership of D. T. Niles as secretary of the WCC Department of Evangelism.

"The Gospel and Man" addresses the questions of the
nature of evangelism, what it is, its motivation, and the
call to evangelize. While universalism was implied in
earlier documents on evangelism, this study openly
affirms the eternal reconciliation of all men. The death
of Christ applied to all mankind:

> This shalom is in Jesus Christ in whom God has
> proclaimed His Gospel. By this proclamation is
> created a new situation for mankind because,
> whether acknowledged or unacknowledged, it
> brings mankind into a decisive relationship with
> God.[84]

Evangelism has been redefined, ignoring its biblical

imperative to proclaim the Gospel, because this theology
sees all of humanity as in "The New Situation in Christ":

> Indeed, the world is already a redeemed world so
> that, whether men discern their true condition or
> not, and even if they deny it, they are still the heirs
> of God's redemption. To proclaim the Gospel is to
> bid them claim their inheritance in Christ.[85]

The gift of the Gospel (possibly meaning "salvation") is
the present appropriation of that which men will inherit
eventually.

The world is redeemed and, consequently, is seen as
alien and in opposition to the Christian only because it is
not aware of, or has not accepted, the Lordship of Christ
over it. The righteousness of Christ in behalf of the
sinner does not apply only to those who believe before
and after Christ's atonement (Rom. 3:22-26), but
eventually to all men. The lostness of man is described in
terms of his inevitable involvement in sinful social and
political institutions whether he is a believer or not:

> Men are in a state of lostness. Even their virtues are
> tainted by sin. There is a common rebellion against
> God in which each man finds himself involved in
> spite of his own faith and obedience. There is sin in
> the concrete political and social institutions in which
> all men are enmeshed.[86]

Sin is described as primarily social and political rebellion
against God's order in His world, not against God
directly: "Evangelistic efforts, consequently, are to be
directed toward the continued establishment of the rule
of God over mankind. The horizontal relationships
become of primary importance because man's vertical
need has already been provided for—sooner or later—in
Christ." Apparently, eternal punishment as "lostness" has
no place in this "new situation in Christ," since God's
present saving concern is temporal in this present age:

> This King has willed to rule as Saviour. Wherever
> His Kingship is proclaimed, His saving concern for
> mankind will be manifest.[87]

This will be "shalom" upon the earth at the
"consummation" of all things. As sin is corporate rather
than personal, so salvation is corporate.

Evangelism was redefined in terms of a
new-universalism and "the new situation in Christ."
Salvation is "found" as a temporal deliverance from
social and political sins, for this is the inheritance in
Christ for all. Evangelism is reinterpreted in evangelical
language as

> the decisive confrontation of men with the Gospel
> in Jesus Christ to the end that they may believe in
> Him and believing find salvation in His service.[88]

Consequently, a personal appropriation of the Cross does
not begin at a moment of evangelistic decision, for this
has already occurred in Christ. Regeneration, conversion,
and personal decision assume an entirely different
theological perspective.

The "newness" of life is in one's converted relationship
to his fellow humans, in a world that is optimistically
becoming the *shalom* "peace" of God. Part of the
evangelistic work of the Church, therefore, is

> to understand what God is doing in these times
> through all the changes that are taking place in the
> ways and circumstances of human life, to penetrate
> into the significance of the new forms of association
> in which persons find their social satisfaction, to ask
> how the Gospel may be related to men in their
> several needs as they seek to come to terms with
> life.[89]

The Christian is to observe what God is doing in His
mission *(missio dei)* upon the earth. In ecumenical theology
of evangelism, God is not going to establish this shalom
when Jesus Christ returns personally again. He is doing

it now! "It opens up for him (man) the hope of a better life in which there shall be plenty for all."[90] It is "a world being recreated in Christ."[91]

The treatment of non-Christian religions was entitled "Unbelief and Other Belief." The historical debate on this question goes back to Jerusalem 1928, the Hocking Report of 1932, and Madras (Tambaram) 1938. Hendrik Kraemer in his book *The Christian Message in a Non-Christian World* concluded that there was a basic discontinuity among all religions: they were unrelated and could not be compared—especially with Christianity. This view now seemed like "merely an echo of the old-time missionary policy, that it was not true to the facts and that it would lead nowhere."[92] The resurgence of non-Christian religions, which at Jerusalem 1928 had been expected to disappear slowly because of the rising strength of secularism, made their discussion relevant again to the WCC. In the WCC studies on universalism and "the new situation in Christ" of all men, they had not yet applied this theology to the WCC relationships with the non-Christian religions.

The new title of the WCC Department of Evangelism study, "The Word of God and the Living Faiths of Men," reveals the changed attitude of the Department of Evangelism under D. T. Niles:

1. The nature of the living faiths of men and the elements in them of appeal and power
2. The nature of the Word of God which is addressed to men who live by these faiths
3. The nature of the relation between the Christian message and these faiths
4. The way in which the Church may be enabled to communicate this word to those who live by these faiths.[93]

After Davos 1955, there is little evidence of conservative evangelical participation in a theology of evangelism that clearly distinguished between that Word of God possibly speaking in or to the non-Christian religions, and that of the Bible.

The study question on "Unbelief and Other Belief"

reveals an absence of historical evangelistic foundations:
1. It spoke of man listening or responding with his "conscience." While this is true, it neglects the immortality of the soul and spirit of man who responds to God and is restored by faith (John 17:3).
2. It saw the Gospel as addressed to the conscience of men in concrete experiences. This method leads to the neglect of the Bible message (1 Cor. 15:1-4) in favor of proclaiming a current social or political injustice which will convict the hearer of his social guilt.
3. The reality of Satan as a person was replaced by the structures of "Powers" real or imagined—political, social, or religious. These are the "false masters" from which the non-Christian is to be delivered, not the supernatural bond of Satan upon those who "by nature" are under his control (Eph. 2:1-3). Response to the Gospel is regarded as "recognition" rather than as regeneration:

> At the proclamation of His Gospel, the Powers are revealed and man's foolish submission to them is disclosed. Henceforth it is sin to submit to them in fear.[94]

A "believer" should decide to reject the social, political, or religious "powers" to which he has been subjected.

Fundamental to the entire study is a Barthian distinction between the Bible and the Word of God. "Biblical theology" of neo-orthodoxy does not limit the Word of God to the Bible. The message of the Bible is in the deeds, the acts of God in history, not in the explanatory material of the Old and New Testaments. Consequently, men who "find their salvation in Jesus Christ" have a message; "their message is the deeds of God wrought for the salvation of men."[95] It is a horizontal and temporal salvation.

Furthermore, according to the study, the Bible is not the only authority, for authority is "from God" and only "witnessed to" by the Scripture. The Church derives authority to evangelize by the authority of Christ and His Spirit.[96] In its practical application, evangelism must

appeal to the Church as an institution established by
Christ, not to the infallible apostolic witness to what
God's Son said and what God's Spirit inerrantly
recorded. If the Church is not united, the testimony of
the Church suffers for it has lost its credentials.[97] The
visible unity of the Church is a prerequisite for
evangelistic credibility. Ecumenical authority to
evangelize is dependent upon the testimony of
ecumenicity, not upon the testimony of the Apostles to
the person and redemptive work of Christ.

The witness of the Church leading to faith, it says, are
by "the spoken, read, and written Word of God."[98]
Besides the "Word of God" spoken or read "the Bible is
the Church's treasure beyond compare."[99] Whereas the
Holy Spirit and the Holy Scripture were the instruments
of salvation in the early Church,[100] this study sees
preaching as in some measure the "open Word of God"
and authoritative for the congregation, "The Word
uttered in obedience and addressed to the congregation
is also an open Word directed to all men who listen to
it."[101]

Evangelism in the WCC changed radically during the
twelve years between 1947 and 1959. The meaning of
the atonement was applied universally, attention was
given to the "acts" of the Scripture instead of entire
content of the Bible. The world was no longer an enemy
but a humanity with which the Christian was to identify.
Salvation was individual, but was seen as a personal
engagement for service for a world already redeemed by
Christ. The mission was God's and Jesus Christ is the
evangelist. It is not the Bible alone that brings men by
the Spirit to the living Christ. The "word" must be
proclaimed with "Christian action in society" in order to
convince the hearers.

> If preaching is the proclamation of salvation then
> Christian action in society is the "pantomime of
> salvation." It reveals the character of love, and it
> convinces those who hear the Word that in Christ
> they truly meet a Lord who loves them.[102]

This requirement has stretched the biblical truth, which requires the personal morality of the witness or the evangelist, to the place where social action or political involvement for a just cause are necessary for an effective personal witness. It has also neglected the biblical truths that "faith comes by hearing" and that the Word written is "living and powerful." Evangelicals believe that God spoke in the entire Old Testament and New Testament revelation as recorded in the Scripture. His Spirit speaks today in, with, and by the Bible. A perfect and complete revelation of God in Christ was concluded with and by the apostolic canon of the New Testament.

This ecumenical theology of evangelism was to continue its theological pilgrimage. Its theology of evangelism was "another gospel" which did not easily commend itself to those whose theology was grounded in a verbally inerrant Bible. The need for another evangelical world conference on evangelism was evident after New Delhi 1961.

AN EVANGELICAL EVALUATION OF THE ECUMENICAL PROCESS AND EVANGELISM

An evangelical evaluation of the WCC theology of evangelism is not an easy task. Evangelicals have been rightfully skeptical of ecumenical theology and evangelism. Whereas the earlier WCC documents from Amsterdam 1948 to Evanston 1954 were generally written in traditional theological language, the triumph of neo-orthodoxy (personified to some extent in the Israel debate and in the prolonged applause for Visser 't Hooft) gave a mandate for the Barthian-oriented general secretary, Visser 't Hooft, to pursue the institutional integration of the IMC into the WCC and to integrate the theology of Barth into the evangelism of the WCC.

The theological language of the liberal-evangelical

synthesis of the period prior to New Delhi 1961 adopted
the equivocal style so characteristic of the earlier IMC
reports. Descriptive theological language made the
synthesis less evident and more satisfying to a
theologically pluralistic constituency.

Evaluation can only be accomplished through an
understanding of the theologian in vogue (Barth, in this
period), a reading of the background study papers
prepared under the WCC direction, an acquaintance of
the theologians selected to prepare them, and a
knowledge of the official publication of these studies
and/or their adoption by a meeting. The effort to "hear
the Word of God speaking" to the conferences or
Assemblies will lead to amendments of a previously
coherent document that frequently results in
contradictory statements. Consequently, only trends can
be observed.

Subsequently, Geneva staff members are able to
research the WCC documents and statements and, within
certain limitations, reconstruct a line of reasoning for the
occasion or for a particular constituency. An example of
this procedure is found in Philip Potter's "Evangelism
and the World Council of Churches," presented to the
Central Committee at Heraklion, Crete, August 1967.[103]
His earlier quotations from Madras 1938, Amsterdam
1948, and Evanston 1954 have an evangelical and biblical
ring to them. Mention of the theological shift to an
essentially Barthian or ecumenical theology of evangelism
is ignored or avoided. Potter responds to critics within
and without the WCC who accuse the WCC of "more
concern about social justice than about evangelism."[104]
First, Potter defends his viewpoint by saying that

> from the very beginning of its life the World
> Council has declared its conviction that speaking
> and acting on social issues is part of the evangelistic
> task of the Church.[105]

A careful examination of the Report of Section II,
Amsterdam 1948 does not sustain this contention,
although the Report of Section II at Evanston 1954

could possibly be interpreted this way. Second, Potter
does not say that the theology of evangelism was
modified to its present horizontal "dimensions." Third,
many within the WCC and many without are unaware of
what the WCC truly understands as evangelism. Either
the WCC has failed to communicate, or it has
camouflaged its decision, or it is so philosophically
oriented in European theology that it cannot be
understood by the world community.

The ecumenical theology of evangelism made some
concessions to modernism in supporting the "growing
presence of the Kingdom in this world" under the
Lordship of Christ. The significance of the incarnation,
death, and resurrection events in creating a "new man"
in Christ appeals to traditional Christianity. If liberalism
was in principle rejected, so was conservative
evangelicalism. The evangelical "literalism" of biblical
interpretation, systematic theology, and propositional
truth were replaced by a progressive and existential
"consensus" theology—that which the authoritative
churches believe. The style of theology became
"descriptive," in order to unite Christian churches whose
theology was "definitive" and, consequently, divisive.

Nine rather essential alterations have been instituted
into the ecumenical theology of evangelism:

1. Emphasis is given to the present Lordship of Christ
in a world of humanity redeemed since Christ.

2. By the incarnation and universalist redemption of
Christ, there is a new situation in the world for the
Church: all humanity is now in the process of
sanctification.

3. A general "universalism" prevails, which
reinterprets the lostness of man in terms of his lack of
involvement in his earthly inheritance.

4. The saviourship of Christ is an event in the past
and receives minimal attention.

5. Conversion became a recognition and an awareness
of what Christ has already done.[106]

6. Salvation, consequently, is seen more in terms of
shalom upon the earth. It is a "now" and a "not yet."

7. The "witness" is primarily that of an authoritative Church whose "Word" of testimony necessarily must address the unjust social and political issues, not only the personal moral and spiritual life of the individual.

8. The Bible is the inestimable treasure of the Church, but not *the* only Word of God.

9. The personality of Satan is minimized, if not rejected, while the "powers" are "real" but illusory social, political, and religious dominations over the new humanity since the Christ-event.

The results of this ecumenical theology of evangelism have had some disturbing influences upon historical evangelism.

1. "Mission" and "evangelism" have lost their historic meaning of "sending" and "proclaiming."

2. Confusion has arisen over the priority and aim of evangelism as proclamation by individual Christians, by evangelists, and by the church.

3. The proclamation of the Gospel has been blunted by an inordinate and illegitimate focus on the *results* of evangelism, the good works and redeeming qualities of regenerate people in society and civic life. The results have been confused with the aim and means.

4. The work of the Spirit in evangelism has been hindered by a lack of confidence in the Scriptures He inspired. Organizational unity and sociopolitical involvement are desirable but not essential. The Spirit and the Word are able in and of themselves to illuminate, regenerate, and convert the sinner to Christ Himself.

5. A reaction against "soul winning" leading to regenerate disciples hinders personal witnessing and evangelism. Evangelicalism has been caricatured by ecumenicals as neglecting the "whole man."

6. The authority of the "church" visible discourages a spontaneous witness whenever the occasion arises to speak of Christ.

7. Christ's present providential work in the world and His Lordship in the Church are confused with Christ's

sovereign authority and ultimate Lordship in the world at His second coming.

Evangelicals have been right in rejecting ecumenical evangelism. Evangelicals within the movement and without have been slow to discern the basic theological deviations. The debilitating effects paralyze a personal verbal witness, church growth, church extension, and mission. The complexity of the philosophical-theological nuances of its Barthian theology, however, is not likely to have an appeal beyond an intellectual elite. Ecumenical theology of evangelism lacks the spirituality and the dynamic of the Word and the Spirit.

4 Contrasting Developments in Evangelical and Ecumenical Evangelism

The post-World War I era saw the
decline of "main street" evangelism in the United States,
the kind of popular evangelism that had been
characteristic of previous generations under the ministry
of Charles Finney and D. L. Moody. People from all
Protestant churches had been able to unite together in
the evangelical, evangelistic outreach so characteristic of
American Christianity. Billy Sunday's outstanding
evangelistic ministry in the first quarter of the century
concluded with his Mt. Holly campaign in May 1930,
when "professional tabernacle evangelism disappeared
from public interest for almost twenty years"[1] This
decline may be attributed to both the Scopes Trial of
1925 which held up fundamentalism to public scorn and
to the 1929 financial depression. McLoughlin maintains:

> By rejecting the scientific and scholarly theories of
> the twentieth century and by insisting upon the
> small-town moral code of nineteenth-century
> America, the evangelists doomed themselves to
> obscurity along with the fundamentalism to which
> they clung. And in the 1930's the political and
> economic conservatism of the revivalists (a
> conservatism which is indissolubly linked to the

individualistic gospel they preach) produced an
even greater abyss between them and the average
American.[2]

It is interesting to note that ecumenical contemporaries
accused "Fundamentalists" of lack of involvement in
social and political action, and yet their involvement
characterized the revivalists of the post World War I era.
They condemned the aggression of Hitler, rebuked
anti-Semitism, and questioned New Deal policies.
Modernists, of course, believed fundamentalism to have
followed the wrong political philosophy. A strong case
could be made, however, that the political and social
involvement of some evangelists limited their ministry,
and that they were prophetic voices rejected by the
people. Nevertheless, the great campaigns—such as the
one held by Sunday in Philadelphia which drew two
million in eleven weeks—had entirely ceased.

Yet the growth of the cities prior to and during World
War II continued to present an evangelistic challenge to
the churches. The suburban trend in Protestantism
continued to increase the urban problems. Many church
and parachurch programs developed which struggled
valiantly against overwhelming social and financial odds.
Latourette observes that a "mass conversion" of North
Americans occurred in those decades between and
including the two world wars. Church membership was
socially popular, yet the individual spiritual quality of
Americans declined.[3] The urban centers, however, were
abandoned and the mainline denominations needed
evangelism, revival, and renewal.

THE REVIVAL OF EVANGELICALISM

During this period, however, evangelicalism did not die.
The historic use of "Evangelical" was replaced by the
pejorative term "Fundamentalist" because of the rejection
of modernism, their tenacious adherence to the

"fundamentals," and their personal commitment to
Christ as prior to—and necessary for—social reform:

> Both the social theology of modernism and the
> political liberalism of progressivism and the New
> Deal maintained that to save the individual it was
> first necessary to save or reform society.[4]

By 1935, leading churchmen began to question the
validity of modernism and the "social gospel." Harry
Emerson Fosdick was quoted in the December 4, 1935,
issue of *Christian Century* as saying that

> the modernistic movement adjusting itself to
> man-centered culture, has . . . watered down the
> thought of the Divine and . . . left souls standing
> like the ancient Athenians before an altar to an
> Unknown God! On that point the church must go
> beyond modernism. We have been all things to all
> men long enough. . . We have at times gotten so low
> down that we talked as though the highest
> compliment that could be paid to Almighty God was
> that a few scientists believed in Him.[5]

Evangelism became unpopular in most of the mainline
churches, but statistics reveal that the numerical growth
of the newer denominations in Northern United States
exceeded that of the denominations in the South.
Evangelical Bible institutes, Christian liberal arts colleges,
youth movements, conference grounds, camps, and
periodicals became centers that regrouped and
reorganized evangelical forces. What appeared to be
ecclesiastical chaos was truly a sign of vitality in
conservative evangelicalism. The professional evangelist
was held in low esteem but evangelism was very much
alive in the growing evangelical churches and parachurch
institutions, such as Moody Bible Institute, Wheaton
College, and Bob Jones University. Evangelists and Bible
teachers such as Charles Fuller, Walter Meier, W. B.
Riley, Oswald Smith, and L. S. Chafer attracted growing
numbers of Evangelicals to Bible conferences in North
America.

THE FOURTH GREAT
AWAKENING IN
AMERICA

The historical key to revivalism in the United States is
not attributed to the personal talent or sincerity of the
evangelist, to the social crisis, wars or economic
distresses, but rather to a shift in the Protestant
theological emphasis, that invariably reoriented American
society as a whole and changed leadership and structures
in the churches.[6] Historians now recognize that the
fourth "Great Awakening" in America, which is still in
progress, became evident in the post-World War II era.
It was characterized by a theological rejection of the
social gospel, modernism, and liberalism.[7] It would be an
error, however, to say that this rise of evangelicalism is
due to a reaction to nonevangelical theology. It is rather
a return to the revivalism of earlier centuries in
American history.[8] Men like Albert Schweitzer (not
neo-orthodox), Karl Barth, and Emil Brunner certainly
contributed to a new theological climate in the mainline
churches, whereby the Bible could be used and
intellectual respectability maintained. But neo-orthodoxy
did not stimulate the renewal or evangelistic activity it
promised. The awakening came through those
representing "fundamentalism" in the first half of this
century, and through conservative Evangelicals during
the last twenty-five years, those within their mainline
denominations and without.[9]

FUNDAMENTALISM
AND
EVANGELICALISM

Many are endeavoring to define evangelicalism today.[10]
The present revival of evangelicalism certainly has its
roots in the *Fundamentals* published in the first decades
of this century to clarify the biblical differences
separating evangelicalism and the liberalism of Harnack
and Ritschl, as well as the modernism of Gladden and
Rauschenbusch.[11] Just as the American pastors in 1868

adopted the "Evangelical Test" concerning the new
Y.M.C.A. movement in the United States, so the
Fundamentals singled out certain doctrines that liberalism
and modernism rejected. The "five points of
fundamentalism" were: (1) the infallibility of Scripture,
(2) the virgin birth, (3) the substitutionary atonement, (4)
the bodily resurrection, and (5) the imminent, bodily
second coming of Christ.

Whereas fundamentalism remained within the
mainline denominations in the 1920s, the denominational
resistance to Fundamentalists moved the Fundamentalist
to separation. The separationists formed minority
groups and acquired a ghetto mentality through their
efforts to defend the Scripture. This defensiveness
hindered an evangelistic advance into the American
society. When the 1949 Los Angeles Crusade received
national news coverage, the defensive ghetto barrier to
the American public was broken [12] As crusade
evangelism increased in popular appeal and acceptance,
Evangelicals increased their evangelistic penetration into
the American society and the world.[13]

The rise of Billy Graham as an evangelist parallels in
many respects the rise and resurgence of North
American evangelicalism. He represents historic
American revivalism. In reply to frequent identification
with fundamentalism, Graham declared his own
theological heritage:

> If by fundamentalist you mean "narrow," "bigoted,"
> "extremist," "emotional," "snakehandler," "without
> social conscience"—then I am definitely not a
> fundamentalist. However, if by fundamentalist you
> mean a person who accepts the authorities of
> Scripture, the virgin birth of Christ, the atoning
> death of Christ, His bodily resurrection, His second
> coming, and personal salvation by faith through
> grace—then I am a fundamentalist.[14]

For many, Graham became the symbol and spokesman
for organized Protestantism. The *Christian Century*

editorialized that "many leading American churchmen
are willing to let him represent the whole American
church."[15] Since the Berlin 1966 and Lausanne 1974
Congresses on evangelism, his influence has been
recognized far beyond the North American borders.

REVIVAL IN
OUR TIME

The evangelical movement restored to national
recognition by Graham's Los Angeles Crusade,
September 25, 1949, was first called a "revival." The
Associated Press of November 2, 1949, reported a rising
new evangelist who "tops Billy Sunday." During the eight
weeks of meetings, some 3,000 reconsecrated their lives
or were restored to fellowship with Christ.

The seventy-two meetings recorded a total of 350,000
people in attendance. After more than eighteen months
of prayer, another era in evangelism was born in the
United States.[16] As in later crusades, Graham attributed
their import and response to prayer, the Holy Spirit, and
the Bible. After the South Carolina campaigns he said,

No credit for this belongs to me. There are three
reasons why God has given us a great harvest time
in Columbia these weeks. The first is, the prayers of
those thousands who prayed one month before we
came. The second reason is the power of the Holy
Spirit of God in convicting men. And the third is
the power of the Word of God. To Him be all the
glory.[17]

Faith and Works. Graham was quick to point out that
revival and evangelism always have social implications.
He said that

a revival brings tremendous social implications. Do
you know what came out of past revivals? The
abolishment of slavery came out of revival. The
abolishment of child labor came out of revival.

When the Wesleys preached in England, people
were working ninety hours a week! As a result of
that revival, sixty working hours became standard,
and our great trade unions were organized. Did you
know that the Y.M.C.A., the Salvation Army, most
of our charity organizations, many of our
educational institutions, slum clearance programs,
the Sunday School, Christian reform, and Women's
Suffrage are revival results?[18]

Graham, as in historical revivalism, had clearly discerned
the biblical necessity of personal faith in Jesus Christ as
essential to one's eternal destiny. He asked the question,

What does a man go to hell for? Not for getting
drunk, cursing, committing adultery, or lying. The
only thing that will send a man to hell is rejecting
Jesus Christ.[19]

Nevertheless, Graham firmly upheld and affirmed the
consequences and fruits of revival in the transformation
of society:

The Bible says that you're not saved by works. The
Bible says that you can't work your way to heaven,
you can't buy your way to heaven. The Bible says
that it's a free gift from God. But after you're
saved, after you believe and are born again by
accepting Jesus Christ as your personal Saviour, you
start working for the Lord Jesus Christ.[20]

The new believer is constrained by the love of Christ
to make service for the Lord his "main business" and his
occupation, profession, or business secondary. The
believer will not be judged at the Great White Throne of
Judgment because his sin was judged at the Cross of
Calvary. Christians—"bought with the precious blood of
Jesus Christ"—and who are living for Christ are going to
be caught up in the air "to be with the Lord forever."
They will stand before the judgment seat of Christ to
"receive rewards for the work that they've done for the
Lord Jesus since the moment they believed."[21]

America's hour of decision. Another early indication of the
evangelical theology of the Graham crusades was
America's Hour of Decision, published in 1951.[22] One
quickly discerns the evangelicalism characteristic of
evangelism in the nineteenth century and the early
decades of this century. Prayer services precede and
accompany the meetings.[23] The necessity of personal
faith—"ye must be born again"—permeates the
message.[24] A personal decision results in immediate
salvation,[25] judgment and hell await the unrepentant,[26]
the return of Christ Jesus is imminent,[27] and the Gospel
is powerful to transform lives and preserve the nation.[28]
A prophetic call to revival, renewal, and evangelism
challenged both "fortress" evangelicalism and mainline
denominationalism.

Peace with God. In the early 1950s, the fears and tensions
of the "Cold War" between the great powers of the West
and Eastern Europe produced in America a certain
receptivity to evangelicalism. Responding to this "age of
anxiety" and the threat of atomic warfare, Billy Graham
wrote *Peace with God,* a book written not for theologians
and philosophers, but for the "man in the street":

> My purpose is to give him a clear understanding of
> a new way of life that was presented by an
> unknown Galilean two thousand years ago. I have
> endeavored to present it in the language of the
> common man, that "the wayfaring men, though
> fools, shall not err therein."[29]

Although it was written as a popular evangelistic
presentation, *Peace with God* possesses a definite and
systematic theology of evangelism. Jesus Christ is man's
only valid answer to sin, sorrow, and death. He is God's
solution to the age-old problems. The results of
repentance, faith, and the new birth are seen in the
believer's transformed life, conduct, and relationship to
the church and society. Peace came to the heart of the

one who trusted personally in Jesus Christ as Lord and Savior, who was "born again." The believer was reconciled to God. His sins have been pardoned, and he has peace in his heart:

> But through the blood of the cross, Christ has made peace with God for us and is Himself our peace. If by faith we accept Him, we are justified by God and can realize the inner serenity that can come to man through no other means. When Christ enters our heart, we are freed of that haunting sense of sin. Cleansed of all feeling of contamination and unfitness, we can lift up our head secure in the knowledge that we can look with confidence into the face of our fellow men.[30]

The great questions of life have their answers in Jesus Christ:

> I know where I've come from, I know why I'm here, I know where I'm going—and I have peace in my heart. His peace floods my heart and overwhelms my soul![31]

Historians may well conclude that the contemporary demise of the deification of science, modernism, and liberal Christianity began at Los Angeles—just as the power of Pentecostal Christianity outgrew the provincialism of Judaism and, ultimately, conquered the paganism of the Empire. The "new evangelism" of neo-orthodoxy was eclipsed by the popular response to a multitude of evangelical movements that arose in the post-World War II era. Evangelical dynamic was directed toward evangelism in its many forms rather than dispensed in the quest for unity. The praxis was evangelism: it was "done," apostolic mission was applied in an apocalyptic age. It worked.

THE THEOLOGICAL CHARACTER OF POST-WORLD WAR II EVANGELICALISM

The message of the Gospel, proclaimed and published by Billy Graham, received widespread national and international acceptance. Few of those on the evangelical "right" will fault his doctrine, although many may not endorse his cooperative evangelism, considering it to be an ecclesiological compromise with unbelievers. Theological liberals remained aloof from Graham's crusades because of their widely divergent views of his message and evangelistic method. American Roman Catholicism, on the other hand, seemed to have widely accepted Graham's ministry, in the spirit of post-Vatican II (1962 to 1965) pluralism.

Graham's theology represents a general continuity with historical revivalism and the evangelicalism of this century. His leadership strongly influenced the theological direction of Berlin 1966 and Lausanne 1974, and deserves particular attention as representative of a worldwide movement. The dynamic of his theology is characterized by world evangelicalism, and the present evangelical awakening will depend upon the continuance of this theology.

Graham's *Peace with God* is profound in its simplicity and directness and, consequently, appeals to a wide spectrum of people throughout North America and the entire world—where multiple translations have penetrated. *World Aflame* (1965) builds upon the more personal *Peace with God,* and applies the same doctrine to the world and the end times. A doctrinal summary of *Peace with God* reveals a growing consensus of popular biblical teaching and of the evangelistic message throughout the world.

Authority. The Bible is God's Word that has been revealed in history and accurately recorded:

> Christianity finds all its doctrines stated in the Bible, and the true Christian denies no part, nor attempts

to add anything to the Word of God. While the
Constitution of the United States may be amended
from time to time, no amendment is ever necessary
for the Bible. We truly believe that the men who
wrote the Bible were guided by the Holy Spirit,
both in the thoughts they expressed and in their
choice of words.[32]

It is God who caused the Bible to be written to reveal His
plan of redemption. The Bible is "the only book in which
God's revelation is contained." Non-Christian revelations
"all begin with some flashes of true light, and end in
utter darkness."[33]

All of the authors of the sixty-six books were so guided
by God that the message they wrote was one. It is
normative for the Christian today and eternally
contemporary. Those who read the Bible

are finding the familiar but almost forgotten
phrases ring with a current meaning that makes
them seem to have been written only yesterday.
This is because the Bible embodies all the
knowledge man needs to fill the longing of his soul
and solve all his problems. It is the blueprint of the
Master Architect, and only by following its
directions can we build the life we are seeking.[34]

Since God speaks to man through the Scripture, it is
important that each person reads the Bible for himself.

God. The Bible is the revelation of God. He is a Person, a
"Spirit, Infinite, Eternal, and Unchangeable." God is
love, but He is also holy and righteous:

God's holiness demands that all sin be punished,
but God's love provides the plan and the way of
redemption for sinful man. God's love provided the
cross of Jesus, by which man can have forgiveness
and cleansing. It was the love of God that sent Jesus
Christ to the cross.[35]

Jesus Christ. The Bible teaches that God is "actually three
Persons, an incomprehensible mystery. There is but one

God expressed as God the Father, God the Son, and God
the Holy Spirit."[36] Jesus "is the Eternal Son of God—the
Second Person of the Holy Trinity, God manifested in
the flesh, the living Savior." He had no beginning and
was never created. All things were created by Him and
for Him. Christ came to reveal God to men:

> He it is who told us of the mercy and long-suffering
> and grace of God. He it is who promised life
> everlasting. . . . The very purpose of Christ's coming
> into the world was that He might offer up His life
> as a sacrifice for the sins of men . . . He suffered as
> no man has ever suffered . . . He died
> voluntarily. . . But the physical suffering of Jesus
> Christ was not the real suffering. . . The awful
> suffering of Jesus Christ was His spiritual death . . .
> He who knew no sin was made to be sin on our
> behalf. . . The sacrifice was penal, substitutionary,
> redemptive, propitiatory, reconciliatory,
> efficacious. . . .[37]

The resurrection assures the believer that Christ was
God, that God accepted His atoning work on the cross,
that mankind will be judged righteously, that our bodies
will be raised in the end, and that death's power has
been broken and abolished and its fear has been
removed.[38]

Sin. Sin entered the world through literal historical
Adam who "was created full-grown with every mental
and physical faculty developed." In his "total freedom"
and sinlessness, Adam, as the "fountainhead" of the
human race, "chose to listen to the lies of the Tempter
rather than to the truth of God!"[39] Generations yet
unborn fell with Adam, who stands as the federal head
of the human race. Adam's original sin has infected all
his children with the "death-dealing disease of sin" that
has been passed on to every generation since then:

> All the sorrow, all the bitterness, all the violence,
> tragedy, heartache and shame of man's history are
> summed up in that one little word—sin.

> Sin—plain old-fashioned sin, the selfsame sin that
> caused Adam's downfall—is what we are suffering
> from today, and it will do us far more harm than
> good to try to dress it up with a fancy, more
> attractive label.[40]

In the Bible, sin is described as a lawlessness, iniquity,
missing the mark, a trespass, and unbelief:

> Sin incurs the penalty of death, and no man has the
> ability to save himself from sin's penalty or to
> cleanse his own heart of its corruption. . . It is only
> in Christ that the remedy for sin can be found. It is
> only Christ who can save the sinner from the fate
> that surely awaits him.[41]

Man's fatal disease, sin, has separated man from his
Maker—resulting in a physical, a spiritual, and an eternal
death in hell:

> The Bible has a great deal to say about hell. No one
> spoke more about hell than Jesus did, and the hell
> He came to save men from was not only a hell on
> earth. It was not only some condition in which men
> are now living. It was something to come. Jesus
> never once taught that anyone was living in hell
> now. He always warned of a hell to come. Whatever
> He meant by hell, essentially it is the separation of
> the soul from God as the culmination of man's
> spiritual death. There are mysteries here and we
> dare not go beyond the teaching of Scripture.[42]

Unbelievers will be neither eventually saved nor
annihilated, for there is a conscious everlasting existence
of the immortal soul of man.[43] God made a complete
and perfect provision for the cure of man's fatal disease
by justification by faith in the blood of Christ.[44]

The Devil. The Scripture warns of a personal Devil who
controls a host of demons and seeks to come between us
and God. God has allowed the Devil to exist, for all his
designs only serve to work out God's own great plan.
The Devil has set up his kingdom upon the earth and
has endeavored to seduce mankind ever since the
Garden of Eden. He opposed the Trinity of God face to
face:

> Never for a second of your waking or sleeping life
> are you without these two powerful forces, never is
> there a moment when you cannot deliberately
> choose to go with one or the other. Always the
> Devil is standing at your side tempting, coaxing,
> threatening, cajoling. And always on your other side
> stands Jesus, the all-loving, the all-forgiving, waiting
> for you to turn to Him and ask His aid, waiting to
> give you supernatural power to resist the evil one.[45]

Salvation. The Devil won a victory over the human race
in the Garden. Because of this, man dies both spiritually
and physically. He has become helplessly lost and his
very nature opposes and even denies God. In the Old
Testament, God taught His people that "man could only
be saved by substitution."[46] Only God's Son, the Second
Person of the Trinity, had the capacity to bear in His
own body the sins of the world. He came to this earth as
a servant, made in the likeness of men:

> He would have to humble Himself and become
> obedient unto death. He would have to grapple
> with sin. He would have to buy sinners out of the
> slave market of sin. He would have to loose the
> bonds and set the prisoners free by paying a
> price—that price would be His own blood.[47]

Jesus' physical sufferings were exceeded by the awful
suffering of spiritual death. It was a voluntary death out
of love for you and me. The Cross reveals the depth of
men's sin, the overwhelming love of God and the way of

salvation. The Blood of the Cross redeems us, brings us nigh to God, makes peace with God, justifies and cleanses the sinner.

Conversion is necessary in order to get to heaven. It may not be a dramatic experience, but it is one of which the believer is certain. It involves:

1. Repentance, to turn away from sin; this involves acknowledgement of sin by the intellect, a godly sorrow of the emotions, and a determination of the will.

> The Bible teaches that when a person comes to Christ a change takes place that is reflected in everything he does.[48]

2. Faith is the "channel through which God's grace to us is received."[49] It is utter confidence in the efficacy of Christ's death for the salvation of the soul, "based upon the best evidence in the world, the Bible."[50]

3. The new birth, a second birth or regeneration. This is a divine work whereby the whole mental process is enlightened, the "heart undergoes a revolution, and the will is changed."

> This new nature that you receive from God is bent to the will of God. You will want to do only His will. You are utterly and completely devoted to Him. There is a new self-determination, inclination, disposition, a new principle of living, new choices.[51]

Of this salvation, the believer may have confidence that his sin was forgiven, that as a new man he is adopted into the family of God, and that the Holy Spirit continually indwells him.[52] By the new birth, he has already become a member of the great universal Church founded by Jesus Christ. Yet Jesus Christ intended that believers should become members in the local church "to glorify God by worship, for fellowship, for the strengthening of faith, as a medium for service, to channel funds for Christian work, to spread the Gospel, and to give wide expression to the humanitarian commands of Christ."[53]

Social obligations. While the Scripture teaches that Christ
may come at any time, they also exhort us "to carry on
business as usual until He comes."[54] Our entire way of
life should honor Christ. Christians are to be concerned
with the welfare of others:

> Many people have criticized the so-called "social
> gospel," but Jesus taught that we are to take
> regeneration in one hand and a cup of cold water
> in the other. Christians, above all others, should be
> concerned with social problems and social
> injustices. . . The Christian is to take his place in
> society with moral courage to stand up for that
> which is right, just, and honorable.[55]

Racial justice, civic responsibility, right
labor-management relationships, and the needs of
suffering humanity deserve the attention and assistance
of Christians as do hospitality, morality, financial
integrity, and mutual love and concern among
Christians.[56]
The coming of Christ and His message has uplifted
womanhood, freed slaves, promoted humanitarian
efforts, and improved society economically and morally:

> Christ has sensitized the life of the world. He has
> pointed man in a new direction. Why then is the
> world in such a desperate plight? The answer is that
> it will not come to Jesus Christ that it may have life.
> The world has rejected Him . . . Christ can save the
> world only as He is living in the hearts of men and
> women. We talk glibly about the establishment of a
> Christian social order of society through legislation
> and social engineering, as though we could bring it
> down from the skies, if only we worked hard
> enough. The Kingdom of God will never come that
> way. If the human race should suddenly turn to
> Christ, we would have immediately the possibility of
> a new Christian order. We could approach our
> problems in the framework of Christian
> understanding and brotherhood. To be sure, the

problems would remain, but the atmosphere for
their solution would be completely changed.[57]

The church in the United States has become too involved
in politics and social issues, to the neglect of the spiritual
issues and other areas in which the church is competent:

There are certain issues we know to be
wrong—racial injustice, crime, gambling, dishonesty,
pornography. On these matters we must thunder
forth as the prophets of God.[58]

The main responsibility of the church in the world is
proclaiming the Gospel which, in turn, will produce
many social changes:

I am convinced that if the church went back to its
main task of preaching the Gospel and getting
people converted to Christ it would have far more
impact on the social structure of the nation than it
can have in any other thing it could possibly do.[59]

The Blessed Hope. God will supernaturally establish His
Kingdom on the earth, because sinning man is incapable
of doing so:

Even the clamor for social justice, which is a biblical
concern, seems to seek an ideal mass society of
highly privileged sinners who keep God at a great
distance. But when the Kingdom of God is
established, it will not be established by social
reforms, democratic principles or scientific
achievement alone. It will be established by the
hand of God in the midst of *the ruins* of our social
and governmental institutions.[60]

In that day when Christ comes back to establish a new
social order, the longing and dreams of mankind will be
fulfilled. Jesus Christ will return unexpectedly and will
bring peace, establish justice, and restore nature to its
original state, so that the will of God will be
accomplished upon the earth.

Christ's return, however, will be preceded by world
distress, moral degeneracy, lawlessness, and a falling
away from true Christianity:

> This all seems to point to a time of widespread
> hypocrisy when multitudes of people will be herded
> into the church without having had a personal
> experience with Jesus Christ. Sects will grow. False
> teachers will infiltrate the church. The Bible will be
> under severe attack.[61]

Christians will be persecuted in a day of affluence,
knowledge and travel, peace conferences and war.

There will be a final great conflict, Armageddon, as a
culmination of the coming dictatorial rule of the
incarnation of Satan, called Antichrist. All men and
nations will stand before God to be judged: the righteous
at the judgment seat of Christ, the unrighteous dead at
the Great White Throne, and the nations at another
time:

> In that great day, men will call upon God for
> mercy, but it will be too late. In that day men will
> seek God, but they will not find Him. It will be too
> late.[62]

Finally, after the entire world "feels" the awful price
paid for sin in both the physical and human realms, "the
new heavens and earth will emerge from a world on
fire."[63] Every vestige of sin and corruption will be
destroyed and God will reshape the earth and heavens
according to His own design. Everything in heaven will
be new. God will have His throne there and the believer
will meet his Lord and Savior Jesus Christ.

THE INTERNATIONAL
FOUNDATIONS FOR
BERLIN

A survey of evangelistic appeal among Evangelicals
reveals a trend from a concern for national evangelism in

America in the early post-World War II era to a
worldwide, international, interracial dimension that
would lead to Berlin 1966 and to Lausanne 1974. The
expansion and extension of evangelical missions of the
West and of the Third World provided a representative
international base for these congresses on evangelism.
The extensive travel of evangelist Billy Graham for
crusades in London, Scotland, and on the Continent in
1954 and 1955, India in 1956, Australia and New
Zealand in 1959, and to Africa in early 1960, proved to
be the catalyst necessary to unite Evangelicals for the
Berlin World Congress on Evangelism in 1966. The
evangelistic declaration of the Gospel—based upon the
authority of the apostolic writings, the Bible—
transcended denominational differences and united
churchmen, evangelists, and missionaries around the
world in a renewed vision to fulfill the Great Commission
of Matthew 28:19, 20. The first—but unconscious—step
toward Berlin 1966 took place in an international
consultation held at Montreux, Switzerland, from August
16 to 19, 1960. It was characterized by heart-searching
revival, prayer, and Bible study under the theme
"Twentieth Century Evangelism."

AN ECUMENICAL
THEOLOGY OF
REVOLUTION
THE
CONTINUING
CRISIS IN
CONCILIAR
EVANGELISM

Ecumenical historians quickly trace their contemporary
origins to their pietistic or evangelical origins of the
nineteenth century. Some Evangelicals were slow to
abandon the various ecumenical movements that had
their roots in the evangelical dynamic of conferences

such as New York 1900 and Edinburgh 1910. According
to the ecumenical tradition, the Evangelicals of the world
should have been able to turn to the International
Missionary Council and to the World Council for
leadership in evangelism. Berlin 1966 should not have
been necessary at all. The doctrinal decline in the IMC
and the WCC has already been reviewed; and to the
Evangelical there seemed to be little, if any, hope for
evangelism in this direction. For evangelism had been
redefined to mean something else.

Was Berlin 1966 truly justified? At New Delhi 1961, a
number of major decisions were made which all but
eroded the basic foundations of the apostolic and
reformation dynamics of evangelism. Between the
Second Assembly at Evanston 1954 and New Delhi 1961,
the WCC theology of evangelism had been elaborated
but not officially endorsed by a WCC assembly. New
Delhi adopted the *principles* upon which this theology was
built and approved by the Central Committee in 1959 at
Rhodes. No official adoption of the 1959 document,
entitled "A Theological Reflection of the Work of
Evangelism," was made—probably because of the delicate
nature of the integration of the International Missionary
Council into the WCC, and of the inclusion of the larger
Eastern Orthodox churches into the ranks of the WCC as
well.

NEW DELHI 1961,
THE TRIUMPH OF
UNIVERSALISM

Evanston 1954 addressed the motive for
evangelism—proclaiming an encounter with Jesus Christ
as essential to eternal life and determining the destiny of
every man.[64] The "lostness" of man had been redefined
to speak of a common rebellion against God
demonstrated in the sin that is enmeshed in concrete
political and social institutions.[65] By contrast, the
horizontal "lostness" of man seems to be considered
more as a cause than as an effect. Because all men are or

will be saved, according to this doctrine of universalism,
the mission of the Church must be directed toward a
transformation of sinful structures! Underlying the
entire theology is the assumption expressed by D. T.
Niles, that the theologian should avoid a "literalistic"
interpretation of the Bible—leading to the eternal
lostness and punishment of man in hell.[66]
New Delhi most fully reflects the brilliant theological
and organizational genius of W. A. Visser 't Hooft. First,
the Basis was amended to satisfy conservative elements in
the WCC as well as the Eastern Orthodox churches, who
had insisted upon them as a condition for membership.
The intervening years since 1961 confirm the
conservative (not evangelical) influence these churches
have exercised in ecumenical theology.
Second, a document entitled "Christian Witness,
Proselytism and Religious Liberty" was received by the
Assembly.[67] This decision had its origins in Eastern
Orthodox concerns at the early Central Committee
meetings regarding the evangelistic activities of
evangelical missionaries among their constituents. In the
WCC relationships the "churchness" of all member
churches is recognized and the eternal "savedness" of all
those within their communions is not questioned. The
proper subjects of evangelism are the unchurched and
those of non-Christian religions unacquainted with the
"fullness" of salvation provided in Christ.
Third, after over two decades of negotiations, the
International Missionary Council was integrated into the
WCC as the Commission or Division of World Mission
and Evangelism.

The adoption of ecumenical evangelism. The "substance" of
the New Delhi "Report of Sections: Witness" was
approved by the Assembly and commended to the
churches for study and appropriate action. "Witness"
represents one of the three theological areas along with
"Service" and "Unity" deemed essential for evangelism.
The Pre-Assembly document was characteristically
amended by numerous recommendations.[68] The final

document reflects a general consensus edited by the
chairman and secretary. The coherence and consistency
of the document is lacking due to the amendments
reflecting differing views on evangelism. In it, some
traces of evangelical theology can be found which are
used by some to justify a continued evangelical presence
and participation in the WCC.

The assembly theme, "Jesus Christ, the Light of the
World" was seen as

> already the light of the world, of which He is Lord,
> and His light has preceded the bearers of the good
> news into the darkest places. The task of Christian
> witness is to point to Him as the true light, which is
> already shining. In Christ was life, and the life was
> the light of men, the light that enlightens every
> man. The work of evangelism is necessary in this
> and in every age in order that the blind eyes may
> be opened to the splendour of light.[69]

The lostness of man can be understood only in terms of
man's inability to see "the splendor of light," the
reconciliation for the atonement, "through Christ
embraces all creation and the whole of mankind."[70] The
new birth, it seems, is an apprehension of a greater
measure of light than that already possessed!

The basis for dialogue. Regarding this Light which New
Delhi asserted to be in every man,

> we have but little understanding of the wisdom,
> love and power which God has given to men of
> other faiths and of no faith, or of the changes
> wrought in other faiths by their encounter with
> Christianity. We must take up the conversations
> about Christ with them, knowing that Christ
> addresses them through us and us through them.[71]

This quotation elucidates the earlier quotation of Jesus as
the Light of the world in that this "Light" may now be
understood as another—though perhaps incomplete or

incognito—revelation of Christ to men of other faiths, the non-Christian religions, or of no faith, as in Marxism or Maoism. These assembly statements are official and form the theological basis for ecumenical mission. They are also the foundation for "dialogue" as an ecumenical evangelistic method. Since God has revealed Himself in Christ to those of "other faiths" and "no faith," through dialogue the Christian also receives additional revelation. It is only the splendor, the identification, of Jesus as that light that remains as the true substance of dialogue.[72]

Christ joins Himself to all humanity and by His death bridges the Church with the world. It is not surprising to find that the declaration questions the contemporary relevance of "judgment and hell" and emphasizes the proclamation of victory through Christ's death "over the power of death itself and the reality of a fuller and richer life than this world knows."[73] How is it that this distinction between the Church and the world has been minimized so that both may work together toward "the realization of our true humanity and eternal destiny"?[74] It is because of the incarnation whereby "our Lord has joined Himself to us all by becoming man."[75] It is also by His death, according to New Delhi, that the world has been reconciled so that this "reconciliation wrought through Christ embraces all creation and the whole of mankind."[76] A solidarity with all men of every nation, class, color, and faith "is a starting point of the renewal of the life and witness of our churches by the Holy Spirit." New Delhi did not emphasize the necessity for the "new birth" as a basis of solidarity and Church renewal. Solidarity was based, rather, upon what God had done independently of man by the incarnation and death of Christ. Man's active and personal faith are not required for reconciliation and Church renewal. An implied universalism almost obliterated the distinction between the Church and the world, between Christianity and non-Christian religions, and between men of the Christian faith and those ideologies of "no faith."

At New Delhi, the incarnation went beyond Jesus

Christ's *identification* with mankind for the purpose of a
substitutionary sacrificial death and help (Mark 10:45;
Heb. 2:14-17). According to New Delhi, Christ came into
union with all men, ". . . our Lord has joined Himself to
us all. . ." in not only our common humanity, but also, it
seems, in our common reconciliation.

Mission is a gathering for community and service.
Consequently, the gathering of the Church in mission is
a demonstration of world community, already reconciled
under the fatherhood of God:

> The gathering of the Church in every age
> demonstrates the loving purpose of God to draw
> men out of isolation and sinful separation into a
> community of brothers with a common Father, God
> Himself. . . Through His Church, God witnesses to
> His purpose to gather all nations, peoples and
> tongues, all sorts and conditions of men into His
> city.[77]

Since God's purpose is collective and national and since
the Church is a demonstration of the new humanity and
the world to come, its mission is *service.* It is not,
according to New Delhi, the gathered church that will
inherit the Kingdom of God, but all men. The Church is
no longer uniquely the body of Christ; for the entire
world, a universe universally redeemed is His body.
There is absolutely no place for evangelical doctrines of
evangelism in the New Delhi ecumenical theology.

Holistic evangelism. The WCC committed itself to another
gospel in a "Christian" context. It is upon these
foundations, however, that Evangelicals are influenced by
national or liberation theologies and unwittingly led to
redefine the Christian mission in ecumenical holistic
terms. First, the historical witness of the believer, by the
apostolic Scripture through the Holy Spirit, can no
longer be effective in evangelism without visible
organizational or ecumenical unity—for "the Bible

teaches us that the Gospel cannot be authoritatively
proclaimed to the world by a disunited Church."[78]
Second, service to the world is *essential* to evangelism:

> Witness to the Gospel must therefore be prepared
> to engage in the struggle for social justice and
> peace, it will have to take the form of humble
> service and a practical ministry of reconciliation
> amidst the actual conflicts of our times. The
> wholeness of the Gospel demands a corporate
> expression, since it concerns every aspect of men's
> lives. Healing and the relief of distress, the attack
> upon social abuses and reconciliation, as well as
> preaching, Christian fellowship and worship, are all
> bound together in the message that is proclaimed.[79]

The Evangelical must recognize that the theological
foundation of holistic evangelism, as noble as it sounds, is
built not only upon the theology of an errant Bible but
also upon the universalism of New Delhi that justifies a
horizontal salvation as equal to, or superior to, the
evangelical concern for the personal and individual
salvation.

Evangelicalism has always been careful to distinguish
between the "roots" and the "fruits" of salvation. The
salvation of the soul inevitably produces a transformation
in lives and society, but holistic evangelism is built upon
universalism: Christ incarnationally in union with all
men, the abolition of eternal punishment, the
redefinition of "lostness" to mean horizontal
hopelessness, and an abuse of the concept of the
sovereign Lordship of Christ that mitigates and
minimizes personal responsibility in favor of that of the
corporate Church. The mission was God's to the world,
missio dei,[80] not the evangelist toward the gathering in of
Christ's body from the world into the Church.

In conclusion, several new directions in evangelism
were officially initiated at New Delhi 1961 that enable
the Evangelical to better understand the theological
structure of the subsequent divisional meetings of the
WCC and their assemblies. Berlin 1966 and Lausanne

1974 reacted to the new theology of evangelism.

1. New Delhi officially adopted in principle the substance of that which the Central Committee at Rhodes received in 1961.[81]
To the ecumenical world, this position has the binding nature of the conciliar actions of the early centuries of the church. Normally, there is no return or revocation possible even though the descriptive language used lends itself to broad interpretations.

2. Mission and evangelism have acquired the additional horizontal responsibilities of pursuing world community by the restructuring of society, because Christ is the Light of all the world and He dwells within it.

3. Dialogue has been adopted as the most effective method of evangelism because of the "savedness" of others in the WCC and the revelation of Christ to those of other faiths and no faith.

New Delhi completely rejected the evangelicalism of Amsterdam 1948 and that of Evanston 1954. The theologically knowledgeable Evangelical could no longer find the essential elements fundamental to his faith.

MONTREAL 1963: THEOLOGICAL UNITY WITH ROMAN CATHOLICISM CONTINUES

The Fourth World Conference on Faith and Order (doctrine and polity) was held in Montreal, July 12-26, 1963, several months before the first meeting of the new Division of World Mission and Evangelism established at New Delhi 1961. These meetings represent one of the subdivisions of Edinburgh 1910 and further the ecumenical study of doctrine and polity.

The Bishop of Bristol, England, informed the impressive body of theologians represented that this conference "would build upon foundations laid in the past: upon the accumulated work of the Faith and Order Movement and of the World Council of Churches, including the New Delhi statement."[82]

Of particular significance was the official introduction of the Eastern Orthodox churches into an ecumenical conference, and the theological preparation that would facilitate the entry of the Roman Catholic Church into the WCC. Cardinal issues for Evangelicals concern biblical inspiration and the authority of Scripture in relation to the "tradition" of these historical churches.

The conferences opened with a discussion of the Orthodox and Roman Catholic views of tradition contrasted with the Protestant Reformation "appeal to Holy Scriptures alone, as the infallible and sufficient authority in all matters pertaining to salvation, to which all human traditions should be subjected."[83] Although the subject was inconclusive, an underlying assumption of higher critical methodology tended to leave the Bible as part of the tradition of the Church. This implies that the Church has not only preceded the Scripture *historically*, but that the Scripture in itself is not an adequate criterion of truth. While the Holy Scripture is central, its authoritative interpretation is dependent upon some hermeneutical principle other than that "any portion of Scripture is to be interpreted in the light of the Scripture as a whole."[84] In the final analysis, it is the verbal inspiration of the Scripture as infallible that underlies the problem, and it was to this issue that the Lausanne 1974 Covenant spoke.[85]

What difference did this conference make in evangelism, one may be asked. In principle, the evangelist can no longer say, "Thus saith the Lord," "The Bible says," or, "Jesus Christ says," for he is obliged to say, "Thus says my church, or my tradition, or the tradition of the Church," etc. His authoritative proclamation and that of the Bible have been diluted, for the evangelist must become an authority on church history, hermeneutics, and ecclesiology before he can "effectively" proclaim the Gospel message. For the Evangelical it is *not* too simplistic to say that the evangelist bears the apostolic message infallibly inscripturated or recorded under the direction (not dictation) of the Holy Spirit. At Montreal 1963, either the authority of a not-as-yet defined Church, or the

authority of ecumenical theological consensus or of
contemporary conciliarity (traditions in Council) was
superimposed upon the Bible. The issues are far
from resolved even today. Must apostolic world
evangelism wait for the unity of the Church on faith
and order? Will evangelism truly be more effectively
accomplished by an ecumenical or conciliar Church?
The record of the past decades leaves grave doubts as
to the values of evangelistic efforts diverted toward
organizational or ecclesiastical unity. Organic unity has
already been "given" to those "in Christ." Would
visible organizational unity contribute *more* to world
evangelization?

MEXICO CITY 1963: ECUMENICAL MISSION TO SIX CONTINENTS

Evangelicals have persistently declared the necessity of
evangelism at home and mission overseas. The
Commission of World Mission and Evangelism conducted
its first meeting in Mexico City, December 8-19, 1963,
and by their title "intended to challenge more radically
than hitherto any assumption that the western world no
longer itself needed to be evangelized."[86] The entire
world with its horizontal needs became a field of
Christian witness and ecumenical evangelism. Witnesses
were to continue crossing national and confessional
frontiers as part of the whole Church. The geographic
lines were erased. The official report of the meeting said,

> The missionary frontier runs around the world. It
> is the line that separates belief from unbelief, the
> unseen frontier which cuts across all other frontiers
> and presents the universal Church with its primary
> missionary challenge. Other frontiers exist. The
> most important of these today are between nations
> and races, between ideological and cultural
> groups.[87]

Mexico 1963 called for the entry of international teams
of "missionaries" into racial, social, and economic
problem areas of the world to "show the world that
God's Kingdom is at hand."[88]

The changed focus upon the "world" (New Delhi
1961)—rather than upon the "church gathered" by
evangelism and missions, and distinct by its nature from
the world (historical and evangelical position)—produced
a different approach, currently reflected in holistic
evangelism. According to Goodall, the difference lies

> between approaching the secular from outside in
> order to change or challenge it and learning from
> the inside its meaning and possibilities. Missions
> have always acted in the conviction that the Church
> is *sent to* the secular with news about God, man,
> history, and destiny. Yet being *sent to* suggests an
> initial separation *from*. In the new emphasis the
> movement is from within the secular as a realm
> which is itself created by God, within which His
> presence is to be discovered and His redemptive
> work realized.[89]

What does this approach imply for the Evangelical? It
says that God is primarily concerned with the
transformation of the abusive social and political
structures of society, that God is redemptively present in
all people (the secular) so that mankind only awaits the
presence, witness, and work of Christians to change the
world structures and alleviate human need. The planting
and growth of churches by conversions is minimized if
not lost—for growing churches have become incidental to
a redeemable world. A theology of world development
and better men replaced evangelical evangelism. These
programs are a direct result of the New Delhi 1961 and
Montreal 1963 "cosmic Christ," who has replaced a
personal Redeemer, while the lostness of man is seen
almost entirely in terms of human need and suffering.

Church renewal seeks to restructure the churches for
these new goals, but it must be recognized that the
theological research for this new "evangelism" rejected

the evangelical view of the inspiration of the Bible. The Department on Studies in Evangelism's "One Year's Discussion on Structures for Missionary Congregations," as commissioned by New Delhi and prepared for Mexico 1963, considered "structured fundamentalism" as opposed to the restructuring of the church that would enable it to go into the world to activate social and political changes. The report said,

> By fundamentalism we usually mean an especially dogmatic position which makes no allowance whatsoever for a historical understanding of the Bible and Christian doctrine. This kind of fundamentalism expresses itself especially in its emphatic defense of verbal inspiration. "Structural fundamentalism" is a parallel phenomenon which . . . removes . . . the form or structure of the congregation from the realm of historical consideration and questioning.[90]

Evangelical theology of scriptural inspiration maintained the normative and permanent nature of the scriptural teachings regarding the Church and its mission. The Lausanne 1974 Covenant position on Scripture has extended implications regarding the place and meaning of evangelism in the local church for it is the Scripture that provides an unchanging apostolic doctrine of the Church and its evangelistic missionary structure between the times of Jesus' ascension and His return.

It is for this reason that in ecumenical terminology the word "mission" has replaced "missions." Long before New Delhi 1961, missions directed their efforts toward individual conversions and mission leaders readily perceived the new concept of "mission" as an effort to attack "society's structure and values more radically than does the average pietist."[91] Eugene Carson Blake saw this conflict arising in Mexico 1963 and culminating at the Uppsala 1968 Assembly where some advocates of "mission" in the new sense espoused only "dialogue" with men of other faiths or no faith and found "proclamation" to be usually triumphalist and

self-defeating. It is enlightening to note that "mission"
finally resulted in a new definition of "conversion,"
where the religious aspect of the new birth may not
appear at all, for it has an ethical and social content that
in essence relates the convert to the "new Humanity" and
the community of mankind![92]
    Evangelicals could find little encouragement for world
evangelism by these trends of "mission." Renewal in
missions, consequently, means the transformation of the
local church and of the universal Church to the new
theology of evangelism and mission. A "revival" of the
former evangelical spiritual life of the church was not
sought in this ecumenical program, but rather was
outdated by the "progress" of theology.

GENEVA 1966: REVOLUTION AS A PART OF EVANGELISM

Shortly before the World Congress on Evangelism in
Berlin in October 1966, the Department of Church and
Society, formerly known as Life and Work in its 1925
origins, held a conference which "made the issue of
world economic development a major concern of the
churches."[93] This subject had been at the heart of the
WCC since the height of the social gospel and the
Oxford Conference of 1937.[94]
    The rising emphasis upon the physical needs of man at
New Delhi 1961 came to a dramatic climax at Geneva
1966, as the conference recognized "the need for
revolutionary change in social and political structures."[95]
Social thought developed from the earlier idea of a
"responsible society" to a "responsible world society"
produced by revolutionary transformation. The
one-sided presentation of socialism as the ideal structure
for a just society revealed the political orientation of the
new evangelism.[96] Christians within and without were
shocked by this overt advocacy of political revolution.
Carl F. H. Henry said the

one dominant emphasis of this initial Geneva
background volume is its *rejection of fixed moral
principles,* irrespective of divine revelation and the
Bible. . . . The revolt against fixed revelation
principles in ecumenical social theory has
increasingly led on toward an unprincipled,
situational ethic.[97]

Paul Ramsay, a Princeton professor and a member of the
co-opted staff for Geneva 1966, in his book *Who Speaks
for the Church?*

castigates the WCC hierarchy for procedures and
conclusions of the Geneva Conference but also
declares that neo-Protestant political incursion
shatters all Reformation precedent and that modern
Roman papacy is in welcome contrast.[98]

Evangelism at Berlin 1966, consequently, appeared on
the world scene as a dramatic alternative to what Alice
Widener called "The Gospel of Revolution."[99] Paul
Abrecht concludes in his review of Geneva 1966,

Christians in a revolutionary situation have a moral
duty to do all in their power to exercise a ministry
of reconciliation to enable the revolutionary change
to take place non-violently or, if this is not possible,
with a minimum of violence.[100]

Ecumenical theology has not accepted the second coming
of Christ and is, consequently, unable to understand the
present patience and meekness of the Christian who will
not bring in the Kingdom by force.[101] The ecumenical
movement first rejected an evangelical theology of
evangelism, and then endorsed a radicalism which
supported violent political revolution if necessary. It
became difficult to see how Evangelicals could support or
identify with a movement even more radical than the
social gospel. Another source and voice of evangelism
was essential.

5
One Race, One Gospel, One Task

The World Congress on Evangelism

held in Berlin in the fall of 1966 was one of the most
remarkable evangelical events in modern Christian
history. Even though previous or subsequent congresses
have had larger attendance, improved methods, wider
representation, or greater prestige, Berlin 1966 was
significant for two reasons. The first is that such a
Congress on evangelism could take place at all. The
second is the graceful simplicity reflected in its theme,
"One Race, One Gospel, One Task": there was a spiritual
mpact transcending organizational or theological
preparation.

Berlin 1966 expressed the concern of Billy Graham for
evangelism throughout the world. Others had spoken to
him about the need for such an assembly,[1] but his vision
and leadership, sustained by the cosponsorship of the
periodical *Christianity Today* and its editor Carl F. H.
Henry, enabled more than 1,200 delegates from 100
different countries to study evangelism.

In retrospect, the entire Congress represented far
more a movement led and implemented by God than a
program directed by men. A review of the articles
revealed the clear, unconfused, dynamic and biblical
simplicity that had propelled a revival of historic

evangelicalism in North America, and then shared this
message with others in Western Europe. It was
predominantly Western in organization and expression,
but generally configured the increase in evangelical
numerical strength and influence around the world. A
biblical "freshness" seemed to dissipate the dense clouds
of theological ambiguity, scholasticism, and equivocation,
so characteristic of Western assemblies. The content of
the Congress was communicable. The average layman,
pastor, or missionary could profit greatly from almost
every paper. It was popularized and lent itself easily to
the adaptation of regional congresses in the post-Berlin
1966 era.

In spite of the predominance of Western speakers and
their unified views of evangelism, theology, geography,
and methodologies, the Western participant was
continually reminded of his evangelical counterparts
from the Third World. Whether by Auca Indians from
Ecuador, or by French-speaking Vietnamese, the
delegates were continually reminded that they were not
only one in Christ, but "One Race"—sinners redeemed
by faith in Christ. A fraternity developed that united all
hearts in the "One Task" of proclaiming the "One
Gospel." Evangelicals giving their lives to evangelism
around the world were seeking together to learn how to
do it better.

What drew this diversified body together? A roll call of
the speakers and participants would reveal that almost all
were involved in evangelism. There was a profound
willingness to share what had been experienced, and an
openness to learn from others. Various mission
organizations used that occasion to meet with
missionaries and national leaders. Any vestiges of
paternalism were overshadowed by partnership in the
spirit of the Congress.

Berlin herself was an attraction, for she symbolized a
world in need, divided, suffering, struggling, helpless,
and hopeless. The "other worldliness" of Christianity was
compared with the brave democracy of West Berlin and
the sullen oppression of Marxist-dominated East Berlin.
Germany and Reformation Sunday were continuous

reminders of the debt Evangelicals owed to the
Reformers and their biblical contributions.

In spite of the theological confusion that characterized
traditional Christianity and paralyzed evangelism, Berlin
1966 showed no signs of "hesitancy" in the message or
the method. It proved to be an historical declaration of
the revival and advance of evangelicalism that had
recovered from the debacle of the 1920s and 1930s. It
was a *demonstration* of the unity inspired and enabled by
the infallible witness to Christ in the Bible. The
evangelical nature of the Congress introduced a spiritual
dimension that both integrated the papers and enabled
the Congress to conclude in a great surge of *inspiration*.
It was evangelical "ecumenicity," a world fellowship at its
best. No continuation committee was formed, but added
momentum was given to the great evangelistic movement
of the Spirit—most dramatically evidenced at the
Graham Crusade seventeen years earlier in Los Angeles
1949.

BERLIN 1966

There is a sense in which Berlin 1966 was initiated at the
Youth for Christ International conference held in
August 1948 at Beatenberg, Switzerland. Youth for
Christ International's perspective for youth around the
world brought together a small group of friends around
Billy Graham because of their mutual evangelistic
concerns. A special time of prayer with Dawson Trotman
of the Navigators, Bob Evans, the organizer of the
conference, and Hubert Mitchell—men of world
vision—gave birth to the idea of a World Conference of
Evangelism, as Berlin was first called.

THE MONTREUX
CONFERENCE ON
EVANGELISM

For years, the vision for a world conference was shared
with Billy Graham by Bob Evans, now European director

of the Greater European Mission; by Larry Love, a pastor in Florida; and by Don Hoke, then president of the Japan Christian College, who in 1955 wrote about a world conference on missions.[2] The December 1958 board meeting of the Billy Graham Evangelistic Association voted to sponsor a world conference on evangelism and appointed Larry Love to act as executive secretary in charge of arrangements. Shortly thereafter, Billy Graham personally wrote to a number of Christian leaders requesting their "thoughts, ideas, and suggestions" for such a conference.

From the beginning the purpose of such a conference was associated with that of D. L. Moody and the "Watchword" of the Student Volunteer Movement for Foreign Missions—"The Evangelization of the World in This Generation." A unity of evangelistic endeavor was sought that would further world evangelization without organizing a new movement. Graham expressed this clearly in his first general correspondence with several leaders outside of his immediate colleagues:

> There is no thought of organizing a new movement; in fact, we are very definite that no organization will come out of such a conference. It will be for prayer, fellowship and study of evangelistic strategy in the face of the problems of evangelism around the world. Our thought is to invite evangelical leaders from every country in the free world, including evangelists, national church leaders and missionaries.
>
> I believe there is a desperate need for such a conference at this time of confusion and the necessary readjustment of evangelism and missions in the face of changing conditions. Perhaps out of this conference could come a new unity among the Lord's people to get the job of world evangelization done in our generation.[3]

As an ardent student of national and world affairs, it was not difficult for Graham to recognize problems arising for missions and evangelism in a shrinking, anticolonialist world, as he conducted crusades in continent after continent.

Dr. V. R. Edman, then president of Wheaton College (Illinois), was designated chairman of the Planning Committee of what was then called the World Conference on Evangelism. The first committee meeting was held on January 15 and 16, 1959, at the Park Street Church in Boston, Massachusetts. The twelve members represented a wide spectrum of evangelical churchmen and parachurch leaders.[4]

In addition to deciding on the conference objectives, a tentative program and personnel, the required financial arrangements and budget, and a plan for securing delegates, the committee chose September 1960 as the date for the conference. Fifteen evangelical leaders throughout the world were polled to recommend delegates to the second meeting, April 23, 1959.[5]

After further preparation, letters of invitation were sent out in June 1960 for a three-day conference held at Montreux, Switzerland, on August 16-18, 1960. Most of those attending were in Europe, but for those leaders unable to secure travel expenses, these funds were made available by the Billy Graham Evangelistic Association.[6] Among the thirty-three world leaders present, twelve nations were represented in addition to missionaries from several others.[7]

Speakers included Billy Graham, Clyde Taylor, Festo Kivengere, Stephen Olford, John Stott, Paul Rees, Larry Love, Tom Allan, Harold Ockenga, David Morken, V. R. Edman. The theme was "God's Strategy in Missions and Evangelism." *Decision* magazine reported,

> Among the subjects of discussion and prayer were "separation" and "identification"; the Christian message to youth in the next five years; "overworked leadership"; the "attestation of the Holy Spirit"; the Church as the witnessing community; Christian unity; Church-State relationships throughout the world; the

communication of the Gospel to the world and
especially to the underprivileged; repentance,
rejoicing and revival.[8]

John Stott of England spoke on "God's Strategy for
This Age." He referred first to the strategy of the Devil,
who attempted physical attacks upon the apostles, who
polluted the inner life of the churches, and who
intellectually perverted its message. "The Spirit's sword is
the Word of God," he said, "and he is anxious to blunt
the sword."[9] The source of power in God's strategy, he
declared, is in the Word of God, in the cross of Christ,
and in the Holy Spirit.

Tom Allan, pastor of St. George's-Tron Church,
Glasgow, addressed the conference on "Theological
Trends as Related to Evangelism." As a member of the
Department of Evangelism in the WCC, he had chaired a
Consultation on Evangelism at the WCC Ecumenical
Institute at Bossey, Switzerland, prior to his arrival at the
conference. Allan spoke of his spiritual pilgrimage to the
ministry beginning in 1945:

> I was posted to France as an intelligence officer and
> on Easter Day I heard a Negro G.I. sing a spiritual:
> "Were You There When They Crucified My Lord?"
> And on that day Christ laid hold of my life. I came
> back without any background to resume my
> interrupted studies for the ministry, and the
> theological training was the same as Chandu Ray
> referred to last night. It was liberal, modernistic,
> and yet I myself knew beyond any shadow of
> peradventure the reality of Jesus Christ.[10]

As he faced the realities of a mission ministry in
Glasgow, the first great influence occurred when he was

> compelled to ask men to decide for Jesus Christ,
> and this brought me to the place of total and
> absolute nakedness;. . . I was driven to two
> discoveries which transformed my own ministry: the
> first was that the preaching of the cross is central. I

> discovered the meaning of the . . . *doctrine of the atonement* and I discovered *the authority of the Word.*[11]

The second influence was the 1955 "Tell Scotland Movement" and the ministry of Billy Graham to him personally, for it was then that he found his "theological feet for the first time." He also paid tribute to Carl Henry and to *Christianity Today* for the "amazing influence" this publication had upon him and, he believed, upon "the evangelical thinking throughout the whole world."

Allan reflected the theological confrontation recently experienced at Bossey. He called for a definition of evangelism, grappled with the problem of communication, struggled with secularism, and labored—unconsciously perhaps—to integrate the ecumenical theology of Christ's "presence." Secular man, he said, could not accept the linguistic symbols of the Word alone:

> And therefore I believe—increasingly and with absolute conviction—that where my work is mainly among people with no church background at all, the proclamation is being made out of a context in which the Word of the Gospel is being made incarnate in terms which secular men recognize and understand. . . The witness of the community of Christ manifesting the life of its risen Lord in the context of the whole life of man—this is where I think the question that Bob Pierce asked yesterday morning is the great burning contention of our evangelistic program.[12]

Allan's evangelistic concern was a reminder of the increasingly secularized world, of the dynamics of the Graham crusades, and of the influence of contemporary ecumenical theology.

For the Planning Committee, the Montreux Conference was an end in itself, a bringing together of those who were the real leaders in evangelism to inspire and instruct them for more effective evangelistic ministries. The atmosphere was "low-keyed," directed toward a world strategy even though some hungered for a revival atmosphere.[13] The assembled leaders gained a new world perspective, and valuable lessons were learned that led to Berlin 1966 and Lausanne 1974.

THE PERSPECTIVE OF BERLIN 1966

The World Congress on Evangelism seemed to have been providentially directed both in the time of its occurrence as well as the place.

Rising nationalism around the world began to give a new sense of purpose and dignity to the former colonies of the West. Third World Evangelicals attended Berlin as full partners with the other nations. Racial discrimination had become a world issue, and Berlin 1966 helped the rising Third World evangelical leadership to have an authentic voice in the evangelical world and to recognize the importance of their contribution to world evangelism.

The anti-institutionalism of disillusioned youth was soon to erupt into violent riots. The Berlin Wall was an ugly but realistic reminder of the major ideological struggles and divisions characteristic of a world that remained to be evangelized.

Several meetings of international significance occurred that year. The Wheaton Congress (USA) produced a Declaration reaffirming the evangelical position on the new theological threats to missionary work. In Africa many of the evangelical churches and missions united to organize the Association of Evangelicals in Africa and Madagascar. The World Council of Churches sponsored in Geneva a Conference on Church and Society that "took its agenda from the world."

Berlin 1966 reminded Evangelicals of their historical roots in biblical history, when Emperor Haile Selassie I, whose spiritual heritage is traced back to the Ethiopian eunuch, participated in the processional. The 16th-century imprint of the Reformers upon modern evangelicalism was celebrated by the march on Reformation Sunday from Wittenberg Square to the Kaiser Wilhelm Memorial Church. Over 10,000 Christians of West Berlin joined the 1,200 Congress participants for a great demonstration of fellowship. Flags of the 100 different nations of the participants revealed the spectrum of evangelical commitment around the world. The presence of the Auca Indian converts from Ecuador was a stirring testimony of the power of the historic Gospel to transform the murderers of five missionaries in 1956 into messengers of love and peace in this generation.

The unity of mankind as created by God and as in common need of redemption by Jesus Christ was expressed by "One Race." The Congress recognized that the love of God in Christ transcends every human barrier and prejudice.

The uniqueness of the biblical Gospel revealing God's nature and will for mankind was expressed by "One Gospel." This Gospel concerns itself with the death of Jesus Christ for sinners, as recorded in the Bible. The Closing Statement rejected

> . . . all theology and criticism that refuses to bring itself under the divine authority of Holy Scripture, and all traditionalism which weakens that authority by adding to the Word of God.[14]

This Closing Statement also defined the "One Task" as the proclamation of the good news of salvation. The world church was implored "to obey the divine commission to permeate, challenge, and confront the world with the claims of Jesus Christ." Evangelism was defined as uniquely proclamation:

> Evangelism is the proclamation of the Gospel of the crucified and risen Christ, the only Redeemer of men, according to the Scriptures, with the purpose of persuading condemned and lost sinners to put their trust in God by receiving and accepting Christ as Savior through the power of the Holy Spirit, and

to serve Christ as Lord in every calling of life and in the fellowship of his Church, looking toward the day of his coming in glory.[15]

Because of the command of Christ who possesses all authority in heaven and earth, Christians are to be witnesses. The multiple motivations for world evangelism in the history of modern missions seem to be reduced to this one motive—obedience to the command of Christ. The glory of God, His love, the lostness of humanity, the imminent return of Christ, etc., are not mentioned:

> In the power of his Spirit, he commands us to proclaim to all people the good news of salvation through his atoning death and resurrection; to invite them to discipleship through repentance and faith; to baptize them into the fellowship of his Church; and to teach them all his words.[16]

"One Task" referred to an evangelism that was concerned about the church. Converts were to find their place in a local church, be baptized, and be taught. The new life style of the convert would be service of Christ in every calling of life and in the fellowship of his church. A decision alone would not constitute personal faith in Christ according to the biblical requirements of evangelism of Berlin. The responsibility of the evangelist extends to the incorporation of the convert into the life of the local church. What "his Church," the Church of Christ, is was not defined, yet it is described as a visible fellowship of those with an identical commitment and related by baptism. This fellowship anticipates the coming of Christ in glory.

WHY BERLIN 1966

The purpose of Berlin is contained in the opening Congress address by Billy Graham himself entitled, "Why the Berlin Congress?" The text reveals a strong sense of continuity with the history and personalities of evangelism in the past, through references to Dwight L.

Moody, the missionary movement in the nineteenth
century, John R. Mott, and the Edinburgh 1910 World
Missionary Conference. Graham asked the Congress to
clarify the theological problems confronting the
Evangelicals.

First, Graham requested a definition of evangelism. He
found the definition of Archbishops' Committee in 1918
to be the most adequate:

> To evangelize is so to present Christ Jesus in the
> power of the Holy Spirit, that men shall come to
> put their trust in God through him, to accept him
> as their Savior and serve him as their King in the
> fellowship of his Church.[17]

The definition contrasted sharply with a popular WCC
viewpoint expressed by one American secretary of
evangelism in 1964, who was saying that

> the redemption of the world is not dependent upon
> the souls we win for Christ. . .There cannot be
> individual salvation. . .Salvation has more to do with
> the whole society than with the individual
> soul. . .We must not be satisfied to win the people
> one by one. . .Contemporary evangelism is moving
> away from winning souls one by one to the
> evangelization of the structures of society.[18]

Graham reminded the Congress that the primary thrust
of evangelism "is the winning of men to a personal
relationship to Jesus Christ." Nevertheless, the Gospel
has social implications. In recent years, sin, reconciliation,
and the task of the Church had been redefined.

Second, Graham found that the biblical motives for
evangelism had been confused. He found the scriptural
basis of evangelism to be in the commands of the Great
Commission, in the example set by the preaching of the
apostles, in the constraining love of Christ, in the
knowledge of an approaching judgment, and in the
spiritual and moral needs of men. Syncretism, he stated,
was rejected in the Bible because of the all-inclusive

nature of Acts 1:8. The command extends to the end of the earth and "represents every conceivable situation—taking account of every possible language, race, color, or even religious belief."[19]

Universalism, likewise, had caused much confusion in the mission of the church because it questioned whether men are really lost.

> The various shades of universalism prevalent throughout the Church have done more to blunt evangelism and take the heart out of the missionary movement than anything else. I believe the Scriptures teach that men outside of Jesus Christ are lost.[20]

Graham believed that a deep conviction of this biblical teaching "would become a burning incentive to evangelize" with zeal and passion. He avoided the debates within evangelicalism concerning the Kingdom, and directed his attention toward the fundamental issue of eternal punishment. The subtle propagation of universalism had eroded or eliminated the eschatological motivation—the return of Jesus Christ and the subsequent judgment to come—to evangelize.

Graham supported social compassion and reaffirmed that evangelism has a social responsibility. He saw, however, an inversion of the divine order when Christians endeavor to exhort people to love one another before these people have the capacity to do so by a regenerating personal relationship with Jesus Christ. In this, Graham replied to the ecumenical error that all men are Christians through a mystical infusion of the "new humanity" into mankind by the Incarnation. He corrected this heresy, emphasizing the importance of social compassion or social responsibility:

> Thus evangelism has a social responsibility. The social, psychological, moral and spiritual needs of men become a burning motivation for evangelism. However, I am convinced if the Church went back to its main task of proclaiming the Gospel and

> getting people converted to Christ, it would have a
> far greater impact on the social, moral and
> psychological needs of men than any other thing it
> could possibly do. Some of the greatest social
> movements of history have come about as the result
> of men being converted to Christ.[21]

Evangelism would bring about social results.

Third, Graham believed that the message of
evangelism had been distorted to resemble humanism.
The normative nature of Scripture makes the truths
announced by the apostolic writers valid for this century
as well. Biblical evangelism requires a proclamation of
the *kerygma* as summarized by the Apostle Paul in
1 Corinthians 15:1-4. This message is relevant and
transforming in every generation and on every continent.
The message of the Gospel works supernaturally to bring
salvation:

> I have found that there is a supernatural power in
> this message that cannot be rationally explained. It
> may appear ridiculous and foolish to the
> intellectuals of our day, but it is the power of God
> unto salvation.[22]

Graham's presentation was an implicit rejection of
national theologies, and a strong affirmation of the
transcultural nature of biblical truth. Evangelism,
consequently, should not be seen as a deviation from
historic Christianity, but as a renewal and revival of the
apostolic message. While this message may be applied
differently to various social, political, and cultural
contexts and needs, the message remains constant and
normative. "While methods may change, the Message
never changes," he said.[23]

Fourth, Graham declared that *the* enemy of evangelism
is Satan, who

> blinds the minds of those whom we seek to
> evangelize. . .His strategy is to use deception, force,
> evil and error to destroy the effectiveness of the
> Gospel.[24]

Confusion surrounded the personality of Satan. "His most successful strategy has been to get modern theologians to deny his existence."[25]

Fifth, the methods of evangelism required clarification and biblical justification. Graham noted that Leighton Ford found six methods, from mass evangelism to literature evangelism, in the New Testament. Technological developments enabled evangelists to keep pace with the present population explosion. Graham advocated flexibility of methods since the goal of evangelism is the penetration of the entire world.

> No one method will be right for every person in every situation at any given time; but some method of evangelism is certainly right for all people in all situations at all times! The Holy Spirit can take any method and use it to win souls.[26]

Graham believed that one of the great questions facing the Berlin participants was the revival of the institutional Church and that this "cannot be organized or promoted by human means."[27] It is the preaching of the Cross and the resurrection that will not only bring the moral reforms and social changes that the world needs, but also bring unity among true believers:

> Do we want unity among true believers throughout the world? Then evangelize. I believe that some of the greatest demonstrations of ecumenicity in the world today are these evangelistic crusades where people have been meeting by the thousands from various denominations with the purpose of evangelizing. There is a dedication, a zeal, and a spirit that is not found in other gatherings.[28]

Revival may be expected by an outpouring of the Holy Spirit because the day of miracles has not passed. Just as there had been a revival at the birth of the Church, Graham looked forward to this blessing as a possibility in the closing day of the Church's witness on the earth.

Graham said that Berlin represented a return to

biblical evangelism as the source of moral and social
reform, and true ecumenicity. The Congress Purpose
was sevenfold:
   1. To define and clarify biblical evangelism for our
day.
   2. To establish beyond any doubt its relevance to the
modern world.
   3. To underline its urgency in the present situation.
   4. To explore new forms of witness now in use
throughout the world and new ways of reaching
contemporary man.
   5. To deal frankly with problems of resistance to the
Gospel.
   6. To challenge the church to renew its own life
through an intensified proclamation of historic faith.
   7. To show the world in a fresh and dramatic way that
God is in truth Lord of all, and that He saves men
through His Son.[29]
   Berlin 1966 was not conceived as an end in itself or as
a demonstration, but as a definition of biblical evangelism
that would inspire and implement the proclamation of
the Gospel throughout the world. Harold J. Ockenga
had the specific assignment of formulating "a definition
of evangelism"[30] by the end of the Congress. The
pre-Congress Executive Committee predicted a
post-Congress era of evangelistic emphasis. The
Committee was not sure whether to set up future rallies
and small conferences by returning participants or to
have major regional congresses.[31] Congress leadership
was concerned about the Gospel's content, evangelistic
methods in a technological society, and the urgency of
evangelism. Church renewal would be accomplished by
historic evangelism permeating the churches from the
inside.

THE PREPARATION
OF BERLIN 1966

   Berlin 1966 required almost three years of planning.
The first meeting of the Executive Committee took place

in Chicago, April 21, 1964.[32] Earlier informal meetings
with Billy Graham named the committee and decided its
name as the World Congress of Evangelism.

The "Call to Congress" included, "the present
condition of the Church," and the "purpose of the
Congress":

1. To define and reaffirm biblical evangelism—its
   theology and methods, and doctrine of the
   Church.
2. To discover the divine strategy of world
   evangelism for our generation, in view of the
   various problems that we face—nationalism;
   population explosion; social, cultural, and
   economic problems.
3. To develop the framework of cooperation
   (discuss our oneness).[33]

The Sponsoring Committee was responsible for
nominating the delegates—to be selected by the final
decision of the Executive Committee.[34] The fifty-four
members of the Sponsoring Committee represented
evangelical leaders of the Third World and of the West,
laymen and theologians, Lutheran and Church of
England bishops, Pentecostals and Presbyterians,
outstanding evangelists and missionary statesmen,
Reformed churchmen of the West, and parachurch
mission directors. They were a cross section of
Evangelicals within the ranks of traditional Protestantism,
the newer evangelical denominations, and the Church of
England. Roman Catholics were invited as observers.[35]
The separatist "fundamentalists" were not represented at
all.

The Executive Committee served as the Invitational
Committee and established criteria for the invitation of
delegates:

1. Evangelicals with a constituency which can be
   influenced
2. Evangelical national church leaders in the same
   position

3. Educators directly related to evangelism through
   writing, teaching, or influence
4. Missionary leaders
5. Missionary service organizations
6. Key pastors and evangelists
7. Lay leaders who have a concern for
   evangelism.[36]

Quotas of national church leaders insured a world
representation. The numerical goal of delegates was set
at 1,262.[37] The benefits of the Congress were directed
toward the delegates who were to pursue evangelism in
the various parts of the world. What they saw and heard
set a pattern for the regional congress to follow. The
impressions received at Berlin 1966 would have their
most decisive impacts on evangelical leaders and
educators in the five to ten years after the Congress.
   The Congress officers named in the next committee
meeting, September 14, 15, 1964, were:
   Honorary Chairman Billy Graham
   Chairman—Carl F. H. Henry
   Coordinator—W. Stanley Mooneyham
   Publicity Director—David Kucharsky[38]
   Rome, Copenhagen, and Berlin were the three cities
considered for the Congress. Rome was eliminated by the
Executive Committee. By a phone conversation between
Billy Graham and members of the Executive Committee
on July 1, 1964, Berlin was selected as the site for the
Congress, to meet from October 26 to November 4,
1966. The Congress coincided with the dates of the
Berlin Crusade, October 16-25, and a concluding
Crusade meeting on November 6 after the Congress.[39]
At the September 1964 Executive Meeting, Carl Henry
proposed a Congress trip to Wittenburg on Reformation
Sunday, but apparently this excursion was not authorized
by the East German government.
   In the third Executive Committee Meeting of
September 14 and 15, 1964, at New York, it was agreed
that *Christianity Today* would sponsor the Congress
instead of the Billy Graham Evangelistic Association, and

that editor Carl F. H. Henry would become a member of
the Executive Committee. Robert Evans remained
chairman of the Program Committee.[40] The Congress
coincided with the tenth anniversary of *Christianity Today,*
of which Wilbur M. Smith was the founding editor.[41]
Billy Graham was closely involved—with his
father-in-law, Dr. Nelson Bell—in the inspiration and
organization of this evangelical periodical.

At the first Executive Meeting for the Congress on
April 21, 1964, Robert Van Kampen, Chairman of the
Finance Committee, proposed a budget of $405,000. The
Committee asked him to reduce it to $350,000!

By February 1966, the gross budget had climbed to
$725,000. Anticipated income was $128,000, leaving a
need of $597,000. Minutes record that "the final
approval of the budget must await action by Dr. Billy
Graham and the finance committee of the B.G.E.A."[42]
The Billy Graham Evangelistic Association paid salaries
to some members of the Congress staff and contributed
considerably toward the Congress expenses.

THE PROGRAM

English, German, French, and Spanish were the official
languages used in the program established in the first
Executive Committee meeting. After early morning
prayer cell meetings in the hotels, the delegates met in a
plenary session for a Bible Hour, followed by a
theological or methodological "position paper" on a
particular phase of evangelism. In the Discussion
Sections, which were divided into special-interest and
language areas, other speakers developed different
aspects of the position paper. A panel in the Discussion
Group responded to questions from the delegates
attending that session. The main addresses, Bible studies,
"Windows on the World" (surveys of the evangelistic
task), and "Strategy for the Future" are published in *One
Race, One Gospel, One Task,* Vol. I. The six major papers
and the one hundred thirty shorter addresses to the
Sections are published in Volume II.[43]

"ONE TASK,"
THE THEOLOGY
OF BERLIN 1966

The theological position and trends of Berlin are evaluated by an examination of the addresses and papers of the Congress. The substance of the congress materials reveals several trends. First, there is the pilgrimage of Billy Graham as part of the theological trend in evangelicalism. A stronger ecclesiological orientation is immediately sensed in Berlin than is characteristic of the former Crusade messages and spirit. The appeal is to the "Church" in its institutional manifestation or as a collection of individuals. The responsibility of evangelism is incumbent upon *the Church,* says Anglican John R. W. Stott. The baptismal and teaching role of *the Church* are rightly interpreted as essential links within the evangelism responsibility. It is *the Church* that needs fresh experience of the Holy Spirit for its life and evangelistic task. The message given by the apostles belongs to *the Church.*[44] The individualistic revivalism characteristic of pluralistic, volunteeristic American evangelism received an ecclesiological dimension. The Congress also desired to introduce a missionary and evangelistic spirit into the paralyzed and secularized denominations of the West.

Second, the theology of evangelism at Berlin 1966 turned from *missions* from the West to the *missions* of the Church around the world. John Stott said that the recipients of missions in past decades and centuries were to see evangelism of their own countries as a divine prerogative issuing from the Great Commission in Matthew 28:20:

> The emphatic "I," who pledges his presence, is the one who has universal authority and who sends forth his people. It remains questionable, therefore, whether a stay-at-home church—disobedient to the Great Commission, and indifferent to the need of the nations—is in any position to claim or inherit the fullness of Christ's promised presence.[45]

With the rise of national church consciousness, the Third
World churches were encouraged to pursue Third World
missions. Berlin 1966 was not the end of Western
missions, but it marked a beginning of Third World
missions to their own people and of their *missions* beyond
their own geographic borders. "World evangelization"
became a more comprehensive term, to describe the
world mission of the Church as the invisible and visible
body of Christ.

Berlin 1966 also struggled on a second front with the
redefinition of the word "mission" by the WCC
theologians. The social gospel in the earlier part of this
century conceived of "the task" of the Church in terms
of a Christianized or Christ-like society. It was a form of
"civic religion" related to the Kingdom of Heaven in the
present, in contrast to the future Kingdom at the second
coming of Christ. The Bible was more ethical in terms of
the present than eschatological. Then, not only did the
use of the word *mission* lend itself to the reality of the
Church on every continent as "the great new fact" of this
generation, but it enabled the WCC to satisfy old
liberalism and modernism by describing the "task" of the
Church as something more than evangelism. *The*
"mission" became primarily the restructuring of society
and "evangelism" became primarily the means toward its
accomplishment. Furthermore, the mission was *God's
missio dei* (Ghana 1958), not that of manmade
evangelistic endeavors by "missions." Stott and
Climenhaga spoke to this issue in an era when both the
significance of "mission" and that of "presence" theology
were little understood by the Evangelicals. In "presence
theology" a verbal witness could only be justified after
"service" *to* the world and *for* an already redeemed
world. Lausanne 1974 would address itself again to this
issue and attempt to reconcile those "insights" of
nonevangelicals into the theology of evangelicalism. The
regional Minneapolis 1969 Congress, caught in the midst
of the Vietnam conflict and in racial and economic
inequities, failed to discern the WCC redefinition of
mission because of Berlin's *lacuna* in this area.

Third, Berlin 1966 spoke of an interdenominational, international, and interracial unity that evangelical evangelism inspired. As the contemporary ecumenical movement of the WCC recognized its modern roots in the pietism and revivalism of the nineteenth century, so the regrouping of world Evangelicals at Berlin restored the image of apostolic unity under the authority of the Holy Scripture, rather than under ecclesiological tradition or denominational traditions. The "given" unity in Christ centered around the authority of Christ as revealed in the infallible Scripture. Complete unity of evangelistic action arose out of unquestioned allegiance to the Bible as the only written Word of God. While not all may have had identical views of biblical inspiration, the communality of their commitment to biblical authority and evangelism enabled them to pursue evangelism from an apostolic perspective. A Bible whose unity, finality, and narrative nature were unquestioned served to transcend historical and cultural barriers in true heart fellowship. This proved to be more of a living conciliarity than an ecumenical idealism.

Fourth, world religious surveys presented as "Windows on the World" gave an excellent capsule presentation of the particular area from an evangelical perspective. While somewhat less sophisticated than the computerized print-out of Lausanne 1974, the human and spiritual dimension of the authors conveyed a heartthrob impossible for statistics to communicate.

The strategy section generally represented the greatest weakness in both theology and depth. Knowing that theology influences the strategy of mission, Lausanne 1974 gave greatest attention to theology and strategy.

Fifth, the question must be raised as to the theological effect of Berlin upon the evangelical constituency it represented. Was a greater spirit of evangelical pluralism evident in the succeeding years? Did this spirit of pluralism extend to nonevangelicals and the historic Eastern and Western churches? Did world issues, such as social concern, raised at Berlin tend to help or confuse evangelistic movements around the world? Some answers

to these questions are found in the regional congresses
following Berlin 1966, and others are answered more
fully by the Lausanne 1974 program. The world
missionary conferences of the nineteenth century
reminded evangelicalism that it is a movement influenced
by theology, methodology, and world events. It may be,
as Harnack suggested, that the codification and
organization of a movement to channel its resources will
lead to its death by institutionalizing it.

Finally, Berlin 1966 must weigh its influence upon the
nonevangelical constituency, toward which some of its
program was directed. Are there evidences that Berlin
1966 renewed some nonevangelicals as the Madras
(Tambaram) 1938 conference of the International
Missionary Council attempted to do? Can a theological
trend be discerned at Berlin 1966 that diluted evangelical
theology? On the other hand, has there been a truly
growing theological and evangelistic unity among the
Berlin 1966 leadership, or did Lausanne 1974 reveal
growing diversities among Evangelicals committed to
evangelism?

A CHRISTOCENTRIC THEOLOGY

The main message of Section I, "The Authority of
Evangelism," was presented by Johannes Schneider of
East Berlin. His study centered around the authority of
Christ as committed to the disciples in the Great
Commission:

> He himself commanded the disciples to proclaim
> the Gospel to all the nations and upon baptism to
> receive those who believe in him into the redeemed
> fellowship of the new covenant. He thus gave a
> comprehensive charge which bound not only them,
> but all others as well who stand in his service, to win
> the world for Christ.[46]

Jesus Christ continues His earthly ministry through His messengers today, so that God's plan of redemption is accomplished (John 20:21). Evangelism is

> intrinsic and essential to God's plan of redemption. It is through evangelism that Jesus' great prophetic vision is being realized. . .[47]

The authority of Christ, it is understood, has the authority of the Scripture as its historic foundation. It is not the authority of the Church, church leaders, spiritual experience, Tradition, or traditions by which the authority of Christ is established.

By contrast, the WCC Fourth World Conference on Faith and Order at Montreal in 1963 said,

> Thus we can say that we exist as Christians by the Tradition of the Gospel (the *paradosis* of the *kerygma*) testified in Scripture, transmitted in and by the Church through the power of the Holy Spirit.[48]

Evangelicals discern two errors in this ecumenical approach. First, the Church exists and is judged by Scripture. God's Word incarnately revealed, proclaimed by the holy apostles, and inscripturated, precedes the visible Church in authority, even though the Bible does not precede the Church chronologically. The Church, by the Holy Spirit, discerned that which God had divinely inspired and also preserved that entire *corpus* of Truth.

Second, there is little evidence that conciliar theology holds to the supreme authority of the Bible as a presupposition used to establish what the content of this "Tradition of the Gospel" is. The place of the Church as the key to the interpretation of Scripture represents a return toward a pre-16th-century Reformation principle.

> The Tradition in its written form, as Holy Scripture (comprising both the Old and New Testament), has to be interpreted by the Church in ever new

situations. Such interpretation of the Tradition is to
be found in the crystallization of tradition in the
creeds, the liturgical forms of the sacraments and
other forms of worship, and also in the preaching
of the Word and in theological expositions of the
Church's doctrine.[49]

As has happened in the history of the Church,
doctrine may be distorted or deformed by an appeal to
tradition about the Bible that makes tradition
authoritative over the Bible (Tradition). In effect, the
Bible becomes subordinate to the Church both by its
alleged chronological acceptance by the Church and by
the historical interpretations of the institutional churches
of Christendom (Roman Catholic, Eastern Orthodox,
etc.). The Church in some way represents a spiritual
synthesis of Christendom and this body reflects the right
interpretation of Scripture as Tradition. Consequently
the content of the Gospel becomes that which this
"Church" understands it to be at this or any particular
period of history. To this error Berlin 1966 consciously,
and perhaps unconsciously, addressed itself as
Evangelicals: authority for evangelism is not grounded in
the Church, but in the historical apostolic witness of the
Scripture.

In the position paper of Section III, Walter Künneth
rightly related the Church and the Gospel:

Actually they stand in an indissoluble relationship.
The Gospel points to the Church, and the Church
derives from the Gospel. . .The Church issued from
this Gospel and not from some system of
ethics. . .The Gospel is the means, the tool, the
instrument through which Jesus Christ reveals
himself as active and alive in the Church.
Everything accordingly depends on whether or not
this Gospel is preserved and carried forward
unclouded and unabridged.[50]

The authority of evangelism today ultimately depends
upon the inspiration and authority of Scripture as the

faithful record of the authority of Christ. The Bible is
the decisive norm in evangelism. In the opening sentence
of the first theological address at Berlin 1966 Schneider
reaffirmed the authority of the Scripture record
concerning Jesus' words. "Authority for evangelism is
grounded most deeply and finally in the risen Lord's
Great Commission (Matthew 28:19)."[51] Authority for
evangelism does not reside in the Church but in the
command of Christ as recorded by the apostles in the
Scripture.

This initial position paper of the Congress finally
established world evangelization as the primary purpose
of God through His servants. Becoming a Christian was
defined as an acknowledgment of Jesus Christ as Savior
and Lord. Schneider applied this requirement to
evangelists and to all witnessing Christians:

> In conversion and regeneration they must have had
> a personal experience of salvation effected by the
> grace of God; they must believe in Jesus Christ with
> their whole being; must be in constant fellowship
> with him, by the power of the Holy Spirit; must live
> a life dedicated to the Lord; and in word and deed
> must show themselves to be living members of the
> body of Christ.[52]

Because the Gospel of Christ is the only salvation for
all mankind,

> evangelism therefore is the determinative saving
> action for a lost world. . .Man's fate in time and
> eternity depends on his acceptance or rejection of
> the offer of redemption (2 Thess. 1:8ff.). There is
> no other way of salvation.[53]

Universalism is rejected, and the proclamation of the
salvation message required the mobilization of all the
powers of the Church of Jesus Christ.

Vital, however, to evangelism is the content of the
Gospel itself. On the basis of 2 Corinthians 5:19-21,
Schneider reaffirms the "determinative substance" of the

Cross of Christ. The Cross was one of the historical
events of revelation accomplished by God:

> By free decree according to the riches of his grace,
> God gave His Son to die as atoning sacrifice for the
> sins of the world; and in obedience to God's will,
> Christ took upon himself the sacrifice that has
> brought redemption to lost mankind. This is the
> unique, once-for-all and unrepeatable fact valid for
> all time.[54]

This is not Bultmann's "goal of being," whereby the
Cross is an example for man's self-realization. Nor, as
Robinson says, is the Cross a proof of Jesus' selflessness
and of a love "that gives itself to and unites itself with
the ground of being (Seinsgrund)."[55] Existential and
secular theology were rejected because they robbed or
denied the historical redemptive act of the Cross of its
worth. Yet it is the proclamation of the incarnation, the
Cross, and the resurrection as historical events that serve
as the necessary facts of evangelistic preaching:

> But it is impossible to speak of the "significance" of
> the salvation facts, that is, of the meaning they have
> for us, if they themselves are disregarded or even
> denied.[56]

Proclamation is the impartation of facts that have
occurred whereby God has reconciled the world through
the blood of the crucified Christ Jesus. This redemption
will have its fulfillment at the return of the Lord of the
Church.

But authoritative evangelism has not fulfilled its
responsibility until it has "confronted men with a final
inescapable decision." Schneider found that existential
theology also calls for a decision, but that it is not based
upon the atonement of Christ "as the
redemptive-historical foundation of God's forgiving
activity."[57] The Gospel has a divine purpose. "Its aim is
to lead man to 'reality,' to a proper understanding of
himself, to a true God-willed existence."[58]

Schneider concludes with the Pauline perspective of "Be ye reconciled to God" as grounded upon the objective work of Christ on the Cross appropriated subjectively:

> Paul does not ask *man* to reconcile himself to God; man is in no position to do this. In Christ, God has accomplished everything needful for man's salvation. Lost in his sin and guilt, man needs only to accept the completed reconciliation and apply it to himself. Through conversion which leads him to living faith in God and Christ, a new existence—life in Christ—is given him by grace. Zinzendorf's watchword is still valid for the evangelist today: "My joy until I die: to win souls for the Lamb."[59]

Schneider's position paper was a clear exposition of New Testament theology built upon the authority of Christ as accurately recorded in the Bible. He dealt with the great issues relating to the atonement and to the historical "message." He declared its continued relevance until the final culmination of redemption at the second coming of the Lord of the Church. Evangelism occupied the central place of the apostolic church and remains that of the Church today. Men with individual eternal souls are the subject of evangelism and their conversion remains the deepest and greatest joy of the evangelist. The paper was an indirect, yet firm, biblical refutation of nonevangelical theology. It spoke clearly to the fundamental presuppositions of ecumenical evangelism in addition to reasserting a biblical theology based upon an infallible Bible.

The subsection I papers dealt briefly with the general topics of "The Teaching of the Bible," "The Lord's Command," "The Spirit's Restraint," "The Destiny of the Lost," "The Return of Christ," and "The Church's Tradition and Practice." Each of the subjects was the basis for a subsection panel involving the delegates in Group Discussion. Their value lies in the diverse cultural, national, and denominational backgrounds generally supporting other evangelical aspects of the main position paper. While the brevity of each paper tended toward a superficial treatment of the subject assigned, nevertheless they represented a fair cross section of evangelicalism in the mid-sixties. Few of the papers made a significant contribution to their subject, but their popular presentation made the Congress and the published papers accessible to the general evangelical constituency of the West, as well as to the Third World. This contribution of Berlin 1966 cannot be minimized, for nonevangelical congresses of this kind had spoken mainly to a theological elite particularly of the West. Berlin 1966 seemed to communicate simply to its delegates without becoming simplistic.

A NEW TESTAMENT CHRISTIANITY

Section II, "The Basic Theology of Evangelism," reviewed systematically the message of Christianity to the world. Harold J. Ockenga built his position paper upon the principles of the sixteenth-century Reformation which, he said, "established Protestantism as a return to New Testament Christianity."[60] Ockenga spoke to the heart of the issues that separated evangelism from ecumenical evangelism since the post-1910 expressions of liberal Protestantism which rejected the Bible as the final and infallible authority in matters of faith and practice:

> The principle of *sola scriptura* has been rejected by liberal Protestantism. For the liberal, the Bible is not authoritative, not dependable, and not authentic. This dismissal of the Bible has resulted from the acceptance of evolutionary naturalism and higher criticism. . . . The removal of the Bible from the central place of authority in Protestantism has debilitated its power to evangelize.[61]

Ockenga upheld the "Scriptures alone," "faith alone," and the priesthood of the believer as fundamental to New Testament Christianity and contemporary evangelism.

Ockenga rightly understood the pluralistic and
conciliar intent of the Third Assembly of the World
Council of Churches at New Delhi 1961 and recognized
its source in the theology of Karl Barth who said that
"the Bible is full of errors" and in Emil Brunner who
made "the Bible a shambles" in his *Revelation and Reason.*

> A liberal Protestantism cannot meet the competition
> of the Roman Church. In order to build a power
> structure comparable to the Roman Church, it has
> embraced the activities of the ecumenical
> movement. This movement not only intends to
> unite the various Protestant churches, but also to
> circumvent the Reformation in order to find a basis
> of theology and tradition for reunion with Rome.
> The 1963 Montreal Conference on Faith and Order
> of the World Council of Churches spent much time
> seeking to discover and express the tradition which
> will bring together the various traditions of the
> individual branches of Christianity and will supply a
> basis for dialogue in the areas of reform and
> reunion.[62]

The alternatives to biblical authority as characteristic of
New Testament Christianity and the Reformation,
Ockenga saw as

> left-wing rationalism in which the human mind is
> the supreme authority in religious matters . . . or a
> return to Rome, where the church is the final
> authority in Christian doctrine and ethics.[63]

It will be a biblical foundation that would support
evangelism in the future as it has in the past. The
Reformation, Ockenga declared, was a revival through
the truths of the New Testament by which the leaders
endeavored to reform the existing church:

> They discovered that the church was unreformable
> and they themselves were excluded by
> excommunication from its membership and
> benefits. Therefore, Martin Luther, John Calvin,

> Ulrich Zwingli and their colaborers returned to
> New Testament Christianity though it meant
> separation from the Roman Catholic church of the
> day.[64]

Major revivals—from the Puritans to the Wesleys,
Whitefield, and Finney—resulted from a recovery of
neglected New Testament truth.

The position paper merits consideration as an
outstanding evangelical summary of the theology of
evangelism. Ockenga upheld the fact that the New
Testament reveals the specific work of each person of
the Trinity in evangelism[65] by showing "that the Father
elects, which is predestination; that the Son redeems,
which is the atonement; and that the Holy Spirit
regenerates, which is salvation."[66]

First, God the Father decreed the plan of salvation
expressed as the "eternal covenant of redemption"
whereby

> the Father agreed to give to the Son a people; the
> Son covenanted to represent this people by
> substitution in a life of obedience and in a death of
> suffering; the Spirit covenanted to apply this
> efficaciously to men so that there would be a
> redeemed people belonging to the Son.[67]

This was grace found in the love of a just God
reconciling the world to Himself through His Son (John
3:16; 1 John 4:10; 2 Corinthians 5:19). Ockenga
reviewed the Calvinist "election" and Arminian
"conditional election" and believed that this biblical
teaching was of great importance to evangelistic fervor,
for it was related to the methodology of evangelism as
well, the giving of an invitation at the conclusion of an
evangelistic sermon. Ockenga holds to a "practical
synergism of affirming prevenient grace, the
responsibility of each individual, and of election in Christ
of all who believe."[68] Salvation is all of God and
reprobation is all of man. The offer of salvation is real,

yet it "is the Spirit's work to attend that offer with
life-giving power."[69] Ockenga concluded that God
sovereignly honors His Word as it is preached, and that
there is no exclusive methodology in the invitation to
unbelievers to receive Christ as Savior and Lord.

Second, Ockenga insisted that "evangelism must center
in the offer of the person of Christ" as the *kerygma,* the
message preached.[70] A lower, liberal view of the person
of Christ than that of the Council of Chalcedon,
upholding His full divinity and full humanity, cuts the
nerve of evangelism and missions. "It is only by
preaching the Christ of the Bible that converts may be
won spiritually."[71]

The substitutionary atonement was seen as central to
evangelism. "The Bible teaches that Christ died for us, in
the place of us, and in behalf of us."[72] The personal and
individual responsibility to accept Christ was contrasted
with universalism—incompatible with biblical
teaching—"which declares that all men are redeemed by
Christ and reconciled to God so that all which remains is
to publicize this to them."[73] The death of Christ was
"sufficient and applicable for all," but "efficacious only to
those who believe." Ultimate restoration after a period of
punishment is just as unacceptable as universalism:

> The plain alternative to this is the state of being lost
> and of suffering eternal torment. . . We must
> remember that the greatest emphasis upon hell and
> suffering as the alternative to salvation was made by
> the Lord Jesus Christ. If we give the proper
> emphasis to the responsibility of man, we have no
> problem with the doctrine of hell.[74]

Third, the ministry of the Holy Spirit was essential to
evangelism. His ministry in "common grace," whereby
He restrains the destructive processes of sin and thus
enables humanity to maintain an orderly life, was
compared with His ministry in "special grace." It seems
that Ockenga also attributes the "renewing process in the

churches and in society" as well as the "emphasis upon
spiritual renewal in the Roman Catholic Church and the
various branches of Protestantism" to common grace. He
participated in every stage of redemption,

> in creation, in revelation, in inspiration, in the
> incarnation, in the atonement, in the resurrection,
> in the formation of the Church, in the missionary
> undertaking, in the prayer life of the believer, in
> the transformation of the believer into the image of
> Christ, and so on. His work is a prerequisite to
> effective evangelism.[75]

Evangelism is defined as public proclamation or
private witnessing to "the Good News of the Gospel, with
the purpose of bringing individuals to faith in and
confession of Christ as Savior."[76] The resultant
conversion has two senses: the *lesser* sense where the
individual actively turns in response to the Gospel, and
the *larger* sense where the Holy Spirit works in
regeneration to convict, convert, and transform the life
of the individual. In contrast to baptismal regeneration,
taught by some Anglicans and Lutherans, and in contrast
to some reformed theologians who teach that
regeneration precedes conversion, the "evangelical
position is that regeneration is conditioned upon
repentance, confession and faith," as necessary to
stimulate evangelism.

The paper stressed the need for revival in the Church
through a visitation of the Holy Spirit. As in the
pre-Pentecostal prayer meetings of the apostles and
disciples, and as in the history of revival, prerequisites
are, first, united confession:

> It is essential that evangelicals confess their
> fragmentization, their divisions, their suspicions,
> their impotencies, their faithlessness, and their
> quarreling. Nothing will break down barriers faster
> than this.[77]

Second is united prayer; third, united believing; and
fourth, united witnessing.

The subsection papers reinforced the main position
paper, revealing the remarkable evangelical unity amid
confessional and denominational diversity. Hans
Rohrbach emphasized the error of transforming the
biblical message so that secular man can accept it. He
believed that rather than "restructure the Gospel"
theologians should "regenerate the sinner."[78] The task
and meaning of the Gospel is

> to prepare co workers for God in Jesus' name, to
> fill them with knowledge of and love for modern
> man's needs, and then to send them with the
> unabridged message of the Cross and resurrection
> under the sure expectation that God by his Holy
> Spirit will use their proclamation to accomplish the
> marvel of quickening man's spiritually dead heart.[79]

Samuel Bénétreau defended the full validity of the
moral law and its relationship to the reality of sin. He
said that sin is not an illusion, or something passive in
man's constitutional weakness, or the residue of
out-of-date mythical thinking. A supernatural God has
given us absolutes. Some theologians think that modern
man "can accept only a relativistic morality tied to the
particular circumstances of his existence."[80] Sin is a
refusal of the divine Lordship, a disobedience of His will,
a transgression of the law, and a state of slavery, leaving
the sinner a guilty being who is cursed by the wrath of
God. John Winston affirmed redemption as grounded in
"Christ's objective work of grace." He rejected Abelard's
awakening of a love that conquers all, Schleiermacher's
disconnection between Christ's sufferings and the divine
punishment for sin, and Ritschl's view that "Christ's
death is an act of solidarity with the human race, not a
substitution for it."[81]

This position paper not only presented the basic
historical message of New Testament Christianity, but it
has gone farther. Ockenga defined biblically what a
Christian is: that salvation is individual rather than
collective, that it involves personal faith rather than just
church membership or baptismal regeneration, that it

involves the supernatural ministry of the Holy Spirit
resulting in transformed conduct. The message is
essentially a "vertical" reconciliation with
God—characteristic of revivalism, nineteenth-century
evangelicalism, and the Great Century of missions.

EVANGELICALISM ADDRESSES THE CHURCH

Section III, "Hindrances to Evangelism in the Church,"
recognized the intimate relationship that evangelism
bears to the Church, but also spoke to the heresies,
errors, and attitudes within the Church. The section
boldly considered itself as a biblical corrective to the
impotencies of world Christianity in general and of
European Christianity in particular. It spoke to
ecumenical Christianity about its heresy of universalism;
to separated Christianity about its sins of
self-containment, parochialism and isolation; to impotent
Christianity concerning its spiritual indifferences and
nonexpectation; to secularized Christianity concerning its
doctrinal deviations and unbelief; and to formalistic
Christianity concerning its sacramental regeneration,
often expressed in infant baptism. Evangelicalism was
telling Christendom that biblical evangelism was not only
possible but that it could be done as the conditions were
met and the corrections were made. This section really
proposed a twentieth-century Reformation that would
enable the Church to regain its spiritual life and
evangelistic momentum.

The position paper of Walter Künneth introduced the
"invasion of God's revelation in history" as the fact and
presupposition leading mankind toward its eternal goal.
This "joyous news" gathered together the body of Christ
and inspired the Christian Church. Consequently,

it becomes evident from this origin of Christ's
Church in the revelational event, that the Church
has a task to do in the world, and that it is

empowered to go throughout the world. . . As a
Church of the Gospel, therefore, the Church is not
called to flee and despise the world, not forced into
a narrowminded isolation, not condemned to a
ghetto existence; just the reverse is true: the
Church is called to be on display before the world.[82]

Künneth found it depressing that opposition to the
Gospel, so closely identified with the Church, should be
found in the Church. He summarized the basic principle
of an obstacle or a hindrance as

anything, everything that bedims the message of the
Gospel, that prevents the heart of the Gospel from
shining through clear and true.[83]

Künneth seems reluctantly to cite these hindrances:
first, the immaturity of traditional or cultural
Christianity; second, poorly equipped Christians without
either the power or knowledge to communicate the
Gospel; the weak and unbelieving among the Church
membership who finally succumbs "to the whisperings of
false spirits, yields to superstitions, and charts his life (sic)
by horoscopes."[84] Lives of Christians appear so
unredeemed that they are false representatives of the
Church and counteract the work of the Gospel.

A second major area of hindrance to evangelism was
the undue importance given the form, structure, and
order of the Church body. Church structure should be
determined on the basis of its suitability to implement a
"purposeful presentation of the Gospel." He believed
that when the Church is under the lordship of the
Gospel it would be constantly self-reforming:

The only valid consideration for the Church to
realize at all times must be what serves the Gospel,
its credibility, its deepening, its propagation.[85]

Forms, ceremonies, rites, and traditions have only
relative value and are "in no way necessary for salvation."
Künneth spoke to all of Christendom when he found it
possible

to retain old religious forms, encrusted traditions
which hinder and do not promote a new vital
development of the Church.

He also said,

There may be a revered language of the Church
that as time passes no longer clearly communicates
the meaning of the Gospel; there may be a jungle
of religious bureaucracy that supersedes the
principle of stated order, that assaults and controls
the course of daily life and embitters people.[86]

The third concern of the paper was the hindrance
resulting from the alteration of the Gospel itself. While
correct doctrine does not guarantee evangelistic
penetration—because of the previously cited
hindrances—nevertheless, to change the content is an
abuse that makes its very essence misunderstood and
misinterpreted. Man substitutes his own discoveries and
experiences because he has not been a listener to, and a
receiver of, the Gospel. He

adjusts the Gospel message to suit his own needs,
corrects them and manipulates them to his own
purposes. In this manner, he at one stroke exalts
himself above the authority of the Gospel, makes
himself lord over the Word, over God's revelation.[87]

Künneth stood strongly against every perversion of the
Gospel by canonizing one way, one method, or one
experience, as necessary to becoming a true Christian.
Even worse than this, or a legalism that is joyless and
depressing, is the distortion of the Gospel "that under
the influence of sóme current philosophy and absolutely
defined scientific arguments and hypotheses has
undergone a content-changing revision."[88] By the
impositions of the presuppositions of contemporary
existentialism, the Gospel loses its transcendent reality:

In the realm of causal relationships, no room then
remains for miracles whose reality is indissolubly

linked with the Gospel. Jesus Christ can be honored
only as a man, not as the world's Redeemer who
died on the Cross for mankind, not as the risen
Lord in whose life rests the basis of eternal hope. In
the last analysis, the Gospel itself becomes a mere
symbol, a code to some new human understanding
of the self, a thrust to help gain some
anthropological meaning for existence.[89]

The changed Gospel has, however, retained the biblical
concepts of Word and Faith, Christ and Redemption,
Pardon and Eschatology, but changed their content and
has given them new meanings which create uncertainty
among Christians. "A Gospel that has become cheap is a
defeated, emasculated Gospel that can no longer sound a
clear trumpet call."[90]

Perhaps the strongest subsection in the Congress was
that rejecting universalism, as characteristic of conciliar
theology or as an aberration within evangelicalism. Leon
Morris rejected universalism because the New Testament
does not teach it, and because much universalism is
based upon a nonbiblical conviction of God's nature of
love divorced from His justice "which may affect the way
love operates."[91]

James I. Packer said, ". . . all statements about 'the
necessity of God's nature' which go beyond Scripture are
speculative."[92] First, it is based upon a speculative and
subjective hermeneutic that goes beyond the intention of
the biblical author.

Second, it speculates about God's purpose of love when
there are clear teachings concerning the ultimate state
expressed in terms of *"inextinguishable* fire, an *undying*
worm, *eternal* punishment and destruction. The hell of
the New Testament has no exit door."[93]

Third, there is speculation concerning the means by
which universal salvation will be fulfilled when the
Scripture witnesses so clearly to election, redemption,
effectual calling, and final glory. It is difficult to
reconcile the biblical probationary character of this life,
requiring repentance and faith for eternal life, with the
universalist doctrine of hell, whereby God will meet with

unbelievers a second time until His "striving" will change their hearts. One who holds to the heresy of universalism can still maintain an interest in evangelism, but this will influence his evangelism in three ways:

> First, he will feel free to argue that in particular situations other ways of loving one's neighbor are more important than seeking to win him to Christ. Second, he cannot help intellectualizing the Gospel, for his message is not "believe on the Lord Jesus Christ, and thou shalt be saved," but rather "believe that the Lord Jesus Christ is your Savior already, and show your thanks." The thought of believing *on* (into, *eis*) Jesus, and coming *to* Jesus, is thus overshadowed. Third, since he does not believe that a decision against Christ is really decisive of anything, his evangelism will lack the urgency which marks New Testament evangelism. He will not preach or pray in terms of the prospect of unbelievers being finally lost.[94]

Although universalism has an attractive optimism, it is very unusual to find universalists who are evangelists.

Arthur M. Climenhaga examined the problem of universalism as it was related to the theological redefinition of words during the last thirty years. Of particular concern was the implicit universalism represented by the change from the use of the word "missions" to "mission" by the ecumenical movement. The ambiguous and equivocal nature of "mission" caused concern for the way in which a totally different orientation of evangelism could replace the historical evangelistic "missions" of earlier centuries.

First, for many Christians the use of "mission" expresses the command inherent within the Great Commission, and means as much as "missions" did in past decades and centuries.

Second, "mission" has come to emphasize "the sense of total Church involvement in witness to a total world."[95] This eliminates the distinctions between home and foreign missions and between evangelistic missions and

service (Inner Church Aid) programs, which are not
related to evangelism and do not have evangelism as
their ultimate goal.

Third, the use of the term "mission" in the new sense
represents an attempt to depart from the narrow verbal
proclamation which evangelism considered to be
ineffectual, or ineffectual.without the wider area of
service. The use of the word "mission" represents a
symbolic departure from the heaven and hell concepts of
historical missions. It represents not only a change of
method but also of the *message* of missions.

Fourth, the use of mission as the "mission of the
church" has been used to describe the penetration of the
values of Christianity into other cultures and religions
and has, consequently, precluded the need of first
winning individuals to Christ.

Fifth, the "church mission" communicates the sense of
brotherhood of man under the fatherhood of God
whereby service becomes an act of reconciliation by the
"church in mission." Sin is not individual but corporate
deeds, alienating man from God and rending or tearing
the human fabric of peace.

Sixth, God, according to D. T. Niles, has performed
reconciling acts in all religions, to which men have
responded in faith without accepting the Christian's God
in Christ.

Seventh, the consequences of this form of universalism
lead to a syncretism of all religions and faith—a new
universalism:

> There is no necessity to challenge men to flee to the
> Lord Jesus Christ from the city of destruction.
> There is no "Woe is me if I preach not the Gospel."
> There is no wishing one's self accursed for his
> kinsmen's sake because they are lost! Instead we
> find a concept of love and service which depends
> on dialogue with the various faiths and practices of
> the world to introduce them to what they already
> are by the grace of God and what they will be
> whether they accept it in this life or not! Thus the

call to the harvest field is muffled, volunteers
dwindle away, and the spirit of evangelism in the
Great Commission is no longer one of urgency.[96]
Jakob Jocz related Jewish missions to universalism. He
insisted that Jewish people are to be considered a part of
missionary strategy, because conversion is as necessary
for the Jew now as it was in the Pauline mission. The
difference between the Jew and the Christian is that the
former is *without* Christ and the latter is *in* Christ.
Humanly, they are both sinners and in need of grace:

> The Christian acknowledges his need and looks to
> Jesus for salvation; the Jew saves himself. These are
> two radically different attitudes and result in two
> utterly different perceptions of God.
>
> We do not say that Israel is without God . . . But we
> do say that the Jewish and Christian knowledge of
> God is *different.*[97]

"To know God in Jesus Christ is to know one's self a
sinner saved by grace."[98] Conversion means an
acknowledgement of one's helplessness.
    Jewish evangelism is not bigotry, but a demonstration
of loyalty to Jesus Christ. Commitment to Him makes
universalism impossible. Jocz believed that the testing
ground in determining universalism is the Jewish mission
field. Man must utterly depend upon God's grace in the
Cross to save him, and not on religious or cultural
achievements. Jewish missions are related to evangelism
among all religions:

> Once we have decided about Judaism we have
> decided about all other religions. If Judaism can
> manage without Jesus Christ, so can the Church
> and so can the world religions.[99]

The remaining papers constituted a challenge to the
Evangelicals to boldly evangelize by faithfulness to the
Scripture, by fully "losing one's self" for the Gospel's
sake, and by a life unspotted by the world. This

"unspotted life," however, does not keep our faith
ineffective in evangelism by imprisoning it behind a wall
of separation and fear. We are to trust the Holy Spirit to
preserve Christ's Church. "This Gospel does not need
protection—it needs proclamation."[100]

ONE GOSPEL IN A PAGAN WORLD

Section IV revived the relevant age-long issues the
Church has confronted since the apostolic age. Harold B.
Kuhn's outstanding position paper on "Obstacles to
Evangelism in the World" served both as a perspective
and philosophy for the Christian and Christianity in the
world, and as a challenge to evangelize the world. The
great obstacles in the world of the 1960s were isolated
and evaluated not only on the basis of their destructive
influence upon world evangelism but also for their
potential for the furtherance of the Gospel. Of particular
significance was Kuhn's perceptibility and balanced
viewpoints on nationalism, totalitarianism, materialism,
the intellectual climate, and alien elements influencing
the Church.

On the basis of the subject presented in the position
paper and in the following studies, it would be a serious
mistake to say that Berlin 1966 did not contribute
directly toward *world* evangelism. Cross-cultural
considerations interlock with the solid basic theological
issues, enabling the missionary as well as the evangelist in
the Third World or in the West to effectively accomplish
"One Task." Kuhn dealt with the obstacles confronting
missionaries and evangelists around the world. It would
have been helpful, however, had he more directly
defined the "world," in a day when cultural values of the
secular world are confused with the ethical norms of
Christianity.

Nationalism was distinguished by Kuhn from
patriotism. It (nationalism) is "a distortion of that
normal love of country, and normal pride which

men and women take in their country's group
achievement."[101]

The reaction to old colonialism in nationalism is
possibly God's providential work, whereby those peoples
historically disadvantaged may share in the freedoms and
comforts of the more prosperous societies. The danger
of nationalism to retain memories of past grievances and
thus hinder the future contributions of Christian
missionaries was compared with the danger that
paternalistic mission leaders may dominate the national
church with their Western brand of "reflex nationalism."
Nationalism may frustrate the mission leaders, but it may
also offer "fore-gleams of promise."

Totalitarian systems generally close mission fields and
hinder evangelism. Nevertheless, Kuhn noted, there are
processes whereby "totalitarian systems modify
themselves from within" and may move away from
disruptive revolution toward stability and the possibility
of renewed evangelistic endeavor. Perhaps unjustly,
Kuhn questioned the tendency of the Church under
totalitarian rule to speak prophetically and to develop a
protective mentality—to remain as inconspicuous as
possible and thus limit their evangelistic outreach. He
did, however, caution against a pessimistic attitude
toward the finality of doors closed by revolution, for
even Paul and the apostles must have felt frustrations
and limitations under the sophisticated totalitarian system
of Rome:

> But they never allowed forbidding external
> circumstances to paralyze them into inaction. Then
> as now, those who view things with eyes of faith see
> God working providentially also in human
> government structures, however imperfect as media
> they may seem for expressing God's activity.[102]

While materialism has been legitimately criticized as it
has swept the world by the industrial and technical
revolutions, Kuhn warned against superficial
explanations and correctives. First, he said that some
have forgotten that God is the Creator of the material

order and uses it providentially toward the
accomplishment of His redemptive purposes:

> Some of the unstructured thinking on this question,
> in the West no less than the East, has failed to
> remember that God is Creator of the material
> order, and uses it to channel and accomplish both
> his providential and redemptive purposes. To be
> thoroughly and characteristically Christian in
> perspective, one must give proper recognition to
> the Divine ordination of the material structures of
> our world; one must see how the New Testament
> emphasizes the placement of Christians as stewards
> within them.[103]

Critics of materialism must recognize that it is not caused
by "assembly line" technology, but that it is a distortion
of a divinely implanted drive

> that impels man to greater heights of human
> comfort and dignity. It must be acknowledged, after
> all, that while the advent of the machine placed
> heavy loads upon mankind at some points, it also
> relieved man of certain heavy and degrading
> burdens.[104]

Materialism should be understood as an outlook and
attitude measuring the values of life in terms of visible
and tangible things, and casting aside those values not
measured by the acquisition of goods. This ideological
materialism may exist "independent of the presence or
absence of the actual symbols of material existence."[105] It
is a basic attitude of covetousness against which our Lord
warned us (Luke 12:15). Where there is
acknowledgement of human worth and dignity,
"materialism becomes unpalatable," yet

> anyone who professes materialism as an overt creed
> is more self-conscious of his position, and therefore
> more susceptible to direct confrontation by the
> claims of the Living Christ.[106]

A more subtle form of materialism is evident in the
mental attitude that desires to withdraw from the
God-given creative effort of work in order to retire and
"enjoy life." Work is not a "necessary but unwelcomed
intruder into the life of man," but rather "a stewardship
to be preserved under the recognition that some day the
Lord of the Harvest will call the laborers to a
reckoning."[107] For those who are exploited and whose
human dignity has been debarred,

> the evangelical cannot reflect the heart of his Lord
> without not only sympathizing with those thus
> bound, but also identifying himself as a Christian
> citizen with movements that offer genuine promise
> of remedying social and economic wrongs. It must
> be remembered, however, that if exploitation by an
> unjust employer has served to dull the worker's ears
> to the Good News, the tyranny of uncreative leisure
> is scarcely much better for opening the heart to the
> Lord's, "Follow me."[108]

The evangelist must recognize that materialism
stimulates the temporal aspirations of man on the one
hand; and, on the other, it tends to make him a prisoner
of his pursuit of leisure, entertainment, spectatorism and
"escapes." This tyranny produces a climate where that
which is transcendent and otherworldly seems antiquated
and dull.

Materialism tends toward the security obtainable by the
welfare state and evades a sense of self-reliance, personal
endeavor, and individual responsibility. It thus opposes
personal evangelism where the individual is isolated from
the crowd and confronted with "the issues between him
and his Maker." It is at this point that Kuhn's argument
has corrective overtones for mass movements, collective
decisions, and even multi-individual decisions in
evangelistic methodology. Kuhn was wary about the
wisdom of involving ecclesiastical structures in specific
social and economic betterment programs and fearful of
neglecting the "Christian mandate" of "bringing the
claims of the sovereign Lord of all life to bear upon the

structures of society."[109]

One of the intellectual obstacles to evangelism was seen as a depreciatory attitude toward mass evangelism. Scientific naturalism had crowded out the supernatural life to come and had excluded the pursuit of that future life as an urgent issue. The secular spirit resents appeals to an absolute authority. A hedonistic spirit regarding pleasure as the highest good has molded the new morality of the "situation ethic," and superficial psychological systems attribute sin to environmental pressures. Historical biblical views of sin have been revised so that "feelings of guilt" are not dealt with by pointing "men and women to him who gave himself to destroy sin and to lift the crushing burden of man's guilt through genuine forgiveness."[110]

The concluding obstacle Kuhn presents is the influence of alien elements impinging themselves upon the Church. He finds that both leaders and members are subtly shaped by forces uncongenial and even hostile to her evangelistic thrust. The surrounding world climate is essentially alien to the Church and yet "the mid-twentieth-century Church has been singularly unaware of the massive, if not glacial incursion of paganism into the contemporary world."[111] Christians have assumed the world to be Christian when it is not. One danger is to assume a defensive attitude that alienates non-Christians; but a

> greater danger . . . seems to lie in uncritically accepting the ideals and norms of the world, and, in doing so, becoming their prisoner. To be specific, it is possible for well-meaning Christians to become immersed in the materialistic *Weltanschauung* to a degree which they do not realize; an experience which leaves them really unimpressed with the urgent claims of the Christian Evangel with its strong insistence upon the reality of the unseen.[112]

The so-called Christian West has been erected upon principles that omit God from their outlook. "But it is

this that lies at the heart of paganism; and seen in this
light, our culture can scarcely be judged in any other
terms."[113] Kuhn saw rightly that this creeping paganism
is not friendly to the facts that underlie biblical
evangelism. The Christian lives in a pagan world.

The subsection papers dealt with issues relative to
evangelization in and around the world: materialism,
world religions, totalitarianism, nationalism, racism, cults,
and persecution. Materialism, for example, was evident
not only in Western civilization but also in Africa.

This Congress spoke strongly against the hindrance to
evangelism under various totalitarian governments, such
as Communism. Dr. Helen Kim of Korea deplored how
in Communist countries

> freedom of religion is guaranteed, at first; but,
> quietly and systematically, church work in welfare
> agencies, hospitals and educational institutions is
> banned. Church literature is restricted, and finally
> only worship is left and this is usually scheduled
> when attendance is demanded elsewhere.[114]

Andrew Ben Loo of Taiwan was equally indignant
concerning the 95 percent of Red China who are unable
to "speak for themselves."[115] Arthur Glasser found hope
in the small Bible studies in Eastern Europe and the
response to the Gospel among the working class there.[116]
The Group Discussion concluded that

> all forms of government, all economic and social
> systems, lie under the judgment of God. Despite the
> wide differences in the environment for evangelism
> in various social structures, the greatest caution
> should be exercised in identifying any one of them
> as *the* Christian structure.[117]

Hudson T. Armerding proposed that efforts be made
to evangelize the leadership of the emerging Third
World nations.[118] Heini Germann-Edey believed that the
new nationalism had actually speeded evangelization.[119]
Of great significance was the call of Bishop Augustine G.

Jebaraj of India, appealing to the churches of the Third
World to send out their own cross-cultural missionaries:

> Each national church should send out and support
> its own missionaries in other lands. Each local
> congregation should have an opportunity to share
> in this missionary outreach.[120]

Attention was called to the cross-cultural missions of
Korea, India, Japan, and the Philippines.

The social question relating to South Africa was
studied by Michael Cassidy, an English-speaking South
African, under the title of "The Ethics of Political
Nationalism." He found that the Christian is called to the
absolute ethic of Christianity, wherein the Church does
not align itself with "the corporate self-interest of any
state or racial group within it."[121] The *group* ethic is
developed by group thinking, in which the group's
political progress toward the desired social end becomes
legitimate and equated with the divine will. This ethic is
relative, idolatrous, anti-Christian, and oversteps its
bounds. "The Christian at this point must preach and
show that Christian commitment involves a superior
allegiance that does not permit the confusion of Christ
and Caesar. . . ."[122] In Africa, the white philosophy of
self-preservation is on a collision course with the African
philosophy of self-realization. ". . . for the African to be
anti-white is no more morally defensible than for the
white to be anti-black."[123] In spite of extravagant
statements that have caused white fear

> . . . the Christian must call upon the white
> nationalist for charity in spite of dangers,
> unselfishness in spite of risks, faith in spite of fear.
> White nationalism has to be reminded that the
> Christian ethic is to "lose one's life in order to save
> it," whereas it is the very reverse of this—save your
> life in order not to lose it—which stands as the
> ethical heart of some white thinking.[124]

The Group Discussion provided some tense, frank,
and open disagreement and a sharp clash of opposing

opinions. An appendage to the subsection paper was submitted by another South African viewpoint— recognizing the complexity of the problem, the historical background of parallel development, and the atmosphere of peace to promote evangelism. The Discussion closed as African Samuel Obaker from the Cameroun paid tribute "to the power of Christian love to break through all and any barriers that rampant nationalism can erect against the free flow of the Gospel."[125]

This section also dealt with manifestations of totalitarianism in Spain, Greece, and Ceylon. Rising cults were recognized as subtle foes of the soul and vicious errors of demonic origin. A strong teaching ministry, emphasizing redemption and coming judgment, was needed to combat these intrusions into the lives of the immature believers.[126]

WINNING THE WORLD BY SOUL WINNING

The movement of the Berlin 1966 program was directed toward the centrality of personal evangelism in the spirit of the apostolic age and of revivalistic evangelicalism as expressed in a variety of historical manifestations. The Section V position paper of Richard C. Halverson, "Methods of Personal Evangelism," upheld that spontaneous evangelism would take place when Christians abide in Christ, recognize evangelism as their vocation, and are rightly related to one another in the fellowship of the Christian community.

Halverson's position paper sustained the thesis that the apostolic church expanded spontaneously because of its inner health.

> Evangelism was somehow "assumed," and it functioned without special techniques or special programs. . . St. Paul does not repeatedly exhort his churches to subscribe money for the propagation of

the faith; he is far more concerned to explain to them what the faith is, and how they ought to practice and keep it.[127]

Nor did Peter and John continue to urge the duty of the Great Commission upon their converts. The spiritual health of the apostolic church enabled "exciting and effective evangelism," which is inevitable in a spiritually robust congregation today as well.

> Failure to be evangelistic or "mission minded" in the New Testament sense betrays a poor spiritual condition. The way to evangelistic vigor is not some special emphasis or program, but rather repentance and healing and nurture.[128]

The necessity of organizing evangelistic efforts revealed the need for renewal. "One might as well exhort a woman with a barren womb to have children as to exhort a sterile church to evangelize or respond to missions."[129]

Evangelism was expected of New Testament believers because they would embody the same Holy Spirit and power who had worked in and through the incarnate Christ.

> In the Spirit-empowered Christian was a witness, not because he elected to be or was compelled to be, but because the divine witness indwelt him and worked through him. They did not witness because they had to, but because they could not help it.[130]

There is only one exhortation to evangelism among the epistles of the New Testament (2 Timothy 4:5). Jesus expected every disciple to be an evangelist in the sense of being a witness.

Halverson implies the necessity of a community of true believers as necessary for evangelism. "Witnessing proceeded out of fellowship, forward and into fellowship."[131] It was out of a true and authentic fellowship that the witness to Christ was born and sustained. "Fellowship is fundamental to effective personal evangelism."[132] This requisite of fellowship is based upon a right relationship with God and between believers.

Concern was also expressed regarding the corporate image of the local church. Those outside ought to be attracted by their love for each other, so that the work of zealous personal evangelists is not neutralized by members who are not concerned for each other's welfare.

Halverson believed that evangelism is the vocation of every believer, and that any method used in the church should not produce either a spiritual elite or a semiprofessional class in the Christian community. Nor should the method used pressure the individual into a mold, where he tends to become like the one from whom he is learning rather than "being himself in the fullness of the Holy Spirit and the fellowship."[133] The New Testament observes a different approach to each person.

The witness of the Christian is reflected in everything he does. It "begins where he is, in what he is doing, among those with whom he associates."[134] The Christian can be prepared for a positive effective witness:

1. By realizing that the work of the ministry belongs to each Christian and not to a few professionals.
2. By instruction in the Scripture.
3. By recognition that the warfare is spiritual and that the only weapon provided by God is the "sword of the Spirit," the Scripture.
4. By understanding one's own weakness, and, consequently, depend upon the Holy Spirit rather than upon a method.
5. By being joined with others in an authentic fellowship.
6. By conceiving of one's lay task as a second vocation ordained by God and considering it as productive for eternity as that of a pastor.
7. By being themselves as God has gifted them because they have given themselves as living sacrifices (Rom. 12:1, 2).

8. By abiding in Christ so as to bring forth much fruit (John 15)."The basic strategy for maximum Christian effectiveness is the abiding life."[135]

Methods of evangelism are as diverse as those who are to be reached, and as those that reach them. Worldwide evangelism will not be accomplished by organizing a department of evangelism, but by a fresh infusion of the Holy Spirit renewing the life of the Church.

Most of the authors of subsection papers from the West were from parachurch organizations, but half of those from the Third World were churchmen. Each was a specialist in his field and qualified to address the question of methods of evangelism on the basis of his gift and ministry.

Lorne Sanny stressed the use of the small group to make disciples.[130] John W. Alexander found that it was important to speak personally with one who, in a Bible study, manifests a hunger to know Christ personally.[137] William Bright believed that training in personal evangelism is imperative and that Christian leaders should set the example.[138] The Discussion group concluded that no amount of training or materials could succeed, however, without the ministry of the Holy Spirit in the life of the evangelist.[139] Ross Hidy gave emphasis to the importance of the period of follow-up after a decision had been made.[140] A Ghana student, Isaac Ababio, said that the soul-winner must have a broken heart.

> If we believe in an eternal Hell, could our eyes be dry and our hearts undisturbed, when we see so many sinners blindly drifting to an eternal doom?[141]

Josip Horak, president of the Yugoslavian Baptist Convention, found that one could always be "fishing patiently with a rod" even if it is not possible to use the large nets of mass evangelism.[142]

Doan van Mieng, president of the Evangelical Church of Vietnam, spoke of the necessity of using the Bible, because our entire lives are engaged in personal

evangelism.[143] He said that the family, as an immediate
and extended unit, should receive special consideration
in a strategy of evangelism in the Orient.[144] James R.
Graham of Taiwan was concerned about the
deteriorating quality of evangelists. Many seem more
concerned about praise for their preaching than with
pricking the consciousness of those who listen!

> Promotion, publicity, personality, politics, popularity
> and even prosperity, we have in abundance. But
> there is a dearth of God-empowered men and
> women with a deep love for the Savior,
> unconditional commitment to him and complete
> indifference to their own well-being.[145]

After stressing the need of visitation evangelism in Japan
even though this is the most difficult method, Shuichi
Matsumura, vice-president of the Baptist World Alliance,
lamented the pastor-centered tendency that limits
evangelism to the pastor's ability:

> A high level of seminary training and the rite of
> ordination have been useful for maintaining the
> ideal of purity of the Gospel, but they cannot
> produce that purity of the Gospel which is based
> upon God's dealing directly with souls through the
> Holy Spirit. Clergy-centeredness has been the
> result.[146]

Methodist Bishop Takesaburo Uzaki of Japan stressed
"The Worth of a Single Soul" and noted that extensive
mass evangelism increases the need for adequate
personal work after the crusade.

   This entire section gave prominence to the spiritual
quality of the believer's life. While methods were not
minimized, it was recognized that where the inner life of
the believer deteriorates, the use of the Bible and holy
living diminishes. The church must then turn to
organization, methodology, and social action. The focus
of Berlin was upon the dynamics of the Gospel,
supernaturally transforming the heart of the believer by

the power of the Holy Spirit. Personal Evangelism was
the essential substructure of the Berlin theology of
evangelism and methodology: this included soul winning,
proclamation, persuasion, and a regeneration leading to
a life of committed discipleship.

Lausanne 1974 would give more attention to the
growth of local churches.

PROCLAMATION EVANGELISM OF "ONE TASK"

Bishop Goodwin Hudson of the Church of England
presented "The Methods of Group Evangelism" as the
final theological position paper, Section VI, concluding
the work of the Congress. As personal evangelism had
been projected as the basic plan for world evangelization,
Hudson's paper was concerned with "how to" principles
and practices of reaching the exploding masses of people
in the "marketplace." The proclamation of the Gospel
was seen as fundamental. It was the message of truth
that must be communicated courageously by all the
means of rising technology at our disposal.

Hudson believed that *how* "we present Christ to a
constantly changing world is a question which should
engage us to the end of our ministry."[147] While methods
of evangelism is a subject that can never be mastered,
experience and spiritual life alone can do for a minister
what training cannot do. It is the principles, not the
methods of the past, that must guide evangelism today;
for "we must not attempt our service for God and man
as if we lived in a pre-television, pre-radio, pre-electronic
era."[148] Whereas the population of the world doubled
between 1900 and 1962, it is now projected to double
again in only eighteen years, between 1962 and 1980!

Group Evangelism was defined as a special effort at
one place for a brief period to convert people to God. Its
purpose is to convert the unconverted by securing a
definite turning of the will and the entire surrender of
the life to God. It is not to "feed" the Christians, but to
seek and save the lost:

We must proclaim, in new tones, the two-fold vision of the love of God, and the loss of God; of eternal life and eternal separation; we must win from the individual that decision on which his salvation now depends. There is no room for shallow universalism, for some vague belief in heaven and hell, which is a product, not of love, but of the self-indulgent morality of our times, and of the invasion of hedonism into the affluent society of the West.[149]

The Church should place conversion to Christ above all other plans for improvement, and special missions should rescue the Christian from lukewarmness and spiritual selfishness. As organized religion has moved toward liberalism and ritualism, the Church must be moving society toward Christ, so that it can say—as was recorded on a missionary's grave:

When he came, there was no light.
When he died, there was no darkness.[150]

Hudson reviewed group or mass evangelism and distinguished it from the one-win-one personal evangelism. *Direct evangelism* of a group is the meeting of people face to face. The message, as exemplified by the biblical prophets, will not vary, but the method used to make contact with his live audience will be influenced by climate, culture, and the character of the audience. Open-air and visitation evangelism may vary in effectiveness, depending upon the situation and country.

Films, newspapers, radio, and television are *indirect or mediated evangelism*. The effectiveness of these media cannot be underestimated. Hudson thought that "it might be debated whether any revival of true religion has ever come without the use of modern means of communication."[151] The great influence of television has made it the marketplace and, consequently, "the Christian Church must be in that marketplace."[152] Television evangelism should give the viewer what the evangelist desires to proclaim *but* packaged as the viewer likes it.

Regardless of the method, group evangelism should involve the new believer in both a personal acceptance of Christ and an open confession of Him:

> To be saved, a man must hear and believe, and call upon the name of the Lord (Rom. 10:13-15). The "chain" that accomplishes this work has five links: sending, proclaiming (that is our task), hearing, believing, calling (these are the listener's responsibility). Over all, of course, is the Holy Spirit of God to bless the effort and the response.[153]

Hudson spoke strongly against those who fail to emphasize the urgency of a decision for Christ. Conviction must be pressed home, but one must move from preaching to personal evangelism without forcing the door:

> Anyone who is content to say "peace, peace," when there is no peace, and who fails to emphasize the urgency of a decision for Christ *now*, is but a spiritual "quack." No one can love more truly nor more deeply than our blessed Lord, and it was he who unveiled the terrible consequences of unrepented sin in a final judgment. The refusal to echo his teaching generally springs from some sin, or weakness, in the evangelist—love of popularity, or failure to realize the extreme holiness of God.[154]

The subsection paper of Oswald Hoffmann stressed the necessity of *active* proclamation as the *primary* task of the Church. It was a basic theology for evangelistic methods:

> Proclamation of the Gospel is the responsible *activity* of a Church committed to Jesus Christ its Lord, and responsive to his atoning work for the whole world.

> The *primary* task of the Church is proclamation of the *Gospel*. Law convicts, Gospel forgives. Law condemns, Gospel saves. Law kills, Gospel gives life.

> The Holy Spirit of God does his work through the Gospel of Christ, proclaiming Christ and testifying to Jesus Christ, Savior of the world.
>
> The Spirit of God also proclaims Christ and testifies to Jesus Christ through the Word of God, given to the world through inspiration of prophets, apostles, and evangelists by the Holy Spirit himself.
>
> The testimony of the Spirit comes to the world today through the people of God, empowered by the Spirit himself to give witness not merely *about* Christ, as he is described in the Scriptures but *to* Christ, as he is embraced and held fast in personal faith, which is also the gift of the Holy Spirit.[155]

Hoffmann asserted that the best methods are those which not only witness to Jesus Christ, but also bring those won into active fellowship with other believers. The media may be direct evangelism, or a pre-evangelism, preparing the way for Christian pastors or people to visit for person-to-person testimony.

Leighton Ford spoke of the evangelist as a gift to the Church and also of his responsibility to the Church. A united evangelistic campaign does not by-pass the local church, but operates as "part of the continuing strategy of evangelism."[156]

Statistics reveal, said Leo Janz, that only 10 percent of the converts survive when their names are given to an indifferent or hostile pastor after the united campaign, whereas 90 percent of the converts remain true followers six years after the campaign when under the spiritual care of a faithful lay counselor.

Francis Schaeffer was concerned about the unevangelized children of Christians, but addressed his paper to "The Practice of Truth." He reacted to the twentieth-century relativism of truth that conceives of the truths of Christianity as abstract "religious" truth, rather than as objective historical things that actually happened in history:

Historic Christianity rests upon the truth of what
today is called the "brute facts" and not just upon
an unknown experience of men in past ages of
which we have only a faulty hermeneutical
interpretation. Behind the truth of such history is
the great truth that the personal, infinite God is
objectively "there." He actually exists (in contrast to
his not being there); and Christ's redemptive and
finished work actually took place at a point of time
in real space-time history (in contrast to this not
being the case). Historic Christianity rests upon the
truth of these things in absolute antithesis to their
not being true.[157]

Because of the danger of falsely communicating to this
generation, Schaeffer insisted that the Gospel must be
communicated by stating the antithesis, lest the message
be misunderstood by the contemporary generation. He
suggested that "One Truth" was necessary for the
Congress theme, but that it had been omitted.

Schaeffer further warned that identification with truth,
and against the enemy of false doctrine, must be
practiced if the next generation of Christians is to remain
faithful. Commitment to truth would be proved by what
it cost us:

Thus—because of our commitment to evangelism
on the basis of the holiness of God and for the sake
of truth—I can visualize times when the only way to
make plain the seriousness of what is involved in
regard to a campaign where the Gospel is going to
be preached, but where men (whose doctrine is
known to be an enemy) are going to be invited to
pray, etc., is with tears not to accept an official part
in that campaign. Evangelism that does not lead to
purity of life and purity of doctrine is just as faulty
and incomplete as an orthodoxy which does not
lead to a concern for, and communication with, the
lost.[158]

Schaeffer here was referring to certain cooperative
crusades where nonevangelical leadership had

participated in the programs.

The group evangelism practiced by the Southern Baptist Convention resulted in 4,334,000 won to Christ and baptized between 1954 and 1964, according to C. E. Autrey. He also recommended using pastors as evangelists in simultaneous local cooperative crusades by local churches in a given area. Success had been noted as a number of pastor-evangelists crossed cultures on a simultaneous crusade in another country.

Two opposing methods of evangelism were represented by José Maria Rico of the Assemblies of God, and Ruben Lores of Evangelism-in-Depth (saturation evangelism). E.I.D. represented a South American strategy "whereby all churches use all available resources to reach an entire country with the whole Gospel of Christ."[159] Rico spoke of the Total Evangelism used by the Assemblies of God which

> has no regard to the number of people that can be reached but places its emphasis on the total power of the Gospel, in every phase mentioned in the Word of God, i.e., salvation, healing, and the baptism of the believer in the Holy Spirit.[160]

Lores spoke of a mobilization of resources, while Rico spoke about the total power of the Gospel. The Assemblies of God, Rico said, commend efforts resulting in benefit to society but

> in no way consider them efficacious in the salvation of men. The Gospel does not consider man to be just one of many cells in a collective social group; indeed, it focuses on the individual as the direct object of the entire divine plan. . . In other words, every time an individual makes a personal decision to belong to Christ, a definite change takes place in the person who is experiencing the birth of a new creature in his own life where old things are left behind. What society needs, therefore, is the multiplication of these new creatures in its fold. When these take control of society, society will experience total and natural renewal.[161]

Rico noted that Jesus did not mention social reforms
used in the popular sense. Jesus rather "projected an
evangelical principle that he desired should become the
social principle."[162] Man was to seek first the Kingdom
and His righteousness and all these material things
would be added (Matt. 6:33). This viewpoint seemed to
prevail among most of the Congress delegates.
Proclamation of the "One Truth" was the beginning of
God's answer to the temporal needs of humanity, even as
the Gospel alone could bring eternal salvation.

THE NEW
INTERNATIONAL
VISAGE OF
EVANGELICALS

Berlin 1966 defined, as well as demonstrated,
evangelicalism. The interdenominational unity of
historical revivalism expressed itself beyond the
institutionalized boundaries of the state religions of
Europe in the tradition of revivalism and pietist
evangelism. A nonsectarian pattern of evangelistic
cooperation was established for the era of postcolonialism
in the Third World. Evangelicals would proclaim the
Gospel. Their first concern would be the spiritual
transformation of individuals, and not the political
restructuring of society.

Interdenominational and international unity. Since the rise of
liberalism and modernism in the nineteenth century,
evangelicalism has receded from public view as a
religious force. Berlin represented a unity and a
cohesiveness that drew not only the small separatist
denominations together, but disclosed significant
evangelical elements within traditional Protestant
denominations and the Church of England. The
evangelistic bankruptcy of nonevangelicalism became
apparent by an examination of the WCC's redefinition of
evangelism.

Future perimeters for world evangelism. Berlin 1966 drew the
perimeters of the theology of evangelism that would

continue to channel its dynamics for the next turbulent decade. Berlin said, "This has been the way in which God has enabled us to see His hand of blessing in the past. The continued proclamation of the One True Gospel will bring His continued blessing in evangelism and church expansion, until Jesus Christ returns again." Berlin became a moral bulwark amid situation ethics and philosophical existentialism and relativism, a theological bulwark against the extravagances of experiential mysticism on one hand, and the "death of God" on the other, and an historical landmark amid the vacuum of biblical authority in Protestantism, papal authority in Catholicism, and the abstract progressive theology of tradition in ecumenical circles.

Evangelical stature. It would be ill-advised to speak of Berlin 1966 or of Lausanne 1974 as "mature" expressions of evangelicalism, for that term is condemnatory of the spiritual stature of the previous generation, and its use may prejudice the future. However, Berlin gave evidence of a restored movement in the history of Christianity. Evangelicalism could now be seen as a significant international body, capable of even greater evangelistic exploits, in an age of technology and population explosion. Evangelicalism slowly began to withdraw from its defensive stance, characteristic since the Scopes Trial of 1925, where its academic credibility and spiritual relevance in a "scientific age" were rejected.

Billy Graham. Without minimizing the contributions of outstanding evangelical leaders and untold unpublicized servants of God, the international leadership and financial backing of Billy Graham enabled him to serve as a catalyst for the evangelicalism represented at Berlin. A study of the pre-Congress Minutes indicates his influence upon the direction of the Congress through policy decisions. Graham's introductory and concluding addresses set the tone of the Congress and outlined the issues of evangelism. Careful study of the planning and program procedures also reveals the cohesive theological

brilliance of the co-sponsor of the Congress, editor Carl
Henry of *Christianity Today.*

Simple Christianity. Berlin 1966 was beautiful and strong
in its simplicity and directness. The position papers were
profound but communicated readily to their audience.
The subsection reports represent a wealth of information
and insights popularly written by men involved with the
public and capable of communicating to the
congregations. The unambiguous approach leaves the
reader without any doubt as to the author's intent, for
there is little ambiguity and none of the equivocation
characteristic of ecumenical statements.

Mainline evangelicalism. With rare exceptions, the position
and subsection papers were written by those who
represented historical evangelicalism around the world.
Berlin 1966 did not flirt with the left and those capable
of importing new "insights" from a Christian theology
built on weak unbiblical presuppositions. Nor did Berlin
compromise with the ultraseparatist right.

Non-Christian religions. In an atmosphere where
universalism in all of its forms is categorically rejected,
the non-Christian religions did not become an issue.
Berlin sought the best methods to reach them for Christ.
In spite of the firm stand (that the Jewish people must
accept Jesus for salvation) taken by Jakob Jocz in his
paper, "Jewish Missions in Relation to Universalism,"[163]
Rabbi Arthur Gilbert welcomed the invitation to the
Congress. He expressed appreciation for the new climate
of Jewish-Christian relationships evidenced at the
Congress. While the lostness of Jews was not denied, the
Congress recognized their privileged place in the history
of redemption, and the light of revelation they possess
that the other non-Christian religions do not.[164] The
world was considered as "One Race" in need of salvation
by faith alone in God's final and full revelation of
Himself in Jesus Christ.

Evangelism and world Christianity. Evangelism at Berlin was rightly related to doctrine for it was, as Halverson said, both the content of the faith and the "inner health" of the church that brought about spontaneous evangelism. This means that all endeavors either to inspire evangelism or to change the definition of evangelism must of necessity imply an acceptance of the apostolic authority of Scripture, the biblical doctrine of sin, Christology, soteriology, and eschatology. Schaeffer is right about "One Truth" as basic to biblical evangelism. Efforts to correct the theology of evangelism and its consequent methodology seem useless for those outside the perimeters of revealed Truth. The purpose of a congress on evangelism is more to inspire, instruct, and channel the forces of interdenominational and international evangelicalism as a movement of the Spirit, rather than to attempt to convince those who are essentially unconvincible, those whose convictions are not built upon biblical authority. As the biblical theology of mission and evangelism is spelled out, and as testimony of God's blessing is evident, the work of a congress will commend itself to the conscience of world Christianity. Bible-believing Christians, for example, can be challenged and channeled to evangelism or church growth, because the dynamics of the Spirit and Word are present even though their lives may be unfruitful.

Personal evangelism. The individualism characteristic of the Scripture and of evangelicalism prevailed at Berlin so that all collectivist concepts of sin or salvation were rejected. Few notes of "triumphalism" were sounded, and they were related to the return of Jesus Christ to establish His Kingdom. His Church during this age would continue to consist of a minority, composed of those saved by personal faith alone. In the face of collective sin and collective belief based upon sociological and anthropological studies of tribes, clans, and families, a strong apologetic for "individualism" might be made—based upon the foundations of the personal worth of man created in the image of God, and upon his

individual moral responsibility and accountability before
his Maker. The Scriptures themselves are responsible for
teaching the personal responsibility of the individual
before God. Evangelism was ultimately not the
responsibility of the Church to do or not to do, but the
personal responsibility of the believer toward his
neighbor near and far.

The new prestige of evangelicalism. Berlin marked, no
doubt, a milestone in the evangelical self-image. Where
previously the defensive ghetto mentality prevailed as a
consequence of the apparent defeat of evangelicalism in
the modernist-fundamentalist controversy in the earlier
decades of this century, the international dimensions of
the Congress ably led by Graham and Henry enabled
Evangelicals to see themselves as a rising worldwide
movement. Evangelism, consequently, was no longer to
be conceived as attacks upon liberalism or modernism,
but as a positive powerful proclamation of Jesus Christ
and His redemption from sin.

Certain dangers accompany this new self-image:
Evangelicals could accept the world as a friend and
forget that they are aliens in it; the world could be
accepted as a domain to be conquered and restructured
for God; theological sophistry could replace the
simplicity of biblical proclamation rather than
complement it; evangelical scholarship might be tempted
to rely upon its intellectual vigor in evangelism rather
than upon the power of the Spirit and the Bible.

Soul winning. Berlin spoke occasionally of "soul winning"
and it was this emphasis upon the immortality of the soul
of man that undergirded its concept of the more current
usage of "personal evangelism." Soul winning recognized
the personal responsibility of every Christian to engage
himself with God in His mission. This responsibility did
not neglect either the inner spiritual life and soundness
of doctrine, or the presence of the believer and his
loving concern for the total person. The soul was not
dissected from the body, but its immortality was kept in
focus and perspective.

Soul winning spoke of the primacy of proclamation evangelism, in the perspective of the population explosion and the needs of man. It saw social action and social improvements as valuable where the new birth had preceded and prepared society to accept and sustain them. The emphasis was on persuasion evangelism, which neither pressured nor proselytized, but nevertheless sought a verdict. Evangelism was more than sharing information and personal experiences, but lovingly and winsomely sought the eternal welfare of the lost person. Soul winning continued its responsibility at Berlin by establishing the new believer into the community of a local church. It saw the goal of evangelism as the discipleship of the believer in fellowship with other believers.

Soul winning was concerned implicitly (Schmidt and Ockenga) and explicitly (Halverson, Hudson, and Schaeffer) with biblical "truth" that convicts and saves. The cause of Christ is not advanced in the life of an individual, a church, or in Christendom, by an unbiblical pluralistic soteriology. A constancy and consistency prevailed throughout the Congress that gave a "certain sound" to the message of evangelism. Denominational and charismatic differences melted before the communality of biblical essentials and the lostness of man.

Weaknesses of Berlin. Certain current issues could have been considered, such as proselytism and evangelism, a biblical view of the world and non-Christian religions, eschatology and evangelism. Cross-cultural problems in evangelism and the evangelism of the growing cities of the world required study in depth. Certainly the Christian attitude toward "racism" received little biblical attention, considering the place that the unity of humanity as "One Race" had received in the motto of the Congress. Race, however, was directed toward the unity of mankind in need of salvation rather than toward issues of racism.

Nevertheless, the strengths and contributions of Berlin

raise it to a significant place in the history of missions
and evangelism during the last one hundred years.
Berlin might well serve as the standard of revived
evangelicalism in this century.

The unfinished business of Berlin. The relationship of social
action and social concern to evangelism required greater
theological expression and application than it received.
While the definition of evangelism clearly related to the
witnessing Christian who verbally proclaimed Christ
Jesus and sought to persuade, Berlin gave little more
than token theological consideration to the social
pressures of the 1960s. Racial issues were considered in a
Supplementary Discussion Group,[165] and the "Social
Program of the Church" was presented as a method of
group evangelism. Berlin did not establish the theological
basis for social action, even though it stood firm on
proclamation evangelism as *the* mission of the Church.

In his Bible study of "The Great Commission," John
Stott was concerned that Christians are willing to
proclaim but not to identify with people as Jesus did.
Stott spoke of the necessity of expressing and
demonstrating love for the secular man or woman, "and
win a right to share with them the good news of
Christ."[166] Similarly, Paul Rees believed that issues of
race, war, intemperance, sex, and other social problems
can erect psychological barriers to the reception of the
Gospel.[167] Theological answers drawn from Scripture
would be needed to place these issues in a balanced
perspective. The subject would receive far more attention
at Lausanne 1974.

Reaction to this question came from a variety of
delegates. Rev. Richard Møeller Petersen, pastor of the
Holy Cross Church (Lutheran) of Copenhagen,
Denmark, challenged Maxey Jarman's statement in a
Sectional meeting saying that the Church should stick to
its business of preaching the Gospel while leaving the
social realm alone. Petersen reacted by saying,

> As a pastor I regard it a great misconception to
> think of evangelization only in the perspective of

> preaching and proclaiming the gospel. Our ministry
> is the ministry of the whole congregation of the
> laity and the clergy. . . . Our ministry is a ministry
> of preaching and a ministry of works. These cannot
> be separated and they are equally important
> because they are equally important to the men to
> whom we are sent.[100]

Petersen did not seem to feel that Berlin had given a
ministry of "works" its proper relationship to evangelism.

Paul P. Fryhling, later to become program chairman of
the Minneapolis 1969 regional congress, wrote how the
Congress had intensified his burden to reach men with
the saving Gospel:

> No one present would have escaped the relevancy
> and importance of God's written revelation, the
> Holy Bible, for effectively proclaiming this saving
> Word to the world.[169]

He believed that the social and human needs of mankind
had a high place of concern.

> . . . delegates realized that one cannot simply preach
> a spiritual gospel without reaching forth a helping
> hand.[170]

It is difficult to see how Fryhling came to this conclusion
on the basis of the printed texts.

Rev. Reynold Johnson, executive director of the
Commission on Evangelism in the Lutheran Church in
America, was enthused by the "One Race" emphasis and
also about the conversion accounts given by two Auca
Indians:

> . . . he thought the greatest inadequacies were, on
> the one hand, lack of continuing attention to social
> problems and to the way the church witness can be
> strengthened by action in these areas; and, on the
> other hand, too easy a dismissal of modern
> theological trends.[171]

Johnson confirmed the need for more biblical treatment
of this subject, of continuing interest to evangelistic
efforts and the Church.

AN INVITATION TO
THIS GENERATION

International evangelicalism carried with it from Berlin
most, if not all, of the characteristics of historical
revivalism and evangelicalism of the previous centuries.
The personal and individual nature of salvation was
consistently upheld, in contrast to the collective and
horizontal positions of ecumenical theology. Berlin 1966
was a strong expression of renewal and revival
characteristic of those movements at the fringes or
outside of the institutional church throughout the history
of Christianity.[172] Contemporary evangelicalism, under
prophetic and charismatic leadership, not only reacted in
the early part of this century to the rejection by much of
Protestantism of prophetic and apostolic authority
historically recorded in the Bible, but also to the rejection
of biblical evangelism by the World Council of Churches
by New Delhi 1961. Evangelical views of salvation must
be called "vertical" and the ecumenical viewpoint
"horizontal." They are bibically and theologically
incompatible. Later conferences, such as the WCC
Assembly at Nairobi, would develop a synthesis approach
known as "holistic evangelism," but this could not prove
to be satisfactory or reconciling because of its theological
foundation upon tradition, its progressive theological
methodology, and its universalism presuppositions.

Berlin stood firmly against totalitarian forms of
government which inhibit Christians' freedom of
religion. A dissatisfaction with the evangelistic inertia of
institutional churches prevailed in the light of the
population explosion, and the rise of technology to be
used in the extension of the Gospel. Biblical
apocalypticism, anticipating the return of Jesus Christ,
gave optimistic encouragement to evangelism, yet
foresaw that judgment would accompany sin in the world

and apostasy in Christendom. The threat of nuclear
destruction intensified the need for world evangelization.
Berlin saw the transcendental nature of the Scripture as
the answer to the spiritual and practical needs of
mankind. New creatures in Christ Jesus bring impressive
changes in society.

The Closing Statement of the Congress, unanimously
accepted by a standing vote, boldly adopted the motto of
the Student Volunteer Movement used three-quarters of
a century before, "The Evangelization of the World in
This Generation."

> As an evangelical ecumenical gathering of Christian
> disciples and workers, we cordially invite all
> believers in Christ to unite in the common task of
> bringing the word of salvation to mankind in
> spiritual revolt and moral chaos. Our goal is
> nothing short of the evangelization of the human
> race in this generation, by every means God has
> given to the mind and will of men.[173]

The Berlin delegates called all believers in Christ to unite
in world evangelization.

6 The Crystallization of Another Gospel

The crisis of Christianity during the period between Berlin 1966 and Lausanne 1974 may be summarized theologically as the definition of the mission of the Church. Evangelical missions continually faced the fact that their evangelistic efforts were culminating in growing national churches seeking independence. Ecumenically oriented churches and missions saw the hope of the Christian faith as applicable to both the growth of the church and to the welfare of the entire creation—a new heaven and earth in which righteousness should dwell. The latter was a distinctly political gospel, concerned with the restructuring of churches for their social mission. The mission of the renewed church is to work for the restructuring of society.

The crisis was most crucially focused upon evangelism. At the Fourth Assembly of the WCC at Uppsala in 1968, John V. Taylor introduced the theme "Renewal in Mission," and isolated the main theological issue as "the apparent opposition between the Gospel of personal conversion and the Gospel of social responsibility."[1] Taylor opposed an "either/or" alternative and recommended a synthesis rather than a compromise. It will be seen that the WCC Commission of World Mission and Evangelism meeting in 1973 at Bangkok and the

Fifth Assembly of the WCC at Nairobi in 1975 both
sought a synthesis to this dilemma in mission. Even the
Lausanne International Congress on World Evangelism
could not escape this debate.

These years were characterized in the West by student
rebellion against the "establishment," the institutions of
contemporary society. Ecumenical theologians took their
agenda from the world. Much of their theologizing
centered around the revolutionary
socio-politico-economic questions of the day. The *Missio
Dei* theology was developed at the Ghana 1958 meeting
of the International Missionary Council—*God* is a
sending God; the *World* is the content and goal of God's
acting and sending; and the *Church* was seen as serving
the sending God. The Church is God's means to bring
shalom (peace, harmony, etc.) as a social event to the
world by the transforming power of the Gospel. The
conversion of individuals is not only a one-sided event,
for salvation should not be understood in a narrow
individualistic sense.[2] God's mission embraces both the
Church and the world, and consequently, the Church is
to be of service to a world in social upheaval.

Four evangelical congresses in different continents
were initiated by national leaders as a means of
disseminating the inspiration and findings of Berlin
1966: Singapore 1968, Minneapolis 1969, Bogotá 1969,
and Amsterdam 1971. They were evangelical responses
to the specific evangelistic needs represented on the four
continents. The Billy Graham Evangelistic Association
supported and made significant financial contributions
to each one. While each adopted a different perspective,
according to the problems each continent faced,
they did much to consolidate evangelical theology and to
strengthen leadership in evangelism in countries facing
social change and revolution. Decades earlier, John R.
Mott found that times of social and political change, and
of national disaster, were especially fruitful occasions for
the proclamation of the Gospel. These congresses, in
general, encouraged evangelism in the midst of riots,
revolution, and wars.

From Uppsala 1968 to the Fifth Assembly of the WCC
at Nairobi in 1975, ecumenical "evangelism" looked
toward *action* rather than only pronouncements
concerning the politico-socio-economic and ecological
needs of the world. Continued lip service was given to
the traditional vocabulary of evangelism but very obvious
differences in meaning confused Evangelicals as well as
Third World members of the WCC.

As the research has shown, these theological changes
were directly related to the historical question of biblical
authority. Since Edinburgh 1910, the abandonment of
the historical doctrine of verbal inspiration of the Bible
has continually resulted in broad hermeneutical
possibilities, which in turn have produced a progressive
theology that accommodates itself to the theologian
popular in a particular WCC meeting. The Louvain 1971
Faith and Order meeting, then, addressed itself to this
question of interpretation as a basis for theological unity
with both Eastern Orthodoxy within the WCC and
Roman Catholicism without. The ultimate result was the
synthesis now known as "holistic" evangelism, now also
adopted by some of the evangelical "left."

Before considering Lausanne 1974, the issues of this
decade must be made more clear by a survey, first, of the
redefinition of mission in the WCC at Uppsala 1968;
next, the congresses resulting from Berlin 1966; and,
finally, the synthesis position of the WCC at Bangkok
1973.

CHURCH FOR
THE WORLD

Stimulated by the Berlin 1966 Congress, the question of
evangelism again became a popular subject in the WCC.
Philip Potter, then director of the Division of World
Mission and Evangelism, reviewed the role of evangelism
in the history of the WCC at the August 1967 Central
Committee at Heraklion, Crete. He saw the differences
between "mission" and "evangelism" as difficult to

maintain. Study revealed "evangelism" had been
"described" in 1959, but not "mission." The older
approach, Potter said, claims

> that mission takes place in continents where the
> Gospel has never been heard, while evangelism is
> directed to those who are alienated from the
> churches and to new generations within the sphere
> of the Christian community.[3]

He saw additional complications in the debate because
many of those who are alienated from the Church have
often been baptized and "as such have been sealed as
members of the Body of Christ."[4] Here it may be seen
that baptism for Potter had a totally different
significance than that expressed at Berlin 1966, where
baptism was not to be confused with baptismal
regeneration, "Nothing here sets aside the necessity of
personal faith for salvation."[5] Bishop Gibson of Jamaica
affirmed that "the grace of salvation is not tied to the
sacrament," but to the new birth.[6]

Potter further noted the interchangeable use of
"mission," "witness," and "evangelism" since Amsterdam
1948. "Mission" tends to speak of the Church's total
involvement in Christ's ministry, while "evangelism" of
calling men to Christ. Yet the word "service" is preferred
to "mission" by some, because of the pejorative use of
"missions" as associated with organized missionary work
of churches or societies.

Potter misinterpreted Berlin 1966 to imply that racial,
cultural, and national divisions were part of the
evangelistic message. He said,

> A very strong statement was made on race and the
> final declaration was entitled "One Race, One
> Gospel, One Task." Here was a tacit
> acknowledgement that it is part of the evangelistic
> message that in Christ the walls which divide men
> into races, cultures, nations and classes have been
> broken down.[7]

Berlin spoke against distinctions based on race or color
that would limit fellowship or proclamation.[8] Berlin
1966, however, insisted that the issue was Jesus Christ
and that by coming to Him the "new birth" would
transform the prejudiced heart. Unity and reconciliation
were for those "in Christ." Fellowship and service were
not part of the message but a result of it.

Furthermore, Potter said the ecumenical movement
strongly advocated "dialogue" and "presence" and
opposed an aggressive evangelical attitude that says we
have everything to give but nothing to receive. Crusades,
missions, and personal evangelism were rejected because

> there is a tendency toward evangelistic campaigns
> or special missions or individual societies aimed at
> winning folk for Christ and rescuing them from the
> world into our apparently unworldly churches,
> which would increase their introversion. These
> attitudes and actions have been rightly condemned
> in all our ecumenical conferences. We are all for
> "dialogue" and "presence."[9]

Potter tacitly acknowledged the need of proclamation in
the dialogue as part of the nature of evangelism, and
returned to the question of the content of evangelism as
"the Good News of the one, new, reconciled humanity in
Christ."[10] Potter's universalism in the atonement as
already accomplished made evangelism a proclamation
which those without a knowledge of Christ needed to
recognize, rather than to *respond* to in repentance of sin
and saving faith by confession of Jesus Christ as Savior
and Lord. Potter, later to become general secretary,
became a sincere, but *habile,* spokesman of another
gospel.

A NEW CATHOLICITY

More delegates and people than ever before met at the
Fourth Assembly of the WCC at Uppsala under the
theme "Behold I make all things new." There were 704

voting delegates representing 235 member churches,
among a total of over 2700 people at Uppsala. The
number of delegates had doubled since New Delhi 1961.
At Uppsala, the Eastern Orthodox churches participated
more freely and contributed more strongly than
previously. The Roman Catholic Vatican Council II
(1902-65) had initiated a Joint Working Group which
had been working together with the WCC for some time.
Norman Goodall described the Assembly's "obsession"

> with the revolutionary ferment of our time, with
> questions of social and international responsibility,
> of war and peace and economic justice, with the
> pressing, agonizing physical needs of men, with the
> plight of the underprivileged, the homeless and
> starving, and with the most radical contemporary
> rebellions against all "establishments," civil and
> religious.[11]

The "world" wrote the agenda for the meeting, and it
was expected to do so.

The "new manhood" or the "new humanity" initiated
by the Christ-event predominated the theology of
Uppsala. For many, Christ is now working redemptively
in society to make it "new." Section I, "The Holy Spirit
and the Catholicity of the Church," presented the new
view of the world for which the Church is a servant:

> We have come to view this world of men as the
> place where God is already at work to make all
> things new, and where he summons us to work with
> him.[12]

The mission of the renewed Church seemed
preoccupied with the horizontal problems of the world at
the local church level.

> Renewal must begin in the local community by
> detecting and dethroning all exclusiveness of race
> and class and by fighting all economic, political and
> social degradation and exploitation of men.[13]

This seemed to be the emphasis of the Gospel message at
Uppsala—instead of the expansion of the Church by
evangelical evangelism.[14]

At Uppsala, the WCC began the implementation of its
own renewal in terms of "the church for the world." A
new structure should be established that would make the
WCC more spiritually responsive to the Third World and
Eastern Orthodox churches.[15] The assembly approved
the restructuring of the WCC because the churches

> . . . need to consider what it means for the World
> Council as an expression of the common life of the
> churches that it has moved away from the
> limitations of the North Atlantic that gave it birth,
> toward the Third World.[16]

Special emphasis was given toward the ultimate
incorporation of Roman Catholics and Evangelicals into
the WCC. The adopted proposal asked,

> How should the structure of the World Council of
> Churches be modified to enable it to pursue with
> the most practical effect and least burden of work
> and finance these opportunities with the Roman
> Catholic Church, with Evangelical Churches and
> organizations not now in fellowship with the World
> Council of Churches, and with the organ of the
> world families of churches, including the
> Orthodox?[17]

Uppsala anticipated the membership of both Roman
Catholics and Evangelicals in a conciliar atmosphere of
theological pluralism.

THE REDESCRIBED
MISSION OF THE
CHURCH

Historic evangelism was almost extinguished as an option
in world evangelism at Uppsala. Section II, "Renewal in

Mission," attracted more Uppsala delegates than any
other[18] because of the controversial nature of the
pre-Assembly draft prepared by the Geneva staff and
modified by consultants and the Central Committee. As
the Assembly opened, two other drafts were submitted
by groups in Scandinavia and Germany. Scandalized
Norwegians threatened to withdraw from the WCC.[19]

The "new humanity" was used as its starting point.
Men were seen as disobedient and alienated "sons of
God, answerable to their Father for one another and for
the world."[20] In this condition, man expresses himself by
the exploitation of others and by alienation in all of his
relationships. Uppsala's theology implies a
universalism—by the forgiveness opened to all men by
the Cross, and by the new creation born in the
resurrection. Sin has not resulted in death and judgment,
making man by nature a child of wrath. Sin is *described* by
the horizontal concerns of mankind and is not *defined* in
terms of regeneration by faith, whereby broken
fellowship with God is restored by personal faith in
Christ.

Uppsala depreciated proclamation in favor of dialogue
used in meeting with men of other faiths, or of no faith.
Dialogue enabled the Christian to share his common
humanity:

> Christ speaks in this dialogue, revealing himself to
> those who do not know him and connecting the
> limited and distorted knowledge of those who do.
> Dialogue and proclamation are not the same. The
> one complements the other in a total witness.[21]

The new manhood is both a goal and a gift,
appropriated by a response of faith when

> the Holy Spirit. . .takes the Word of God and makes
> it a living, converting word to men. Our part in
> evangelism might be described as bringing about
> the occasions of men's response to Jesus Christ.
> Often the turning point does not appear to be a
> religious choice at all.[22]

The conversion experience involved, for Uppsala, a turning to one's fellow man in a new way. Sin was considered to be on the horizontal level and the decision experience, consequently, involved a change of attitude and relationship in "putting on the new man."

The observations of Eugene Carson Blake, then general secretary of the WCC, clarified the ambiguities of the Section II report on this heavily debated "mission" definition. First of all, he identified part of the problem as being a question of terminology, for the sociologists who wrote the first report had not used theological language. The integration at New Delhi 1961 brought sociologically oriented IMC mission administrators into the WCC.[23] Yet foreign mission leaders believed that home mission leaders had capitulated to a secularized description of the mission of the Church and had betrayed the Gospel.[24]

Second, Blake acknowledged that the continuing unresolved problem was the

> real theological differences among the membership
> of the churches. "Pietists" understand conversion
> and evangelism in highly individualistic terms and
> expect that the resultant Christians will be obviously
> "not of this world." Many other Christians see
> conversion in the context of "this world"
> conforming much more to the ways of the world in
> an external sense, but, on the other hand, attacking
> society's structures and values much more radically
> than does the average pietist. All churches have
> within their membership both kinds of members.[25]

This dichotomy between evangelical and ecumenical theology was also expressed in the last section, "Toward New Styles of Living." Evangelicals were associated with revivalist personal ethics; and the ecumenical life style toward a commitment to social justice:

> In our times many efforts of renewal are
> identifiable by their commitment to the struggle for
> social justice. Other revival movements see the new
> life style in the refusal to smoke, to drink alcohol, to

dance, to use make-up and to gamble, and in the
eagerness to attend church regularly.[26]

In effect, the evangelical struggle for existence, which
had been fought and lost in the Jerusalem 1928 meeting
of the IMC, was now revived in the WCC at
Uppsala—and they lost again. The Uppsala documents
could give Evangelicals little consolation or comfort. The
secularized content of Section II prepared by the Geneva
staff of the DWME was significantly modified by
conservative Evangelicals in the WCC and by the Eastern
Orthodox. These modifications would have little
significance when Philip Potter moved from director of
the DWME to general secretary of the WCC and
continued to exercise the prophetic role he believed
Geneva should have in leading the churches in mission.[27]
    Third, Blake pointed to the eschatological differences
"between those who see salvation in other worldly terms
primarily and those who believe that otherworldliness is
an escape."[28]
    Fourth, Blake isolated the proclamation or dialogue
debate at Uppsala:

> . . .there are some Christians who believe that
> "proclamation of the gospel is usually triumphalist
> and self-defeating," while there are others who
> believe that "dialogue" with non-Christians is
> engaged only by Christians who have already lost
> their faith.[29]

"Mission" as defined or described at Uppsala was
unquestionably interpreted by the Geneva WCC staff as
in favor of the struggle for social justice. Evangelical
evangelism and church growth are denigrated as a
primary mission of the Church. Uppsala said,

> The church is rightly concerned for the world's
> hundreds of millions who do not know the Gospel
> of Christ. It is constantly sent out to them in witness

and service. But that concern becomes suspect when the church is preoccupied with its own numerical and institutional strength. It is called to be the servant body of Christ given to and for the world.[30]

Blake believed that Uppsala revealed the dilemma of its mission by stating that the growth of the Church "both inward and outward, is of urgent importance."[31] Uppsala escaped

> the horns of a dilemma by stating concretely and positively that the mission of Jesus Christ includes both purposes and that you dare not choose between them.[32]

While "mission" became wholistic (later holistic) at Uppsala by a synthesis of proclamation and social justice, the first priority for missions was toward centers of power, "For the sake of the new humanity the powerless must exercise power."[33] The second priority was revolutionary movements. Christians were warned of their tendency to be deeply concerned for law and order, while the revolutionary movements represented the "longings for a just society." Furthermore, the new humanity cannot fully come without the revolutions necessary to establish just order. "The Christian community must decide whether it can recognize the validity of their decision and support them."[34]

Uppsala led the churches into political theology, and its mission would become involvement in "valid" revolutions! If Uppsala decreed a mission of social justice and proclamation as necessary complements, the latter received little consideration in terms of evangelical mission. Proclamation evangelism was interpreted in terms of the new humanity and social justice. Perhaps it would not be too strong to say that evangelical evangelism died in the WCC at Uppsala. Nevertheless, some Evangelicals in the WCC continue to attend WCC meetings and attempt a futile modification of the Geneva evangelism syndrome that began at Edinburgh 1910.

EVANGELICAL EXTENSION ON FOUR CONTINENTS

Four congresses met on four different continents as regional expressions of Berlin 1966—Singapore 1968, Minneapolis 1969, Bogotá 1969, and Amsterdam 1971. It is impossible to assess the importance of the many other developments in evangelism inspired by Berlin 1966, but these congresses strengthened evangelical proclamation and helped to dissipate the confusion over evangelism disseminated by the WCC meetings at Geneva 1966 and Uppsala 1968.

SINGAPORE 1968: NON-CHRISTIAN RELIGIONS AND THE MISSION OF THE CHURCH

Representatives from twenty-four Asian nations, representing two-thirds of the world's population, convened at Singapore from November 5 to 13, 1968, for the Asia-South Pacific Congress on Evangelism. In addition to making a substantial financial contribution to the Congress as at Berlin 1966, the Billy Graham Evangelistic Association assigned their then staff man, W. Stanley Mooneyham, to be the coordinating director for its preparations and organization under Asian leadership. Max D. Atienza of Manila served as the associate coordinator. He later recalled the challenge to evangelize received at the Congress. The closing meeting in the National Theater, attended by 3,500 people, indicated greater spiritual blessings and wider ministries in Asia's future. There were ten Asian cochairmen responsible for bringing together 1,100 delegates from twenty-four nations.

The Congress was called to facilitate the proclamation of the Gospel in Asia and the South Pacific. The

Congress Purpose was unified and directed toward the
non-Christian populations on Asian continents:

> To *discover* ways of implementing the proposals of
> the 1966 World Congress on Evangelism in our
> area, challenged by an exploding population and
> social upheaval.

> To *expand* the relevance of the Christian evangel
> and stress the urgency of its proclamation to the
> two billion people living in this region.

> To *summon* the Church corporately, and its
> members individually, to recognize and accept the
> priority of evangelism.

Other objectives were to develop specialized methods
amid cultural diversity, tools and techniques, ways of
vitalizing evangelism, and cooperation in evangelism and
outreach.[35]

No one else. After decades of leadership in Korean
education, the United Nations, government service, and
the former International Missionary Council, Dr. Helen
Kim declared that the most important problem for the
churches of Asia was how to preach the Gospel to people
of other faiths:

> Some scholars in theology and some church leaders
> in Asia say that the Holy Spirit is already working
> in these non-Christians through their faiths so that
> they need not be considered as people to whom we
> need to preach. I cannot follow this way of
> thinking. It has been said and written clearly in the
> Scripture that ". . . there is salvation in no one else,
> for there is no other name under heaven given
> among men by which we must be saved" (Acts
> 4:12). Therefore we ought to make very plain in
> our encounter with other religions that only Christ
> is our Savior.[36]

Methods may include dialogue, she said, but with the
frank explanation of salvation through Christ alone. The
Spirit of Christ will speak to their hearts and open their
hearts to this message.[37]

The alienation of non-Christian religions. Akbar
Abdul-Haqq, born in India, delivered the major position
paper on "A Theology of Evangelism." He quoted
literature of the West but reflected the Asian context of a
non-Christian world. Haqq centered his position paper
on the Old and New Testaments and directed his
attention toward the need of "religious" mankind in
Asia:

> This particular Congress on Evangelism deals with a
> part of the world which is inalienably religious in its
> outlook on life. In this regard it stands in contrast
> to the West, where science and material values have
> for many persons become normative of all truth
> while spiritual values are being discarded as
> irrelevant for everyday life.[38]

Haqq's adaptation of the Berlin theology reaffirmed the
contention that the evangelistic message of the Bible
becomes "contextualized" as theologians of a particular
region speak to the demands of their own culture. He
emphasized the alienation of natural man from God in
non-Christian religions. God's self-revelation and grace
were necessary for a saving knowledge of God. The Bible
is concerned, he said, that alienated seekers after truth
come to a living experience of God. The Bible

> . . . considers it an idle presumption to prove the
> existence of God, making the spiritually distorted
> reason of man normative of all truth. . .(Heb. 11:6).
> None can excuse himself from believing that "God
> is" (Rom. 1:19, 20). But when it comes to the
> business of establishing a contact with God thus
> recognized, a person is invaded by diabolical forces
> operating through the depravity of his sin. As a
> result, instead of worshiping the Supreme God, a

man succumbs to idolatry. . .(Rom. 1:23). Due to
idolatry the natural faith of man becomes a blind
faith mistaking superstition for spirituality and
fanaticism for righteousness.

The twin phenomena of idolatry and homage to the
Unknown God completely overshadow man's search
for God. Idolatry and its concomitant blind faith
constitute sickness unto death. There stands an altar
to the Unknown God in the innermost secret
chambers of every religion. . . But the nature of
God remains unknown and the face of God
unseen.[39]

A person must be exposed to the light of the Gospel in
order to come by "saving faith." Hence,

alienation from God means that man is in original
sin and. . .despite all talk about God in natural
religion and theology, man is in sin so long as he
does not meet his God in a personal experience of
Jesus Christ.[40]

This sin results in alienation not only from God, but also
"from nature, from one another, and from one's own
self." Sin in the unregenerate individual and society
grows cumulatively. Our twentieth century has inherited
the collective guilt of previous centuries, during which
Satan has had control over the natural man and his social
structure (1 John 5:19). "A society without God is bound
quickly to degenerate into a demoniac society."[41] The
help of God is required to save man from his
enslavement to sin, because man's moral depravity has
kept him "under the sway of a powerful and
superhuman enemy."[42] The ancient worship of an idol,
the contemporary worship of one's own self, and
practically all forms of mysticism are expressions of
man's self-alienation on the spiritual level leading to
Freudian "neurosis of mankind."

The Kingdom of God is the only way out of man's
social and personal predicament. It is opposed to the

civilizations and kingdoms man has built upon the
structures of alienation:

> This world system is an "arrangement" under which
> Satan has organized the world of unbelieving
> mankind upon his cosmic principles of force, greed,
> selfishness, ambition and pleasure.[43]

The Gospel of the Kingdom of God is the good news
that the King has given His own life as a ransom for His
subjects, who will no longer live for themselves but for
Him. By the new birth alone, one becomes a member of
His Kingdom. God rules supreme in this heaven-born
order.

The Kingdom of God, therefore, is diametrically
opposed to the kingdom of the devil and the powers of
darkness controlled by the prince of this world (John
14:30):

> The kingdom of God in Christ is waging a
> relentless but bloodless crusade against the powers
> of darkness of this age to win the hearts and minds
> of men and women (Matt. 10:34). In this context all
> godless kingdoms of this world are diabolical. But
> then there are societies and systems of government
> which give direct or indirect recognition to God. To
> the extent that their structures are alienated from
> Him or tend to become so, they are demoniac. The
> measure of alienation obtaining between the
> individual and his society is the measure of the
> godlessness of a given social system. The kingdom
> of Christ is a reign of peace for those who are His
> own, and good will toward all who hear His gospel
> (Luke 2:14).[44]

The true Church is composed of the whole number of
regenerate believers from Pentecost to the first
resurrection. It is not coextensive with the organized or
visible church. "To the extent the visible church makes
concessions to the alienated world and society around
her, she ceases to battle on the side of Christ."[45] The

truth of God in Christ will march forward to the end of this age.

> The church militant looks forward to the return of the Lord when He shall deliver the final blow to the prince of this world. This interegnum between the first and second coming will not be too long.[40]

The Church is not the building or traditions. Petrus Octavianus of Indonesia attributed the closing of the door in China to the compromising of God's churches with the world and their loss of the spirit of evangelism. Chinese converts were taught the traditions of the church and that the church consisted of a building with four walls, but

> it would seem that a majority of ministers from the west (sic) did not teach that the church symbolized the body of Christ and that, where two or three are gathered together "in his name" there was He in the midst.[47]

He believed that it was now God's time for Asia to advance the Gospel throughout Asia and the world—even though "the Communist system is not only a threat to nationalism in Asia, but also the biggest hindrance and obstacle to the Gospel here."[48]

Witness or survival. Presbyterian Professor Jong Sung Rhee of Korea summarized evangelism in his paper as "soul winning" in "Theological Dilutions Which Hinder Evangelism." He feared that the church had forgotten its mission, which causes the church to stand or fall. He recalled how Dr. Sam Moffett at the Berlin Congress warned the participants of the lesson taught by the Nestorian church that was forbidden to propagate the Gospel under Islamic rule.

> Faced with a choice between survival and witness, the church chose survival. As the inevitable result it survived, but what survived was no longer a whole church. It was a sick, ingrown community.[49]

Speaking as an Asian, Rhee concluded that there were
two groups of opponents of evangelism—those who are
from the non-Christian world, and those who are from
within the church itself.

> The former is easily identified and recognized. The
> latter is not so easily distinguished since this group
> is inside the gate. They look like orthodox
> Christians but when they are pressed to confess
> their faith—whether they really believe in Jesus
> Christ as their Savior or in the Bible as the living
> Word of God—they are found wanting.[50]

Rhee had established a theocentric view of man rather
than the anthropocentric view that attributes the
existence of man to natural law. He isolated humanism,
liberalism, syncretism, and universalism within the
Church as the crucial hindrances to evangelism in Asia.

The cultural and evangelistic mandates. At Singapore, Dòn
Hoke, then president of Tokyo Christian College, made
a distinct contribution to the continuing century-old
debate on the relationship of the mission of the
church—evangelism—to social action, justice, and
revolution. He declared that the preaching of the Gospel
to the world is the reconciling mission of the church. He
distinguished between this proclamation of the Gospel to
the world, and the "whole counsel of God" which should
be taught in the local church. This distinction was based
upon the "cultural mandate" given by God to man at
creation (Gen. 1:28) whereby God calls man to
responsible participation in human society, and the
"evangelistic mandate" (Matt. 28:18-20; Acts 1:8) as
God's command to His people to participate with Him in
His redemptive activity.[51]

The cultural mandate involves man's obligation to
fulfill his responsibilities to his family and community, to
law and order, and to his culture and civilization. The
life of Jesus Christ on earth witnesses to His fulfillment
of this mandate by His concern for the physical and
social needs of men. The Sermon on the Mount and the

epistles of the New Testament exhort Christians to
express their faith outwardly in acts of *individual*
compassion and love. First, then, the individual Christian
is to obey what God the Creator has commanded all
mankind to do—

> to exercise all God-given intellectual and physical
> powers in subduing the earth for man's good and
> God's glory. This involves responsible Christian
> citizenship, participation in government, and
> assumption of legitimate social obligations to see
> that the law is upheld, order maintained, wrongs
> righted, justice assured and that all of God's
> image-creatures are given equal opportunity to
> enjoy His grace and to serve Him under His
> *sovereignty.*[52]

Second, he will also

> seek to meet the needs of the sick, the poor, the
> unfortunate, the down-trodden. The divine *agape*
> shed abroad in the heart of the Christian by the
> Holy Spirit should put him in the forefront of
> concerned activities to meet the needs of
> underprivileged men.[53]

Hoke emphasized that the cultural mandate was not
given to the Church but to man as man, God's regent
over His creation. In the New Testament, the *individual*
was to go out into society and achieve the goals, not the
Church.

The evangelistic mandate was the last word of Jesus
Christ to Christians and the church. By the proclamation
of the good news, men may come to repentance and
faith, and receive eternal life by the Holy Spirit. By the
evangelistic mandate, a church is gathered out of the
nations. Every individual Christian is to share God's good
news of redemption in Christ. The laity must be taught
that they are ministers of God and witnesses of Christ in
the world.

> Were every Christian a minister, witnessing to God's
> redemptive work in Christ, he would bring the
> healing power of the gospel to bear on the
> problems of society, and Christ's purifying influence
> would more actively guide the destinies of
> communities and nations.[54]

The Spirit-filled disciple goes forth daily to "shine" in
society and "season" it where he is.

Essential to Hoke's position is his view of the Church
as a spiritual building in which each stone is a believer. It
is the mystical body of Christ, of which each Christian is
a member. It is the bride, for union and fellowship with
the heavenly Bridegroom, Christ. It is an international
spiritual body, not a social or national group—as was
Israel of the Old Testament with a human king,
geographical boundaries, and a body politic. The
functions of the apostolic church were worship, teaching,
fellowship, witness and proclamation, and service.
Consequently,

> (1) no nation, race or political group can claim to be
> the people of God; (2) the civil prerogatives and
> laws of Israel are not applicable to the spiritual
> people of God; (3) since it is supra-national, the
> church is not a competitive political body with other
> nations nor a political party within a nation; (4) the
> church has never been given the authority or
> mandate to legislate politically, or to revolt socially
> as a unit. It is not a lobby or a pressure group.[55]

History seems to indicate that when the church has
departed from its biblical ministry and functions, it has
inevitably declined—both in its spiritual power, and in its
influence upon the society it sought to uplift. Although
apostolic Christians lived under despotic Rome, under
cruel and arbitrary military power, with economic
injustice, exorbitant taxes, and limited political freedom
in an empire where two-thirds of the population were
slaves, the New Testament gives no clear words except to

admonish slaves to be obedient to their masters.
Christians are to obey their government, for God has put
it there. Hoke was biblical and brave in an era when this
message was not the palatable answer to this "agenda"
from the world.

A Christianized world at Singapore? Benjamin E. Fernando,
a Methodist layman from Ceylon, spoke to the issue of
social upheaval, stressing the importance of social
reformation as well as the redemption of individuals. He
quoted Leighton Ford's article in the *Ecumenical Review,*
that "Evangelicalism has been atomized by some
conservative Evangelicals whose key word is 'decision,'
and who tend to regard evangelism merely as an isolated,
individualistic religious experience."[56] Fernando
expressed deep commitment to the absolutely essential
place of individual salvation, for which there is no
substitute. He saw hunger, overpopulation, disease, social
disabilities, war and violence as areas requiring not only
individual action but social reform. In his aspirations to
see social evil cured and prevented, he did not make the
distinctions that Akbar Abdul-Haqq and Hoke did.
Fernando saw the world of men in human relationships,
and physical needs as requiring compassion. Inspired by
Jesus' example, he seemed to sustain the ideal of a
Christianized or a Christlike world, reminiscent of some
ecumenical Evangelicals in the era between Edinburgh
1910 and Jerusalem 1928. The church would gradually
achieve the social reformation of the world, just as the
trickle of water from the sanctuary would ultimately
touch the entire city (Ezek. 47).

Social concern in the local church. Korean pastor Kyung
Chik Han held strongly to evangelism as the supreme
mission of the Church. Consequently "a healthy church
should spend about one-half of its budget for out-reach,
namely evangelism."[57] In addition to many other
requirements for growth, a church ought to be
structured to serve, for

the most serving church is the most growing
church. The church which is alert in helping the
poor, the sick, the needy, orphans, widows, and all
people—in other words, the church which has the
most earnest social concern—is always the most
thronged with people. This does not mean that we
should help the people with a selfishly evangelistic
purpose, i.e., merely for the sake of our church's
growth, but it does mean that when we are
concerned about people's bodily needs and meet
their physical needs, we are usually also on the way
to saving their souls.[58]

The Congress Declaration asked God's pardon for
their failure in "giving as strong and urgent a witness as
our Lord demands amongst Asia's millions."[59] The
participants decided to be more united, compassionate,
involved, and outgoing. In addition to forming
international and interdenominational evangelistic teams,
the delegates from the twenty-four countries pledged "to
initiate some form of united evangelistic effort within
each country to preach the Gospel to the whole nation."
Berlin 1966 gave great encouragement and direction to
Asia's Evangelicals.

MINNEAPOLIS 1969: CHURCH RENEWAL FOR EVANGELISM BY REVIVAL

The second major regional conference supported by
Billy Graham was held in Minneapolis, September 8-13,
1969. Concern for the Congress was born in the hearts
of Christian leaders in Minneapolis as a result of Berlin.
At their request, Billy Graham assumed responsibility as
honorary chairman and Oswald Hoffmann accepted the
chairmanship.[60] In the difficult days of the Vietnam
War, racial turbulence, and student anti-institutionalism,
this Congress convened under the theme "Much Is
Given—Much Is Required" (Luke 12:46). A National
Committe sponsored the Congress, and accepted the
invitation of Minnesota Governor Le Vander and the

Honorary Committee of One Hundred to convene in
Minneapolis. In addition to the program of Bible study,
position papers, and forty-five workshops for more than
5,000 delegates, a Friday Youth Night attracted 18,000.
On the closing Saturday night, hundreds of the 22,000
capacity crowd responded to Billy Graham's evangelistic
appeal. Paul Fryhling chaired the executive committee,
Victor Nelson of the Billy Graham Evangelistic
Association served as executive secretary, and George M.
Wilson, also of the B.G.E.A., was treasurer.

Personal purity, discipline, separation. Minneapolis 1969 was
not characterized by strong biblical exposition (although
it was present) nor by a biblical exegesis of the
theological issues facing the nation. In the historical
evangelical tradition, Minneapolis turned to preaching in
a revivalist spirit as the primary solution for the social ills
of the day. Billy Graham's welcoming address appealed
for a renewal in the churches of an evangelistic urgency,
based upon a new unity and fellowship. He rejected
social action, public demonstrations, or wars of liberation
as evangelism, for the content of the Gospel had not
changed. He saw the need of God's people in America
for a renewed life style—required because of the morally
degrading influence of television:

> I believe, ladies and gentlemen, that we need, in the
> church today, a new Puritanism, a new discipline in
> our personal lives. We need to know what it means
> to be separated from the world and separated unto
> God again. The nightclub is now in our homes, the
> burlesque is now in our homes. We've become more
> and more tolerant to it all. How much has it robbed
> us of our spiritual power?. . .Our problem today is
> not so much personnel and money, our problem
> today is the power of the Holy Spirit. I'm convinced
> that the evangelist is not a man, the evangelist is the
> Holy Spirit.[61]

Graham's prophetic note was founded upon good
theology, for it saw the primary solution to national
problems in the work of the Holy Spirit in the churches.

This was Graham's answer to the theological confusion over evangelism, revolution, decadent morals, and the restructuring of churches in Christendom.

In blunt words, Oswald Hoffmann's keynote address claimed that the church has been sidetracked from evangelism and has been "playing around." He recognized that

> for some people the word "evangelism" has a bad odor. Some find it distasteful because they resent the very idea of personal commitment which the Good News of Jesus Christ commands, which it demands of a man. . .Still others have a view of the church which makes it seem like a social club, consisting of first-class snobs *who want to make others over in their own image.*[62]

He pleaded for a new image of the Church, where Christ means everything, so that He can mean everything to those who are without Him.

Holiness of life. Archbishop Marcus L. Loane of Australia turned to the gracious mercy of God as the source of personal salvation.[63] He dwelt upon the need for love in the inner man as the fountainhead of an effective ministry.[64] Harold Lindsell emphasized the necessity of the power of prayer, love, and the Holy Spirit. He was concerned that the delegates be filled with the Holy Spirit as something *God* does in the believer. Regenerated Christians may be spiritual or carnal. They have been sealed by the Spirit when justified by faith, but the fullness of the Spirit is also their birthright. This is not sinless perfection but a sense of the presence of Jesus Himself intimately abiding in our hearts day by day, the important work of sanctification in the Christian's life:

> Now sanctification is a matter of holiness. It has to do with the quality of my life. It is supposed to be progressive in the sense that I should go from grace to grace and glory to glory. Every day I should be making advances in my Christian walk, but

> unfortunately . . . it is possible for me to go
> backward. It is possible for me to become
> backslidden . . . In this Congress, we have heard a
> great deal about what the Christian ought to be
> doing. I am deeply concerned, not only with what
> we ought to be doing, but with what we are in our
> inner man. Before you *do* something you must *be*
> something, and I suggest that being is more
> important than doing.[65]

Quite unconsciously, perhaps, Lindsell was giving the
evangelical response to the praxis theology of this
decade, as well as consciously adjusting the spiritual roots
of social activism. The abundant life of the Spirit (John
4:14), Lindsell said, was not characteristic of many
Christians in Paul's day (Eph. 5:18). Believers must be
emptied of sins by confession and forgiveness through
the blood of Christ (1 John 1:9). Pet personal sins,
whether of immorality or racism, must be repented of
and restitution be made where necessary. Finally, there
must be a total laying of one's life upon the altar.
Lindsell prayed this prayer on his knees during his
college days, "I am yours, all of me. Take me, use me,
make me what you want. Send me where you want me to
go. I'm yours forever."[66] This revival spirit permeated
the Congress.

Leighton Ford recognized the revolutionary
atmosphere of the sixties in America and declared that
conversion was a complete revolution in the individual
life.

> When a man meets Jesus Christ, God begins to heal
> all his broken relationships, to put him right with
> God, and with himself and with his fellowman.[67]

Conversion was, however, only the beginning of the
Christian life and not the end. By understanding the
need for Christian growth after conversion and the
completeness of the Gospel message the Church can
avoid the polarization between "soul savers" and "soul
reformers." A church made up of redeemed people with

a personal commitment *to* Christ, with a unique
fellowship *in* Christ, and a clear mission *for* Christ, will
take the message to people where they are. He believed
that revolutionary evangelism would be possible among
those "bruised and battered by social upheaval" when
Christians have "earned the right to speak" by love that
seeks for justice in society. Ford did not promise a
perfect world by Christian efforts.

> We can make some things better, but the new world
> will not come until Christ returns. Nor am I saying
> that the Church should stop giving priority to
> evangelism and become a political lobby. What I am
> saying is that God wants to give through our lives as
> Christians a kind of preview, an advance
> demonstration, of the love and peace and justice
> that will mark His eternal kingdom.[68]

Ford failed to distinguish between the lay activity of a
man involved in the creation mandate, such as William
Wilberforce who was characterized by "fierce debate and
political action," and the "evangelistic mandate" given to
the apostles by Christ. While he believed that social
action should not be confused with evangelism, he did
not believe that it should be separated from it. He did
not distinguish between the social *action* of the layman in
his political responsibility as a member of the human
community and the social *concern* on the personal level
that should characterize the Christian as a member of the
community of Christ. Ford's call for the Church to
become involved in social action as well as evangelism
was not supported biblically or theologically. This debate
would continue at Lausanne 1974, and in the
post-Lausanne era.

Black evangelist Tom Skinner and Ralph D. Abernathy
of the Southern Christian Leadership Conference gave
eloquent and forceful pleas against racism in the
churches, and for evangelism as the beginning of God's
solution to social and economic injustices. Skinner said,

> There is no community on the North American
> continent that is so hurting and so lacking the

Gospel, and in such desperate need for all that
Jesus can mean as the black community. I plead
with you on the grounds that to deny a brother a
place to live because of the color of his skin is one
thing, he can recover from that; to deny him a job
based on his qualifications is something else,
because he can recover from that; to deny him
social position because of the color of his skin is
something else, he can recover from that; but to tell
me that I can't hear of the unsearchable riches of
Jesus, to deny me the truth of Calvary, to deny me
participation in the body of Christ, to deny me the
privilege of being a joint heir with Jesus to be
seated together with Him in heavenly places, to
deny me the right of participating in every spiritual
gift in heavenly places is a blow that I can never
recover from.[69]

Abernathy also asked the Congress to demand rights of
life, liberty, and the pursuit of happiness for all men,
regardless of color or religion. He challenged "the
church to be the church" and to take evangelism beyond
the four walls of its sacred sanctuaries. He spoke of the
personal cost that he suffered, and warned that "if you
will be a Christian, it may be that you will be crucified on
your Calvary. . ."[70] Nevertheless, the delegates were
exhorted to "evangelize until men will live together as
brothers."[71]

In his concluding address, Billy Graham expressed his
fear that the evangelical reaction to liberalism in the
earlier half of this century tended to overemphasize the
vertical and forget the horizontal. As an illustration, he
told how in the southern United States he had seen
racism overcome in many integrated evangelistic
campaigns. He believed that the preaching of the Cross
as the everlasting Gospel has a "built-in power to
transform individuals and society." The man of God
must place his hope in God's plan for the world, and
should work and pray for permanent world peace,

but it's not going to be accomplished. It'll only be
accomplished when the Prince of Peace is reigning

as King of kings and Lord of lords. That's when
peace is going to come. And that will come by the
intervention of God once again in history in
supernatural power, when Christ comes back.[72]

In Minneapolis, the evangelicalism in this century was
built upon the apocalyptic hope of the visible bodily
return of Jesus Christ. It was not the anticipation of a
New Jerusalem in the United States, nor an idealistic
social activism that will usher in a utopian order of
restructured churches and governments. It was, rather,
an evangelism alert to its social responsibilities as
members of the human race created by God, and was
committed to the fulfillment of its evangelistic mandate
as churches "to whom much has been given." Revival
would bring the dynamic from the Holy Spirit to
evangelize. He would then bring His power through a
redeemed people to transform society and government.

A BLUNTING OF THE
CUTTING EDGE:
BOGOTÁ 1969

The First Latin American Congress on Evangelism
(CLADE) convened in Bogotá, Colombia, from
November 21-29, 1969. The Congress motto was "Action
in Christ for a Continent in Crisis." The theme was
evangelism, for the Congress was inspired by Berlin
1966. Billy Graham encouraged the Congress and, at the
request of the Latin American delegates at Berlin,
appointed Clyde Taylor and Ephraim Santiago to
organize it with an Executive Committee of fourteen
leaders in Latin America. There were 920 delegates from
twenty-five countries who met at the International Fair
Grounds in Bogotá. The prevailing language was
Spanish.[73]

CLADE took place at a very strategic time in Latin
America. The influence of the spirit of *aggiornamento*
developing out of Vatican II (1962-1965) was becoming
apparent in a new tolerance of Protestants that even led
to ecumenical overtures. Evangelicals were uncertain how

to adapt to the new biblical orientation of many within the Roman Church. Evangelism-in-Depth had increased interest in a more cooperative and aggressive evangelism, resulting in fruitfulness in some places and reaction in others. The growth of Pentecostalism in Latin America raised questions among Evangelicals regarding their own methods and doctrine of the Holy Spirit. In addition, the ecumenically oriented mainline denominations appeared to be building up a powerful regional organization which stressed ecumenical "evangelism."[74]

Incarnate evangelism. The most popular address of the Congress was that of Samuel Escobar, who declared that evangelical evangelism and social action were the responsibility of the Church.[75] Ruben Lores' two papers on reconciliation with Roman Catholics and the future of the charismatic movement in Latin America were the most controversial. The scholarly and studied paper by Emilio Antonio Núñez gave balanced perspective on evangelical attitudes toward both the Roman Catholic Church and the ecumenical movement.

In Escobar's position paper on "The Social Responsibility of the Church," he stated that he believed the inclusion of this subject on the agenda of the Congress is a sign of Christian maturity and "indicates a healthy change of attitude in evangelical ranks."[76] Because the Latin American Protestant churches had Anglo-Saxon pietist mission origins, he maintains, there is a misunderstanding that evangelism and social action contradict one another.[77] He concludes that

> any evangelism which does not take into consideration social problems and which does not proclaim the salvation and lordship of Christ within the context in which those who listen live, is a deficient evangelism which is traitor to biblical teaching and does not follow the example set forth by Christ, who sends us forth as evangels.[78]

These strong words contend that the evangelical pietistic separation from the world was made more acute

by the hostility of a Catholic or semipagan environment.
He questions the motives of those involved in evangelism
alone by declaring,

> Any concern for social and political issues came to
> be identified as an attempt to introduce a "social
> Gospel" and finally came to the point where lack of
> compassion and obedience were excused by an
> attitude of "defending the faith."[79]

Furthermore, he finds that the growth of denominations
and churches has *diminished* earlier evangelical sensitivity
to social needs. Of Latin America, even "the economic
and political solutions" which continued "in the beliefs of
our Anglo-Saxon brethren" did not work "in this
explosive situation."[80] Escobar, however, did not answer
the question of whether evangelical Christianity would
have arisen to its present numerical and spiritual stature
in Latin America, if his proposed social and political
involvement had been adopted. Nor has he refuted the
possibility that the proposed contemporary inclusion of
social and political action with evangelism as the mission
of the church may indicate its spiritual demise rather
than its maturity. For evangelism has traditionally
resulted in remarkable social and political
transformations when its mission remained evangelism.
Political and social changes in Latin America may be
attributed, as in Africa, to the evangelical subculture
necessary to initiate, support, and sustain more just and
equitable social and political structures. Escobar seemed
unwilling to admit the danger of blunting the evangelistic
edge, which enables the continued growth and influence
of Latin American evangelicalism. Unbelievers in an
alienated world with a heart and life alienated from God
cannot long stand with, or support, the unalienated social
and political justice of the Gospel introduced by
Evangelicals.

The final Evangelical Declaration of Bogotá approved
by the Congress called for the contextualized
proclamation of a total Gospel,

> Together we have recognized the necessity of living
> the Christian life to the full and proclaiming the
> total Gospel to the Latin American man in the
> context of his many needs.[81]

This approach was further amplified in terms of social
responsibility and evangelism as a process:

> The process of evangelization must occur in
> concrete human situations. Social structures have
> their influence on the Church and on those who
> receive the Gospel. If this fact is not recognized, the
> Gospel is betrayed and the Christian life
> impoverished. The time has come for us
> evangelicals to take seriously our social
> responsibility. In order to do this, we must build on
> a biblical foundation which implies evangelical
> doctrine and the example of Jesus Christ carried to
> its logical implications. Christ's example must
> become incarnated in the critical Latin American
> situation of underdevelopment, injustice, hunger,
> violence, and despair. Men cannot build the
> Kingdom of God on earth, but evangelical action
> will contribute toward the creation of a better world
> as a foreshadowing of that Kingdom whose coming
> we pray for daily.[82]

CLADE voted to appeal to Evangelicals to become
involved in social concern and action. It fell short of
stating that social and political involvement was part of
the mission of the Church. Some confusion certainly
would arise in the minds of the delegates, since the
biblical and theological foundations were not clear. For
example, what place does the ministry of the Spirit have
in His work "in, with, and by the Scriptures" to bring
men to Christ and salvation? To what extent is the
"incarnation" of Christ's example essential for Latin
America or anywhere else, when one looks primarily to
the power of the living Word, the Bible, to authenticate
the Truth, Christ Jesus?

Partial cosmic reconciliation now. In his paper, "Upon All Flesh," Ruben Lores describes the various charismatic manifestations in Latin America as classic Pentecostalism, "Pente-Protestantism, and Pente-Catholicism." He opposes propositional formulations when dealing with the Holy Spirit as a person, for He is not a thing, a doctrine, or a phenomenon. He implied that denominations and missions had established exclusive and dogmatic positions on the person and work of the Holy Spirit that threaten His freedom and sovereignty "in His present relationship with the Church and with the world."[83] Lores believed that Latin America would be threatened by a proliferation of schismatic sects, as in Africa, unless there was a new environment of freedom and love given by the Holy Spirit. The task of evangelism, he declared, would be hindered in its mobilization of all believers for an effective witness (Evangelism-in-Depth) because mission boards, Geneva-or-New York-tutored denominations, and even autochthonous churches, are not utilizing the power of the Spirit in His autochthonous charismatic manifestation in Latin America.

In another paper entitled "Reconciliation," Lores compared the unity between the Jewish and Gentile believers with the relationship that should exist between Roman Catholics and Evangelicals! He did not discuss the doctrinal unity of the Jewish and Gentile believers in Jesus as the Messiah, but looked rather to an ultimate cosmic dimension of reconciliation that seemed to justify a spirit of pluralism among all who call themselves Christians. Lores went further than that to entertain the ecumenical idea of a dynamic process whereby creation (mankind?) and the structures of society will be reconciled to God at least partially in the present age. But how and when does this take place?

> We know that it is "through the blood of his Cross." But this is only a partial answer and we need to know more. Undoubtedly the reconciliation of man includes certain eschatological aspects which will be the culmination of a process.[84]

Lores gave the impression of struggling to reconcile
the ecumenical position of the atonement in an
evangelical context. The death of Christ transcends
individual justification in this present age and applies to
the "justification" and "sanctification" of present social
and political structures as well. According to this view,
Christians should work toward the reconciliation of
society and politics with God. According to
evangelicalism, however, Christians—by the strength of
their presence in society—will be the salt that preserves
and purifies it, but society and politics under the
prince of this world cannot and will not be reconciled
until Christ returns. This return is contingent upon
proclamation evangelization (Matt. 24:14). The
uncertainty of Lores' soteriology and eschatology caused
this confusion in his ecclesiology and served,
unconsciously perhaps, to blunt the Latin American
understanding of what evangelicalism is. Wagner
reported this new problem.[85] Lores wrestled with the
ecumenical theology—and lost.

The extended hand from Rome. Emilio Núñez had the
delicate and demanding task of spelling out the position
Evangelicals should take toward the Roman Catholic
Church in his paper entitled "The Position of the
Church Toward Aggiornamento." He claimed that this
subject had been imposed on Evangelicals by the
socio-religious realities resulting in the post-Vatican II
conciliar church. A marked difference exists between the
preconciliar church in liturgy and biblical renewal.
Evangelicals could be most encouraged by the latter:

> Of all the changes in post-conciliar Catholicism
> there is none more promising of better things in the
> lives of thousands of Catholics than that related to
> the new attitude of the Roman Church toward the
> Sacred Scriptures. We must confide in the
> redeeming power of the Scriptural Revelation
> "Faith comes by hearing, and hearing by the Word
> of God," (Rom. 10:17).[86]

He believed that the renewal sought by John XXIII had
become a *revolution* threatening the very foundations of
traditional Catholicism.

Three well-defined tendencies have developed in
contemporary Catholicism:

> *First,* traditionalism that closes the door to any
> fundamental change in doctrine; *second,*
> progressivism with its concern to reinterpret
> Catholic doctrine and effect a basic transformation
> in the structure of the Church; and *third,* moderate
> Catholicism in the style of John XXIII, who wanted
> to renew the Church within the context of
> traditional theology.[87]

This inner struggle for self-renewal is further
complicated for Latin American Evangelicals by the
unexpected hand of ecumenical friendship extended by
the Catholics to the Protestants.[88] Evangelical churches
cannot, Núñez said, remain indifferent to this extended
hand.

Núñez then entered into the interevangelical debate
that begins with the confusion created in the mind of
one who is converted from Catholicism to Protestantism.
It is natural to ask, "If the Roman Catholic Church is our
sister, why was I invited to leave it to embrace
Protestantism?"[89] Some Protestants favor closer relations
with Rome; many others do not:

> Those who favor the ecumenical encounter
> say. . .that the Holy Spirit is moving in an unusual
> way in the Roman Church, and that the
> Evangelicals should be very careful in their
> anti-ecumenism, or they may be opposing the work
> of God. The other group asks if it is possible that
> the Spirit should approve an ecclesiastical relation
> that can compromise certain truths that He Himself
> has inspired. Besides, they say, if the Spirit has
> begun an extraordinary work among the Catholics,
> is it not certain that an anti-Biblical ecumenism
> would hinder it rather than help it?[90]

Supporters of the ecumenical dialogue affirm that
opposition to it demonstrates a serious lack of love
toward Catholics. Opponents say that out of love for
Catholics they desire to preserve the integrity of the
Gospel—and who has demonstrated more love (for in the
Scripture love is not divorced from truth) than those who
have given their lives as pioneers or martyrs in South
America?

> Another argument in favor of Catholic-Protestant
> ecumenism is the affirmation that the Perfect
> Church doesn't exist on the face of the earth. The
> reply to this argument is that although it is
> conceded that there is no perfect ecclesiastical
> community, this doesn't oblige anyone to unite with
> a Church whose errors are evident in the light of
> the Bible.[91]

Evangelical uncertainties about the future of Catholicism
should not pressure them into rejecting it, some say, for
it is not known what is going on inside. Others disagree
with the principle of "waiting," because there are norms
in God's Word "that guide the Church along paths of
right doctrine and morals, or must she depend only on
the march of human events to determine her way?"[92]
The path of evangelical relativism, Núñez fears, and "the
parenthesis of waiting may send many souls into an
eternity without God, without Christ, and without
hope. . . ."[93]

Aggiornamento should not lead to an unfounded
optimism that minimizes the postconciliar differences
and maximizes the similarities, for *aggiornamento* has not
ushered in any fundamental changes in questions of
tradition, authority of Scriptures, papal infallibility,
synergism, sacramentalism, mariology, purgatory, and
prayers for the dead. Other confessions are considered
incomplete, and Roman Catholicism is *"the Church* par
excellence" for "the *ecclesia semper reformanda* is also the
ecclesia semper eadem."[94] Núñez agreed with Francis
Schaeffer's belief that Roman Catholicism was moving
more and more toward a humanism that would make a

THE BATTLE FOR
WORLD EVANGELISM
262

relationship with ecumenical Protestantism more compatible. The latter affirms that it is "not necessary or even correct to evangelize Catholics" because "they are already incorporated into the redeemed community as a result of their baptism in the Catholic Church. . . ."[95]

The Evangelical must be positive in his teaching and practice but "relevant proclamation of the Christian Message includes also the clear and conclusive denunciation of error, wherever this threatens the life of the Church that Christ bought with His blood."[96] Individual friendships with Roman Catholics are to be encouraged but ecumenical dialogue was discouraged.

> In reality, to maintain burning in our hearts the flame of evangelistic zeal is one of the best antidotes against any theological or ecclesiastical movement that threatens the Church with paralysis in her missionary function.[97]

The official translation of the final "Evangelical Declaration of Bogotá" decided by a vote of the Congress that

> in a continent where the majority are nominal Catholics, we cannot shut our eyes to the ferment of renewal within the Church of Rome. The "aggiornamento" faces us up both with risk and opportunity: change in liturgy, ecclesiology, politics and strategy still leave untouched the dogmas which separate evangelicals from Rome. Nevertheless, our trust in the Word of God, the distribution and reading of which continue to accelerate within catholicism, cause us to hope for fruit of renewal, and they present us with an opportunity for dialogue on a personal level. This needs to be an intelligent dialogue, and it demands from our churches a deeper and more consistent teaching of our own evangelical heritage, so as to avoid the risks of a false and misunderstood ecumenism.[98]

CLADE opted to persevere in evangelism. CLADE's work would not terminate with the Bogotá evangelistic emphasis. An interim coordinating committee was named until the continental evangelism committee composed of 100 persons could elect an Executive Committee to coordinate future congresses. The continent was divided into six regions, with a regional congress to be held in one each year beginning with the 1970 Hispanic-American Congress, ultimately scheduled for October 27-November 1, 1970, at San Antonio, Texas. In 1976 a second CLADE in Brazil would become the first phase of a thirty-year plan for the total evangelization of Latin America.[99]

AN EVANGELISTIC ECCLESIOLOGY FOR EVANGELICAL MISSION — AMSTERDAM 1971

The Lausanne International Congress on World Evangelization was delayed until 1974 to enable Europeans to hold their European Congress on Evangelism from August 28-September 4, 1971, at Amsterdam, Holland. This fourth and final post-Berlin 1966 congress was sponsored by the European Evangelical Alliance and attracted 1064 participants from eighteen denominations in thirty-six European nations. Notably absent were representatives from East Germany and Russia. Of the participants, 462 were laymen and 120 were women; 565 were under forty years of age and 499 were forty or over. A minority were clergymen.[100] Official languages of the Congress were French, German, and English. No official religious body was represented at the Congress.[101]

Gilbert W. Kirby (England) and Peter Schneider (Germany) were the chairman and vice-chairman of the executive committee. Victor Nelson (USA) served as secretary and coordinator of the Congress. From the beginning of the Congress, it was made clear that the nature and validity of the Gospel were not open for debate since the participants were united in the essentials of the Christian message. A basic unity, consequently,

characterized the Congress, enabling the participants to
interact in Christian love and united action, concerning
the social implications of the Gospel, the need for
institutional flexibility to bridge the generation
communication gap, and the rediscovery of the
importance of the New Testament pattern of
person-to-person witnessing.[102]

The Statement of Purpose was simple and direct, and
was reflected throughout the program in the devotions,
papers, and workshops:

1. To reaffirm the fact that the Gospel of Jesus
   Christ is still the power of God unto salvation to
   all who believe.
2. To alert individual Christians to their personal
   responsibility to evangelism.
3. To recognize the social implications of the
   Gospel.
4. To seek ways and means of effective cooperation
   in evangelism in Europe.
5. To discover ways and means of communicating
   the eternal Gospel in the context of
   contemporary society.[103]

Amsterdam 1971 may be compared with the
pre-Amsterdam 1948 Conference on Evangelism held at
Geneva in February 1947. Since that predominately
evangelical meeting, Europe has come to be recognized
as secular, neo-pagan and post-Christian. Western
Europe had become the front line of evangelical defense
against non-Christian ideologies as well as conciliar
Christianity and secularism. Student riots and the drug
culture now marred the charm of the "old world." In
contrast with the "new world" of North America, with its
religious pluralism and volunteerism, and with the
younger churches of the Third World, the state churches
of Europe still dominated the religious scene—this in
spite of the rapidly growing secularism on the one hand
and the rise of non-Christian ideologies, and even
non-Christian religions, on the other hand. Post-World
War II affluence seemed to contribute to the prevailing

indifference to historic institutionalized Christianity.
Evangelicalism (not in the German sense) appears to be a
"remnant" theology hardly worthy of note in European
Christendom.

Ma Ma Maism in Europe. For this reason, Gerhard
Bergmann's position paper on "The Relevance of the
Gospel Today" was of special significance in explaining
the political or theological resistance to evangelical
evangelism encountered by the participants. He rejected
the unrealistic optimistic belief in the emancipation of
man based upon utopian visions:

> The intellectual content of this "principle of hope"
> and the euphoric vision of the future is largely
> *embedded in a neo-marxist ideology.* Three intellectual
> leaders, all starting with a capital M, are worshipped
> on a large scale: Marx, Marcuse, Mao. If you wish,
> you might speak today of "Ma Ma Maism."[104]

Man is neither free nor good, but selfish, sometimes
brutal, dependent, "and very limited and restricted in his
knowledge and will."[105] Liberation comes to man
individually through God and a knowledge of His will.
Consequently,

> The gospel is relevant today in that it keeps us from
> the illusion of a paradise-like future here in this
> age, which man might achieve by his own efforts. In
> contrast to this, the gospel directs our eyes to him
> who, by his return visibly, overcomes the powers of
> sin and death and thus brings to fulfillment his
> kingdom, in which justice and peace will finally be
> united. . . . That is our imminent future. But we
> cannot help feeling that this rose-coloured,
> optimistic, futuristic dream is, in the last analysis,
> escapism and evasion from a depressing fear in the
> light of the horrible possibilities of permanently
> rising armaments, mass weapons of destruction and
> space bombs.[106]

Jesus Christ is the Lord of the world; He is our
unshakable certainty and we may live by His promises.

Therefore we can be certain that the future under
the sceptre of Jesus Christ will be that sin, death
and the devil will be overcome.[107]

Man without Christ is already lost: a decision is necessary.
Henri Blocher said that "The Lost State of Man" was
twofold: first, man has lost his way and severed his tie
with the "father's home." He is without guidance and an
easy prey to all possible ideologies. Second, he is
condemned and in a lost state comparable to death (Luke
15:24), to destruction, and to damnation. He must be
saved, for he is already lost. Many preachers, Blocher
said, falsely deduce that by the incarnation the lost state
has ceased to exist. The Barthian insistence that salvation
is completed in Christ and granted to each man whether
he knows it or not is a seductive interpretation for many.
For these preachers,

evangelism is no longer a rescue operation but
rather the declaration of the news that deliverance
has already taken place. It is simply the
communication of joy in the light of knowledge.[108]

Barth had rejected the view that a decision must be
added to the work of God in salvation. This is an
unwarranted addition to grace, he felt. Blocher insisted
that to accept the work of Christ upon the cross is not to
add to it. "Faith is the fruit of the Spirit" and faith adds
nothing to grace for faith is also a gift (Eph. 2:8).

To separate faith from salvation as the new
universalists do, means to juggle away the original
role of the holy ghost (sic) and to sin against the
Trinitarian distinction. It is also to de-personalize
the covenant-relationship. God did not want to
include us automatically in Christ. He wants us as
responsible partners and he allows us to enter his
kingdom by bringing us to a place of decision. . . .[109]

Expect great things from God. Billy Graham, the only
non-European to speak at Amsterdam, was concerned
about the millions of professing Christians who have
never entered into real fellowship with Jesus Christ. The
Church itself was one of the most fruitful fields for
evangelism. He found that one of the great problems for
evangelism is the relationship between baptism,
confirmation, and conversion.

> Many Anglicans, Lutherans, Orthodox and Roman
> Catholic clergy have agreed that those within the
> church need "converting" even after baptism and
> confirmation.[110]

If confirmation is rightly understood and applied, it can
become conversion, but for tens of thousands baptism
and confirmation are only a "form."

> They have led many to believe that they need no
> further experience and in many cases no further
> relationship with God until they get married and go
> to the church for marriage, or until they die, and
> go to the church for the funeral.[111]

Graham urged that the Gospel be proclaimed in
Europe with authority, simplicity, and urgency. It is the
message and the life behind it that really counts, and this
message is relevant to each generation.

> This gospel is not a set of ideas to be discussed; it is
> a declaration. What the gospel needs, the early
> church concurred, was not a philosopher, but a
> witness—not a lawyer but a herald![112]

He implied that the Holy Spirit was able to use the
simple message of the Gospel and transcend the human
communication gaps so that it was contextualized to
widen social, educational, and age groups:

> When I preach the gospel, I do not have one
> message for the intellectuals and another for the
> simpleminded. When I first started out as an

evangelist I thought I had to tailor my message to various groups. I soon learned by experience that I was not to speak to a working man as a working man or to an intellectual as an intellectual, or to a black man as a black man or a white man as a white man. I spoke to them as men and women who had sinned against God and were in need of a Saviour.[113]

Europeans were encouraged to expect a "new and great and mighty thing" in Amsterdam that would begin a new era of evangelism in Europe. As William Carey preached, so the Amsterdam participants were to "expect great things from God. Attempt great things for God."[114]

Personal salvation precedes service. Racism, unjust economic practices, and the needs of others, Paavo Kortekangas said, are the areas of Christian social concern. Nevertheless, the winning of people to Christ must be the one passion of Christians. Then those who have experienced personal salvation in Christ have a new impetus for reforming society, for their love goes beyond the Christian community to those who are outsiders. "The history of 'diakonia' shows that unselfish serving began and was strongest where personal salvation had been received."[115] Christianity, consequently, through successful evangelism had raised the cultural level, revived the arts and sciences, and stimulated national economies. But he affirmed, "It is not possible to reform society without renewing the individual."[116] The Christian life after conversion is not one of idle waiting for the new heaven and earth promised by God, but

a time for spreading the gospel and carrying out God's will. This sinful world is the place where we are to live as Christians and which we are to try to reform by the power of the Holy Spirit, and through the courage arising from our faith.[117]

Christians cannot, or should not, try to make a heaven out of this world.

The Holy Spirit is the chief evangelist. John Stott spoke to
the primary place of the Holy Spirit in evangelism:

> For the Holy Spirit is himself the chief evangelist,
> the chief witness, the chief communicator of the
> gospel. . .Evangelism is the witness of God the
> Father to God the Son, through God the Holy
> Spirit.[118]

He saw the absence of evangelism as an evidence that the
Holy Spirit is at least paralyzed—if not entirely
absent—in the self-contained inward-looking church, for
it is the nature of the Spirit to transmit life in
ever-widening circles.

Stott proposes that the visual nonverbal community of
Christians is used by the Spirit to communicate the
Gospel. Their demonstrations of Christian love must
always be interpreted by words. Here, Stott was
grappling with the ecumenical "presence theology" and
endeavoring to show that there is a place for "visual
communication," but that it must always be accompanied
by "verbal proclamation."

Stott could be misunderstood regarding the place and
value of contemporary evangelistic crusades, as he
rightfully rejected its abuses:

> With the development of modern psychology and
> the use of psychological knowledge in advertising
> (both over- and sub liminal), in propaganda, in the
> deliberate inducement of mass hysteria, and in the
> most wicked assault on the human personality called
> "brainwashing," we Christians make it clear beyond
> all doubt that evangelism is an entirely different
> kind of activity. We refuse to bludgeon people into
> the kingdom of God by human pressures.[119]

He said that the work of the Holy Spirit in evangelism
may not be replaced by a human manipulation, which
violates the personality of the individual. Nor does the
Holy Spirit "bludgeon" people. We are helpless to
convert people by ourselves, and must reject pressure

techniques. A public decision, as a human response to the Gospel, would appear to be inappropriate if, as Stott says, "it is true that conversion is the work of God and is frequently represented in scripture in terms which seem to eliminate the need for any human response."[120] Stott affirms that the evangelist is to communicate the Gospel. This Gospel, God's Word, is the instrument of the Holy Spirit in evangelism. He concludes that the Holy Spirit is the chief evangelist, and the work of conversion is essentially the Holy Spirit's work. Evangelism is the witness of God the Father to God the Son through God the Holy Spirit. The church in Europe needs to "let God be God and to look again to the Holy Spirit for power."[121] In all likelihood, Stott was reacting to the debate in the DWME (WCC) on conversion which tended to relegate "conversion to a *recognition* (of what has already been done) rather than *repentance and faith* in Christ."

Believers only: evangelical ecclesiology in Europe. The most significant contribution at Amsterdam 1971 was that of Carl Wisløff of Norway on "The Church, Its Nature and Mission." He affirmed that the biblical view of the Church is that of the *people* of God, of believers who are "living stones," and not of a building—in which people sit—or of an institution:

> The church is a building that is built up of believers as living stones! The walls do not enclose the faithful, but rather the faithful are the walls. No one.knows the exact number of stones in that spiritual house. And yet I can tell you one thing: in God's living church on earth there are as many stones as there are living hearts that believe in Jesus as their Saviour. Not a single one more, not a single one less![122]

Luther explained the nature of the Church by the text "I am the good shepherd. My sheep hear my voice and I know them, and they follow me (John 10:11-27)." Calvin was quoted as saying that "the Lord furnished us with an unfailing test when he said, 'I am the good shepherd, and I know my sheep, and am known of mine (Inst. IV. 2:4).' "[123] The church, then, is a fellowship of believers "added" (Acts 2:47) by an act of God's grace through belief in the Gospel, and the ministry of the Holy Spirit.

The unity of this fellowship of believers is created by the one true Gospel of Christ and the unity of the Trinity. There is *one* Church, the body of Christ (Eph. 1:23; 4.16), which is His bride (Rev. 21:9)

> The Christian church consists of people who believe in Christ, people who have faith and the Holy Spirit in their hearts. There are many denominational bodies, but there is only one Christian Church, the body of Christ.[124]

Wisløff stated that this position is consistent with an article of faith, and that the oneness and unity of the body prevail in spite of the objections raised by a bishop, who deplored the divisions of the church and claimed the one Christian Church does not exist for the time being. Wisløff replied,

> We do not need to be that pessimistic. It exists all right! It can be found. God sees it. Christ knows it and loves it. It is his body. It is composed of all who are living in faith in Christ on earth and in heaven. . . . No single church, no single denomination or organized body can claim to be identical with that church which is the body of Christ. The body of Christ consists of all those who believe in Christ and have accepted him as their personal saviour—that is the church of God.[125]

True church unity is not achieved by joining together organized church bodies, nor is the witness of large organized church bodies more effective in evangelism than that of smaller ones.

> An ocean liner might not be very suitable for fishing purposes. Unity in the Spirit is one thing,

unification is another. If all of Christendom were
united in one single church organization, this would
still not be the only holy Christian Church we
confess in the Apostles' Creed.[126]

The essential question today is, "Who are the Church?"
The answer is not found in beautiful buildings, great
scholars, eloquent speakers, numerous clergymen, or
large congregations. The crux of the matter is: "Is the
Word of God proclaimed, are sinners called to
repentance, and believers admonished to lead a Christian
life according to the Word of God?"[127]

Wisløff related the duty and function of the church to
its nature:

> The true church lives by the word of God. Its
> mission is to proclaim the word of God. . .(Matt.
> 28:18, 19). . .The people of God are sent to
> proclaim the gospel. . .(2 Cor. 5:20). . .This is the
> great commission: to preach the gospel, the word of
> God, to all nations, and so to call all men to repent
> and believe in Christ. This is God's great plan for
> the salvation of sinners. . .(Acts 15:14). . .That is the
> mission of the church. God is visiting all nations
> making one people of those who will believe in his
> blessed name. Our commission is to preach the
> gospel.[128]

Two consequences flow from this evangelistic
proclamation mission in the light of the concept of
"presence" theology. First, the presence of a Christian
can never replace his verbal witness, for "there is no
salvation in meeting me as a Christian."[129] Second, there
is a life to be lived in the world that does not conform to
the world, because Christians are God's people living as
foreigners in this world (1 Peter 4:4).

The Christian moral standards of previous centuries
no longer exist in Europe, but Christians must remain
true to God's standards.

> If they join in with the world, and the way the
> world lives, Christianity will disappear from Europe

as a drop of clean water on blotting-paper, and
Christ will remove our lampstand from its place.[130]
Wisløff quotes Gregory Nazianzus, (335-394) who wrote
concerning his devotion to the Church and education
during his student days in Athens:

> We knew only two streets of the city, the first and
> most excellent one to the churches—the other to
> the schools and teachers of science. The streets to
> the theatres, games and places of unholy
> amusement, we left to others. We didn't even know
> them.[131]

So the Christian must be prepared to be alone and to be
different from the world.

Wisløff called European Christianity back to the
spiritual nature of the Church, essential to its renewal for
biblical evangelism. He recognized the Church's pilgrim
character which looks forward to a better country as a
citizen of heaven, without retreating from dual
citizenship in one's own country on earth. He respected
the institutional manifestation of the Church without
surrendering the biblical soteriology of the necessity of a
personal and living faith which transcends
sacramentalism.[132] Wisløff had reached the heart of the
historical errors that have hindered the revival of the
nominal Christianity imposed on the populations of
medieval Europe by "mass conversion." Christianity
became the "opiate" of the people, because social conduct
was not sustained by a regenerate populace but rather by
a hierarchical sacramentalism. With a breakdown in
ecclesiastical authority—as in the Roman Catholicism of
Western Europe, or the decimated authority of the
Scripture in Protestantism and the Anglican Church—the
vacuum of authority opened the door to rampant
secularism and non-Christian ideologies. Wisløff
concluded that faithfulness to the Word of God and to
the true nature of the Church, as a professing
evangelizing community, were the only road back to
revival and renewal in a neo-pagan Europe, threatened
by atheism and engulfed in materialism.

ANOTHER GOSPEL WITH ANOTHER MISSION— BANGKOK 1973

The utter contrast between Amsterdam 1971 and the World Conference on "Salvation Today" called by the Commission of World Mission and Evangelism of the WCC (Dec. 29, 1972—Jan. 8, 1973) is readily apparent. If the Fourth Assembly of the WCC at Uppsala 1968 had established "another gospel," this conference codified "another mission" for the ecumenical and conciliar movement. The Bangkok 1973 theology of mission and missiology required a theological response from Evangelicals, a response which was given by the International Congress on World Evangelization at Lausanne in 1974.

The importance of Bangkok 1973 resided in the fact that this was the first full expression of the conciliar theology of mission in the WCC. The Mexico 1963 meeting was still feeling its way in expressing the new ecumenical theology of evangelism—because of the recent integration with the International Missionary Council at the WCC Third Assembly at New Delhi 1961, and because of the avowed large "conservative" voice of Eastern Orthodoxy which had joined the WCC at New Delhi. As in the almost "revelatory" nature of the Conference on Church and Society at Geneva 1966 regarding the work of God in non-Christian ideologies, of the Uppsala 1968 Assembly on the concern of God that His Church restructure society by revolution if necessary, and by the Louvain 1971 Faith and Order meeting on the problem of conciliar hermeneutics or interpretation of the Bible, so God would continue to "speak" to the 325 carefully selected delegates—co-opted delegates and consultants—which included sixteen Roman Catholics, twenty-seven women, and sixteen youth.[133] Undisguised desire for the inclusion of Roman Catholics and conservative Evangelicals among the ranks

of the CWME and the WCC permeated the preparations
and proceedings.

The vigorous ecumenical-evangelical debate at
Bangkok had its historical roots in the pre-Edinburgh
1910 debates in the Student Volunteer Movement
provoked by nineteenth-century liberalism.[134] A revived
and revised "Salvation Today" concept was contained in
the Oxford 1937 Life and Work Conference, now
entitled "Let the Church be the Church," drafted by J.
H. Oldham and William Temple, and developed from a
document originally written by John MacKay of
Princeton. In the 1957 Report of the General Secretary,
W. A. Visser 't Hooft explained,

> This phrase, 'Let the Church be the Church,' has
> sometimes been misunderstood as if it meant 'Let
> the Church stick to its own internal affairs.' That is
> a completely wrong exegesis. What was meant was:
> 'Let the Church be what it was called to be: the
> community of the new age, the spear-head of the
> Kingdom of God, the voice and the instrument of
> the Lord who is King, Priest and Prophet.' For the
> Oxford and Edinburgh (1937) Conferences were
> held at a time when the Church, after a long period
> of relative calm, was openly and aggressively
> challenged by anti-Christian totalitarian ideologies.
> And this challenge could only be met with a
> rediscovery and re-affirmation of the all-embracing
> claim of Jesus Christ as Lord. 'Let the Church be
> the Church' in the context of that year was a call to
> the renewal of the Church and to a more faithful
> fulfilling of its whole calling in and to the world."[135]

Jürgen Moltmann, influenced by Ernst Bloch, "a
Marxist with a Bible in his hand,"[136] developed his own
political hermeneutics and became one of the leading
theological contributors to the political theology of
Bangkok. Moltmann's "creative eschatological hope" was
founded upon Bloch's concept of "historical activity in
the sphere of that-which-is-not-yet (*des Noch-Nicht-Seins*)."
In the absence of an evangelical eschatology, it seems

that Moltmann resisted the existential tendency of his
day to live only for the moment, but he directed the
"open future" toward a "hope" that is action-oriented:

> Christian eschatology has to maintain a constant
> question mark and keep the future open, in order
> that man will not take life as it comes (in *den Tag
> hinein leben*), but will "live for more than the
> moment" (*uber den Tag hinaus leben*).[137]

Moltmann traced the development of his hermeneutics
from the historical relativism of Wilhelm Dilthey to the
existential hermeneutics of Sören Kierkegaard and from
the *kerygma* of Rudolf Bultmann to the revolutionary
hermeneutics of the young Karl Marx and, finally, to his
own political hermeneutics. Theology should criticize
history and its institutions:

> Theology serves future freedom to the degree that
> it prepares the way for it in historical criticism, in
> ideological criticism and, finally, in criticism of
> institutions.[138]

Moltmann followed what Karl Marx had said about
praxis—that philosophers would be unable to reach a
correct interpretation of the world without becoming
involved in the process of engagement with the world. As
a respectable theologian, he committed himself to action.
God is present, Moltmann believed, in revolution. But
for him, revolution was different from evolution, or
reform, because it was "a transformation of a
system—whether of economics, of politics, of morality, or
of religion."[139] He believes that new possibilities are
occurring that enable the Christian and people in general
to make a qualitative improvement of the present.
Moltmann strongly contributed to the South American
"national" theology of liberation that was predominant
and encouraged at Bangkok. The dramatic difference
between evangelical "hope" and ecumenical "hope"
would be seen in the Lausanne presentation of
Moltmann's professional colleague at Tübingen, Peter
Beyerhaus.

The first draft in 1968 of "Salvation Today"
unhesitatingly delineated the ecumenical-evangelical
tension as it considered the objective of Section I:

> The Section's point of departure is the
> disagreement between those who plead for an
> unreserved involvement of Christians at all points
> of tension in modern society for the sake of a
> greater humanization of life, and those who ask for
> a faithful proclamation of the salvation offered by
> God in Christ so that as many as possible may be
> saved.[140]

In the Canterbury Consultation, Potter said that he
desired to "bring the debate to full expression" in
1972.[141]

In 1971, Potter defended his view of the "fundamental
crisis in mission" in the WCC which the evangelical
"Frankfurt Declaration" had exposed. He attempted to
dismiss the differences with Evangelicals as largely that
of a Western cultural expression of theology which
causes confusion in the understanding of the Gospel
among other Third World cultures.[142] On another
occasion, however, Potter recognized that the real debate
began on the theological level at Jerusalem 1928—a
taking of the best in non-Christian religions and
crowning it with Christianity, in contrast to those who
completely reject them and take Christ alone.[143] The
debate was an old one, and clearly defined by Potter.

Walter Hollenweger, as Director of Evangelism,
DWME, bluntly questioned whether personal conversion
and piety were essential:

> Is personal piety and conversion a pre-condition for
> Christian social engagement? Is an explicit
> confession of Christ a conditio sine qua non for the
> unity of the church, if not for the unity of
> mankind?[144]

The continued controversy was reflected by a
"Resolution on Conservatives," approved by the recently

structured Program Unit I—Faith and Witness. This
report, which was not forwarded to the Central
Committee, gave

> serious attention to the Christians, who, because of
> "conservative" theological conviction, are not in
> sympathy with some contemporary trends in the
> ecumenical movement. Whether Orthodox or
> Evangelical, many of these are communicants of
> member churches of the World Council of
> Churches while others belong to churches which are
> not members.[145]

Consequently, the committees and staff of the sub-units
were instructed

> to keep in mind the implications of these continuing
> disagreements and to maintain communication and
> dialogue between Christians who represent a
> diversity of perspectives and convictions on the
> issues with which they are obliged to deal.[146]

The Unit recommended to the Central Committee that,
in view of the differing theological positions, Bangkok
keep "before it those millions who as individuals and
groups do not yet know and confess Jesus Christ, and
who seek salvation in their own setting."[147] This concern
of the WCC found little expression at Bangkok. It
seemed that the Geneva staff reinterpreted the New
Delhi 1961 CWME constitution—"to further the
proclamation to the whole world of the Gospel of Jesus
Christ, to the end that all men may believe in him and be
saved"—toward an entirely different orientation of
mission. Instead of providing "an opportunity for
working together with the churches and groups not
associated with the World Council but which share a
concern for mission," as the Central Committee
hoped,[148] conservative Evangelicals were confronted with
a theological "synthesis of opposites" which they could
not approve.[149]

Preparation for the subject "Salvation Today" began

four years before the actual meeting. The theological
preparation is recorded by Thomas Wieser in the
IRM.[150] He recognized that the Conservative Evangelical
debate was a continual issue during the entire conference
when he explained the "substance and basis" of the
ecumenical faith:
1. *"The Bible, tradition and 'Salvation Today.'"* Weiser went
to the heart of the issue by recognizing "how the Bible
(is) to be understood as norm and authority for the
contemporary affirmation of salvation in Christ." He
refers to the Dutch group who found authority in the
Scripture because of a *cantus firmus,* a continuing theme
in the biblical history, whereby "the unity of the theme
and the continuity of this in history provide the power
and the authoritative basis on which to proclaim and
believe in salvation."[151]

Having conceded a central continuing theme, the next
question arises as to whether biblical history, including
the death and resurrection of Jesus, applies to us today.
That is, can we depend upon the validity of this history?
A report from Tübingen's Ecumenical Seminar found
only a *qualitative* difference between the history of the
Bible and other history, because the biblical story and
"the revelation of His plan of salvation can only be found
in the particular history of His people Israel and the
founding of the Church of Jesus Christ."[152] The
uniqueness of the story of the Bible, however,
accentuates "the discontinuity between the biblical story
and our historical situation today."[153] This raised the
question as to whether the Bible has normative authority
over Christian life and mission today.

European theology had been preoccupied by the
difference between the normative *content* of the Gospel
message as recorded in the Bible and the *form* of its
presentation which "might be allowed to differ according
to time and circumstances."[154] This separation between
the message and the text endeavors to avoid certain,
literal interpretation of the Scripture. It allows for some
alterations in what the text says, and so far as what truly
happened in history, it allows greater breadth of

interpretation. Nevertheless, this hermeneutical concept was rejected because of the resultant ambiguity in the text and in the biblical doctrines of the atonement, adoption, and justification. But Wieser's explanation for the content and form hermeneutic has further implications. The whole scheme was seen as a philosophical tradition of Western or European Christianity and as a part of Western theological culture! It may "be useful in some, but not in other, parts of the world." By this last statement, European theology said that the Bible does not have normative standards that apply throughout the world. Each nation must apply the Bible according to its own needs. This position justified the introduction of "national theologies" into ecumenical thought. The core of evangelical belief, however, united on a common understanding of Scripture, which is applicable to national needs in every continent. Ecumenical theology, however, found itself more divided than ever.

This rejection had not been consistently applied. When Peter Beyerhaus questioned Philip Potter's report as general secretary of DWME as to why mention was not made of the Wheaton Declaration, the World Congress on Evangelization, and the Frankfurt Declaration, Jacques Rossel replied that this was because there is "a conflict between two biblical interpretations. . .it is a hermeneutical problem similar to that found in the Reformation."[155] Rossel's reply very accurately and specifically recognizes (1) the basic hermeneutic differences encountered by those with divergent views on the authority of the Scripture and the authoritative traditions of the Church. (2) It was also tacit rejection of the principles of interpretation governing the early Church councils and the sixteenth-century Reformation authority of *sola scriptura*. The WCC had adopted a non-Protestant moderating position on authority of Scripture, in theological preparation for the entry of the Roman Catholic church.

This view is further supported as Wieser discusses "The Role of Tradition." Since the admission of the

Eastern Orthodox churches, this question had already shifted the conciliar movement toward a more committed stance on the relationship between the Church and the Scripture.[156] For our present consideration, it is sufficient to note the rising role of the Church as the ecumenical interpreter of the Scripture. Wieser admits that

> the question of the norms concerns not only the Bible but also the Church's tradition, in fact the two are for many inseparable. The tradition, based on scripture, can be drawn upon to serve as norm.[157]

It is this total Tradition of the Church which constitutes the authority by which the consensus theology of the conciliar movement is developed and codified from conference to conference, assembly to asssembly.
2. *"Salvation in/and history."* Liberation theology became the current orientation of this decade in ecumenical life. On the basis of the cosmic Christ, the entire creation has been saved, or is in the "cosmic process" of being saved. An attempt was made *not* to identify the personal/individual realm with the communal, political, historical salvation and humanization. The "humane level" and the "whole of history is the battlefield between the forces of God's kingdom and the demons. . .a part of the history of salvation or the history of the evil on earth."[158] Based upon incarnation theology, the work of God in redemption is not seen as opposing creation, but should "be seen as a completion and a perfection of the creation."[159] On this ground, the humanization of society was theologically justified as evangelism.

Since little need remains for the final eschatological *redemption* and *restoration* of creation, Wieser explains that through the leadership of the Church this present mission is "by no means a purely secular or this worldly process."[160] After interpreting the mission of the Church in this way, Wieser hastened to add, "But we should at least be freed from the pietistic concept of salvation as primarily a private affair between the individual and

God."[161] Evangelical evangelism was theologically and categorically renounced. According to the theologians of the CWME of Bangkok, the Cross has universally saved both humanity and man's social environment. All will be saved some day and the ecumenical task is to work toward both. But in any case, the evangelical understanding of the salvation of individuals is not for today.

3. *"Salvation and the Church."* After decades of strong emphasis upon the Church as a "saving community," the contemporary focus upon the cosmic Christ, anti-institutionalism, and the Church's own need of renewal led the DWME studies to speak of the "predicament of the Church" and its "credibility gap." God works *outside* of the Church, and the role of the Church has now become the "responsibility to identify and support all secular movements which contribute to the completion and perfection of creation and to the full development of mankind according to the image of God."[162]

4. *"Salvation and situation."* The problem of this new mission of the Church within socialist states, such as the German Democratic Republic, increased with the rising atheism represented in cultural and political revolutions. Wieser proposes that God is in this and other liberation movements. He has sent these political "saviors" to direct them in their deliverance from colonialism. These social liberation movements are acts of God that Christians are not to oppose, for "the refusal to accept the new historic situation as given by God inhibits the articulation in new ways of the Christian hope and proclamation of salvation."[163] "Salvation Today" at Bangkok was prepared horizontally, not vertically.

The report of Philip Potter, as director of the CWME (1967-1972), gave almost undivided attention to the humanitarian aspect of missions today. He reviewed the context in which mission takes place in the world with its political divisions, economic inequities, racism, and violence, and cavalierly declared that the debate concerning the proclamation of the Gospel to the two billion, or to other lands, or to the whole world, "is totally futile."[164] He dismissed the Mexico City 1963 concerns over secularization because "man was coming of age and the Christian faith had to be reinterpreted to allow for a God who is in the midst of history rather than beyond it."[165] On the contrary, Potter saw secularization as "thoroughly biblical in its emphasis."[166] Secularization, he said, is the process by which man exercises control over nature, and this is substantiated by two new biblical insights. The first is that ". . .man should become responsible for himself and for his neighbor, and not place the blame on nature or on his heritage, or call on God in desperation to fill in the gaps, or be a *Deus ex machina.* . . ." The other biblical insight is "man's inveterate tendency to treat his own creations as transcendent, permanent realities, and to make idols of them which he worships and invests with eternity."[167] The secular world is an arena in which the Christian is to act, not one from which he should withdraw. He observes that the language of salvation has been used in the cultural revolutions in China, and he considers it to be a

> conscious and determined experiment. . .to change radically the character of a whole people towards ends of community responsibility. This same process in Latin America is called *conscientization,* the means by which people become conscious of themselves as human beings capable of shaping their destiny and of doing so for the common good.[168]

The role of mission in the present rise of "submerged peoples" in so-called "mission lands," calls for a change in the policies governing the International Missionary Council since its beginnings in 1921. These changes involve the pain of theological and ecclesiological controversy, because of the struggle between national denominational bodies and their national churches, but "we dare not look or go back."[169] He called for a complete break with the missionary past, and a change in the whole understanding of mission. Consequently,

methodologies of mission must change, because "we live
in a religiously and culturally pluralistic world
undergoing rapid changes."[170] Instead of the
confrontation of traditional witness and proclamation,
dialogue should be "the major element in witnessing to
our faith."[171] Proclamation evangelism was categorically
rejected again.

M. M. Thomas, chairman of the WCC Control
Committee, described "Salvation Today" as:

1. bodily health and beauty of bodily form for the
   youth.
2. development of material abundance.
3. security from aggression and peace of the
   frontier between peoples.
4. social justice among the people.[172]

As a spiritual being, man is to experience self-realization.
Thus the Christian mission is primarily concerned

> with the salvation of human spirituality, with man's
> right choices in the realm of self-transcendence, and
> with structures of ultimate meaning and
> sacredness—not in any pietistic or individualistic
> isolation, but related to and expressed within the
> material, social and cultural revolution of our
> time.[173]

Even more radical, however, were Thomas' statements
regarding the future place of the church. He questioned
whether the church should be a separate religious
community among the non-Christian religions:

> But it is a moot question whether the fellowship
> should be a separate religious community among
> others, where most of the primary levels of social
> living of the believers are confined to the Christian
> circle, where there is even a Christian law governing
> their conduct and recognized by the State, as is the
> case today in many countries of Asia, and certainly
> in India.[174]

He recommended that Christians become new sects
within "the movements of cultural creativity and social
liberation" rather than trying to bring about one
organized church that threatened to make several small
ghettos become one large ghetto and so not influence the
structures of society! In earlier years the International
Missionary Council spoke of the *problems* of missions,
then before integration Dr. Freytag of Ghana 1958
began to speak of missions as *the problem,* and now the
new theology of evangelism has led Thomas from
considering the *problems of the church* to *the church* as a
problem!

The "Report of the Commission on World Mission and
Evangelism 1963-1973" provided a kaleidoscopic view of
Commission activities around the world. Of particular
interest was the little growth in church unions during
this period, the weakening of the institutional churches
of the West, the penetration of the WCC into Latin
American Pentecostalism, and the relatively small growth
rate (82 percent) of NCCC/DOM-related bodies in the
USA since 1945, as compared with Evangelical
Associations (270 percent) and unaffiliated groups (900
percent).

THE DECISIONS
OF BANGKOK

Decisions are divided into two categories—those
expressing the theological trends of the Conference, and
the binding decisions of the Assembly of the Commission
which were influenced by the Conference.

The Section I Report from the Conference on Culture
and Identity said that white racism has deprived other
cultures of their own identity, and, therefore, foreign
models of conversion are not to be copied, because one's
social and cultural identity are divine gifts. The West is
not to determine what is theologically acceptable for a
Christian community in a particular place at a particular
time. Theology will be contextual.

The description of evangelical conversion was rejected

because "in order to express this experience one has to seek other ways of communication than just report-language."[175] Conversion introduces people into the Christian community, whose structure varies from one culture to another. As "personal conversion always leads to different forms of social action," so a group growing "almost inevitably enters into full civic life at the local level."[176] As the group gains political power through growth, it may align itself with either political conservatives or progressives. The community should not be a counter-culture for this would cut it off from the communities of men of which it is a part.[177] Recognition is given to charismatic groups, with which the traditional groups can live and witness together.

The Section II Report on "Salvation and Social Justice" provided more balance to "salvation" than Section I, by giving a primary and equal attention to the soul and the body, to the individual and society, mankind and "the groaning creation" (Rom. 8:19).[178] While the personal and individual conception of salvation in this section is conditioned by the interpretation of Section I, the salvation of the soul does not seem to be ruled out completely. The church is to initiate social action in liberating people:

1. from exploitation to economic justice
2. from oppression to human dignity
3. from alienation to solidarity
4. from despair to hope.[179]

"Churches Renewed in Mission" in the Section III Report[180] served to fragment the strong institutional systems which bind the Third World churches to international denominations such as the centralized Eastern Orthodox and Roman Catholic churches, or the world confessional bodies.

The local congregation should have a steady "Conscientization" in joint preparation for the action of mission in the life of the world. Local churches operating freely in ecumenical mission will become "agents of catholicity." A foreigner or a foreign worker in another

church represents the catholicity of the church and the
wholeness of the world. This also prevents the church
from becoming self-sufficient and inward-looking. Even
the sending churches are themselves deficient without
the witness and presence of the foreigner. Ways and
means are to be sought for the missionary exchange to
be completely mutal and international.[181] Yet each
church is free to be itself within its own national and
cultural milieu, and thus they are to acknowledge their
interdependence within the world Christian fellowship.

One of the significant theological developments was
the definite way in which European theology—and
especially higher criticism of the Bible—was dethroned
by a rejection of Western theology and the adoption of
national theologies. Dr. Jacques Rossel said, "If we take
cultural identity seriously, then we will have somehow to
break away from Anglo-Saxon ecumenism."[182] This may
have indicated the beginning of the end of higher
criticism since this apparently has met with little success
in Eastern Orthodox tradition, but made some inroads
into Vatican II declarations.

Efforts to give the "Evangelicals" or "Conservative
Evangelicals" within the WCC a voice in all decisions
were emphasized, yet the document warned that there
may be contradictory areas unacceptable to the WCC:

> It is the aim of the World Council of Churches to
> be fully representative of all ecclesiastical and
> theological positions *which are consistent with its basis.*
> (italics mine)[183]

Evangelicals are concerned, of course, that the Basis is
too inclusive. Meetings had been held with evangelical
leaders, and mention was made of the debate with
conservative Evangelicals that took place at Uppsala in
Section II. A careful study of the Bangkok 1973
documents and decisions, however, leads to the inevitable
conclusion that an evangelical synthesis or theological
concessions are either illusory or hypocritical for
ecumenical theology does not begin with an infallible
Bible—nor end with a biblical Gospel.[184]

7 Let the Earth Hear His Voice

The magnitude and significance
of the Lausanne, Switzerland, International Congress on
World Evangelization, July 16-25, 1974, overwhelms the
careful student of the history of Christianity. Its
theological depth was not only apparent in the plenary
papers, but also evident throughout the Congress and,
especially, in the Lausanne Covenant. The ethnic and
national diversity become apparent when it is
remembered that 2,700 participants gathered from more
than 150 nations, necessitating translation into a
minimum of six languages. This denominational diversity
revealed evangelicalism as a significant unifying element
in Christendom. The logistic and financial dimensions of
such a gathering required thorough preparation and
outstanding leadership.

The Lausanne Covenant will remain the outstanding
document of the Congress. Leadership in the major
branches of Christendom have considered seriously its
contents, and the World Council of Churches brought it
to the attention of the Fifth Assembly delegates at
Nairobi 1975. As a document, it defined, in a large
measure, evangelicalism within and without the conciliar
movement today. Historically, it may have been very
representative of a great majority of those who were at

the World Missionary Conference at Edinburgh 1910. While it is not a doctrinal statement, it stands in the best traditions of pietism, revivalism, and evangelicalism. Theologically, it has reasserted the authority and inspiration of Scripture, two bulwarks of apostolic and historical Christianity. While it was especially weak in not speaking to the great issue of "Tradition" as it related to Roman Catholicism, Eastern Orthodoxy, and the Church of England, this *lacuna* made its contents more acceptable to these bodies.[1] Non-conciliar-minded Evangelicals may be more concerned by this omission.

Lausanne 1974 was conceived as a "process" rather than as an isolated event.[2] The intent of this objective is understood in the post-Lausanne publications, regional congresses on evangelism, the Continuation Committee, and the impetus given to evangelism by each participant. The planning and program reflected this vision. The encouragement and inspiration of biblical evangelism was the obvious concern of originators of the Congress. The theme of the Congress expresses the continuing concern that the entire earth hear the proclamation of the biblical Gospel as *the* voice of the risen Christ, "Let the Earth Hear His Voice."

PLANNING FOR A "TOTALLY AND THOROUGHLY EVANGELICAL" CONGRESS

Concrete plans for Lausanne 1974 began at White Sulphur Springs, West Virginia, on December 2, 1971, when Billy Graham met with sixteen international leaders to initiate plans for a "World Evangelization Strategy Consultation." Previous preparation had been delayed until the Amsterdam 1971 Congress on Evangelism was finished. From the beginning a Covenant was anticipated by Harold Lindsell who suggested that a "statement should be prepared during the Congress to go from the Congress to the world setting forth the

challenge agreed upon at the Congress."[3] He believed
that the "goal should be the full evangelization of the
world."[4] Leighton Ford presented a tentative program
development schedule, and Billy Graham requested that
Bishop Jack Dain (Australia) be the chairman of the
Central Steering Committee.

At the next meeting in Vero Beach, Florida, March 23
and 24, 1972, Billy Graham concluded with a survey of
the world in general, following seven area reports on the
progress and obstacles to evangelism around the world.
In the minutes he summarized:

> The trend of the general population is not moving
> enmasse (sic) towards evangelism. Our assignment is
> to be faithful in proclamation and witness. God's
> time-piece is on schedule. There is a vacuum
> developing in the world church. Radical theology
> has had its heyday. The question before us is: Has
> God spoken to this vacuum and is He guiding us to
> have another World Congress on Evangelism and
> Mission? In the next world congress, "Every
> participant must be totally and thoroughly
> evangelical."[5]

The Vero Beach Minutes record that Graham repeated
on two other occasions his concern that the Congress be
thoroughly evangelical. After Leighton Ford suggested a
canvass of the thinking of strategic evangelical leaders
around the world, Graham stated:

> This must be a gathering of those totally committed
> to the evangelical position as we understand it. This
> should not be a gathering of those committed to
> liberal or to controversial positions.[6]

The Consultative Congress of the ICOWE agreed that
the Convening Committee should be selected from
among those world leaders "who are thoroughly
evangelical."[7] Any participation of nonevangelicals at
Lausanne was only accidental and incidental. The first
printed qualification for nomination was that "each

participant must be committedly evangelical, true to the
Bible as the inspired Word of God, and holding to a
Biblical view of evangelism, salvation, and conversion."[8]
The Invitation Committee chaired by Clyde Taylor
planned for a minimum of 3,000 participants and sought
facilities adequate for 5,000 people. Since it was to be a
"working congress" requiring at least sixty rooms, many
desirable locations in the Third World were eliminated
and Lausanne was finally chosen. Billy Graham was
selected Honorary Chairman of the Congress to be
assisted by "six outstanding evangelical church leaders, as
co-chairmen, each representing a continent. . ."[9] Donald
Hoke accepted the invitation to be Congress Director;
and Paul Little became Associate Director (Programme).
Leighton Ford was chairman of the Programme
Committee and ultimately responsible for giving
direction to the Congress program. The amended Report
of the Programme Sub-Committee was adopted at Los
Angeles, August 24 and 25, 1972, by the Planning
Committee.

Several preliminary observations on the program may
be made.

1. ICOWE would build upon the foundation of Berlin
1966 and, consequently, would focus upon the personal
aspects of evangelistic responsibility rather than the
ecclesiological orientation which called upon the Church
to evangelize. According to a further statement, there
was to be an emphasis in the Congress on God's plan for
the world that "Every Christian is responsible for
evangelization of the entire world."[10] Lausanne shifted
from the Berlin emphasis upon personal evangelism to a
focus upon the growth of the Church. It became more
"community"- and "Body of Christ"-conscious through
plenary papers such as "The Church as God's Agent in
Evangelism" by Howard Snyder. The Lausanne
Covenant stated, "The church is at the very center of
God's cosmic purpose and is his appointed means of
spreading the Gospel."[11] A strong ecclesiology permeated
the Congress, Covenant, and Continuation Committee
deliberations; the Planning Committee declared their

intention to convene the Congress "as members of
Christ's body."

2. Lausanne would focus upon the two billion
unevangelized so that each participant would be helped
to develop a strategy for E-1, E-2, and E-3 evangelism in
his area. The *evangelization of the world* in this century
would undergird the objectives of the Congress. In his
introductory message, Billy Graham said that while many
people are sincerely interested in *evangelism* in their own
communities, evangelism is

> *God's big picture* of "world need" and the "global
> responsibility" that he has put upon the church in
> his Word. . .God's heartbeat is for the world.
> Churches of every land, therefore must deliberately
> send out evangelists and missionaries to master
> other languages, learn other cultures, live in them
> perhaps for life, and thus evangelize these
> multitudes.[12]

"Near neighbor" evangelism alone is an inadequate
strategy for reaching at least one billion people.
Evangelism must be cross-cultural. The comprehensive
nature of world evangelization requires the rejection of
the moratorium on missionaries. The Covenant
responded by suggesting that a form of financial and
missionary moratorium may be necessary to facilitate
growth of self-reliance and "to release resources for
unevangelized areas."[13]

3. The Congress planners clearly recognized man's
need for reconciliation with God as the root cause of his
alienation from his fellow man. The first aim of the
Congress, however, centered upon utilitarian values of
the Gospel for man, rather than a focus on the eternal
destiny of the individual without Christ. The Congress
would

> reaffirm the primacy of world evangelization by the
> proclamation of the Gospel which adequately meets

the deepest spiritual and human needs of
contemporary man and society.[14]

The Congress aims responded directly to the ecumenical
theology of evangelism, but they seemed to distract the
Congress from the individual and personal motive, and
to further emphasize the community and the social and
self-fulfillment values inherent in salvation.

The "Call to the International Congress on World
Evangelization" adapted or changed the aims: "We
purpose

1) To proclaim the Biblical basis of evangelism in a
day of theological confusion.
2) To examine our message and methods by this
standard; to relate Biblical truth to crucial issues
facing Christians everywhere.
3) To share and strengthen our unity and love in
Christ.
4) To identify those who are as yet unreached or
alienated from the Gospel.
5) To learn from each other the patterns of
evangelism the Holy Spirit is using today in our
churches, fellowships, and missionary societies.
6) To awaken our Christian consciences to the
implications of expressing Christ's love in attitude
and action to men of every class and color.
7) To encourage cooperative strategies toward
reaching all men for Christ.
8) To pray together for world evangelization in this
century, asking that the Congress may contribute
significantly to this end.
9) To be God's people, available for all His
purposes in the world."[15]

The decision of the Planning Committee was first, to
enable each Christian to see his responsibility for the
evangelization of the entire world as God's plan. It began
personally, E-1, and ended in cross-cultural missions,
E-3. Second, the church was to be involved in this
strategy; and, third, these goals were to be substantiated
by biblical principles.

The controlling aim endorsed by the Committee was to "rediscover and re-examine in the light of our times the basic biblical evangelistic message."[16] The aim concerning the message, however, was somewhat changed to a proclamation of the biblical basis of evangelism. This change enabled the Congress to examine the word "evangelism," rather than present a biblical exposition of the message of evangelism. The first plenary paper of John Stott, consequently, placed evangelism in the context of mission, and proceeded to unravel the new ecumenical knots in the historical evangelical vocabulary of evangelism. The basic biblical message received an almost incidental treatment in the paper.

This redefinition of evangelism within the context of the mission of the church recalled the theological arguments used by the WCC to justify the integration of the International Missionary Council with the WCC during the 1950s, which culminated in the integration at New Delhi 1961. The WCC said that the *Church* is mission, and it is not *missions* that should be independently involved in evangelistic missions to the world, for the Church is the sending agency and *missions* independent of the WCC concept of the Church are outdated, anachronistic, and without theological support. Valid biblical mission, according to the WCC, should be so much a part of the Church that one no longer speaks of the missions of churches, but of the mission of the Church as a uniting body on all six continents. This basic theological deviation from the theology of the successful pietist missionary movement of the nineteenth century was incorporated into the Lausanne Covenant, and, after the Congress, caused confusion in the Continuation Committee's conception of their mandate. Henceforth, evangelism would be theologically subject to the Church (in whatever form it is understood) rather than subject to the mandate of the Great Commission to make disciples *and then* incorporate them into the visible fellowship of believers. The *responsibility* of each church to evangelize must be recognized and obediently practiced, but the authority for world evangelism does not reside with the Church.[17] Believers *are* to be incorporated into a visible

local church, but as they are not regenerated because of
their relationship to the local visible church, so their
responsibility to be witnesses is not received from the
authority of the local church but from Christ Himself.

In a very consistent manner, the Covenant clearly gave
evangelistic responsibility to the *Church* as the people of
God, rather than to *individual witnesses* as members of the
Church. This point is not a theological nuance or
triviality. The IMC and the WCC used much of their
theological energies in establishing the primacy of the
Church between Oxford 1937, Edinburgh 1937, and
Madras 1938, until New Delhi 1961. It took twenty-four
years for the WCC to accomplish what Stott's paper at
Lausanne accomplished in the two years after Lausanne:
authority for evangelism is an authority derived from the
Church, not a direct command incumbent upon
individual believers based upon the exegesis of the Great
Commission (Matthew 28:19). The IMC and the WCC
devoted much of their theological energies to establish
the theological primacy of the ecumenical Church at
Oxford 1937, Edinburgh 1937, Madras 1938, and New
Delhi 1961. Lausanne 1974, in comparison with Berlin
1966, gave greater responsibility for evangelism to the
Church as a visible institution and, consequently, seemed
to remove some of the individual responsibility
characteristic of evangelicalism during the past century.

The Congress goals also contained a note of optimism
and realism that is often misunderstood or misconstrued
as "triumphalism." It spoke of the present unusual work
of the Holy Spirit in the world, of the millions of
searching peoples, of the "multiplied numbers"
responding to the Gospel invitation, of the churches and
Christians that have been renewed, of the threshold of a
new era, and of the manifold means "at our command to
proclaim the Gospel."[18] While there were many sobering
concerns expressed at Lausanne for the unreached,
underprivileged, and the oppressed, yet the address of
Billy Graham, Waldron Scott, and others recognized the
blessing of God upon those in our generation who have
been faithful in adhering firmly to biblical

evangelicalism. This is an implicit and explicit cause for
rejoicing over what God has done by His Spirit through
His written Word. While all movements, churches, and
individuals have had moments of backsliding, the
Covenant should have reminded Evangelicals and all
Christendom that God was continuing to bless the simple
proclamation of the Gospel, and the Holy Spirit was
transforming countless lives and adding them to the
Church in Indonesia, Korea, South America, Africa, and
North America. A more evident spirit of gratitude to
God in the Covenant would have captured the spirit of
the Planning Committee and encouraged the participants
to remain loyal at any cost to the evangelical stand for
divine Truth. This note was replaced in the Covenant by
an acknowledgement of the ecumenical criticism of
evangelical triumphalism, and the adoption of a
dispirited plea for penitence because of past failures.[19]

Lastly, the Lausanne principle of a "process" led both
to the pre-Congress study of plenary papers by the
participants and to the post-Congress implementation of
evangelistic strategy by the participants. While it may be
argued that the Congress participants themselves should
fix their own priorities and principles, the historical
evangelicalism reaffirmed at Berlin 1966 and the goals of
the organizing committees would become the guidelines
of the Continuation Committee as part of this
evangelistic "process." The Lausanne changes in the
theology of evangelism and in the "process" and the
influence of the Covenant upon the future
responsibilities of the Continuation Committee remain
for later consideration.

It has already been observed that planning a "totally
and thoroughly evangelical congress" is one thing, but
the implementation of it is another. This observation
could be misinterpreted as underestimating or
minimizing the remarkable contribution that Lausanne
made to evangelicalism throughout the world. The
planning of Lausanne truly isolated the heretical views of
the ecumenical movement, exposed their nonbiblical
foundations, and strongly reaffirmed the primacy of

proclamation evangelism. In this area, Lausanne
rendered an invaluable service to the Third World
churches in particular, who may have been unaware of
the large theological gulf separating them from the WCC
and European theologians. Equivocal "salvation"
language in the 1959 theology of evangelism even
confused knowledgeable Western Evangelicals, to say
nothing of the problem confronting those whose native
tongue is not English and whose culture is not Western.
But Lausanne did modify the historical revivalism and
pietism of evangelicalism.

LAUSANNE 1974: EVANGELICAL CONCILIARITY IN TRUTH

Lausanne 1974 spoke far more eloquently and biblically
to the theological threats to evangelicalism than did
Edinburgh 1910 and, as a result, preserved many from
the theological equivocation of ecumenical pluralism.
The basic theology of Lausanne was sound and clear,
even though it opened the door to broad evangelical
viewpoints. It is impossible to summarize the vast scope
of evangelical theology and missiology given at Lausanne.
While there is some overlapping and duplication of
material, the contents possess a remarkable theological
coherence and consistency based upon a high view of
Scripture. Consequently, only the main trends can be
considered in anticipation of other more detailed studies.

EVANGELISM IN PARTNERSHIP WITH SOCIAL RESPONSIBILITY

John Stott presented a critique of the ecumenical
theology of evangelism in his introductory study entitled
"The Biblical Basis of Evangelism."[20] He lucidly
distinguished the biblical exegetical content of such

words as mission, evangelism, dialogue, salvation, and conversion from their ecumenical usage, and thus rendered an invaluable service to contemporary evangelical theology. "Mission," however, was reinterpreted in a broader sense, to include both evangelism and service. Stott recognized that the traditional view of missions as central in the life of the Church had been modified when the International Missionary Council became the Division of World Mission and Evangelism at New Delhi 1961, but he saw "no reason why we should resist this development."[21] This use of the IMC definition of "mission," however, had its origins in the *missio dei* theology of the 1950s that declared the mission to be God's and not ours, to be that of the Church and not of missions or parachurch agencies, to be God's action in the world He has cosmically redeemed and not our "soul-winning" activities, and to be the incarnational nature of God in the world in Christ, and not to be the redemptive work of the Cross for personal salvation.

Stott supported his synthesis of historic evangelicalism and the WCC concept of mission by John 20:21, one Gospel expression of the Great Commission wherein, he believed, Jesus not only sends us into the world to proclaim but also, according to Jesus' example, to serve. Jesus' mission of the

> supreme atoning sacrifice was the climax of a life of service. . . Our mission, like his, is to be one of service. He emptied himself of status and took the form of a servant (Phil. 2:7). So must we. He supplies us with the perfect model of service and sends his church into the world to be a servant church.[22]

Stott in a later book, *Christian Mission in the Modern World,* explained that at Berlin 1966 he argued that the cumulative emphasis of the Great Commission texts was on preaching, witnessing, and making disciples, and that one could conclude from his exposition there that the mission of the church is "exclusively a preaching,

converting and teaching mission."[23] Previously, he had
seen social responsibility as one of the duties to be taught
to converts, not as an integral partner with evangelism in
the mission of the church.

> Today, however, I would express myself differently.
> It is not just that the commission includes a duty to
> teach converts everything Jesus had previously
> commanded (Matthew 28:20), (sic) and that social
> responsibility is among the things which Jesus
> commanded. I now see more clearly that not only
> the consequences of the commission but the actual
> commission itself must be understood to include
> social as well as evangelistic responsibility, unless we
> are to be guilty of distorting the words of Jesus.[24]

Stott recognized that Jesus' ministry of bringing eternal
life (1 John 4:9, 10, 14) and seeking (Luke 19:10) was
unique, but that He deliberately and precisely made His
mission the *model* for ours. He concludes that these
statements of why Jesus came, "bringing eternal life" and
"seeking" are inadequate in themselves and that "it is
better to begin with something more general and say that
he came to serve."[25]

In this new conception of evangelical mission, Stott
believed that the truly Christian relation between
evangelism and social action is

> that social action is *a partner of evangelism.* As
> partners the two belong to each other. Each stands
> on its own feet in its own right alongside the other.
> Neither is a means to the other, or even a
> manifestation of the other. For each is an end in
> itself. Both are expressions of unfeigned love.[26]

This, he notes, was also the conclusion of the National
Evangelical Anglican Congress at Keele, England, in
1967. Stott built a rather substantial superstructure on
the limited foundation of his interpretation of John
20:21 and John 17:18. The influence and implications of
this new theology of mission remain to be seen. Stott has

dethroned evangelism as *the* only historical aim of mission. The mission of the Church *must* include some measure of social action. The principle of the complete self-authentication of the Gospel in mission through the ministry of the Holy Spirit in evangelism (Heb. 4:12, 13) is modified by the necessity of some incarnational sociopolitical actions. These actions are different from the personal "fruits of the Spirit" (Gal. 5:22, 23). Sociopolitical actions have become as essential to mission as proclamation evangelism. If it could be shown that the work-signs of Jesus were primarily to *identify* Him and produce faith (John 20:31) in a world hostile to Jesus and to His disciples (John 17:15), and that the works and words of Jesus were to be written and proclaimed (Rom. 10:17), then mission would retain its historical conception of E-1, E-2, and E-3 evangelism. The primacy of evangelism in the mission of the Church has rarely hindered, however, many philanthropic acts and ministries of loving service to human need. The mission of the Church is evangelism. To say that mission is a comprehensive word "embracing everything that God sends his people into the world to do" may be too great a concession to ecumenical theology and without biblical foundations.[27]

Evangelism, Stott reaffirms, is presenting Jesus crucified and resurrected. The apostles were primary witnesses to the Gospel events, while the postapostolic believer renders a secondary witness to what the apostolic authors of Scripture recorded.

> The only Christ there is to preach is the biblical Christ, the objective historical Jesus attested by the joint witness of the prophets in the Old Testament and the Apostles of the New (cf. Acts 10:39-43). Our witness is always secondary to theirs.[28]

Stott follows J. I. Packer in separating evangelistic proclamation from evangelistic results and, in so doing, rejects the famous definition of 1919 by the English Archbishops' "Committee of Enquiry into the Evangelistic Work of the Church." This definition defines

evangelism in terms of success. But to evangelize is
not so to preach that something happens. Of course
the objective is that something will happen, namely
that people will respond and believe. Nevertheless,
biblically speaking, to evangelize is to proclaim the
Gospel whether anything happens or not.[29]

He later recognized persuasion as a goal or purpose of
evangelism, but does not include it within the strict
definition of evangelism because it is not for us to
determine the results of our evangelism, but God.[30]

Stott seemed to have been influenced by "presence"
theology or "contemporary communication" theory, by
his illustrations of the statement that "evangelism must
not be defined in terms of *methods.*"[31] In addition to
verbal methods, he included some *nonverbal*
announcements, such as "good works of love, a
Christ-centered home, a transformed life," or even
"speechless excitement about Jesus."[32] He later balanced
the nonverbal viewpoint by reaffirming that "if we want
to be biblically accurate, we must insist that the essence
of evangelism lies in the faithful proclamation of the
Gospel."[33] The Covenant therefore, distinguished
evangelism from dialogue and, then, unequivocally
defined evangelism:

> Our Christian presence in the world is
> indispensable to evangelism, and so is that kind of
> dialogue whose purpose is to listen sensitively to
> understand. But evangelism itself is the
> proclamation of the historical, biblical Christ as
> Savior and Lord, with a view to persuading people
> to come to him personally and so be reconciled to
> God.[34]

Lausanne stood firm on the historical, biblical doctrine of
proclamation evangelism and the need of persuasion.

In Stott's summary of salvation he rejected the
psychophysical or wholeness view, because

> Salvation by faith in Christ crucified and risen is
> moral not material, a deliverance from *sin*, not from

harm. . .and his works of physical rescue (from
disease, drowning, and death) were intentional
"signs" of his salvation, and were understood by the
early Church to be such.[35]

The importance of biblical eschatology was again
apparent, as he recognized divine healing from
psychosomatic conditions as a present consequence of
salvation, but new bodies in a new society will be given at
the consummation—". . .the salvation offered in and
through Jesus Christ today is not a complete
psycho-physical wholeness; to maintain that is to
anticipate the resurrection."[36]

Stott rejected sociopolitical liberation, or the
humanization of salvation, at Uppsala 1968 and Bangkok
1973. He approved the goals of humanization,
development, wholeness, liberation, and justice as
activities in which Christians should be involved, but
denied that these things constitute the salvation offered
the world by God through Jesus Christ, for that is a
gross theological confusion.

> It is to mix what Scripture keeps distinct—God the
> Creator and God the Redeemer, justice and
> justification, common grace and saving grace, the
> reformation of society and the regeneration of
> man.[37]

He accused Bangkok 1973 of misusing Scripture to
support national liberation movements today:

> The Exodus was the redemption of God's covenant
> people. It is used in Scripture as a foreshadowing of
> redemption from sin through Christ. It offers no
> conceivable justification or pattern of national
> liberation movements today.[38]

Stott concluded that biblical "salvation. . .is a personal
freedom from sin and its consequences, which brings
many wholesome consequences in terms both of health
and of social responsibility."[39] First, the believer has been
saved from the wrath of God. Our objective guilt before

God was borne by Christ, who was condemned in our place. We were "slaves" under the curse of the law and have become "sons." Second, salvation is a process whereby the indwelling Spirit of Christ is gradually but surely "subduing the flesh within me and is transforming me into the image of Christ. . ."[40] This is no longer a slavery to sin and self but a new willing slavery to God for Jesus' sake in selfless service. Third, final salvation is future, the object of the Christian "hope of salvation." The whole creation will experience with us our new bodies, in a new heaven and a new earth.

> We rejoice and we groan: this is the paradoxical experience of Christians who have been saved and are being saved, and at the same time are not yet saved.[41]

Conversion is the necessary response to the Gospel of those who are still "perishing." Stott rejected universalism:

> We proclaim to them the good news of Christ not because they are saved already but in order that they may be saved. It is impossible to be a biblical Christian and a universalist simultaneously.[42]

While the precise nature of hell is not known, it is an awful reality that should be thought of with tears. Conversion is not a work that man does by himself, nor is it a renunciation of one's cultural heritage. It is a turning to God, that sends the believer back into the world as a new person. It is the beginning of growth by a life of discipleship, maturity, church membership, and involvement in the world.

THE BIBLE IS MOST NECESSARY

Susumu Uda spoke on "Biblical Authority and Evangelism," because the concept of revelation is under attack, and the content of faith and evangelization are intimately related. Because all men are totally incapable spiritually, God's written special revelation is most necessary

> in order that men, thus blinded by sin, may learn his (God's) will, works, and ways with respect to this saving, restorative work. God's special communication to them became a necessity (2 Timothy 3:17).[43]

The Scripture enables man to interpret nature correctly, to think of God and properly describe Him in human language, to know Him as a Person and a personal God, and to constantly renew the degenerating forms of faith and worship in the Church that always come under temptation from evil forces.

The evangelical approach to the Bible gives first priority to the self testimony of the Bible. The Bible speaks for itself.

> It has been the faith of the people of God from the very foundation of the church until today that the Bible is the Word of God in such a sense that whatever it says, God says.[44]

This attitude of entire trust is warranted because the entire Bible is inspired by the Holy Spirit (2 Tim. 3:16). According to the words of Christ in Matthew 5:18,

> this book is perfect to the smallest detail. . . . What the Scripture says will stand steadfast (cf. Heb. 2:2) and cannot be annulled. If the Scripture speaks, the issue is settled once and for all.[45]

This teaching is not a creation of late Judaism or the Reformation, but was the one held by the Jews, the early church, and throughout the centuries. Uda cites the CWME Bangkok Conference on "Salvation Today" where the Bible was viewed by many

> as merely a collection of fallible human witnesses to the experience of the so-called authentic way of

human existence (a mode of living with true
humanness).[46]

Eui Whan Kim (Korea) elaborated the differences
among the Roman Catholic, old liberal, neo-orthodox,
and evangelical views of the Bible. He quoted the Belgic
Confession which emphasized the Bible's inherent
authority:

> We receive all these books, and these only, as holy
> and canonical for the regulation, foundation, and
> confirmation of our faith; believing without any
> doubt all things contained in them, not so much
> because the church receives and approves them as
> such, but more especially because the Holy Spirit
> witnesses in our hearts that they are from God, and
> also because they carry the evidence thereof in
> themselves.[47]

He said that Christ did not teach the "dynamic
inspiration of the writers of the Bible" but He did teach
the "inspiration of their entire writings."[48] That the
entire Bible was the Word of God was the united
testimony of Clement of Rome, Justin Martyr, and
Irenaeus:

> Such a high view of inspiration carries with it
> certain concomitant truths. That is the doctrine of
> inerrancy and infallibility of the Bible. Infallibility is
> a necessary inference to be drawn from the doctrine
> of inspiration. Inspiration is incompatible with
> errors in the Bible. If the words of Scripture in the
> original autographs are the very words inspired by
> the Holy Spirit, they must of necessity be inerrant
> and infallible. This was the attitude toward the
> Scriptures that was held by the historical evangelical
> Christians through the ages till the present day.[49]

Kim warned against the trend of certain "conservatives"
among "American ministers" who do not subscribe to
inerrancy or who have doubts about the doctrine:

> Nowadays we are beginning to hear from some
> evangelicals a cry for a reinvestigation of biblical
> inerrancy, thus creating a new theological
> climate. . . . Perhaps the basic reason for such a
> dissatisfaction against contemporary orthodoxy
> resides in the desire of some evangelical scholars to
> win a new respectability for orthodoxy in the
> academic community.[50]

The "Authority and Uniqueness of Scripture Report"
by Kenneth Kantzer responded to Kim[51] in the valuable
summary included in Appendix III. In the group, many
of the conflicts of a recognizable minority were
eliminated as the discussion progressed over the
three-day periods, and as cross-cultural and
cross-disciplinary communications increased. A joyous
note of encouragement related the infallibility of
Scripture to continued blessing in world evangelization:

> The task of *world* evangelization demands a message
> from God for *all the peoples of the world*. The
> experiences of an individual or group cannot be the
> base for the universal Gospel; rather our message
> must be based in God's divine Word of revelation,
> the Bible, which is applicable to all men (Matt.
> 24:14). It is this Word, not personal opinions (2
> Tim. 4:2), that we are to preach. Such witness God
> has promised to bless (Isa. 55:11), and he will not
> deny his promise (Num. 23:19).[52]

CHURCH GROWTH

Lausanne 1974 introduced a new strong element of
church growth into the evangelical bloodstream. The
successful expansion of national churches around the
world offered ample evidence that Evangelicals have long
been involved in "church planting," but Lausanne added
"church growth" by Western and Third World missions
to their international evangelistic agenda for the first

time. Don Hoke said that Lausanne was concerned that
world evangelization be accomplished by the "cutting
edge of evangelism from *every* country," not from the
West alone.[53] There can be no question that this
contemporary church growth emphasis had been
spearheaded prior to, as well as during, Lausanne by
Donald McGavran who gave the plenary paper on "The
Dimensions of World Evangelization."

In essence, McGavran modified Stott's partnership of
evangelism and social responsibility, by seeing personal
and social improvements as a *fruit* of salvation which
issue from sound conversion. There are varying aspects
of "radical discipleship" inherent in Escobar,[54] and
Padilla which seem to minimize repentance from
personal moral sins of the "world" and, instead,
emphasize repentance from social sins.[55] An
undesignated group of participants prepared a response
entitled "Theological Implications of Radical
Discipleship," to which McGavran, in a measure,
addressed the response to his plenary address. In
replying to questions like "Can we evangelize in today's
world without vigorously engaging in social action? Can
men be saved as individuals, if the social order is bad?
Must not evangelism aim to change evil social
structures?"[56] McGavran replied:

> Of course, Christians engage in social action. Social
> structures, when evil, must be changed. Christians
> have always done this, are doing it, and always will.
> Ethical improvements, both personal and social, are
> the fruit of salvation. They issue naturally from
> sound conversion. The Holy Spirit leads Christians
> into all righteousness—both individual and
> corporate. Biblically well-instructed Christians are
> the world's greatest reformers. The most potent
> forces for social change are Bible-reading,
> Bible-obeying churches.
>
> But first, my friends, you must have some
> Christians and some churches. First, you must have
> reborn men. . . . Evangelism is not proclaiming the
> desirability of a liquorless world and persuading

people to vote for prohibition. Evangelism is not
proclaiming the desirability of sharing the wealth
and persuading people to take political action to
achieve it. Christians who judge these and others
like them to be good ends will of course work for
them, pray for them and fight for them. And I will
enthusiastically back such Christians. Make no
mistake about that. But evangelism is something
else. Evangelism is proclaiming Jesus Christ as God
and only Savior and persuading men to become his
disciples and responsible members of his church.
That is the first and basic task. Calling people to
repent and to become disciples of the Son of
Righteousness is the most important political act
that anyone can perform. Until politicized
Christians realize that, our politics will be terribly
inadequate.[57]

McGavran's debate on the primacy, rather than the
partnership, of evangelism extends back at least ten years
before Lausanne 1974. In his 1958 preparation for the
IMC integration into the WCC, Lesslie Newbigin (IMC
and later the DWME director) first advocated the Madras
1938 "Larger Evangelism" strategy whereby service is a
partner with evangelism.[58] Günter Linnenbrink, in the
October 1965 International Review of Missions, said that
the resurrection of Jesus "must not be understood as a
'better land beyond' which will provide consolation for
life on earth. The Kingdom is a present historical
reality."[59] He then divides Moltmann's "hope" into three
categories of: (1) the pietist missions who save souls for
eternity and have no hope for God's present creation, (2)
the church-centered missions who do not see the need of
personal conversion, and who restrict the Kingdom of
God to the Church, and (3) those who hold a
"cosmocratic" hope for the Church and also for the
whole creation. Mission, he said, "is the participation of
the Church of Jesus Christ in our Lord's assumption of
His sovereignty in the world."[60] This "cosmocratic" view
is the theological presupposition of Newbigin's definition,
and led Linnenbrink to say,

It is therefore clear that proclamation (the verbal or
written proclamation of the Christian message) and
service (the proclamation of the Christian message
through works of love) are equal partners in the
mission of the Church.[61]

Harold Lindsell replied in the same issue of the IRM
that Linnenbrink had made a serious error by separating
pietistic, church-centered, and cosmocratic hope, because

Biblical mission has always included all three ideas
in its total outlook. Individuals are to be gathered
from the mass of men. They constitute the Church,
visible and invisible, that lives "between the
times"—that is, of its creation and consummation.
There is no hope for the present world as we know
it, but the Christian looks for a recreated world with
a new heaven and a new earth, where righteousness
dwells.[62]

Lindsell concludes that the redefinition is unwarranted
because service follows proclamation, as an expression of
a redeemed heart:

The role of service is twofold. First, it is a means to
an end. By service it is possible to confront men
with the Gospel of Christ. All means that make this
possible are legitimate, if they are otherwise
legitimate in themselves—education, medicine,
social action, for instance. The only test is whether
they remain as means and do not become an end in
themselves. As long as service makes it possible to
confront men with the Gospel, it is useful. The
second role of service is as a fruit that grows on the
gospel tree and leads the people of God to fulfil
the law of God.[63]

Lindsell then concluded with the historical evangelical
view of mission:

The mission of the Church, first and foremost, is
proclamation for the salvation of men, some of

whom will respond and others of whom will not. Secondary to this primary goal is service, a means to bring about the salvation of men and an expression of an embraced and a committed faith.[64]

McGavran's later article in the same issue contended that the IMC-WCC "strategy of the fifties" was defective, even though mission to the world had achieved a position of "unique authority" and had been accepted as a "consensus of intelligent thinking";[65]

1. This view of mission tried to take in everything that the Church and the Christian faith ought to do. It was a confusion of the responsibility of the Church in plenary session and not of mission.

2. It tends to resist focusing upon church planting and growth as partisan and narrow.

3. This view really has no answer to the pressing problems of population explosion, the static younger churches, or responsive areas.

4. It was really a defense of the existing bureaucratic machinery and the massive service aims under slogans of "the whole Gospel," "all its fulness," and "the whole man." "The whole Gospel for all mankind means little, unless it is preceded by stupendous church planting," for while the whole Gospel is good, "the only balanced rations that can be given are to sheep that have been found and brought into the fold."[66]

5. Finally it is wrong theologically and biblically because

it does not throb with Christ's passion for men's eternal redemption. It makes haste to point out that there are many kinds of redemption and appears equally in favour of all. It does not blaze with certainty that man, the immortal soul, was created in the image of God, is not in that image now and must regain it through the saving work of Christ. It does not seem to know which part of the Christian religion is the centre and which is periphery.[67]

Now Lausanne was caught up in the ecumenical debate!

McGavran at Lausanne was concerned for the two
billion with no knowledge of Christ, an appeal unheeded
at Uppsala 1968 and Bangkok 1973:

> Let us think of the little clusters of churches in most
> Latfricasian countries as existing on ethnic islands,
> surrounded by oceans of men and women who have
> never heard of Jesus Christ, never seen a Bible, and
> never talked to a Christian. This is the brutal fact
> confronting world evangelism. This is the basic
> evangelistic problem faced by the World Church.[68]

Yet there is unprecedented receptivity to Christianity
which calls for evangelism on a greater scale:

> God has spoken to these multitudes. The Holy
> Spirit has turned them receptive. They hear the
> voice of the Great Shepherd and seek to follow him.
> Christ's church in all six continents must look to her
> Master and follow his lead in proclaiming the Good
> News of salvation and incorporating believers in
> multiplying thousands of Christian cells, churches
> of Christ, congregations of the redeemed.[69]

He pleaded for four modes of church growth:
one-by-one-against-the-family, family movement to
Christ, people movement to Christ, and the
multiplication of house churches in cities and villages.

Many valuable Lausanne papers reflected concern that
evangelism lead converts into the local church. Howard
Snyder said that the Bible places the Church at the very
center of God's cosmic purpose.[70] Henri Blocher
wrestled with the question of "The Nature of Biblical
Unity" and affirmed that "the Bible also establishes a link
between the unity of the church and its growth through
the addition of new members."[71] Peter Beyerhaus found
that biblical evangelism "leads into the church as the new
messianic community of the Kingdom."[72] Yet the church
is not identical with the Kingdom of God but rather "the
transitory communal form of it in the present age, and
through his church Christ exercises a most important

ministry toward the visible coming of the Kingdom."[73]
This understanding is important, Beyerhaus says,
because

> the *goal of evangelism* is not only to make individual
> believers. The goal of evangelism is to persuade
> these believers to be incorporated as responsible
> members into the church as God's messianic
> community.[74]

The time of world evangelism is limited, Beyerhaus said,
because of the prophetic restitution of Israel, when the
full number of Gentiles has come in (Rom. 11:25).

> Israel's conversion will mark the transformation
> from world-evangelization to world-Christianization.
> The church's assignment in the present
> dispensation is not to take the world of nations
> politically under the law of Christ as expressed in
> the Sermon on the Mount. Under the present
> conditions where Satan still is unbound, this is
> simply not possible. . . . Meanwhile, however,
> world-evangelism has only one direct purpose. It is
> to call and to gather the eschatological community
> of the elect out of all nations.[75]

Lausanne saw church growth as an essential fruit of
evangelism in all its forms and methods. Because of the
Holy Spirit within it, the Church grows through
proclaiming the Gospel, multiplying congregations,
building the Christian community and exercising
spiritual gifts. Howard Snyder concluded that

> evangelism and the growth of the Church are not a
> matter of *bringing to* the church that which is
> needed for success in the way of methods,
> techniques, or strategies. *Evangelism is rather a matter
> of removing the hindrances to growth.* Once these
> hindrances are removed—not only individual sin
> but also human traditions, worn-out structures, and
> fundamental misconceptions about the nature of

the Church—then the Church will grow through
the power of God within it.[76]

Church growth is normal because it is indwelt by the
dynamic of the Holy Spirit.

THE
CONCILIARITY
OF THE
COVENANT

Over 1,500 of the 2,200 participants signed the Covenant
at Lausanne—following the example of Bishop Dain and
Billy Graham. Over 80 percent, or 2,200, eventually
signed it.[77] The signatories are assured of anonymity by
a decision of the post-Lausanne Planning Committee that
placed them "under embargo" for fifty years.[78] That the
Covenant represents Evangelicals is generally assumed.
Hans-Lutz Poetsch concluded:

> The Congress has been called the great event of the
> "Evangelicals," and so we may expect that "The
> Lausanne Covenant" reflects the beliefs and
> convictions of those who call themselves
> "Evangelicals."[79]

Poetsch observed its impressive theological uniformity
and asks whether the editorial committee, while taking
note of the suggestions, did not have a preconceived
notion as to what the final result should look like. John
Stott, the main architect appointed by the Program
Committee, recounts how the document was produced:

> A first and fairly short statement was produced two
> or three months before the Congress and submitted
> by mail to a number of advisers. Already this
> document may truly be said to have come out of the
> Congress (although the Congress had not yet
> assembled), because it reflected the contributions of
> the main speakers whose papers had been

published in advance. The document was revised in light of the advisers' comments, and this revision was further revised at Lausanne by the drafting committee. So what was submitted to all participants in the middle of the Congress was the third draft. . . . Some proposed amendments cancelled each other out, but the drafting committee incorporated all they could while at the same time insuring that the final document was a recognizable revision of the draft submitted to participants.[80]

The obvious brevity of the Covenant, in contrast to the 1,471 pages of moderately fine print of the ICOWE Official Reference Volume, assures its relative popularity and its representative nature as an evangelical theology of evangelism that will unquestionably have a distinctive place in contemporary history.[81]

Acceptance of the Covenant will vary according to the *milieu* considering it. Knowledgeable evangelical theologians may be more critical of important details than those who founder in the ambiguities and equivocation of other conciliar statements. Regardless of the reactions, the Covenant represents one of the finest documents on evangelism that has ever been produced in response to the confusion and crisis in ecumenical and conciliar evangelism. Its value should not be underestimated.

CONTENT OF THE COVENANT

Among the highly condensed and succinct statements of evangelical truth, a number deserve special consideration.

1. *Identity.* Not only the international multicultural and interracial aspect is immediately introduced, but also the bold assertation of the relationship of Evangelicals to the Church: "We, members of the Church of Jesus Christ. . ." This declaration of identity is founded upon a later declaration of ecclesiology which states, "The church is the community of God's people rather than an

institution. . . ."[82] The transcendent spiritual nature of
the Church is implied, while its visible manifestation is
recognized as biblical and necessary. The unity of
catholicity "in truth" marked this identity as important
for continued evangelistic witness. A later paragraph
began:

> We affirm that the church's visible unity in truth is
> God's purpose. Evangelism also summons us to
> unity, because our oneness strengthens our witness,
> just as our disunity undermines our gospel of
> reconciliation.[83]

Evangelical identity is associated directly with its
adherence to the apostolic witness to Jesus Christ, the
Bible, as the only authority which Evangelicals possess. It
provides a unique source of the apostolic truth that
unites and identifies them.

In addition, Evangelicals identified themselves as the
Church in its mission of evangelism. "We need to break
out of our ecclesiastical ghettos and permeate
non-Christian society. In the church's mission of
sacrificial service, evangelism is primary."[84] The
Lausanne Covenant did not identify itself as a
parachurch movement of the Church, or as an
evangelistic arm of the Church, but as *the Church* of Jesus
Christ united by the "given unity" in the Truth of Jesus
Christ as revealed to the prophets and the apostles.
There was no defensiveness or sectarianism—simply a
quiet but firm declaration of the conclusions inherent
within obedience to the living Christ. This identity was as
important to Western evangelicalism, recently emerging
from its defensive minority attitude, as it was to the
Third World churches, emerging from a colonial past
and seeking for their identity in an ecclesiological
context.

2. *The Bible.* There can be no question that the most
crucial historical issue in the Covenant was that of the
doctrine of Holy Scripture, for—in the tradition of the
Church—the entire Congress appealed to the Bible alone
for its authority for the numerous theological principles

and practices governing evangelism and world missions.
The Covenant asserted:

> We affirm the divine inspiration, truthfulness and
> authority of both Old and New Testament
> Scriptures in their entirety as the only written Word
> of God, without error in all that it affirms, and the
> only infallible rule of faith and practice.[85]

Because of the intricacies of contemporary controversies,
the only adequate interpretation of this brief definition
can be found in the expositions of Uda (Japan), Kim
(Korea), Kantzer (USA), and the hermeneutical overview
of Saphir Athyal (India). Each contributed to the
affirmations of the doctrine of Scripture defined in the
Covenant. To isolate the statement of the Covenant from
the expositions of the Congress *and from the usage* of the
speakers and participants is to *decontextualize* the
Covenant. John Stott has clearly endeavored to "unpack"
the tight content by his explanation, in which he
summarized the divine method of inspiring the entire
Bible as *verbal.*

> This does not mean that God somehow breathed
> into words which had already been written, or into
> the writers who wrote them, but rather that the
> words themselves were "God-breathed" (2 Tim.
> 3:16, literally). Of course, they were also the words
> of men who spoke and wrote freely. Yet these men
> were "moved by the Holy Spirit" (2 Pet. 1:21) to
> such an extent that it could be said *of their words*
> (italics mine), "the mouth of the Lord has spoken it"
> (Isa. 40:5).[86]

The ground of "infallibility" and of the hermeneutical
"without error in all that it affirms" must be seen as
God-breathed *words* incapable of error in the original
texts.

"Without error in all that it affirms" deals with the fact
that amid the inspired authoritative text are accurate
records of what Satan, demonic-inspired men, and others
have truly said—but which are lies and distortions of

truth not to be believed. Christians may learn from their errors and God's reply to them, but it is that which *God* teaches that "is without error in all that it affirms."

By this, Councils, Tradition (as historical interpretation), dogmas and traditions of denominations and cultures (whose conclusions are to be respectfully and gratefully considered and, in many cases, believed and practiced), are eliminated—for they can never possess the finality of the *magisterium* for all ages, the Bible. The Lausanne Papers should have said something more about Tradition, tradition and traditions—and the Covenant could have declared in a positive way that the Scripture alone is "Infallible Tradition"—but in-depth consideration of the entire work of the Congress reveals that it left little to add in the area of inspiration and authority.[87] In essence, the paragraph on "The Authority and Power of the Bible" is beautiful, powerful, and relevant. In the context of the entire Congress, Evangelicals need not be apologetic or ashamed because of it.

3. *Revelation and Non-Christian Religions.* No world congress in this century—and perhaps in the last—has treated the questions of the universality of Christ, the heresy of universalism (although Berlin 1966 was excellent), the extent and limits of general revelation to the nations, and the lostness of man as thoroughly, theologically, and biblically as Lausanne 1974. After Edinburgh 1910, and despite the warning letter of the aged Gustav Warneck sent to that World Missionary Conference, the great nineteenth-century missionary movement stumbled and foundered on these issues, which led the ecumenical movement from the extremes of syncretism to cosmic universalism, a biblically untenable aberration.[88] The Covenant statement rejects dialogue with non-Christian religions and ideologies as a search for truth because of its abuses as an evangelistic method precluding proclamation.

General revelation cannot save man's eternal soul—or his earthly existence, for that matter—because his sinful nature suppresses the truth communicated by it. Here

again, the Official Reference Volume must be the
commentary on a vast and extensive subject that finds its
roots in the biblical view of divine revelation by Uda
(Japan), Kim (Korea), Runia (Netherlands), and Lindsell
(USA). The Covenant affirms the lostness of man in
non-Christian ideologies and religions, and directs
Evangelicals to the need of proclamation:

> We also reject as derogatory to Christ and the
> Gospel every kind of syncretism and dialogue which
> implies that Christ speaks equally through all
> religions and ideologies. Jesus Christ, being himself
> the only God-man, who gave himself as the only
> ransom for sinners, is the only mediator between
> God and man. . . . All men are perishing because of
> sin, but God loves all men, not wishing that any
> should perish but that all should repent. Yet those
> who reject Christ repudiate the joy of salvation and
> condemn themselves to eternal separation from
> God.[89]

An ambiguity in the text gives the impression that the
Gospel must be heard and rejected before man
condemns himself to eternal separation, but the full text
speaks of men as "perishing" (while they live) until
responding to Him as Saviour and Lord in repentance
and faith. Man is judged by his sinfulness and
condemned eternally to hell whether he has heard the
Gospel and rejected it, or has not even heard it.
Purgatory, conditional immortality, and annihilation are
among some of the errors and heresies rejected along
with universalism. This life is probationary, and one's
decision here regarding his personal and individual
commitment to Jesus Christ determines his eternal
destiny. The proclamation of Jesus as "the Saviour of the
world" means

> to invite all men to respond to him as Savior and
> Lord in the wholehearted personal commitment of
> repentance and faith.[90]

THE COVENANT AND
THE CONGRESS

The Covenant should be separated from the content of
the Congress papers, which synthesized the Covenant.
Yet the Covenant introduces more of a "conciliar"
statement than was expressed by the Congress:

1. It did not take sharp issue with the relationship of
"Tradition" to the authority of Scripture, at a moment in
Church history when it has become increasingly
significant. Consequently, biblical guidelines were not
established to clarify the interpretative role of the
magisterium of Roman Catholicism, of Eastern Orthodox
Tradition, and of the ecumenical councils.

2. Several papers in the Congress communicated a
more precise position on the inspiration and authority of
Scripture than that which was incorporated into the
Covenant. The task of the drafters of the Covenant was,
admittedly, difficult, for while the Covenant was not to
be considered as a doctrinal statement or a confession of
faith, yet it was intended as a serious statement of
evangelical consensus. Consequently, a balance was
required to discern that which was essentially evangelical
and that which was not. The doctrine of inspiration, in
this case, has been recognized by some to be a crucial
area of debate in the dialogue with ecumenical theology.
Others unfamiliar with this theology or unthreatened by
it may believe the debate to be a Western one or merely
a "fundamentalist" touchstone. Ecumenical authors have
been quick to caricature those believing in a high view of
the inspiration of Scripture as holding to a dictation
theory which neglects the personality of the authors so
evident in the biblical text.

Rather than use the word *inerrancy,* therefore, the
Covenant said: "We affirm the divine inspiration,
truthfulness and authority of both the Old and New
Testament Scriptures in their entirety as the only written
Word of God, without error in all that it affirms, and the
only infallible rule of faith and practice." For theological
specialists in the doctrine of inspiration the use of the
word *written* implies its verbal inspiration. These same
specialists also find that "without error in all that it

affirms" preserves the Christian from a commitment to
such things as the errors Satan asserts and the heresies of
evil men recorded in the Bible. It is a way of saying that
the *truths* taught by the Scripture are without any error,
are infallible, or inerrant. The specialist finds this mode
of expression adequate because of his understanding of
the use of the word *written* as applying to the *words* in
which the truth was affirmed. Those less convinced that
the word *written* applies to verbal inerrancy find a *lacuna*
or weakness. They have observed the agility of those who
hold to a lower view of inspiration to find—perhaps in
all honesty—a loophole and to debilitate, weaken, and
erode the objective authority of written revelation. Even
the word *inerrancy* can be restricted to mean "inerrant
truth" or "inerrant faith and practice" rather than
describe the inerrancy of a verbally inspired text.
Consequently, some find the Covenant to be adequate in
its basic refutation of nonevangelical views of inspiration
and authority, but inadequate to protect evangelicalism
from theological deviation within its own ranks. Others
believe that the whole issue is overstated and can only
lead to an unnecessary division in evangelicalism and the
loss of evangelical gains since World War II. Since the
first text of the Covenant presented to the participants
was even weaker, an unexpected credibility gap arose
between the drafters and those Evangelicals familiar with
the issues. The papers of the Congress and its
committees did not seem to be reflected fully in either
the first or second drafts of the Covenant.

3. The Covenant recognized the spirit of unity in
Christ sensed at the Congress and it appealed for visible
unity—but not at the expense of truth. The affirmation
was made in a spirit of evangelical inclusiveness that
recognized the churches of the Third World as well as
those evangelicals within the historic churches of
Christendom. Those signing the Covenant pledged
themselves "to seek a deeper unity in truth, worship,
holiness, and mission." On one hand this has excluded
any organizational unity outside of truth, but on the
other hand it seeks a stronger commitment to evangelical
unity. There is a given unity under the sole authority of

Scripture and the essentials of the Gospel that is not
necessarily institutional. Expressions of future unity were
seen more through regional cooperation for strategy in
evangelism and mission than in a world organization with
unity as a criterion for effective evangelism. This
paragraph of the Covenant could not be compared with
the euphoristic benefits of unity expressed at Edinburgh
1910 although both Edinburgh 1910 and Lausanne 1974
sought world evangelization. Edinburgh 1910 sought it
by *organizational* unity while Lausanne 1974 sought a
functional unity to accomplish regional evangelization
and, ultimately, that of the world.

4. Several Congress speakers followed Stott in his
redefinition of mission, but the Covenant in this case
clearly held to the historic position of the primacy in
time and in rank of evangelism. The Covenant said that
"in the church's mission of sacrificial service evangelism
is primary" and it also declared the church to be at the
very center of God's cosmic purpose and to be God's
appointed means of spreading the Gospel. It must be
recognized, therefore, that the mission of the church in
the minds of the participants related primarily to
evangelism and not to social or political action as a
partner of evangelism. Stott's commentary, *The Lausanne
Covenant,* does not make this completely clear.[91] This
primacy became important in establishing the mandate of
the Continuation Committee for several in the committee
desired to define its work in terms of Stott's view of
mission, the partnership of evangelism and social action,
while others insisted upon the evangelistic mandate alone
as the primary work.

THE CONGRESS
IN RETROSPECT
STRENGTHS AND
WEAKNESSES OF
LAUSANNE'S
COVENANT

In many circles, as well as in the course of history,
Lausanne 1974 identified much more with the Covenant

than with the plenary papers, in-depth theological studies, evangelism strategies reports, and geographical reports. This is unfortunate, even though the Covenant has as much to contribute as the Congress. For this reason, a summary of the strengths and weaknesses of the Covenant may help to chart the course for Evangelicals.

Strengths. Because of the inherent stand for the verbal inspiration and infallibility of the Scripture, evangelical papers in general were able to correct many theological errors and repudiate heresies in the area of evangelism. The Covenant reflects this discernment in a coherent, cohesive way. The process of its production was responsible for this.

In spite of concerns raised by Congress papers, the Covenant gives primary consideration to evangelism without neglecting social responsibility as a duty of the Christian, an essential viewpoint that Evangelicals have always maintained. It was a nonsacramental evangelism, a spiritual ministry that even neglected to give an appropriate place to baptism.

Evangelism was seen as responsible for incorporating believers into Christ's Church as a visible institution. Christians were not to withdraw from the world into the Church, but to go back into the world to evangelize.

The personal nature of faith in the historical Jesus as Savior and Lord is the conclusion of proclamation and persuasion evangelism. "Radical discipleship" was not adopted, for a distinction was made between personal faith and deeds of sanctification. The return of Christ alone will consummate salvation.

A high view of the Bible was maintained, a higher view than many European participants in particular may have cared, at first, to support.

Weaknesses. The first weakness is related to the inspiration of the Bible. There could not have been a Lausanne were it not for the tenacity of a generation which upheld the infallibility of the Scripture and meant thereby verbal plenary inspiration (not dictation) resulting in an infallible content. Much contemporary

theology does not submit to the meaning of a word in
the text and in its context. Inerrancy limits the
possibilities of interpretation and also limits the
interpreter to an objective body of truth. For this reason
some Evangelicals found a weakness in the Covenant,
first, because of the question of divinely inspired words
that are the symbols upon which theology is built and,
second, the "without error in all that it affirms" appears
to leave an opening for another *subjective* authority on
what the Bible teaches: a theologian, a Church, a
Tradition or a tradition, etc. Some of the evangelical
Anglicans at Nottingham 1977 and several of the
evangelical alliances in Europe have adopted a "hands
off" policy on spelling out this issue. Consequently,

> the objections to inerrancy by members of these
> groups accounted in part for the somewhat watery
> statement on Scripture that came out of the 1974
> Lausanne evangelical congress.[92]

The importance of this issue cannot be minimized, for it
reappears within evangelically-oriented Christianity,
whose theology still remains evangelical, just as it
reappeared, with disastrous results to missions and
evangelism, in the first decade of this century.

The second weakness was the theological blurring of
the evangelism focus that has characterized
evangelicalism in the nineteenth and twentieth centuries.
While social responsibility has always been a concern
among Evangelicals, their numerical weakness in the
1930s and 1940s made extensive financial contributions
difficult; yet they were heavily involved in medical work,
literacy, and education as "bridges" for the expansion
and extension of the Gospel. They did not have far to
look in the Scripture to find the Great Commission. An
equally passionate involvement in social and political
affairs of this world is less obvious in the New Testament
to those untutored in the Constantinian liaison between
church and state, even though it is one of many
Christian duties. While evangelism remains the general

focus of the Covenant to many, those who desire to
equate the importance of sociopolitical involvement with
evangelism will be able to justify it by Stott's paper and
by the Covenant statement ". . .we affirm that evangelism
and sociopolitical involvement are both part of our
Christian duty." A good case may be made that an
evangelical commitment to the infallibility and authority
of Scripture leads to a primary concern for evangelism
and also to a loving concern for others. The Scriptures
obviously teach both evangelism and sociopolitical
responsibilities. It is also possible, however, that a
departure from verbal inerrancy leads away from
evangelism as the mission of the Church, then to a
singular interest in social concern and, finally, to a
this-worldly or horizontal preoccupation.[93]

The third weakness is derived from the church growth
emphasis. The evangelical reaction against the
institutional church resulted in a proliferation of
parachurch movements. The Covenant spoke of these,
and even hinted as to their continued value. Stott, in his
commentary on the Covenant, said regarding parachurch
agencies:

> Although the right of such agencies to exist is
> agreed, and God is thanked for their work, yet the
> wisdom of their indefinite survival is not taken for
> granted.[94]

The Covenant also spoke to the WCC focus upon the
world, by stressing the *Church* as the very center of God's
cosmic purpose. But the restored emphasis upon the
Church since Berlin 1966 seems to have taken the
evangelistic responsibility away from the individuals that
comprise the Church, and to have given it to their
institutionalized representation. The mandate has been
transferred from the individual's responsibility as a
witness to the collective responsibility of the "community
of God's people." Lausanne had an overdose of historical
ecclesiology, induced by the influence of conciliar
theology and the multiple publications sponsored by the
WCC.

A fourth weakness is associated with the third—the strong institutionalized ecclesiology that characterizes the entire Covenant. The interdenominational nature of historic evangelicalism, characteristic of the spiritual nature binding believers together in truth, has almost disappeared while an implicit organizational ecclesiology has appeared at Lausanne that, first, proposes visible unity in truth; and, second, pledges itself to deeper unity in truth, worship, holiness, and mission. Third, it asserts that disunity undermines the gospel of reconciliation. This could be interpreted very easily as a mandate to futher church union among Evangelicals, or with others who agree upon the content of "truth" implied in the phrase "visible unity in truth." The conception of what "in truth" means among the plurality of Evangelicals represented among the participants would vary considerably according to the denominational background, theological convictions, and historical antecedents.

The reported vote of the second National Evangelical Anglican Congress at Nottingham, which was chaired by John Stott, strengthens this concern, for the Congress statement declared:

> The "visible unity of all professing Christians should be our goal" and. . ."evangelicals should join others in the Church of England" in working toward "full communion" with the Roman Catholic Church.[95]

This pattern is an almost identical repetition of what happened to the missionary movement at Edinburgh 1910, as churchmen replaced the evangelical "ecumenicity" of New York 1900. In the process, evangelism became submerged by church problems and the primacy of evangelization, both theologically and practically, was dissipated in the sociopolitical burdens of the denominations and state churches. Attempts to revive it within the framework of missions at Madras 1938 and at New Delhi 1961 are notable for the redefinition and reorientation of evangelism. At Madras 1938, it became the "Larger Evangelism," supposedly the best of both worlds of "fundamental" evangelism and modernistic "social gospel." New Delhi 1961 simply adapted the horizontalism of their gospel, and called the restructuring of the world "evangelism." A post-Constantinian ecclesiology diminished evangelism.

The root solution, however, lies in an attitude toward Scripture that not only recognizes its inspiration and authority, but also recognizes its self-authentication and its inherent power by the Holy Spirit to convict men of sin and enable them to come to an understanding of the Scripture, personal faith, and conversion. It is the testimony to Christ in the Bible that transcends the collective witness of the churches by their unity, incarnation, deeds, and sociopolitical involvement. Authority and the power of the Spirit are always related to the Bible. The Church was filled with the Spirit, to preach the Word with boldness.

THE THEOLOGY OF LAUSANNE

Lausanne's theology could have been strengthened in at least four areas. First, in the theology of mission, evangelism should have retained not only its priority and primacy, but also the unique status it held from the nineteenth century to Berlin 1966. The Covenant corrected the Congress papers on this point. The Great Commission does not denigrate the importance of a *Weltanschauung*, the cultural mandate, social concern and action, or the two kingdoms; but the Covenant recognized that the Scripture simply supports evangelism as the primary mission of the Church—making disciples "between the times" of Christ's First and Second Coming. Several Lausanne papers made unnecessary concessions to the pressure of the incarnational theology fadism current within the nonevangelical institutionalized churches since the days of Jerusalem 1928 and the rejection of historic evangelism by a horizontal salvation

based upon "modernism."[96] This debate is by no means
new or over. The Lausanne theology of evangelism was
blunted, nevertheless, and lost some of its historical
"cutting edge" by introducing issues related to the duties
of the church—and then describing this change as an
evidence of "evangelical maturity" by a tacit comparison
with ecumenical assemblies and conferences!

There is a correlation between this issue and the
concept of a state church beginning with Constantine:
that the Church is under some measure of obligation to
fulfill its functions to the state which supports it
financially. It is related to the question of the "world." If
the state has adopted Christianity as the official religion,
then the "world" cannot be as bad as the Bible says. It is
also related to eschatology and the return of Christ. Is
the Church those "gathered out of " a world inhabited by
a mankind which is progressively degenerating until the
Second Coming? The unwarranted emphasis upon the
Church as the "sign" of the future Kingdom—rather
than a bodily gathering of the elect—seems to expect a
more optimistic view of the "last days" as well as a more
benevolent view of man's sins.

Sin is seen as provoked by sinful societal structures,
rather than by the response of man's sinful nature
inherited from Adam.[97] It is related to the atonement.
Certain aspects of the cosmic and universal atonement
doctrines of Blauw, Niles, and Visser 't Hooft tended to
the supposedly naive, simplistic, and narrow concept of
substitutionary atonement. It obviously relates to the
social concern in society, and rejects evangelism as the
primary mission of the church. Social concern and
action, as a fruit of evangelism and as a result of
conversion, did not satisfy the "radical discipleship"
advocates—who want instant social involvement as much
as the older fundamentalists were caricatured as
expecting instant moral perfection and social separation!
This is indeed a new legalism that eliminates both the
doctrine of salvation by grace alone (sola gratia) and the
doctrine of sanctification as growth in grace.

The Gospel that brought evangelicalism to Berlin 1966 and Lausanne 1974 was repeatedly accused of withdrawing from society, of "ghettoism." Yet it was also this supposedly naive and immature evangelism, led by the Spirit and faithful to the authority of the Scripture, that brought Evangelicals out of the extreme minority position in the early part of this generation! The problem of withdrawal was as much psychological as theological. Evangelical abuses or inconsistencies do not require *theological* changes, but rather improved *exegetical, prophetic, and pastoral ministries;* for despite their shortcomings, Evangelicals are committed to the authority of Scripture.

Second, Lausanne could have been strengthened by a plenary paper on "Evangelism and the World" that was more representative of historic evangelical theology and, especially, soteriology. In Padilla's study the roots of an ecumenical theology of evangelism were developed that went beyond a South American expression of evangelicalism and into "holistic" evangelistic theology. Participants of the Congress needed a plenary session on this subject uncluttered by overtones of nationalism and of the ecumenical cosmic atonement, with its special terminology. While it is true that both Stott and the Lausanne Covenant corrected many errors of ecumenical theology of evangelism,[98] yet the Radical Discipleship minority response—finding support from Stott, Padilla, and Escobar—indicates a clear call for evangelicals to enter into the sociopolitical action as a partner with evangelism.[99]

Third, Lausanne could have been strengthened by a Covenant statement on inspiration that expressed what the Bible meant to earlier generations. It has already been mentioned that the "without error" of the *affirmations* of the Bible refers to its truthfulness, but not to the inspiration of the *words* that form the exegetical foundations of these true affirmations.[100]

Fourth, little was said about the great contemporary issue of postapostolic and sixteenth-century origins of the relationship between Tradition and Scripture. Uda's excellent plenary treatment of "Biblical Authority and Evangelism" implied an independence of the believer from the authority of Tradition,[101] and the fine sectional theological study on hermeneutics by Saphir Athyal affirmed the sufficiency of the written Word,[102] but the *conciliar issue lies with how the canon was accepted by the early Church.* If the Church as an institution formed the canon, then the Church historically precedes the Scripture, it is argued; and the Scripture and its interpretation is part of the Tradition of the Church.[103] According to Lukas Vischer, the issue since Vatican II is no longer one of two sources; it is an inspired decision of the Church council—"the Scriptures and the Church are interwoven."[104]

While it may be rightfully argued from the Covenant that the Scriptures are "the only infallible rule of faith and practice" and, consequently, rule out the authority of tradition, yet the current questions of authority in the Anglican-Roman Catholic dialogue and those in Faith and Order (WCC) require a sensitivity to them and a corresponding clarification for Evangelicals.

The basic theology of evangelism at Lausanne was sound, but further attention needs to be given to the trends within it that tend to divert Evangelicals from the centrality of evangelism and divert or blunt its present momentum.

8
The Decisive Decade

No one can seriously deny the

remarkable evangelistic impact of Lausanne 1974 upon the world. Many areas of the world have since recorded unusual responsiveness to the Gospel. Evangelistic conferences and campaigns seem to be multiplying beyond all expectations of the 1960s. Nationalism, nuclear armaments, national disasters, the world energy crisis, and social upheavals have led to a renaissance of fear and uncertainty. Countries like the United States have been disillusioned by breaches of confidence by elected officials, while Canada staggers under the threat of Quebec nationalism. John Mott once observed that in difficult circumstances like these, God always provides unusual evangelistic opportunities. The Lausanne Congress has provided the roots and impetus for a reversal of the nonevangelistic theology of the world conciliar bodies. These bodies are aware of their diminishing spiritual momentum and growth and many of them have expressed their concern about it. Evangelicals themselves have risen to a place of national prominence and international recognition. Lausanne inspired them and sharpened their evangelistic tools.

Yet in the midst of the greatest harvest in history lie the seeds of division that may disrupt the harvest—the conciliar elements within the Lausanne Committee, the

battle for the Bible against the left wing of
evangelicalism, the "radical" discipleship elements within
evangelicalism, the new pluralism of "charismatic"
Evangelicals within the WCC and the Roman Church,
the conflicts within the Lausanne Committee for World
Evangelization and those within more conservative
groups of the World Evangelical Fellowship and their
Barthian counterparts. While the "fundamentalists" have
not given up their separatism, or abandoned their
criticism of Lausanne, their division on the right has
become so decisive that the intensity of their polemic has
subsided. The sources of dissension within evangelicalism
are from those of the theological left, who have
abandoned the historic inspiration of Scripture and
adopted a spirit of latitudinarianism and who envisage a
visible conciliarity within the limits of minimal and
inclusive truth.

The decade 1970-1980 may well be recorded in history
as one of the most decisive of this century. In reviewing
the history of the ecumenical movement, the decade that
culminated in the death of D. L. Moody in 1899 has
been considered as the most decisive for the direction of
the Church and mission since the Reformation. This
decade, in like manner, contains the earlier dramatic
theological elements that finally led to the
Fundamentalist-Modernist controversy which erupted
within Protestantism about sixty years ago. It also
contains the serious threat of nonbiblical conciliarity
within Christendom. Since Lausanne, evangelicalism is
clearly seen as partially within the WCC and partially
outside of it—a fact not yet evident at Berlin.

The year 1980 will be decisive, for both the Lausanne
Committee, and the CWME of the WCC are anticipating
major conferences. The decisions made in the theological
preparation and programming will indicate the direction
the next generation will take. In any case, however,
"middle of the road" evangelicalism has strong
ecclesiastical and evangelical institutions which will not
permit the demise characteristic of the earlier decades of
this century. This decade also has the potential of

becoming an era of unprecedented harvest. Evangelical theology must remain faithful to the Scripture, and leadership must maintain an unwavering solidarity concerning the inspiration of Scripture in the midst of the dissenting voices from the evangelical left. The responsibility for dissension is theirs, for *they* have drifted from the inspiration of Scripture, while the Evangelicals of this century have remained faithful to their historical heritage.

THE LAUSANNE PROCESS

Lausanne stimulated and implemented the ongoing process of evangelism by a regionalization that delegated the preparation of evangelistic strategy on a continent-wide or national level. Lausanne 1974 introduced Evangelicals to those previously separated by linguistic, cultural, racial, or denominational barriers—and a new evangelical consensus and cooperation arose. Because a heavy interdenominational superstructure was avoided, initiative emerged on every level—from individual to regional—encouraged by the inspirational, theological, and instructive nature of Lausanne. The Congress itself not only stimulated other significant congresses on evangelism, but also new evangelistic agencies and Third World missions.

CONTINUITY

The planning Committee of Lausanne 1974 met on October 16-18, 1974, in Honolulu to receive reports from the chairman, the directors, and the associate directors, and to select the continental nominations to the Continuation Committee. The Committee expressed its appreciation to Billy Graham for his fund-raising efforts:

> . . .This Planning Committee, on behalf of the participants of the Congress, expresses its profound

and joyous gratitude to Billy Graham, who initially
financed and ultimately contributed half of the total
budget of the Congress.[1]

George Wilson, Congress Financial Consultant, reported
in the next meeting of the Continuation Committee,
January 20-23, 1975, in Mexico City, that the total
audited expenses through December 31, 1974, were
$3,117,000 and that the total income was $3,365,729,
leaving a balance of $247,979. Of the $3,365,729 raised
for Lausanne, $2,272,000 came directly from the Billy
Graham Evangelistic Association. Various others in
countries around the world responded to the support
committee, led by Maxey Jarman, a member of the
B.G.E.A. Board of Directors, by contributing
one-and-one-quarter million dollars. The unused portion
of the funds raised for the Congress was made available
to the Continuation Committee. It was agreed, however,
that additional funds for the Continuation Committee
would not be requested from the Billy Graham
Evangelistic Association.[2] Therefore, provision was made
through the Congress contributions for further assistance
to the Lausanne process.

The contributions were a remarkable testimony to the
deep evangelical concern for world evangelization and to
the confidence of Evangelicals in Billy Graham's
theology, methodology, and parachurch ministry. He was
voted "Convening Chairman" for the first meeting of the
Continuation Committee, which was expanded from the
original twenty-five members to forty.[3]

PRAYER

Mildred Dienert, who organized the important prayer
base for Lausanne 1974, reported the continued
outreach of the Congress to the constituency. Contact
was maintained with the prayer coordinators, sharing the
reports of praise and requests for future evangelistic
efforts. Reports were received from throughout the
world indicating such activities as newly-formed prayer

fellowships in Bandung, Indonesia, which were
concentrating on prayer for the evangelization of the
world.[4]

The Executive Committee meeting of September 1976
at Berlin gave extended consideration to the
"Recommendation for the Intercessory Ministry of the
LCWE" presented by the executive secretary, Gottfried
Osei-Mensah. The responsibilities for "the production
and dissemination of prayer and information" were
passed over to the staff in Nairobi which was to maintain
contact with the working group on intercession. In
addition to an annual worldwide day of prayer at
Pentecost, the working group was requested to
encourage intercession "for the freedom of our brethren ·
who are suffering for their testimony to the Lord Jesus
Christ. . . ." both as an encouragement and as one of the
best means of publicizing their needs.[5]

EVANGELISTIC
ACTIVITIES

By April 1976, Donald Hoke was able to report an
immense number of evangelistic activities as a direct
outgrowth of Lausanne. Europe had at least twenty-five
new organizations or missions that had been organized in
addition to Mission '76, a student missionary conference
attracting 800 Europeans, an evangelistic crusade in the
historic cathedral in Lausanne in which an African, Rev.
Festo Kivengere, had participated, and the distribution
of 100,000 copies of the Lausanne Covenant in Norway.

Africa had been challenged to a cross-cultural mission,
and leadership conferences held in Nairobi and South
Africa. Among many evangelistic efforts, Asia was
encouraged by: a Chinese Congress on World
Evangelization in August 1976, at Hong Kong, which
attracted 1,600 from all over the world; an All-India
Congress on Mission and Evangelism in January 1977;
and an Asian Evangelization Conference planned for
1978. Congresses on Evangelism were held in Cuba
1975, and renewed evangelistic efforts were initiated in

Nicaragua, Jamaica, and the Bahamas. The first
cooperative evangelistic campaign in the history of the
Bahamas resulted in 1,500 decisions, by combining group
meetings with church evangelism. Donald Hoke reported
that Latin America had "the least direct spin-off activities
from the Congress,"[6] which may have been due to the
extensive evangelism in Latin America prior to
Lausanne, or to the Latin American participants at
Lausanne who felt that Padilla's and Escobar's viewpoints
were not representative of theirs. A North American
Continuation Committee gave special emphasis to church
growth. Austria and Papua-New Guinea had conferences
on the Lausanne Covenant, student evangelism, and
evangelism. Many innovative methods of evangelism
have developed, and conferences on the theology of
evangelism have been held.

Considerable documentary evidence has been
continually accumulating which refutes the allegations of
Margret Nash that Lausanne has not initiated any new
evangelistic outreaches toward the 2,700 million living
outside the direct influence of Christianity and that "new
pioneering methods" from Lausanne have not been
forthcoming.[7]

Throughout the world, delegates have met together to
form national continuation committees and congresses.
For example, ninety-eight Lausanne Congress
participants from all the major denominations in Brazil
met in Rio, November 12 and 13, 1975, to present
papers on evangelism and missions. A committee was
appointed to promote and coordinate evangelical efforts
and to convene a Latin America Evangelization Congress.

In England, nearly 800 ministers, Sunday school
superintendents, teachers, and youth workers attended
the largest Christian education convention in decades in
Great Britain. Lillian Swanson of Scripture Press and
Jean Wilson of Gospel Light Press were inspired by the
Lausanne Congress and requested that the Scripture
Union be represented at the convention which was held
in the Metropolitan Tabernacle, London, December
12-13, 1975.

A survey of the evangelistic activities resulting directly from Lausanne can only conclude that the Congress was effective in stimulating evangelism throughout the world, and that thus far only the tip of the "iceberg" has become visible. Lausanne Evangelization has become regionalized. There is considerable evidence that the participants have taken the evangelistic challenges of the Congress seriously, and that the "process" of evangelizing the world by the year 2000, of completing the Great Commission in this generation, has been earnestly undertaken.

THE LAUSANNE COMMITTEE

The Continuation Committee first went through a two-year period of inner conflict over both purpose and personnel—what it should be and who should lead it. Bishop Jack Dain served as the chairman for the first year. The present structure began to emerge at the January 1976 Lausanne Committee Meeting when Leighton Ford was chosen unanimously to be the chairman. The Executive Committee meeting which was held the following September established the administrative structures which have now begun to function.

"OUR MANDATE FROM LAUSANNE '74"

The address given by Billy Graham to the Mexico City meeting of the Lausanne Continuation Committee on January 20, 1975, expressed his understanding both of the accomplishments of Lausanne and the mandate committed to the Continuation Committee. He recalled the dream that he and a small number of Evangelicals had had at Montreux, nearly fifteen years ago, to "somehow be used by God to bring together the terribly divided evangelical forces of the world, to finish the task

of world evangelization."[8] Lausanne had taken a new
look at the world's need, at world opportunity, and at
Christian responsibility—". . . The whole Church must be
committed to reach the whole world."[9] He believed that
Lausanne had also provided Christian leaders with a
clearer and more balanced perspective on evangelism
and social responsibility. Whereas Protestantism had been
a giant corrective to the Church of the sixteenth century,
over the years parts of it had "degenerated into a lifeless
formalism, nearly as bad as that against which it
revolted."[10]

> Thus evangelicalism was raised up by God not just
> as a corrective but as a vigorous reaffirmation of
> historic first-century Christianity.[11]

Graham foresaw the "challenge, responsibility,
opportunity and danger" confronting the newly elected
committee.

> There is every possibility that this committee could
> influence the direction of the Church in evangelism
> and missions for the next generation.[12]

After stating nine opportunities and challenges, Graham
explained the specific danger of expanding committee
responsibilities beyond the Lausanne evangelistic
mandate. He introduced the danger first by considering
the Great Commission and its relationship to the second
coming of the Lord in Matthew 24:14. The proclamation
of the Gospel as a witness to all nations will precede the
end—thus world evangelization is essential. Secondly, the
Committee received the distinctive "call and mandate
from the participants to further the cause of world
evangelization."[13]

Two concepts required Committee decisions:

> *Concept One* is that the paramount need of the world
> is for reconciliation with God and that nothing will
> benefit men here and now more than for them to
> become convinced followers and obedient disciples

of the Lord Jesus Christ. We need more effective
propagation of the Gospel, more speedy and sound
discipling of the nations. It was this kind of
evangelism that pulled evangelicals together at
Berlin and Lausanne.[14]

Graham did not see any possibility of uniting on any
other subject than this concept at this stage. The
Continuation Committee would, consequently, become

a global clearing house and implementation center
for evangelization for thousands of churches both
inside and outside the conciliar movement.[15]

The second concept contains the danger of proposing
that "this committee ought to get involved in all the
things that God wants done in our generation."[16]
Through global and regional headquarters, the
Committee would "promote a variety of good ends in a
thoroughly evangelical way."[17] While Graham did not
oppose this, he believed that the second concept "would
be off the mandate given at Lausanne," and that
"Concept Two should be carried out by. . .evangelical
organizations dedicated clearly to those ends."[18] He
counseled that the Committee "stick strictly to evangelism
and missions."[19] By this last word he meant missions of
evangelism in its historic sense.

The carefully worded "Guidelines for the Continuation
Committee," however, accepted the Covenant "duty" as
evangelism *and social responsibility,* a duty the Covenant
committed to the Church. It was a circumvention of both
Graham's and McGavran's counsel. The "Basis of Our
Coming Together" stated,

We recognize that we are coming together on the
basis of our common commitment to biblical
doctrine *and duty,* especially as expressed in the
Lausanne Covenant, and we desire to communicate
and interpret these to the church throughout the
world. (italics mine)[20]

The Committee understood from the Covenant that their
mandate transcends the call to Lausanne as a Congress

on World Evangelization. However, in the Congress, world evangelization was clearly distinguished from the Christian duty of social responsibility by both Stott and the Covenant.

The Committee voted that its basis would be the newly defined *mission* of the *Church* as evangelism *and* social responsibility. The evangelical commitment was rightfully included, but a doctrinal statement of what evangelicalism is had never been adopted. The Covenant implied fundamental doctrinal truths, but it was never intended to be confused with a doctrinal statement.[21] In essence, the basis commits the Continuation Committee to the combined responsibilities of the former International Missionary Council, Life and Work, and by extension, Faith and Order! The mission of the Church is *service* in which evangelism is primary among unspecified areas of service. Nor does the "Aim of the Committee" eliminate the broad potentials adopted by the Committee:

> The aim of the committee is to further the total biblical mission of the church, recognizing that "in this mission of sacrificial service, evangelism is primary," and that our particular concern must be evangelization of the 2,700 million unreached people of our world.[22]

Any means may be justified in accomplishing the *mission* of the Church. "The Role of the Committee" was

> to communicate what God is doing and what we believe He wants to do in the world, and to stir up people of God to more effective action.[23]

No negative vote was voiced, but Harold Lindsell requested to have his abstention recorded.

An objective review of the guidelines reveals that it has assumed an almost unlimited mandate, providing that its activities are justified by the evangelization of the 2.7 billion unreached peoples! It is doubtful that this was the avowed intention of the large majority who voted for it.[24] Another text states that "The Lausanne Covenant" is the promise to be "fully dedicated to evangelism and mission work in accordance with the mandate of Christ."[25] It is difficult to support the view that the Continuation Committee limited its work to proclamation and kept the duty of social action subordinate to the discipling mandate of the Great Commission.

It is true that, for a Congress on evangelization, Lausanne gave a disproportionate emphasis to the social aspects of Christian duty. However, it is also true that the soteriological significance of political involvement was avoided.[26]

THE IMPLEMENTATION OF THE MANDATE

The Mexico City meeting proposed the formation of regional committees, as authorized by the Lausanne Covenant,

> by all the members of the Continuation Committee from that region acting as a unit, being sensitive to already existing groups which are prepared to cooperate, allowing each regional committee the flexibility necessary for internal organization, structuring and programming in ways appropriate to its culture and geared specifically to its task.[27]

A flexible budget of $110,000 was adopted to support the program for the first year, and Gottfried Osei-Mensah was appointed the chief executive officer for an initial period of two years.

Strong differences of opinion emerged regarding the leadership of the Continuation Committee, when several joined John Stott in supporting the mission of the Church as the mandate of the Committee. Differences were finally solved by the unanimous request that Bishop Jack Dain continue to serve as chairman pro tem, and Billy Graham accepted the unanimous invitation to become honorary chairman of the Consultative Council, a wider body representing all those nominated by the Lausanne participants.[28] The meeting added a subtitle to their temporary name, "Lausanne Continuation Committee For World Evangelization."[29]

The next meeting was held at Atlanta, Georgia, U.S.A., from January 12-16, 1976. The untimely deaths of Paul Little and Byang Kato were recalled in a service of prayer. The name of the Continuation Committee was modified to be "The Lausanne Committee for World Evangelization."

Some editorial changes were made in the "Aims, Roles and Functions of the Lausanne Committee for World Evangelization." The Preamble stated that the Covenant both defines and defends the biblical doctrine and duty of the common evangelical commitment, and that it is determined to communicate biblical doctrine and duty, duty being *both evangelism and sociopolitical involvement.* Poetsch's theological analysis of "duty" in the Covenant, paragraph 5, concludes:

> Socio-political involvement stands side by side with evangelism and is not of second rank. Christian action in political societies, is, therefore, a part of the mission of the church.[30]

He considers the paragraph as an affirmation of the classically Reformed view of the mission of the church:

> Not only the offer of the saving Gospel for the forgiveness of sins constitutes mission work (sic), but also the Christianization of the structures in the societies of various nations and cultural realms.[31]

The committee adopted four guidelines: intercession, theological interpretation and training for service, research and strategy, and communication and pooling of resources. The function of "Theological Interpretation and Training for Service" has the greatest importance, for it determines the future theological and practical directions the Lausanne Committee may take in the three other functions:

> Theological Interpretation and Training for Service
> is to interpret the meaning and implications of the
> Lausanne Covenant in rapidly changing situations
> with theological analyses of contemporary
> movements and trends which are related to the
> mission of the Church.[32]

This flexibility in the new standing committee, now
called the "Lausanne Theological and Education Group"
and chaired by John Stott,[33] permits both the definition
and defense of the Covenant against contemporary
distortions, but also seems to have few if any limitations
placed upon its interpretation of "mission" beyond
review of the annual meeting of the Executive
Committee, or that of the entire Committee when it
normally meets every two years, or the occasional call of
the Consultative Council, now scheduled for 1980.[34] The
direction of the Committee is essentially vested in the
Executive Committee and its chairman. A retirement
system will renew approximately a third of the Lausanne
Committee at the meeting every other year, but the
minutes do not specify how replacements are to be
selected.

The unreached 2.7 billion stands out as the primary
concern of the Committee and this will be implemented
by committees on intercession, research and strategy
development, and the pooling of resources and
communication. In this area, the Committee has assumed
those responsibilities which the International Missionary
Council and the Division of World Mission and
Evangelism should have assumed after Edinburgh 1910.

HOLISTIC EVANGELISM

While "holistic" became current usage at the time of
Nairobi 1975, this word quite accurately represents the
concept of evangelism developed implicitly by the
Continuation Committee. In his Berlin Report on the
Hour of Decision, Leighton Ford reviewed the Berlin
Executive Committee meeting and assured his audience:

> We must keep our message clear. We must not
> compromise the Gospel by adding to it or taking
> from it. We must ask, "Are we committed to the
> whole Gospel? And do we know what the whole
> Gospel is today?"[35]

At the Chinese Congress on World Evangelization in
August 1976, the missiologist-reporter Ralph Covell was
concerned about the stress given by Stanley Mooneyham
to a *new* vision of the Cross and a fresh understanding of
the physical, social, and spiritual plight of a lost world.

> Noticeably missing from the content of "vision" was
> any detailed plenary presentation of the exact
> spiritual needs either of the entire world or the
> Chinese diaspora.[36]

The Nairobi office of the LCWE reported that the
Rhodesian Congress on Evangelism, May 1976

> dealt with winning the nations to Christ and being
> relevant to the communities of South Africa. A
> prophetic "Call to the Churches and Nations of
> Southern Africa" was issued by the Congress. The
> Call pleads with the leadership of the churches and
> nations of Southern Africa "to recognize the
> interrelatedness of our problems and to tackle them
> theologically and socially from the overall
> perspective." Copies of the Call have been
> presented to heads of government, heads of
> churches, Christian politicians, and other persons of
> influence in Southern Africa.[37]

A beneficial influence of Lausanne upon Roman
Catholic-Protestant unity in evangelism was reported at
the National Seminar on Evangelism, Papua, New
Guinea, in May 1976. Stott's commentary was studied by
160 participants at the annual Evangelical Alliance
Conference. Osei-Mensah, a guest speaker, clearly
distinguished between Christian service and evangelism:

> Social action and evangelism are distinctive
> commands from our God and they are both our

responsibility. . .Evangelism has a redemption base.
It is distinctively Christian and we cannot involve
the non-Christian in it.[38]

He also called Christians to lead the fight against
corruption and to serve in a "disinterested" way. "He
attacked those who believe evangelism and social concern
are polarized."[39] Pastor Joshua Daimoi said that the
conference came to three areas of agreement:

1. The churches must share in a better way their
   gifts and personnel.
2. The churches must begin to send their own
   missionaries to other nearby countries, especially
   to Southeast Asia.
3. Evangelism and social responsibilities go
   together, for we have learned that evangelism is
   not an isolated concept.[40]

He was quoted further as calling the Roman Catholic
presence a "first."

> It was a very unique experience because this was
> the first seminar of its kind in Papua, New Guinea,
> and perhaps in the world-wide Christian Church
> when Protestants and Catholics met side by side,
> thinking and discussing about evangelism. It helped
> us all to know each other's ideas about evangelism.
> Right through the seminar it became very clear that
> we should work unitedly in proclaiming the
> Gospel.[41]

Osei-Mensah believed the expression of "growing thirst
for biblical teaching and commitment to biblical
evangelism among many Catholics today is bound to
challenge evangelicals to re-think their attitudes to these
brethren."[42]

The Devlali Letter from the All-India Congress on
Mission and Evangelism in January 1977 confessed
spiritual coldness, failure to work together, and failure to
become personally involved with the poor and oppressed,
and believed that the evangelization of the 620 million in
India was a great, but achievable, goal![43] An Asian

Leadership Conference on Evangelism sponsored by the
LCWE is scheduled for November 1978:

> . . .the conference will review and evaluate
> evangelization progress of the past decade, identify
> the unreached and unevangelized sections in Asian
> society, examine and clarify theologically the issues
> and realities that help or hinder the mission of the
> church, pray for renewal and guidance in planning
> united strategy, and seek to understand anew the
> implications of total obedience to Christ in
> understanding Asian evangelization.[44]

The Lausanne Committee has adopted "holistic"
evangelism and is implementing its understanding and
acceptance around the world.

DYNAMIC TENSIONS WITHIN

Tensions within any growing movement are normal, yet
the ones to be mentioned in the LCWE had their origin
in the Program Committee prior to Lausanne. The
Committee took what John Stott called a "brave" view, by
taking risks with Padilla and Escobar. There was to be no
party line, no manipulation of the speakers, he said, and
"a willingness for debate to arise" which represents a
maturity "without an artificial front of unity."[45] He
believed that it was the wide acceptance of the Covenant
that had troubled Evangelicals, for even a Roman
Catholic group has accepted all but two points. Peter
Beyerhaus, he said, finds that liberals have twisted the
Covenant because it was not safeguarded by negative
terms at points of disagreement. The "without error in
all that it affirms" phrase has troubled Francis Schaeffer.
Stott replied that the Covenant does have several forms
of negatives. It does reject the Bangkok position and, "if
God could not protect the Scripture from abuse, then
how could he preserve a Covenant?"[46]

The LTEG sponsored a "Consultation on the
Theological and Ethical Issues of the Homogeneity

Principle of Church Growth Philosophy," held at
Pasadena in May 1977. It debated the multi-individual
conversion concept of the Church Growth school as
opposed to the "radical discipleship" concepts of
Lausanne. Further tension arose because of the invitation
of participants such as Victor Hayward, an advocate of
ecumenical theology.[47] The mandate for the Lausanne
participants was clearly to Evangelicals involved in a
"process." One might well ask: What are the limits of
interconfessional consultation and dialogue? Bishop Jack
Dain, chairman of the Lausanne Congress, in addressing
the question of what kind of Evangelicals were invited,
replied that Lausanne 1974 was "far more radical than
any other world congress of evangelicals that has ever
been held."[48] Some will wonder what direction future
LCWE meetings may take.

A similar problem arises from the motion of Peter
Wagner to the Lausanne Committee requesting LCWE
support for a joint Evangelical WCC-Roman Catholic
conference on mission and evangelism in 1980. Wagner
saw an increased interest in evangelism at Geneva, and
believed that the evangelistic resources within the orbit of
the Roman Catholic Church should be recognized. A
September 1975 Executive Committee decision had
already considered this type of meeting as inadvisable,
for nonconciliar participants of Lausanne are concerned
by these latitudinarian overtures.[49] At the Executive
Meeting in September 1976, the question of the LCWE
relationship with the 1980 meeting of the CWME (WCC)
was raised again by Peter Wagner.[50]

The participation of John Gatu and John Mbiti, noted
WCC voices, at the Pan African Christian Leadership
Assembly (PACLA) in December 1976 again created
serious difficulties for the LCWE. Financial appeals to
Evangelicals avoided mention of these and other
ecumenical speakers. In defending these speakers, some
received the impression that those opposing these
PACLA speakers were Western evangelical missions
interfering in African problems.[51] Subsequent
correspondence helped to relieve the tension, but doubts

were raised and some questioned the firm adherence in
practice of African Enterprises—as the sponsor for the
LCWE—to the Lausanne Covenant.[52]

The continual problem within the LCWE relates to its
relationships with the World Evangelical Fellowship.
Waldron Scott, general secretary of the WEF, was invited
to the September 1976 meeting of the LCWE Executive
Committee, and expressed his desire to clarify
misunderstanding, explain the present WEF direction,
and create a greater sense of unity and cooperation.[53]
The WEF began over twenty years ago as an evangelical
alternative to the WCC, while the LCWE attempted to
include all Evangelicals around the world under a large
umbrella. John Stott, Peter Wagner, and Waldron Scott
drew up a News Release, approved by the Executive
Committee, expressing the WEF hope to broaden its
constituency without compromising its evangelical
commitment. Even though the LCWE represented a
somewhat different constituency and possessed different
functions, the LCWE expressed its intention not to
establish an evangelical fellowship, or even compete with
the WEF. Mutual responsibilities were to be respected:

> We cherish the hope that in the providence of God
> our two constituencies, indeed all evangelical
> Christians throughout the world, may grow
> together in mutual understanding and trust, and in
> common prayer, thought and action.[54]

The inner tensions of LCWE helped to clarify its role
and define its responsibilities among world
evangelicalism.

PRESSURES
WITHOUT

The Fifth Assembly of the World Council of Churches
meeting at Nairobi, Kenya, from November 23 to
December 10, 1975, constituted a pressure for the
Evangelicals who were either conciliar-oriented or
unaware of the ecumenical theology of mission and

evangelism that supported the Assembly decisions. M. M.
Thomas, the retiring moderator of the Central
Committee, devoted over one-third of his report to a
comparison of potential areas of synthesis among the
"Salvation Today" report of the Bangkok 1973 DWME
meeting, the Lausanne 1974 Covenant, and the 1974
statement of the Bishops' Synod in Rome on Evangelism
in the Modern World.[55]

Bishop Mortimer Arias (Bolivia) introduced the subject
of "holistic" evangelism in "That the World May
Believe."[56] The areas in which Evangelicals essentially
disagree were outlined by John Stott, who said that he
also agreed with many things Arias said.[57] David Patton
has summarized what Stott stated that the WCC needs to
recover:

1. A recognition of the lostness of man. According to
the New Testament, men and women are not
"anonymous Christians" already in Christ and only
needing to be told so. They are "dead in their trespasses
and sins." Universalism is a deadly enemy of evangelism.

2. Confidence in the truth, relevance, and power of
the Gospel of God.

3. Conviction of the uniqueness of Jesus Christ. There
is truth in other religions and ideologies, but Paul's
argument in Romans is not that this knowledge of God
saves men, but that they are without excuse because they
suppress it.

4. A sense of urgency about evangelism, which might
begin by agreeing on vocabulary. It seemed to Dr. Stott
that mission is the comprehensive word to include both
sociopolitical action and evangelism. The Lausanne
Covenant drew clear distinctions not only between
evangelism and social action, but also between salvation
and political liberation. Dr. Stott was neither urging the
WCC to drop its social and political concerns nor to
"administer a fresh dose of opium to the oppressed" but
to be truly concerned with the *total* demands of justice
and love and with the *fullness* of God's freedom.

5. A personal experience of Jesus Christ—the greatest
of all obstacles to evangelism is the poverty of our own
experience.[58]

The WCC gave special attention to Stott's critique, although at the Assembly they seemed unwilling to hold a floor discussion of his response. Stott asked what could be done to restore the wide gap in confidence and credibility existing "between ecumenical leaders and Evangelicals, between Geneva and Rome."[59]

Hendrikus Berkhof brilliantly assessed the ecumenical-evangelical relationships and found them dormant until 1970:

> But from at least 1970 onwards it became a burning issue, and today it is not just a problem we have on our hands, but a war. On both sides people have come to the conclusion that one is *either* an evangelical *or* a friend of the World Council of Churches.[60]

Members of the WCC within the LCWE certainly must experience a measure of divided loyalty because of their historic ecclesiological roots in the sacraments and the ministry.[61] The WCC Faith and Order studies endeavor to show the importance of the historic episcopate and that "these new insights are enabling churches without the historic episcopate to appreciate it as a sign of the continuity and unity of the Church."[62] By the unity of creation and the reintroduction of the Church as a "sacrament" (a mystery), as well as a sign (of the future), Faith and Order continues to develop an ecumenical theology leading Protestants, Roman Catholics, and Eastern Orthodox one step closer to unity. Those Evangelicals who are without the anchor of verbal infallibility logically turn sooner or later toward a sacramental symbol of the historical church to find assurance of salvation from it and from its "historical" ministers rather than from the words of the apostles themselves in the Bible. An accompanying pluralistic spirit leads again toward conciliarity and catholicity.[63]

The 1976 Central Committee received the "Report of the Core Group of World Mission and Evangelism" which is planning the 1980 conference:

CWME proposes to hold its conference in 1980 in the general area of "mission today." It is not yet ready to propose a specific theme since this can only be done after a process of consultation. This process should include not only the constituency of the WCC, but Roman Catholics and Conservative Evangelicals.[64]

Will the 1980 CWME conference adopt the mission of the Church as proposed by Stott as an adapted form of their holistic *mission*?

The other pressure has been referred to on several occasions—that of the post-Vatican II Roman Catholic Church. The Synod of Bishops on October 25, 1974, confirmed anew that "the mandate to evangelize all men constitutes the essential mission of the church."[65] Archbishop S. E. Carter said:

There has been some stress in Roman Catholic theology upon the positive values to be found in non-Christian religions and in the fact that many non-Christians acting in good faith are not far from the Kingdom of God. But speakers at the Synod placed great emphasis on the necessity to preach the Gospel to every creature, and so upon the necessity to preach the Gospel to those not yet baptized. Great stress was laid upon the fact that this is the duty of the *entire Church* to proclaim the message of Christ. . .[66]

Lukas Vischer believes that the "two sources" of revelation have been dropped since Vatican II.[67] In the Faith and Order Study prepared for the 1976 Central Committee, Dom Emmanuel Lanne noted that the 1870 definition of papal infallibility extends not only to the pope but also to the teaching of the bishops. In addition to those authorities, the people of God have still another authority in which they play an active role. "The assured consensus of 'the People of God' forms part of the infallibility of the Church."[68] An increased emphasis was placed in Vatican II upon the local church assembled around its legitimate pastor, rather than the Church as a worldwide organization. These new Roman Catholic concessions toward conciliarity place greater pressure upon the Lausanne Committee through conciliar-minded leadership in dialogue with Rome.

Evangelicals are confused to hear of the 2,000 Evangelicals who, led by John Stott at Nottingham, April 14-18, 1977, endorsed the rapprochement of the Church of England with the Roman Catholic Church.[69] English Evangelicals at this National Evangelical Anglican Congress were reported as rediscovering the nature of the church, and reacting "against the pietistic inward-looking attitude of the past." Nurtured within the new stream of thought within Evangelical Anglican circles, "politics, race, the arts, and media are now all considered worthy subjects for a Congress of Evangelicals."[70] The definitions of subjects related to evangelism are continuing to expand.

CONCLUSION

Contemporary evangelicalism owes a great debt to the earlier decades of this century. This century, in turn, has built upon the centuries from the Reformation to the Great Century of world mission, the nineteenth, sometimes called the Pietist century. The rise of evangelicalism in its diverse expressions in different countries and cultures reaffirms the eternal truth taught by the apostles that "the word of God is quick, and powerful" (Heb. 4:12). Evangelistic power is intimately related to the Bible which is "living and "energizing" by the power of the Holy Spirit.

Contemporary reports of revival and church growth generally owe little to the united programs popularized during the past decade. Generally, the reports and evaluations of growth have their origins in simple pietist proclamation evangelism and the sacrifices consciously made for Christ in the earlier years of this generation. It is hypocritical and deceptive to report as ours that which

we have not done. Many reports of church growth are
the result of the Seed faithfully sown and watered in past
decades. The present generation will be judged for its
faithfulness to that which it has received, and the way in
which it builds upon this evangelical heritage.

Evangelicals need to be aware of their recognition by
Eastern Orthodoxy and Roman Catholicism because of
their evangelism and the Lausanne Congress. A measure
of renewal within the WCC-affiliated churches and
within Roman Catholicism has come through various
expressions of evangelicalism: from revivalism and
charismatic expressions within, and parachurch
evangelism from without. New waves of institutionalism
in the forms of apostolic succession and Tradition are
beginning to invade evangelicalism as the historical
evangelical confidence in the absolute sufficiency of the
Scripture, *sola scriptura,* begins to fade. The theological
"left" of evangelicalism is in danger of placing the
authority of Scripture into the authority sphere of
Tradition. The answer is not in synthesis, but in
faithfulness to the Bible transmitted by the holy apostles
to us and for us. Our prayers and desires ought to be for
biblical renewal and spiritual revival in the great
institutional churches of Christendom, but revived
evangelicalism has not had its origins in the false
ecclesiological vision of visible unity. There is a "given"
unity in Christ and by the Spirit, transcending its
unlimited manifestations in the local churches.[71]
Apostolic successionism of the ministry and ecclesiastical
institutionalism have never provided for the institutional
churches that for which some Evangelicals are now
seeking. The greatest contribution evangelicalism can
make to historic churches is to retain its apostolic identity
in love, *and evangelize* anywhere and everywhere.
Revivalism and evangelism remain God's program and
God's answer to the need of the human heart and to
society.

Evangelism is central and essential to the earthly body
of Christ living between the times of the ascension and
the second coming. This evangelism, whether at Los

Angeles 1949 or at Berlin 1966, maintains its momentum by its *spiritual* impact upon individual lives. The proclamation of the Word of God, in the power of the Holy Spirit, in a godly life produces divine results. This evangelism is its own best defense and the greatest legacy willed to the next generation. Tom Allan in Scotland was a good example of a minister convinced by what he saw God doing in evangelism. The greatest good can be done for the world by a proclamation evangelism that penetrates all levels of society with the Truth in Christ Jesus.

Adequate theology that defends and corrects is necessary to maintain biblical guidelines or perimeters, but the end in view must be the glory of God expressed in "much fruit" (John 15:8) and "many brethren" (Romans 8:29). A worship of Christ that does not culminate in witness by word and deed has become abortive, sterile, ritualistic. The Spirit makes witnesses (Acts 1:8).

The worldwide advance of the Gospel does not seem to have been greatly advanced—if at all—by a negative polemic preached against the conciliar movement. The Message is Christ. Nor have efforts to penetrate the WCC from within, so as to modify an ecumenical pronouncement, yielded much fruit. Evangelical evangelism has spoken more forcibly. Subtle efforts of sophisticated evangelicalism to penetrate and unite the forces of "unenlightened" and "simplistic" revivalism can only crush and stifle the Evangel enthroned within sincere, committed hearts. Sophistication needs to demonstrate its own dynamic by its own true evangelistic praxis. The errors of darkness are best revealed by more Light. The bats disappear with dawn.

History joins the Scripture in teaching that from generation to generation there will be drifts to the "right," into ingrown nonevangelizing legalism, and drifts to the "left," into latitudinarianism and broad nonevangelical theological pluralism. Active biblical evangelism may well be one of the best major solutions to both drifts.

Evangelicalism by its very naure is ecumenical. It loves

and seeks fellowship with "born-again" believers
wherever they are found. Parachurch evangelical
evangelism, however, may be most vulnerable to the
post-Vatican II theological relativism expressed in
multiple forms of conciliarity—from councils, assemblies,
and synods to the new congeniality on the local levels.
This raises the legitimate question as to the point when
evangelical cooperation becomes compromise and
complicity in error and "another gospel." There are
biblical guidelines beyond which evangelicalism cannot go
without falling into evangelistic impotency and,
eventually, self-destruction. The complete truthfulness
and final authority of Scripture provides the essential
parameters for evangelicals.

Berlin 1966 pointed directly from "The Authority for
Evangelism," the basic study, to personal and group
evangelism. Repeatedly, the value and worth of a human
soul and the "night" of judgment and eternal
punishment were emphasized. Berlin rightly saw the
primary answer to world evangelization rooted in soul
winning on the personal or group level. It was this
essential method of evangelism on an individual or a
group level that revived evangelicalism from the
obscurity of the 1920s.

The Lausanne Covenant shifted the emphasis on
Christian responsibility from the individual to the
Church body and personal responsibility became blurred
in group responsibility. Lausanne, in its desire to reach
the exploding masses, became more technological,
methodological, and sophisticated. What was gained in
depth and technique became less comprehensible and
communicable to the "common man" and less
inspirational to the leaders. The "grace" of New
Testament simplicity—a personal reproduction and
multiplication of spiritual life in Christ—was lost in a
technological and sociological approach to the growth of
the Church. An aristocratic approach to evangelism
made some from South America wonder if the Holy
Spirit was receiving His rightful place in Western
Christianity. The very strength of evangelicalism has
been in the enviable simplicity of its Message and methods.

Furthermore, Lausanne may have served more the needs and goals of conciliar-minded evangelical churchmen. In its effort to be stimulating, unfettered, and somewhat controversial, it opened a door to what was described as the most radical of evangelical congresses. This direction came through the program committee and the selection of speakers. Berlin did not sidestep thorny theological questions, but it gave a united and historical reply to them. Lausanne established a congressional method and approach that invited changes in the present evangelistic thrust. Evangelicals need to evaluate continually the direction in which these trends in mission and evangelism are taking them—toward a more biblical evangelism or away from it.

The acceptance and impact of the redefinition of mission in the Congress papers (but not in the Covenant) is of particular concern. Sociopolitical action had always been a duty of the Christian as a member of a church even though in the "struggle for survival" and building or rebuilding of churches the Evangelical could not devote much time and money to it. It is indeed a cavalier caricature of Evangelicals who were reduced to an extreme minority position, around the world, to accuse them of withdrawal from society because of their reaction to the social gospel. If their efforts had been diverted in this direction, there would not have been a Berlin! Sociopolitical action was always part of "teaching them to observe all things whatsoever I have commanded you" (Matt. 28:20). The mission of the Church was evangelism by its members at home, and by its missions at home and abroad. Expressions of love and compassion in evangelism at home and abroad are evident in dispensaries, hospitals, schools, and orphanages, which contribute to that mission of evangelism. Robert Speer needs to be read before naively accusing Evangelicals of using social concern as evangelistic bait. That is a strongly judgmental accusation to make against Evangelicals, who for centuries have long looked with compassion upon the deprived and oppressed as created in the image of God, and have loved them in Christ into

the dignity and decency of the redeemed family of God.
Much "redefinition" seems to be more of a desire to
establish greater evangelical credibility among ecumenical
critics than a dedicated commitment to world
evangelization.

Interconfessional dialogue by the Lausanne Committee
with those whose theology is built upon the hermeneutic
elasticity of an errant Bible, or upon Tradition, have few
valid insights to contribute to the evangelical concern for
world evangelization. Wrong theological presuppositions,
based upon divergent views of authority, lead to
confusing principles and practices of mission and
evangelism. McGavran is particularly right when he
speaks to the theological and practical priority of
evangelism and church growth. The Lausanne
Committee must reexamine the direction in which it is
taking world evangelization by its theological
contributions to congresses on evangelism and Christian
leadership around the world.

The question of theological relativism leads back finally
to the inspiration and authority of the Scripture as the
watershed issue in evangelism. The Lausanne Covenant,
isolated from the theological studies of the Congress, *did
have* a "somewhat watery statement on Scripture,"[72]
because of the hesitancy of some Evangelicals in Europe
to publicly embrace a stronger position on inspiration.
This, however, has been a cornerstone of evangelicalism
with theological roots in the apostolic Word written, and
historical roots in the early Councils of the Church and
the sixteenth-century Reformation.[73] Many ecumenical
theologians have recognized the issues of not only the
infallibility, but of the verbal inerrancy of the Scripture
in their original text.[74]

Eugene L. Smith, reporting on the ecumenical
situation in the United States to Geneva in 1966, astutely
observed the first basic softening on Scripture since the
first decade of this century:

> One theological issue often cited is that of Biblical
> authority. It promises to be less and less important

in the future as a divisive issue. An important and growing body of conservative Biblical scholars increasingly affirms that Biblical "inerrancy" has to be interpreted, that Scripture must be read for the essential message it seeks to proclaim and understood in the light of the situation in which it was written.[75]

This question is inherent within the Lausanne Committee's work, and within its relationships with the World Evangelical Fellowship troubled with this problem. It is related to the growing question, "What is an Evangelical?"

Evangelism has progressed and advanced under the leadership of the Holy Spirit as the Scripture has been believed and proclaimed by those "born again." This generation is facing three great threats to evangelism: the inspiration of Scriptures, the relationship of Scripture to Tradition, and the mission of the Church. Evangelicals of the post-World War II generation may look back with gratitude to God for His blessing upon their endeavors to evangelize faithfully the world in this generation. These areas constitute the contemporary battle for world evangelism.

Appendixes

APPENDIX I
One Race,
One Gospel,
One Task
Closing Statement of
The Berlin World Congress
on Evangelism

As participants in the World Congress on Evangelism, drawn from 100 nations and gathered in Berlin in the Name of Jesus Christ, we proclaim this day our unswerving determination to carry out the supreme mission of the Church.

On behalf of our fellowmen everywhere, whom we love and for whom our Savior died, we promise with renewed zeal and faithfulness to bear to them the Good News of God's saving Grace to a sinful and lost humanity; and to that end we now rededicate ourselves before the sovereign King of the universe and the risen Lord of the Church.

We enter the closing third of the 20th century with
greater confidence than ever in the God of our fathers
who reveals himself in creation, in judgment and in
redemption. In his holy Name we call upon men and
nations everywhere to repent and turn to works of
righteousness.

As an evangelical ecumenical gathering of Christian
disciples and workers, we cordially invite all believers in
Christ to unite in the common task of bringing the word
of salvation to mankind in spiritual revolt and moral
chaos. Our goal is nothing short of the evangelization of
the human race in this generation, by every means God
has given to the mind and will of men.

ONE RACE

We recognize the failure of many of us in the recent past
to speak with sufficient clarity and force upon the biblical
unity of the human race.

All men are one in the humanity created by God
himself. All men are one in their common need of divine
redemption, and all are offered salvation in Jesus Christ.
All men stand under the same divine condemnation and
all must find justification before God in the same way: by
faith in Christ, Lord of all and Savior of all who put
their trust in him. All who are "in Christ" henceforth can
recognize no distinctions based on race or color and no
limitations arising out of human pride or prejudice,
whether in the fellowship of those who have come to
faith in Christ or in the proclamation of the Good News
of Jesus Christ to men everywhere.

We reject the notion that men are unequal because of
distinction of race or color. In the name of Scripture and
of Jesus Christ we condemn racialism wherever it
appears. We ask forgiveness for our past sins in refusing
to recognize the clear command of God to love our
fellowmen with a love that transcends every human
barrier and prejudice. We seek by God's grace to
eradicate from our lives and from our witness whatever
is displeasing to him in our relations with one another.

We extend our hands to each other in love, and those same hands reach out to men everywhere with the prayer that the Prince of Peace may soon unite our sorely divided world.

ONE GOSPEL

We affirm that God first communicated the Gospel of redemption, and not man; we declare the saving will of God and the saving work of God only because we proclaim the saving Word of God. We are persuaded that today, as in the Reformation, God's people are again being called upon to set God's Word above man's word. We rejoice that the truth of the Bible stands unshaken by human speculation, and that it remains the eternal revelation of God's nature and will for mankind. We reject all theology and criticism that refuses to bring itself under the divine authority of Holy Scripture, and all traditionalism which weakens that authority by adding to the Word of God.

The Bible declares that the Gospel which we have received and wherein we stand, and whereby we are saved, is that "Christ died for our sins according to the scriptures; and that he was buried, and that he arose again the third day according to the scriptures" (1 Corinthians 15:3-4). Evangelism is the proclamation of the Gospel of the crucified and risen Christ, the only Redeemer of men, according to the Scriptures, with the purpose of persuading condemned and lost sinners to put their trust in God by receiving and accepting Christ as Savior through the power of the Holy Spirit, and to serve Christ as Lord in every calling of life and in the fellowship of his Church, looking toward the day of his coming in glory.

ONE TASK

Our Lord Jesus Christ, possessor of all authority in heaven and on earth, has not only called us to himself; he has sent us out into the world to be his witnesses. In the power of his Spirit he commands us to proclaim to all people the good news of salvation through his atoning death and resurrection; to invite them to discipleship through repentance and faith; to baptize them into the fellowship of his Church; and to teach them all his words.

We confess our weakness and inadequacy as we seek to fulfill the Great Commission; nevertheless we give ourselves afresh to our Lord and his cause. Recognizing that the ministry of reconciliation is given to us all, we seek to enlist every believer and to close the ranks of all Christians for an effective witness to our world. We long to share that which we have heard, have seen with the eyes of faith, and have experienced in our personal lives. We implore the world church to obey the divine commission to permeate, challenge, and confront the world with the claims of Jesus Christ.

While not all who hear the Gospel will respond to it, our responsibility is to see that every one is given the opportunity to decide for Christ in our time. Trusting our Lord for strength and guidance, we shoulder this responsibility.

Finally, we express to Evangelist Billy Graham our gratitude for his vision of a World Congress on Evangelism. To the magazine *Christianity Today* goes our debt of thanks for bringing it into reality. As we return to our many fields of labor for Christ we promise to pray for each other; and we extend our love and affection to the whole wide world of men in the matchless name of our Savior.

World Congress on Evangelism
Kongresshalle, Berlin, Germany
4, November 1966

APPENDIX II
The Lausanne
Covenant

Introduction. We, members of the Church of Jesus Christ,
from more than 150 nations, participants in the
International Congress on World Evangelization at
Lausanne, praise God for his great salvation and rejoice
in the fellowship he has given us with himself and with
each other. We are deeply stirred by what God is doing
in our day, moved to penitence by our failures and
challenged by the unfinished task of evangelization. We
believe the Gospel is God's good news for the whole
world, and we are determined by his grace to obey
Christ's commission to proclaim it to all mankind and to
make disciples of every nation. We desire, therefore, to
affirm our faith and our resolve, and to make public our
covenant.

1. *The Purpose of God.* We affirm our belief in the one
eternal God, Creator and Lord of the world, Father, Son
and Holy Spirit, who governs all things according to the

purpose of his will. He has been calling out from the
world a people for himself, and sending his people back
into the world to be his servants and his witnesses, for
the extension of his kingdom, the building up of Christ's
body, and the glory of his name. We confess with shame
that we have often denied our calling and failed in our
mission, by becoming conformed to the world or by
withdrawing from it. Yet we rejoice that even when
borne by earthen vessels the Gospel is still a precious
treasure. To the task of making that treasure known in
the power of the Holy Spirit we desire to dedicate
ourselves anew. (Isa. 40:28; Matt. 28:19; Eph. 1:11; Acts
15:14; John 17:6, 18; Eph. 4:12; I Cor. 5:10; Rom. 12:2;
II Cor. 4:7)

2. *The Authority and Power of The Bible.* We affirm the
divine inspiration, truthfulness and authority of both Old
and New Testament Scriptures in their entirety as the
only written Word of God, without error in all that it
affirms, and the only infallible rule of faith and practice.
We also affirm the power of God's Word to accomplish
his purpose of salvation. The message of the Bible is
addressed to all mankind. For God's revelation in Christ
and in Scripture is unchangeable. Through it the Holy
Spirit still speaks today. He illumines the minds of God's
people in every culture to perceive its truth freshly
through their own eyes and thus discloses to the whole
church ever more of the many-colored wisdom of God.
(II Tim. 3:16; II Pet. 1:21; John 10:35; Isa. 55:11; I Cor.
1:21; Rom. 1:16; Matt. 5:17, 18; Jude 3; Eph. 1:17, 18;
3:10, 18)

3. *The Uniqueness and Universality of Christ.* We affirm that
there is only one Savior and only one Gospel, although
there is a wide diversity of evangelistic approaches. We
recognize that all men have some knowledge of God
through his general revelation in nature. But we deny
that this can save, for men suppress the truth by their
unrighteousness. We also reject as derogatory to Christ
and the Gospel every kind of syncretism and dialogue

which implies that Christ speaks equally through all
religions and ideologies. Jesus Christ, being himself the
only God-man, who gave himself as the only ransom for
sinners, is the only mediator between God and man.
There is no other name by which we must be saved. All
men are perishing because of sin, but God loves all men,
not wishing that any should perish but that all should
repent. Yet those who reject Christ repudiate the joy of
salvation and condemn themselves to eternal separation
from God. To proclaim Jesus as "the Savior of the
World" is not to affirm that all men are either
automatically or ultimately saved, still less to affirm that
all religions offer salvation in Christ. Rather it is to
proclaim God's love for a world of sinners and to invite
all men to respond to him as Savior and Lord in the
wholehearted personal commitment of repentance and
faith. Jesus Christ has been exalted above every other
name; we long for the day when every knee shall bow to
him and every tongue shall confess him Lord. (Gal.
1:6-9; Rom. 1:18-32; I Tim. 2:5,6; Acts 4:12; John
3:16-19; II Pet. 3:9; II Thess. 1:7-9; John 4:42; Matt.
11:28; Eph. 1:20,21; Phil. 2:9-11)

4. *The Nature of Evangelism.* To evangelize is to spread the
good news that Jesus Christ died for our sins and was
raised from the dead according to the Scriptures, and
that as the reigning Lord he now offers the forgiveness
of sins and the liberating gift of the Spirit to all who
repent and believe. Our Christian presence in the world
is indispensable to evangelism, and so is that kind of
dialogue whose purpose is to listen sensitively in order to
understand. But evangelism itself is the proclamation of
the historical, biblical Christ as Savior and Lord, with a
view to persuading people to come to him personally and
so be reconciled to God. In issuing the Gospel invitation
we have no liberty to conceal the cost of discipleship.
Jesus still calls all who would follow him to deny
themselves, take up their cross, and identify themselves
with his new community. The results of evangelism
include obedience to Christ, incorporation into his

church and responsible service in the world. (I Cor. 15:3,4; Acts 2:32-39; John 20:21; I Cor. 1:23; II Cor. 4:5; 5:11, 20; Luke 14:25-33; Mark 8:34; Acts 2:40, 47; Mark 10:43-45)

5. *Christian Social Responsibility.* We affirm that God is both the Creator and the Judge of all men. We therefore should share his concern for justice and reconciliation throughout human society and for the liberation of men from every kind of oppression. Because mankind is made in the image of God, every person, regardless of race, religion, color, culture, class, sex or age, has an intrinsic dignity because of which he should be respected and served, not exploited. Here too we express penitence both for our neglect and for having sometimes regarded evangelism and social concern as mutually exclusive. Although reconciliation with man is not reconciliation with God, nor is social action evangelism, nor political liberation salvation, nevertheless we affirm that evangelism and socio-political involvement are both part of our Christian duty. For both are necessary expressions of our doctrines of God and man, our love for our neighbor and our obedience to Jesus Christ. The message of salvation implies also a message of judgment upon every form of alienation, oppression and discrimination, and we should not be afraid to denounce evil and injustice wherever they exist. When people receive Christ they are born again into his kingdom and must seek not only to exhibit but also to spread its righteousness in the midst of an unrighteous world. The salvation we claim should be transforming us in the totality of our personal and social responsibilities. Faith without works is dead. (Acts 17:26, 31; Gen. 18:25; Isa. 1:17; Psa. 45:7; Gen. 1:26, 27; Jas. 3:9; Lev. 19:18; Luke 6:27, 35; Jas. 2:14-26; John 3:3, 5; Matt. 5:20; 6:33; II Cor. 3:18; Jas. 2:20)

6. *The Church and Evangelism.* We affirm that Christ sends his redeemed people into the world as the Father sent him, and that this calls for a similar deep and costly

penetration of the world. We need to break out of our ecclesiastical ghettos and permeate non-Christian society. In the church's mission of sacrificial service evangelism is primary. World evangelism requires the whole church to take the whole Gospel to the whole world. The church is at the very center of God's cosmic purpose and is his appointed means of spreading the Gospel. But a church which preaches the Cross must itself be marked by the Cross. It becomes a stumbling block to evangelism when it betrays the Gospel or lacks a living faith in God, a genuine love for people, or scrupulous honesty in all things including promotion and finance. The church is the community of God's people rather than an institution, and must not be identified with any particular culture, social or political system, or human ideology. (John 17:18; 20:21; Matt. 28:19, 20; Acts 1:8; 20:27; Eph. 1:9, 10; 3:9-11; Gal. 6:14, 17; II Cor. 6:3, 4; II Tim. 2:19-21; Phil. 1:27)

7. Cooperation in Evangelism. We affirm that the church's visible unity in truth is God's purpose. Evangelism also summons us to unity, because our oneness strengthens our witness, just as our disunity undermines our gospel of reconciliation. We recognize however, that organizational unity may take many forms and does not necessarily forward evangelism. Yet we who share the same biblical faith should be closely united in fellowship, work and witness. We confess that our testimony has sometimes been marred by sinful individualism and needless duplication. We pledge ourselves to seek a deeper unity in truth worship, holiness and mission. We urge the development of regional and functional cooperation for the furtherance of the church's mission, for strategic planning, for mutual encouragement, and for the sharing of resources and experience. (John 17:21, 23; Eph. 4:3, 4; John 13:35; Phil. 1:27; John 17:11-23)

8. *Churches in Evangelistic Partnership.* We rejoice that a new missionary era has dawned. The dominant role of western missions is fast disappearing. God is raising up

from the younger churches a great new resource for
world evangelization, and is thus demonstrating that the
responsibility to evangelize belongs to the whole body of
Christ. All churches should therefore be asking God and
themselves what they should be doing both to reach their
own area and to send missionaries to other parts of the
world. A re-evaluation of our missionary responsibility
and role should be continuous. Thus a growing
partnership of churches will develop and the universal
character of Christ's Church will be more clearly
exhibited. We also thank God for agencies which labor in
Bible translation, theological education, the mass media,
Christian literature, evangelism, missions, church
renewal, and other specialist fields. They too should
engage in constant self-examination to evaluate their
effectiveness as part of the Church's mission. (Rom. 1:8;
Phil. 1:5; 4:15; Acts 13:1-3; I Thess. 1:6-8)

9. *The Urgency of the Evangelistic Task.* More than 2,700
million people, which is more than two-thirds of
mankind, have yet to be evangelized. We are ashamed
that so many have been neglected; it is a standing rebuke
to us and to the whole church. There is now, however, in
many parts of the world an unprecedented receptivity to
the Lord Jesus Christ. We are convinced that this is the
time for church and para-church agencies to pray
earnestly for the salvation of the unreached and to
launch new efforts to achieve world evangelization. A
reduction of foreign missionaries and money in an
evangelized country may sometimes be necessary to
facilitate the national church's growth in self-reliance and
to release resources for unevangelized areas. Missionaries
should flow ever more freely from and to all six
continents in a spirit of humble service. The goal should
be, by all available means and at the earliest possible
time, that every person will have the opportunity to hear,
understand, and receive the good news. We cannot hope
to attain this goal without sacrifice. All of us are shocked
by the poverty of millions and disturbed by the injustices
which cause it. Those of us who live in affluent

circumstances accept our duty to develop a simple life-style in order to contribute more generously to both relief and evangelism. (John 9:4; Matt. 9:35-38; Rom. 9:1-3; I Cor. 9:19-23; Mark 16:15; Isa. 58:6, 7; Jas. 1:27; 2:1-9; Matt. 25:31-46; Acts 2:44, 45; 4:34, 35)

10. *Evangelism and Culture.* The development of strategies for world evangelization calls for imaginative pioneering methods. Under God, the result will be the rise of churches deeply rooted in Christ and closely related to their culture. Culture must always be tested and judged by Scripture. Because man is God's creature, some of his culture is rich in beauty and goodness. Because he has fallen, all of it is tainted with sin and some of it is demonic. The Gospel does not presuppose the superiority of any culture to another, but evaluates all cultures according to its own criteria of truth and righteousness, and insists on moral absolutes in every culture. Missions have all too frequently exported with the Gospel an alien culture, and churches have sometimes been in bondage to culture rather than to the Scripture. Christ's evangelists must humbly seek to empty themselves of all but their personal authenticity in order to become the servants of others, and churches must seek to transform and enrich culture, all for the glory of God. (Mark 7:8, 9,13; Gen. 4:21,22; I Cor. 9:19-23; Phil. 2:5-7; II Cor. 4:5)

11. *Education and Leadership.* We confess that we have sometimes pursued church growth at the expense of church depth, and divorced evangelism from Christian nurture. We also acknowledge that some of our missions have been too slow to equip and encourage national leaders to assume their rightful responsibilities. Yet we are committed to indigenous principles, and long that every church will have national leaders who manifest a Christian style of leadership in terms not of domination but of service. We recognize that there is a great need to improve theological education, especially for church leaders. In every nation and culture there should be an

effective training program for pastors and laymen in
doctrine, discipleship, evangelism, nurture and service.
Such training programs should not rely on any
stereotyped methodology but should be developed by
creative local initiatives according to biblical standards.
(Col. 1:27, 28; Acts 14:23; Tit. 1:5, 9; Mark 10:42-45;
Eph. 4:11, 12)

12. *Spiritual Conflict.* We believe that we are engaged in
constant spiritual warfare with the principalities and
powers of evil, who are seeking to overthrow the church
and frustrate its task of world evangelization. We know
our need to equip ourselves with God's armor and to
fight this battle with the spiritual weapons of truth and
prayer. For we detect the activity of our enemy, not only
in false ideologies outside the church, but also inside it in
false gospels which twist Scripture and put man in the
place of God. We need both watchfulness and
discernment to safeguard the biblical Gospel. We
acknowledge that we ourselves are not immune to
worldliness of thought and action, that is, to a surrender
to secularism. For example, although careful studies of
church growth, both numerical and spiritual, are right
and valuable, we have sometimes neglected them. At
other times, desirous to insure a response to the Gospel,
we have compromised our message, manipulated our
hearers through pressure techniques, and become
unduly preoccupied with statistics or even dishonest in
our use of them. All this is worldly. The church must be
in the world; the world must not be in the church. (Eph.
6:12; II Cor. 4:3,4; Eph. 6:11, 13-18; II Cor. 10:3-5;
I John 2:18-26, 4:1-3; Gal. 1:6-9; II Cor. 2:17, 4:2;
John 17:15)

13. *Freedom and Persecution.* It is the God-appointed duty
of every government to secure conditions of peace,
justice, and liberty in which the church may obey God,
serve the Lord Christ and preach the Gospel without
interference. We therefore, pray for the leaders of the
nations and call upon them to guarantee freedom of

thought and conscience and freedom to practice and propagate religion in accordance with the will of God and as set forth in The Universal Declaration of Human Rights. We also express our deep concern for all who have been unjustly imprisoned and especially for our brethren who are suffering for their testimony to the Lord Jesus. We promise to pray and work for their freedom. At the same time we refuse to be intimidated by their fate. God helping us, we too will seek to stand against injustice and to remain faithful to the Gospel, whatever the cost. We do not forget the warnings of Jesus that persecution is inevitable. (I Tim. 1:1-4; Acts 4:19, 5:29; Col. 3:24; Heb. 13:1-3; Luke 4:18; Gal. 5:11, 6:12; Matt. 5:10-12; John 15:18-21)

14. *The Power of The Holy Spirit.* We believe in the power of the Holy Spirit. The Father sent his Spirit to bear witness to his Son; without his witness ours is futile. Conviction of sin, faith in Christ, new birth, and Christian growth are all his work. Further, the Holy Spirit is a missionary spirit; thus evangelism should arise spontaneously from a Spirit-filled church. A church that is not a missionary church is contradicting itself and quenching the Spirit. Worldwide evangelization will become a realistic possibility only when the Spirit renews the church in truth and wisdom, faith, holiness, love and power. We, therefore, call upon all Christians to pray for such a visitation of the sovereign Spirit of God that all his fruit may appear in all his people and that all his gifts may enrich the body of Christ. Only then will the whole church become a fit instrument in his hands, that the whole earth may hear his voice. (I Cor. 2:4; John 15:26, 27, 16:8-11; I Cor. 12:3; John 3:6-8; II Cor. 3:18; John 7:37-39; I Thess. 5:19; Acts 1:8; Psa. 85:4-7; 67:1-3; Gal. 5:22, 23; I Cor. 12:4-31; Rom. 12:3-8)

15. *The Return of Christ.* We believe that Jesus Christ will return personally and visibly, in power and glory, to consummate his salvation and his judgment. This promise of his coming is a further spur to our

evangelism, for we remember his words that the Gospel must first be preached to all nations. We believe that the interim period between Christ's ascension and return is to be filled with the mission of the people of God, who have no liberty to stop before the end. We also remember his warning that false Christs and false prophets will arise as precursors of the final Antichrist. We, therefore, reject as a proud, self-confident dream the notion that man can ever build a utopia on earth. Our Christian confidence is that God will perfect his kingdom, and we look forward with eager anticipation to that day, and to the new heaven and earth in which righteousness will dwell and God will reign forever. Meanwhile, we rededicate ourselves to the service of Christ and of men in joyful submission to his authority over the whole of our lives. (Mark 14:62; Heb. 9:28; Mark 13:10; Acts 1:8-11; Matt. 28:20; Mark 13:21-23; John 2:18, 4:1-3; Luke 12:32; Rev. 21:1-5; II Pet. 3:13; Matt. 28:18)

Conclusion. Therefore, in the light of this our faith and our resolve, we enter into a solemn covenant with God and with each other, to pray, to plan, and to work together for the evangelization of the whole world. We call upon others to join us. May God help us by his grace and for his glory to be faithful to this our covenant! Amen, Alleluia!

FOOTNOTES

Chapter One **The Decline of Evangelism**
1. Bernard de Vaulx, *History of the Missions* (New York: Hawthorn Books, 1961), pp. 69-72. Originally published in France under the title *Les Missions: Leur Histoire* (Librairie Artheme Fayard, 1960).
2. *Ibid.*, pp. 121-125.
3. *Ecumenical Missionary Conference New York, 1900* (New York: American Tract Society, 1900), pp. 19, 20.
4. It must be remembered that the national churches were comparatively small in this era of history.
5. *Encyclopedia of Missions*, Vol. II, Rev. Edwin Munsel Bliss, editor, "Missionary Conferences" (New York: Funk and Wagnalls, 1891), pp. 106, 107.
6. Delavan Leonard Pierson, *Arthur T. Pierson* (New York: Fleming H. Revell, 1912), pp. 192, 193.
7. Discussion arose over the title of the Edinburgh 1910 conference. There was a recorded diversity of opinion in which some saw "ecumenical" in terms of the plan of campaign which proposes to cover the whole area of the inhabited globe. A civic leader saw it as "ecumenical" "because all Protestant Christendom is to take part in it," and he prophetically looked forward toward a united purpose of all Christendom. Another, speaking for the German delegation, saw that it demonstrated "before the world, and especially in the face of Rome, the unity of all evangelical mission people, and by that also the unity of all Protestant Christendom." "Minutes of the International Committee," July 14-20, 1908, World Missionary Conference 1910, Third Ecumenical Missionary Conference (Geneva: World Council of Churches Archives), pp. 9, 10, 15, 34.
8. *Ibid.*, p. 67.
9. *Ibid.*, p. 70.
10. *Ibid.*, p. 75.
11. *Ibid.*, pp. 74, 75.
12. Arthur P. Johnston, *World Evangelism and the Word of God* (Minneapolis: Bethany Fellowship, 1974), pp. 70-82.

13. *Maintaining the Unity* (Proceedings of the Eleventh International Conference and Diamond Jubilee Celebration of the Evangelical Alliance, London, July 1907) (London: Religious Tract Society, 1907), pp. 143, 144.

14. C. Howard Hopkins, *History of the Y.M.C.A. in North America* (New York: Association Press, 1951), pp. 362-369.

15. A summary of the decline and death of the Student Volunteer Movement for Foreign Missions (which later became the Student Christian Movement) is made by David Howard. Among the ten causes for the decline Howard extracted from the 1941 University of Chicago doctoral dissertation of W. H. Beahm, three are significant to this study:

   1. "Revivalism had given way to basic uncertainty as to the validity of the Christian faith, especially of its claim to exclusive supremacy. Accordingly, the watch-word (the Evangelization of the World in This Generation) fell into disuse and the argument for foreign missions lost its force.

   2. "Their emphasis shifted away from Bible study, evangelism, life-work decision, and foreign-mission obligation, on which the SVM had originally built. Instead they now emphasized new issues such as race relations, economic justice and imperialism.

   3. "The rise of the social gospel blotted out the sharp distinction between Christians and the 'unevangelized portions of the world.' " David Howard, "The Rise and Fall of the SVM," *Christianity Today* (November 6, 1970), pp. 15-17.

16. Tissington Tatlow, *The Story of the Student Christian Movement of Great Britain and Ireland* (London: SCM Press, 1933), p. 220.

17. Franklin H. Little, *The Theology of the Christian Mission*, Gerald H. Anderson, editor (New York: McGraw Hill, 1951), p. 115.

18. Yoder, *A History of the Ecumenical Movement* (1917-1948), Ruth Rouse and Stephen Charles Neill, editors (London: S.P.C.K., 1954), p. 254.

19. W. A. Visser 't Hooft, *The Background of the Social Gospel in America* (Haarlem: H. D. Tjeenk Willink & Zoon, 1928), p. 11.

20. For an example, see *World Missionary Conference 1910*, Vol. IV (Edinburgh: Oliphant, Anderson and Ferrier, 1910), p. 268. This weakness also appears in A. H. Strong's *Systematic Theology*.

21. James Orr, *Ritchlianism* (London: Hodder and Stoughton, 1903), p. 25.

22. Stephen Neill, *Christian Missions* (Middlesex: Penquein, 1964), p. 455.

23. Ernest Troeltsch, *Die Absolutheit des Christentums und die Religionsgeschichte* (Tübingen: B. C. Mohr, 1902), p. 94.

24. Tatlow, *The Story of the Student Christian Movement of Great Britain and Ireland*, p. 213ff.

25. *Ibid.*

26. *Ibid.*

27. *Ibid.*, p. 381.

28. *Ibid.*, p. 220.

29. Forming the Inter-Varsity Christian Fellowship and, ultimately, the International Fellowship of Evangelical Students.

30. Tatlow, *The Story of the Student Christian Movement of Great Britain and Ireland*, p. 383.

31. "Minutes of the Meeting of the General Committee of the World's Student Federation," July 13-17, 1909, at Oxford, England (Geneva: WCC Archives).

32. Tatlow, *The Story of the Student Christian Movement of Great Britain and Ireland*, p. 335.

33. John R. Mott, *Addresses and Papers*, Vol. II (New York: Association Press, 1946), p. 117.

34. Ruth Rouse, *The World's Student Christian Federation* (London: SCM Press, 1948), p. 139.

35. It must be acknowledged that John R. Mott, a man of great intellectual stature and charisma, always considered himself a layman and that he long exercised a strong biblical and evangelistic emphasis in the International Missionary Council until his retirement in 1942.

36. Adolf Harnack, *What Is Christianity?* (New York: Harper and Brothers, 1957), p. 199.

37. "Minutes of the International Committee," n.p.

38. "Education in Relation to the Christianization of National Life," World Missionary Conference 1910, Report to Commission III (Geneva: WCC Archives), p. 407.

39. *Histoire Doctrinale du Mouvement Oecumenique* (Paris: Desclee de Brouwer, 1962), p. 15.

40. W. H. T. Gairdner, *Echoes from Edinburgh 1910* (New York: Revell, 1910), p. 50.

41. "Minutes of the International Committee," n.p.

42. "Minutes of the Executive Committee," World Missionary Conference 1910, June 30, 1909 (Geneva: WCC Archives), p. 44.

43. L. S. Albright, "The International Missionary Council, Its History, Functions, and Relationships" (New York: IMN, 1946), p. 8. Pastor A. Boegner, however, made a heart-stirring plea for foreign missionary assistance in France at the conference. See *World Missionary Conference 1910, The History and Records of the Conference* (New York: Revell, 1910), 231.

44. The original title of the conference was "The Third Ecumenical Missionary Conference." It was amended to World Missionary Conference in July 1908.

45. "In those years, Protestant missionary endeavor in Latin American lands, and in lands associated historically with the Roman Catholic Church, was regarded by most European churchmen as being merely anti-Catholic. Missionaries to those lands were dubbed bigots, members of an uncouth and unlettered proletariat, whose work should be repudiated." John A. Mackay, "The Latin American Churches and the Ecumenical Movement," brochure of the Committee of Cooperation in Latin America (Division of Foreign Missions, National Council of Churches in the U.S.A., 1963), p. 11. A large official delegation of Latin American Protestants was first admitted to the Madras 1938 Conference.

46. Tatlow, *The Story of the Student Christian Movement of Great Britain and Ireland*, pp. 404-410.

47. *World Missionary Conference 1910, The History and Records of the Conference*, pp. 164-172.

48. When Mott visited Korea in December 1925, Miss Helen Kim, later a delegate at Jerusalem, spoke of the differences between the fundamentalists and the modernists and asked, "What is the central thing in Christianity, the heart of the message? This, I hope, the Council will find and state." Alfred W. Wasson, *Church Growth in Korea* (New York: International Missionary Conference, 1934), p. 126.

49. The lucid evangelical theology of New York 1900 spoke so clearly that evangelism was neither blunted nor threatened. President John Barrows of Oberlin College spoke with respect and recognition of non-Christian religions and their followers, but left no opening for any accusation of syncretism. In addressing the subject of "The Wider Relations of Missions to Non-Christian Religions and Apologetic Problems," Barrows acknowledged the limited values of these religions. Judaism, he said,

"has pre-eminently stood for the best, and the highest, and the truest in the knowledge of God, and it is historically certain that the Judeo-Christian revelation has been the mainstream of history. There is no second Bible; there is no second Christ; there is no second Calvary. Heathenism is without Christmas and without Easter. All other streams are tributary to Christianity. It has already absorbed most of them. It does not need to go to India to learn of the omnipotence of the Deity. It does not need to go to Egypt to learn from tomb and pyramid, or Book of the Dead, that life continues beyond the grave. It does not need to sit at the feet of Athens to find the splendor of beauty, and the sacredness of the intellect. Whatever is true in the thought of Persia or in the social ethics of China, has been a part of Christianity. . . . But, although we who know the Christian and study the non-Christian faiths may, for a time, be amazed and dazzled by similarities, it is only to discover, in the end, the profound divergencies. There can be no close sympathies between Christianity and Buddhism, for example, which has no knowledge of the just and holy God seeking after men with purposes of love and reconciliation, and through atonement removing every obstacle on the part of men to the highest blessing which heaven can offer. It is only a beggarly salvation, after all, which Buddha can offer, an almost worthless salvation. It is not an escape from guilt and pollution, it is not receiving the Spirit of God and divine life, holy and immortal; it is only a release from the bondage of desire and the final sinking of the spirit into a quiescence bordering on extinction; and even this salvation, according to the original teaching of Gautama, can be obtained by a very few." *Ecumenical Missionary Conference New York, 1900*, p. 361.

"Missionaries are keenly alive to the fact that some of the non-Christian faiths are keeping their place in the world because they minister to some of the needs of the human heart. They are preserved from utter condemnation by the great truths which, amid all errors and perversions, they undoubtedly contain. There is much beauty in Confucian morals. There are Christian elements, if not a Christian spirit, in Buddhist ethics. Christian theism, teaching the Divine unity and omnipresence of the Spirit, is not wholly out of touch with the monotheism of Islam, or the pantheism of the Hindu philosophies, but the uniqueness of Christianity is the historical

Christ and the one incarnation of God in man for redemption through sacrifice. There is no second Jesus. The best claims which others can make for their faiths is some likeness to the Christian in some particulars. But who else is sinless? Who else brings together God and man? Who else has cleansed the conscience from the perilous load? Who else has brightened the darkness of the grave with sure revelations of a personal immortality?" *Ibid.*, p. 358.

While nineteenth century missionaries did not always retain the national cultural values, their insistence upon a "clean sweep" or a complete break with the non-Christian religion not only avoided the threats of syncretism but also rooted the believers more deeply and permanently even though the growth may not have been as rapid.

50. Report of Commission IV, World Missionary Conference 1910 (Geneva: WCC Archives), pp. 214-274, 324-326.

51. "Carrying the Gospel to All the Non-Christian World," Report of Commission I, World Missionary Conference 1910 (Geneva: WCC Archives), pp. 434-436. In 1900 at New York, Oldham said, "Christianity does not ask for a 'tabula rasa' for the writing of its golden words, but seeks rather to present Him as the 'fulness' and the 'fulfiller,' who is already everywhere present in all the faithful in the measure in which they hold religious truth and spiritual values." *Ecumenical Missionary Conference New York, 1900*, Vol. II, p. 86.

52. Hendrick Kraemer's *The Christian Message in a Non-Christian World*, second edition (London: Edinburgh House Press, 1947), is well-known. Madras turned to the more biblical emphasis of faith.

53. *World Missionary Conference 1910, The History and Records of the Conference*, n.p. *Report of Commission VII, Cooperation and the Promotion of Unity* (New York: Revell, 1910), p. 131. World Missionary Conference 1910, Report of Commission I, "Carrying the Gospel to All the Non-Christian World," p. 48ff.

54. The Scriptures alone, grace alone, faith alone.

55. It is, of course, recognized that God *progressively* revealed Himself to mankind, and that this history is recorded in the Bible. This revelation, however, culminated with the death of the apostles, so that the interpretation of the words and works of the Word made flesh were finalized, leaving the Christians with an infallible Book as the source of their theology and faith.

56. The Basis of the Evangelical Alliance was carefully and prayerfully concluded in 1847 by nearly forty leaders of high spiritual and theological repute. They agreed upon the following evangelical views:
"That the parties composing the Alliance shall be such persons only as hold and maintain what are usually understood to be evangelical views, in regard to the matters of doctrine understated, *viz.*:
1. The divine inspiration, authority, and sufficiency of the Holy Scriptures.
2. The right and duty of private judgment in the interpretation of the Holy Scriptures.
3. The Unity of the Godhead, and Trinity of Persons therein.
4. The utter depravity of human nature in consequence of the fall.

5. The incarnation of the Son of God, His work of atonement for sinners of mankind, and His mediatorial intercession and reign.
6. The justification of the sinner by faith alone.
7. The work of the Holy Spirit in the conversion and sanctification of the sinner.
8. The immortality of the soul, the resurrection of the body, the judgment of the world by our Lord Jesus Christ, with the eternal blessedness of the righteous, and the eternal punishment of the wicked.
9. The Divine institution of the Christian ministry, and the obligation and perpetuity of the ordinances of baptism and the Lord's Supper.

"It being, however, distinctly declared: First, that this brief summary is not to be regarded, in any formal or ecclesiastical sense, as a creed or confession; nor the adoption of it as involving an assumption of the right authoritatively to define the limits of Christian brotherhood, but simply as an indication of the class of persons, whom it is desirable to embrace within the Alliance: Secondly, that the selection of certain tenets, with the omission of others, is not to be held as implying that the former constitute the whole body of important truth, or that the latter are unimportant."

57. As stated by the International Missionary Council Committee, September 30-October 6, 1921, at Lake Mohonk (Geneva: WCC Archives, Box 16). See also *International Review of Missions*, Box XII, 1923, pp. 491, 492. Also, Johnston, *World Evangelism and the Word of God*, pp. 131-134.
58. William Ernest Hocking, *Rethinking Missions: A Layman's Enquiry After One Hundred Years* (New York: Harper, 1932), n.p.

Chapter Two **The "Larger Evangelism"**
of the International Missionary Council 1921-1961
1. W. A. Visser 't Hooft, *The Background of the Social Gospel in America*, n.p.
2. *Ibid.*
3. Robert T. Handy, *The Protestant Quest for a Christian America* (Philadelphia: Fortress, 1967), p. 15.
4. The liberal-modernist camp slurred that of the "fundamentalists" as having a "slaughter-house religion" because of their commitment to the efficacy of the blood of Christ.
5. Wilhelm Anderson, *Towards a Theology of Missions*, International Missionary Council Research Pamphlet No. 2 (London: SCM Press, 1955), p. 23.
6. G. W. H. Lampe, "The Bible Since the Rise of Critical Study," in *The Church's Use of the Bible*, D. E. Nineham, editor (London: S.P.C.K., 1963), pp. 125-144.
7. *The Social Gospel in America 1870-1920*, Robert E. Handy, editor (New York: Oxford University Press, 1966), p. 255.
8. Walter Rauschenbusch, *Christianizing the Social Order* (New York: Macmillan, 1919), pp. 464, 465.
9. Walter Rauschenbusch, *The Righteousness of the Kingdom*, edited and translated by Max L. Stackhouse (Nashville: Abingdon, 1968), pp. 18, 45. Also see *The Social Gospel in America 1870-1920*, Handy, editor, p. 260.

10. *The Social Gospel in America 1870-1920*, Handy, editor, p. 388.
11. *Ibid.*, p. 385.
12. Rauschenbusch, *The Righteousness of the Kingdom*, p. 263.
13. *The Social Gospel in America 1870-1920*, Handy, editor, p. 326.
14. *Ibid.*, p. 12.
15. J. Edwin Orr, *Campus Aflame* (Glendale, Calif.: Regal, 1971), p. 101.
16. Fundamentalism in that era represented evangelicalism. The trial of John T. Scopes, accused of violating the statutes of Tennessee by teaching evolution in the public schools, was prosecuted by the champion of evangelization, William Jennings Bryan. The public image of the Evangelicals was marred by brilliant attacks of defense lawyer Clarence Darrow and by the biased reporting of the New York *Times* and other papers. See *The Evangelicals*, David F. Wells and John R. Woodbridge, editors (Nashville: Abingdon, 1975), pp. 12, 127, 194-197.
17. "Report of the Jerusalem Meeting of the International Missionary Council," March 24-April 8, 1928, Vol. I, p. 490ff.
18. Oliver Chase Quick, "The Jerusalem Meeting and the Christian Message," *International Review of Missions*, XVII (1928), p. 46ff.
19. *Ibid.*, p. 446.
20. Letter of J. H. Oldham to J. R. Mott, "Comments on the Book on Co-operation," in *Salvation and Social Conditions* (Geneva: WCC Archives, approximately 1935), p. 126.
21. Wasson, *Church Growth in Korea*, p. 126.
22. *Ibid.*
23. See Johnston, *World Evangelism and the Word of God*, pp. 176, 177.
24. So J. Edwin Orr oversimplifies and underestimates the gravity of the controversy. He fails to correlate the fact that the subsequent revivals and awakenings of the student movements at Wheaton and other institutions from the 1930s to 1970s were concentrated in *evangelical* academic institutions. "Even in the United States, the phenomenon of Evangelical Awakenings occurred only in those colleges committed to an Evangelical Christian position." Orr, *Campus Aflame*, pp. 144, 215.
25. James Orr, *The Ritschlian Theology and the Evangelical Faith* (London: Hodder and Stoughton, 1897), pp. 142, 143; James Orr, *Sin as a Problem of Today* (London: Hodder and Stoughton, 1900).
26. W. A. Visser 't Hooft and J. H. Oldham, *The Church and Its Function in Society*, Vol. I in Church, Community and State Series (London: George Allen and Unwin, 1937), p. 172.
27. *Ibid.*, p. 229.
28. William John Schmidt, "Ecumenicity and Syncretism: The Confrontation of the Ecumenical Movement with Syncretism in Special Reference to the International Missionary Council and the World Council of Churches" (unpublished Ph.D. thesis, Columbia University, University Microfilms, Inc., Ann Arbor, Mich., 1966), pp. 146-148. Also see Henry P. Van Dusen, "The Missionary Message Since Madras," *Christendom*, IX (Winter 1944), p. 29.
29. Karl Barth, *The Doctrine of the Word of God*, translated by G. T. Thomson, Vol. I, Part 1 (Edinburgh: T. and T. Clark, 1936), n.p.
30. Kraemer, *The Christian Message in a Non-Christian World*, p. 73.
31. *(Madras) Tambaram Series*, Vol. I (London: Oxford University Press, 1939), p. 189.

32. *Ibid.*, p. 185.
33. *Ibid.*, p. 420.
34. *Ibid.*, p. 423.
35. *Ibid.*, p. 429.
36. *Ibid.*, p. 430. In a later work, Latourette takes a far more pessimistic outlook on the value of mass conversions and speaks much more positively of the necessity of "receiving Christ" and of the new birth wrought by God through the Holy Spirit. Kenneth Scott Latourette, *A History of Christianity* (London: Eyre and Spottiswoode, 1954), pp. 375, 405, 406, 476. Cf. William Paton, *Studies in Evangelism* (London: The Sheldon Press, 1940), pp. 28ff., 58-111.
37. *(Madras) Tambaram Series*, Vol. III, p. 432.
38. William Richey Hogg, *Ecumenical Foundations* (New York: Harper and Brothers, 1952), p. 298.
39. The Basel Mission in India is an example. This approach in China produced "rice Christians," those who became Christians because of the availability of food in times of need—but who abandoned Christianity as conditions improved.
40. Robert Evans, *Let Europe Hear* (Chicago: Moody Press, 1964).
41. Dean M. Kelley, *Why Conservative Churches Are Growing* (New York: Harper and Row, 1972).
42. Brunner called this experience a "subjective immediacy which takes into account the 'living voice of the Church.'" Emil Brunner, *Revelation and Reason*, translated by Olive Wyon (London: SCM Press, 1947), pp. 237-276.

Chapter Three Developments in Evangelism Before Berlin 1966

1. "Minutes of the Meeting of the Provisional Committee," January 28-30, 1939, at St. Germain-en-Laye, France (Geneva: WCC Archives), mimeographed, p. 8.
2. "Jesus Christ and Our World, an Interpretation of the Programme at Whitby" (Geneva: WCC Archives), p. 5.
3. *Renewal and Advance*, C. W. Ranson, editor (London: Edinburgh House Press, 1948), p. 217; Johnston, *World Evangelism and the Word of God*, pp. 209-217.
4. *Renewal and Advance*, Ranson, editor, p. 215.
5. *Ibid.*, p. 218.
6. *Ibid.*, p. 213.
7. *Man's Disorder and God's Design*, Vol. II in The Amsterdam Assembly Series (New York: Harper and Brothers, n.d.), p. 165ff.
8. *The Ecumenical Advance: A History of the Ecumenical Movement*, Vol. II, Harold E. Fey, editor (Philadelphia: Westminster, 1970), p. 5.
9. "Guiding Principles for the Interpretation of the Bible," *Ecumenical Review*, II, No. 1 (Autumn 1949), pp. 81, 82; Wolfgang Schweitzer, "The Bible and the Church's Message to the World," *Ecumenical Review*, II, No. 2 (Winter 1950), p. 132.
10. Richard C. Rowe, *Bible Study in the World Council of Churches* (Geneva: WCC, 1969), pp. 24, 25; Johnston, *World Evangelism and the Word of God*, pp. 221-223; *Biblical Authority for Today*, Alan Richardson and Wolfgang Schweitzer, editors (London: SCM Press, 1951), p. 141.
11. Suzanne de Dietrich, "The Bible, a Force for Unity," *Ecumenical Review*, II, No. 4 (Autumn 1949), p. 410.

12. See Klass Runia, *Karl Barth's Doctrine of Holy Scripture* (Grand Rapids, Mich.: Eerdmans, 1962), pp. 18, 41, 153.
13. W. Lillie, "The Universal Missionary Obligation of the Church in Relation to the Present Historical Situation" (Geneva: WCC Archives, n.d.), mimeographed, p. 1.
14. *Ibid.*
15. "The Second Report of the Advisory Commission on the Theme of the Second Assembly of the World Council of Churches," *Ecumenical Review*, V, No. 1 (October 1952), p. 73. See also Johnston, *World Evangelism and the Word of God*, pp. 223-235; *Missions Under the Cross*, Norman Goodall, editor (London: Edinburgh House Press, 1953), p. 15.
16. Schmidt, "Ecumenicity and Syncretism: The Confrontation of the Ecumenical Movement with Syncretism in Special Reference to the International Missionary Council and the World Council of Churches," p. 237.
17. "Minutes of the Enlarged Meeting and the Committee of the International Missionary Council," July 5-21, 1952, at Willingen, Germany, p. 143.
18. *Ibid.*, p. 54.
19. *The Student World*, 1957, p. 336.
20. *Ibid.*, p. 333.
21. Bengt Sundkler, "The Missionary Obligation of the Church; a Memorandum Prepared by the Research Secretary for Consideration by the IMC Research Committee at Oestgeest on September 7, 1948," August 30, 1948, Holland.
22. *The Ghana Assembly of the International Missionary Council*, December 28, 1957 to January 8, 1958, Ronald K. Orchard, editor (London: Edinburgh House Press, 1958), p. 21ff.
23. Lesslie Newbigin, "The Organization of the Church: Mission to the World," June 1958 (Geneva: WCC Archives), mimeographed, p. 1. Newbigin was Secretary of the IMC from 1959 to 1961 and Director of the WCC Division of World Mission and Evangelism from 1961 to 1965.
24. Based on author's interview March 10, 1969. Also see Philip Potter, "Evangelism and the World Council of Churches," *Ecumenical Review*, Vol. XX, No. 2 (April 1968), p. 174.
25. *The First Assembly of the World Council of Churches*. W. A. Visser't Hooft, editor (London: SCM Press, 1949), p. 197.
26. The history of the Basis goes back to the "Paris Basis" established at the first World Conference of the Y.M.C.A., Paris 1855. See Johnston, *World Evangelism and the Word of God*, pp. 66, 67.
27. *The Ecumenical Advance: A History of the Ecumenical Movement*, Fey, editor, p. 35.
28. *Ibid.*, Vasil T. Istavrides, "The Orthodox Churches in the Ecumenical Movement 1948 to 1968," pp. 306, 307.
29. *Ibid.*, H. Kruger, pp. 35, 36.
30. *Ibid.*, W. A. Visser 't Hooft, "The General Ecumenical Development Since 1948," pp. 6-10.
31. W. A. Visser 't Hooft, "The Significance of the World Council of Churches," in *The Universal Church of God's Design* (New York: Harper and Brothers, 1948), p. 193.

32. *The Ecumenical Advance: A History of the Ecumenical Movement,* Vol. II, Fey, editor, W. A. Visser 't Hooft, "The General Ecumenical Development Since 1948," pp. 4, 5.
33. *Ibid.,* p. 19.
34. "Conference of Evangelism," February 11-19, 1947 (Geneva: WCC Archives), mimeographed, p. 6.
35. *Ibid.,* p. 14.
36. *Ibid.,* pp. 14, 15.
37. *Ibid.,* p. 13.
38. *Ibid.,* p. 15.
39. *Ibid.,* E. G. Homrighausen, p. 2.
40. *Ibid.,* p. 32.
41. *The First Assembly of the World Council of Churches,* W. A. Visser 't Hooft, editor, p. 53.
42. *Ibid.,* p. 64.
43. *Ibid.,* p. 68.
44. *Ibid.*
45. *Ibid.,* p. 70.
46. *The Ecumenical Advance: A History of the Ecumenical Movement,* Vol. II, Fey, editor, p. 307.
47. By Department of Studies in Evangelism, WCC, Geneva, 1959, and reprinted in 1963 without additions or changes.
48. *The Ecumenical Advance: A History of the Ecumenical Movement,* Vol. II, Fey, editor, W. A. Visser 't Hooft, "The General Ecumenical Development Since 1948," p. 38.
49. *Ibid.*
50. John Stott, *Christian Mission in the Modern World* (London: Falcon, 1975; Downers Grove, Ill.: InterVarsity, 1976), pp. 22-30 (British edition).
51. "Study Conference on Evangelism," March 2-8, 1949, at Ecumenical Institute, Chateau de Bossey, Celigny, Switzerland (Geneva: WCC Archives), mimeographed, n.p.
52. *Ibid.,* p. 2.
53. *Ibid.*
54. *Ibid.,* p. 3.
55. *Ibid.,* p. 2.
56. *Ibid.,* p. 18.
57. "The Evangelization of Man in Modern Mass Society. An Ecumenical Enquiry" (Geneva: WCC, The Study Department, September 1949), p. 14.
58. *Ibid.,* p. 15.
59. *Ibid.*
60. "Ecumenical Studies, the Bible and the Church's Message to the World" (Geneva: WCC, The Study Department, October 1952).
61. "The Evangelization of Man in Modern Mass Society. An Ecumenical Enquiry," pp. 15, 16.
62. "Minutes of the Meeting of Study Department Committee," July 31 to August 4, 1951, at Rolle, Switzerland (Geneva: WCC Archives), p. 3.
63. *Ibid.*
64. Minutes of the: Meeting of the Business Committee of the Study Department Committee, August 5 and 9; Joint Meeting of the Business Committee of the Study Department Committee and

officers of the Preparatory Commission for Evanston, August 6-9, 1952, at Norrevang, Denmark (Geneva: WCC Archives), mimeographed, p. 4.
65. *Ibid.,* p. 12.
66. "Ecumenical Studies. The Meaning of Hope in the Bible" (Geneva: WCC, The Study Department, October 1952).
67. "Evangelism, the Mission of the Church to Those Outside Her Life" (Evanston assembly study, first draft [Geneva: WCC Archives]), mimeographed, p. 5. See also *The Christian Hope and the Task of the Church,* six ecumenical surveys and the report of the Assembly prepared by the advising Commission of the Main Theme (New York: Harper, 1954).
68. "Evangelism, the Mission of the Church to Those Outside Her Life," p. 16.
69. *Ibid.*
70. *Ibid.,* p. 34.
71. *Ibid.,* p. 29.
72. "Ecumenical Studies. Introducing the Assembly Topic Evangelism" (Geneva: WCC, The Study Department, n.d.), p. 3.
73. *Ibid.,* p. 4.
74. *The Evanston Report, the Second Assembly of the World Council of Churches 1954* (New York: Harper, 1955), p. 6.
75. *Ibid.,* pp. 74-79.
76. *Ibid.,* p. 327.
77. *Ibid.,* p. 1.
78. *Ibid.*
79. *Ibid.,* p. 99.
80. *Ibid.,* p. 101.
81. *Ibid.*
82. *Ibid.,* p. 106.
83. *Ecumenical Review,* Vol. XX, No. 2 (April 1968), p. 175.
84. *A Theological Reflection on the Work of Evangelism* (Geneva: WCC, 1963), p. 6.
85. *Ibid.,* p. 7.
86. *Ibid.*
87. *Ibid.,* p. 6.
88. *Ibid.,* p. 7.
89. *Ibid.,* p. 6.
90. *Ibid.,* p. 12.
91. *Ibid.*
92. "Consultation on Christianity and Non-Christian Religions," July 21-25, 1955, at Davos, Switzerland (Geneva: WCC Archives), mimeographed, p. 4.
93. "The Word of God and the Living Faiths of Men," Division of Studies, Department on Evangelism, Department of Missionary Studies (Geneva: WCC Archives, July 1958), mimeographed, p. 3.
94. *A Theological Reflection on the Work of Evangelism,* p. 10.
95. *Ibid.,* p. 5.
96. *Ibid.,* p. 17.
97. *Ibid.,* pp. 17, 18.
98. *Ibid.,* p. 21.
99. *Ibid.,* p. 22.

100. Michael Green, *Evangelism in the Early Church* (Grand Rapids, Mich.: Eerdmans, 1970).
101. *Ibid.*, pp. 40, 41.
102. *Ibid.*, p. 24.
103. *Ecumenical Review*, Vol. XX, No. 2 (April 1968), pp. 171-182.
104. *Ibid.*, p. 180.
105. *Ibid.*
106. In the 1970s, the "radical discipleship" advocates would call for a commitment to sociopolitical involvement at "conversion."

Chapter Four **Contrasting Developments in Evangelical and Ecumenical Evangelism**
1. William G. McLoughlin, *Billy Sunday Was His Real Name* (Chicago: University of Chicago Press, 1955), p. 287.
2. William G. McLoughlin, Jr., *Billy Graham, Revivalist in a Secular Age* (New York: Ronald Press, 1960), p. 20.
3. Kenneth Scott Latourette, *Advance through Storm, a History of the Expansion of Christianity*, Vol. VII (New York: Harper, 1945), pp. 142-145.
4. McLoughlin, *Billy Graham, Revivalist in a Secular Age*, p. 10.
5. *Ibid.*, p. 23.
6. *Ibid.*, p. 7.
7. *Ibid.*, p. 10. Also see George M. Marsden, *The Evangelicals*, Wells and Woodbridge, editors, pp. 124-139.
8. Marsden, *The Evangelicals*, Wells and Woodbridge, editors, pp. 134, 135.
9. One of a number of recent studies is that of Lowell D. Streiker and Gerald S. Strober, *Religion and the New Majority* (New York: Association Press, 1972), pp. 120-168. This study seems to reveal an unexpected number of "Fundamentalists" within the mainline denominations and, possibly, Roman Catholicism.
10. Harold Lindsell, *The Battle for the Bible* (Grand Rapids, Mich.: Zondervan, 1976), pp. 10, 11, 210.
11. Johnston, *World Evangelism and the Word of God*, pp. 41-46, 65-69.
12. John Pollock, *Crusades, Twenty Years with Billy Graham* (Minneapolis: World Wide Publications, 1966), pp. 59-70.
13. A comparable phenomenon occurred in the eighteenth century during the pietist renewal through Philipp Spener and Herman Franke. "While the pietistic movement under Spener was still on the defensive, under Franke's direction it now took on an offensive position. For forty years he and his pietist co-workers manifested an unequaled evangelical missionary activity. . . Under the Spirit's prompting, Franke had only one purpose: that Christ be glorified in him by the winning of souls in every place and by every possible means." Paulus Scharff, *History of Evangelism*, translated by Helga Bender Henry (Grand Rapids, Mich.: Eerdmans, 1966), p. 29.
14. Billy Graham, *Look* (February 7, 1956), p. 49.
15. McLoughlin, *Billy Graham, Revivalist in a Secular Age*, p. 205.
16. *Revival in Our Time* (Wheaton, Ill.: Van Kampen, 1950), pp. 12, 13. J. Edwin Orr said 400,000 attended and that there were 2,703 first-time decisions among the 4,178 people who responded to the invitation.
17. *Ibid.*, p. 51.

18. *Ibid.*, p. 79
19. *Ibid.*, p. 165.
20. *Ibid.*, p. 155.
21. *Ibid.*, p. 156.
22. *America's Hour of Decision* (Wheaton, Ill.: Van Kampen, 1951).
23. *Ibid.*, p. 61.
24. *Ibid.*, pp. 126, 132, 138.
25. *Ibid.*, p. 138.
26. *Ibid.*, pp. 118, 119, 121, 132.
27. *Ibid.*, pp. 146-148.
28. *Ibid.*, pp. 116, 127.
29. Billy Graham, *Peace with God* (New York: Pocket Books, 1953), p. vii.
30. *Ibid.*, p. 205.
31. *Ibid.*, p. 209.
32. *Ibid.*, p. 17.
33. *Ibid.*, p. 14.
34. *Ibid.*, p. 16.
35. *Ibid.*, p. 30.
36. *Ibid.*, p. 77.
37. *Ibid.*, pp. 79-84.
38. *Ibid.*, p. 34.
39. *Ibid.*, p. 40.
40. *Ibid.*, pp. 46, 47
41. *Ibid.*, pp. 50, 51.
42. Billy Graham, *World Aflame* (Minneapolis: Billy Graham Evangelistic Association, Crusade Edition; Doubleday edition 1965), p. 69.
43. Graham, *Peace with God*, p. 61.
44. *Ibid.*, pp. 72, 73.
45. *Ibid.*, p. 49.
46. *Ibid.*, p 75.
47. *Ibid.*, p. 78.
48. *Ibid.*, p. 106.
49. *Ibid.*, p. 115.
50. *Ibid.*, p. 117.
51. *Ibid.*, p. 125.
52. Graham, *World Aflame*, pp. 149-152.
53. Graham, *Peace with God*, pp. 165-171.
54. *Ibid.*, p. 174.
55. *Ibid.*, pp. 176, 177.
56. *Ibid.*, pp. 177-189.
57. Graham, *World Aflame*, p. 165.
58. *Ibid.*, p. 168.
59. *Ibid.*, pp. 168, 169.
60. *Ibid.*, p. 178.
61. *Ibid.*, p. 201.
62. *Ibid.*, p. 223.
63. *Ibid.*, p. 230.
64. *The Evanston Report, the Second Assembly of the World Council of Churches 1954*, p. 101.
65. *A Theological Reflection on the Work of Evangelism*, p. 7.
66. The D. T. Niles prepublication document, *Upon the Earth*, was studied July 1-10, 1961, at the Bossey, Consultation of the Commission on Theology of Mission (Geneva: WCC Archives). The

preconsultation paper said that eternal punishment (reprobation) had been essentially rejected by previous consultations: "A number of discussions suggest that missions cannot be based upon the idea that men who live and die without knowing or confessing Christ are thereby necessarily subject to penalty—either in terms of God's consigning them to eternal punishment, or even in terms of a life without value. The gospel is a truer, fuller, more adequate saving revelation." Niles had already affirmed that "the Holy Spirit is working everywhere, including in the religions" and that "no theoretical Yes or No can be given to the question, Are all saved?"

67. *The New Delhi Report*, The Third Assembly of the World Council of Churches, 1961 (London: SCM Press, 1961), p. 151.
68. *Ibid.*, pp. 91-93.
69. *Ibid.*, p. 77.
70. *Ibid.*, p. 81.
71. *Ibid.*, p. 82.
72. The rejection of syncretism at the 1975 Nairobi Assembly—on the basis of these doctrines—can only mean an expressed desire to retain the unqualified *identity* of Christianity among world religions.
73. *The New Delhi Report*, p. 80.
74. *Ibid.*
75. *Ibid.*
76. *Ibid.*, p. 81.
77. *Ibid.*
78. *Ibid.*, p. 79.
79. *Ibid.*, p. 86.
80. Personal letter of Philip Potter to Arthur Johnston, August 3, 1972.
81. *The New Delhi Report*, pp. 77-90.
82. *The Fourth World Conference on Faith and Order, Montreal 1963*, P. C. Rodger and L. Vischer, editors (London: SCM Press, 1964), p. 13.
83. *Ibid.*, p. 51.
84. *Ibid.*, p. 53.
85. Cf. John Stott, *The Lausanne Covenant* (Minneapolis: World Wide Publications, 1975), pp. 10-13; *Report on Tradition and Traditions*, Faith and Order Paper No. 40 (Geneva: WCC), p. 21. The North American study said that "modern critical studies, both in biblical and church history, have furnished additional evidence for the generalization that *tradition is primordial.* The primitive church created its Scriptures in the light of what had been handed down by and about Jesus Christ." The European Section saw the Bible as the "primary evidence of God's acts and words . . . as owing its existence theologically to the Church, and in a relative sense subordinate to the Church and in an absolute sense as the bearer of God's Word superior to the Church," p. 53. There is no question that liberal theology has lost its influence since New Delhi 1961, but the issues of Reformation and the Council of Trent between the doctrines of the Scripture and the Church have been revived.
86. Norman Goodall, *Ecumenical Progress, a Decade of Change in the Ecumenical Movement 1961-71* (London: Oxford University Press, 1972), p. 38.
87. *Witness in Six Continents*, Ronald K. Orchard, editor (London: Edinburgh House Press, 1964), p. 161.
88. *Ibid.*, p. 165.

89. Goodall, *Ecumenical Progress, a Decade of Change in the Ecumenical Movement,* p. 37.

90. Hans Jochen Margul, "One Year's Discussion on Structures for Missionary Congregations," mimeographed for appearance in a slightly different version for *International Review of Missions* (October 1963) (Geneva: WCC Archives), pp. 3, 4. This was further clarified in a memo to the Central Committee: "Any fundamentalism, however much it may be understood as a protest against appearances of dissolution of the doctrine of the church, overlooks the fact that the Holy Spirit has neither been petrified in the letter of Holy Scripture, nor in the organization of the church, and that this has never happened in the course of church history." "Memorandum to the Central Committee," First Draft for Discussion, Enlarged Meeting of the Working Committee, Department on Studies in Evangelism, April 9-16, 1964, The Ecumenical Institute, Bossey (Geneva: WCC Archives), mimeographed.

91. Eugene Carson Blake, "Uppsala and Afterwards," in *The Ecumenical Advance: A History of the Ecumenical Movement,* Vol. II, Fey, editor, p. 424.

92. *Ibid.,* p. 425; *The Uppsala Report 1968* (Geneva: WCC, 1968), p. 28.

93. *The Ecumenical Advance: A History of the Ecumenical Movement,* Vol. II, Fey, editor, p. 252.

94 *Foundations of Ecumenical Social Thought,* J. H. Oldham, editor (Philadelphia: Fortress Press, 1966).

95. *Ibid.,* p. 254.

96. The socialist views of Emil Brunner are not as well-known as his views of revelation, nor are those of Walter J. Hollenweger, former Director of Evangelism in the Department of World Mission and Evangelism of the WCC. Hollenweger writes that in his first sermon as vicar in Switzerland he "describes mockingly those Christians who believe that the Gospel has mainly to do with the salvation of the soul, the hereafter. . . The Socialists' materialism is all wrong, but they are like the son in the parable: they say 'No' but do it. . . It is God who stands behind revolutionary movements, as God is always the revolutionary force in history." Hollenweger then further surveys approvingly Brunner's critique, "The church wrongly trains her ministers by trying to teach them objective doctrine. . . She shamefully hides her critical results from her people and is guilty of many an unnecessary conflict between faith and science in the ranks of the Christian intellectuals. She 'simply disregarded the fact that the Bible gives us the Word of God in a multiplicity of doctrines in part very different and even contradictory' . . . That humanity does not descend from Adam, and the virgin birth is not an integral part of Christian belief should belong to the elementary knowledge of every Christian. 'Genuine biblical faith . . . self-evidently belongs together with biblical criticism.' " Walter J. Hollenweger, "The Roots of Emil Brunner's Theology," (Geneva: WCC Archives, September 1966), mimeographed, pp. 1, 2.

97. Carl F. H. Henry, *Christianity Today* (July 8, 1966), p. 3.

98. *Christianity Today* (September 15, 1967), p. 3.

99. *Christianity Today* (February 17, 1967), p. 19. Reprint from *U.S.A.,* Vol. XII, Nos. 24-25 (November 25-December 9, 1966).

100. Paul Abrecht, "The Development of Ecumenical Social Thought and Action," in *The Ecumenical Advance: A History of the Ecumenical Movement*, Fey, editor, p. 255.
101. John 18:36; see Edward P. Clowney, "A Critique of the 'Political Gospel,' " *Christianity Today* (April 28, 1967), pp. 7-11.

Chapter Five **One Race, One Gospel, One Task**
 1. Based on author's interviews of Billy Graham, December 29, 1976, and of Robert P. Evans, June 19, 1976.
 2. Based on authors's interviews of Don Hoke, June 23, 1976, Robert P. Evans, June 23, 1976, and Billy Graham, December 28, 1976.
 3. Letter from Billy Graham to Rev. Tom Allan, December 9, 1958.
 4. Letter from Larry Love to L. Nelson Bell, December 29, 1958. The list included Dr. V. R. Edman, Wheaton College; Dr. L. Nelson Bell; Dr. Jess M. Bader, World Convention of Churches of Christ; Dr. Thomas A. Carruth, Prayer Life Movement, the Methodist Church; Rev. Robert S. Denny, Baptist World Alliance; Dr. Darby Fulton, Presbyterian Board of World Missions; Dr. Ross F. Hidy, St. Mark's Lutheran Church, San Francisco; Dr. Harold J. Ockenga, Park Street Church, Boston; Rev. J. O. Percy, International Foreign Mission Association; Dr. Bob Pierce, World Vision; Rev. R. Kenneth Strachan, Latin America Mission; Dr. Clyde Taylor, National Association of Evangelicals.
 5. Program: "Second Meeting of Planning Committee for World Conference on Evangelism," April 23, 1959.
 6. Letter from Larry Love to Emmanuel Gabre Selassie, June 27, 1960.
 7. Based on letter and delegate list from Larry Love to the delegates, August 26, 1960 (Minneapolis: BGEA Archives).
 8. *Decision*, September and October 1960.
 9. Typed copy of notes taken by Sherwood Wirt (Minneapolis: BGEA Archives), p. 2.
10. Typed text of notes taken by Sherwood Wirt, August 17, 1960 (Minneapolis: BGEA Archives).
11. *Ibid.*
12. *Ibid.*
13. Based on author's interview of Sherwood Wirt, October 15, 1976.
14. *One Race, One Gospel, One Task*, Vol. I, Carl F. H. Henry and Stanley Mooneyham, editors (Minneapolis: World Wide Publications, 1967), p. 6.
15. *Ibid.*
16. *Ibid.*
17. *Ibid.*, p. 25.
18. *Ibid.*, p. 23.
19. *Ibid.*, p. 26.
20. *Ibid.*, p. 27.
21. *Ibid.*, p. 28.
22. *Ibid.*, p. 29.
23. *Ibid.*
24. *Ibid.*, p. 30.
25. *Ibid.*, p. 29.
26. *Ibid.*, p. 33.
27. *Ibid.*, p. 32.
28. *Ibid.*

29. "Program and Information" (Berlin: World Congress on Evangelism, Kongresshalle, October 26-November 4, 1966), p. 4.
30. Executive Committee Meeting at New York City, World Congress on Evangelism, December 14, 1965 (Minneapolis: BGEA Archives), p. 1.
31. Executive Committee Meeting at Berlin, World Congress on Evangelism, December 14, 1965 (Minneapolis: BGEA Archives), p. 7.
32. It was comprised of Dr. Clyde W. Taylor, Dr. Robert P. Evans, Robert Van Kampen, and Rev. W. Stanley Mooneyham. "First Meeting of Executive Committee for World Congress of Evangelism," April 21, 1964, at LaSalle Hotel, Chicago, p. 1.
33. *Ibid.*
34. "Minutes of the Executive Committee," December 14, 1965, p. 7.
35. "Executive Committee Minutes," February 20, 1966, p. 3.
36. *Ibid.*, p. 2.
37. Memo of W. Stanley Mooneyham to Executive Committee, July 9, 1965.
38. *Ibid.*, p. 1.
39. Meeting of the Executive Committee and Program Committee for World Congress on Evangelism, London, July 1-2, 1964, p. 1.
40. Meeting of Executive Committee, World Congress on Evangelism, New York, September 14-15, 1964, p. 1.
41. Based on author's interview of George Wilson, April 1, 1977.
42. Meeting of the Executive Committee, World Congress on Evangelism, Berlin, February 20, 1966, p. 1.
43. *One Race, One Gospel, One Task,* Henry and Mooneyham, editors, Vol. II.
44. *Ibid.*, pp. 37-43.
45. *Ibid.*, p. 49.
46. *Ibid.*, p. 1ff.; see also Matthew 28:18, 19.
47. *One Race, One Gospel, One Task,* Vol. II, Henry and Mooneyham, editors, p. 1.
48. *The Fourth World Conference on Faith and Order, Montreal 1963,* Faith and Order Paper No. 42, P. C. Rodger and L. Vischer, editors, p. 52.
49. *Ibid.*, p. 53.
50. *Ibid.*, pp. 173, 174.
51. *One Race, One Gospel, One Task,* Vol. I, Henry and Mooneyham, editors, p. 1.
52. *Ibid.*, p. 3.
53. *Ibid.*, p. 6.
54. *Ibid.*, p. 7.
55. *Ibid.*
56. *Ibid.*, p. 9.
57. *Ibid.*, p. 10.
58. *Ibid.*
59. *Ibid.*
60. *Ibid.*, p. 95.
61. *Ibid.*
62. *Ibid.*, pp. 95, 96.
63. *Ibid.*
64. *Ibid.*

65. Lesslie Newbigin had approached the subject from a more historical view and endeavored to relate the Trinity to evangelism in the history of the International Missionary Council in the study pamphlet *The Relevance of Trinitarian Doctrines to Today's Mission* (London: Edinburgh House Press, 1963).
66. *One Race, One Gospel, One Task,* Vol. II, Henry and Mooneyham, editors, p. 96.
67. *Ibid.,* p. 97.
68. *Ibid.,* p. 99.
69. *Ibid.*
70. *Ibid.*
71. *Ibid.,* p. 100.
72. *Ibid.*
73. *Ibid.*
74. *Ibid.,* p. 101.
75. *Ibid.*
76. *Ibid.*
77. *Ibid.,* p. 103.
78. *Ibid.,* p. 115.
79. *Ibid.,* p. 118.
80. *Ibid.,* p. 123.
81. *Ibid.,* p. 132.
82. *Ibid.,* pp. 174, 175.
83. *Ibid.,* p. 175.
84. *Ibid.*
85. *Ibid.,* p. 177.
86. *Ibid.*
87. *Ibid.,* p. 178.
88. *Ibid.*
89. *Ibid.,* p. 179.
90. *Ibid.*
91. *Ibid.,* p. 181.
92. *Ibid.*
93. *Ibid.,* p. 183.
94. *Ibid.,* pp. 183, 184.
95. *Ibid.,* p. 185.
96. *Ibid.,* p. 187.
97. *Ibid.,* p. 190.
98. *Ibid.*
99. *Ibid.,* p. 191.
100. *Ibid.,* p. 202.
101. *Ibid.,* p. 251.
102. *Ibid.,* p. 254.
103. *Ibid.*
104. *Ibid.*
105. *Ibid.,* p. 255.
106. *Ibid.*
107. *Ibid.,* p. 256.
108. *Ibid.*
109. *Ibid.,* p. 257.
110. *Ibid.,* p. 259.
111. *Ibid.,* p. 260.
112. *Ibid.*

113. *Ibid.*, p. 261.
114. *Ibid.*, p. 291.
115. *Ibid.*, p. 296.
116. *Ibid.*, p. 299.
117. *Ibid.*, p. 301.
118. *Ibid.*, p. 304.
119. *Ibid.*, p. 305.
120. *Ibid.*, p. 311.
121. *Ibid.*, p. 314.
122. *Ibid.*
123. *Ibid.*, p. 315.
124. *Ibid.*
125. *Ibid.*, p. 317. The issues of racism also found expression in other sections of Section V, "Spiritual Needs of the Negro," William Pannell, pp. 376-380, 390.
126. *Ibid.*, pp. 319-329.
127. *Ibid.*, p. 343.
128. *Ibid.*, p. 344.
129. *Ibid.*
130. *Ibid.*
131. *Ibid.*, p. 345.
132. *Ibid.*, p. 346.
133. *Ibid.*, p. 348.
134. *Ibid.*, p. 350.
135. *Ibid.*, p. 352.
136. *Ibid.*, p. 355.
137. *Ibid.*, pp. 361, 363.
138. *Ibid.*, p. 372.
139. *Ibid.*, p. 375.
140. *Ibid.*, p. 385.
141. *Ibid.*, p. 392.
142. *Ibid.*, p. 398.
143. *Ibid.*, pp. 401, 402.
144. *Ibid.*, pp. 403-405.
145. *Ibid.*, p. 413.
146. *Ibid.*, p. 422.
147. *Ibid.*, p. 432.
148. *Ibid.*, p. 437.
149. *Ibid.*, p. 433.
150. *Ibid.*
151. *Ibid.*, p. 439.
152. *Ibid.*
153. *Ibid.*, p. 438.
154. *Ibid.*, p. 440.
155. *Ibid.*, p. 441.
156. *Ibid.*, p. 468.
157. *Ibid.*, p. 453.
158. *Ibid.*, p. 455.
159. *Ibid.*, p. 495.
160. *Ibid.*, p. 494.
161. *Ibid.*
162. *Ibid.*
163. *Ibid.*, p. 188.

164. *Ibid.*, p. 523; *Anti-Defamation League Bulletin*, Vol. 23, No. 10 (December 1966), pp. 3, 6.
165. *One Race, One Gospel, One Task*, Vol. II, Henry and Mooneyham, editors, p. 523.
166. *Ibid.*, Vol. I, p. 41. He would address himself more fully to this issue at Lausanne 1974.
167. *Ibid.*, Vol. II, p. 307.
168. Møeller Petersen, *Crusader*, The American Baptist Newsmagazine, Vol. 21, No. 11 (December 1966), p. 7.
169. Paul P. Fryhling, *The Covenant Companion* (December 16, 1966), p. 15.
170. *Ibid.*, p. 14.
171. *The Lutheran* (December 21, 1966), p. 32.
172. Cf. Kenneth Scott Latourette, *A History of Christianity*, pp. 416-444. These pre-sixteenth century Reformation movements found expression in orders such as the Franciscans, Dominicans, and Augustinians within the institutional church. Lutheranism, Calvinism, and Zwingliism, for example, have found their corrective contribution to Christianity outside of the Western church at Rome.
173. *One Race, One Gospel, One Task*, Vol. I, Henry and Mooneyham, editors, p. 5. The entire text of the closing statement is found in Appendix II.

Chapter Six The Crystallization of Another Gospel
1. *The Uppsala Report 1968*, Official Report of the Fourth Assembly of the World Council of Churches, Uppsala, July 4-20, 1968, Norman Goodall, editor (Geneva: WCC, 1968), p. 21.
2. "The Driebergen Papers," *Concept IX* (July 1965) (Geneva: WCC, Department on Studies in Evangelism), pp. 7, 8.
3. Philip Potter, *Ecumenical Review*, Vol. XX, No. 2 (April 1968), p. 176.
4. *Ibid.*
5. *One Race, One Gospel, One Task*, Vol. I, Henry and Mooneyham, editors, p. 245.
6. *Ibid.*, p. 246.
7. Potter, *Ecumenical Review* (April 1968), p. 176.
8. *One Race, One Gospel, One Task*, Vol. I, Henry and Mooneyham, editors, p. 5.
9. Potter, *Ecumenical Review* (April 1968), p. 177.
10. *Ibid.*, p. 181.
11. *The Uppsala Report 1968*, Goodall, editor, p. XVII.
12. *Ibid.*, p. 12.
13. *Ibid.*, p. 18.
14. One must use the words "seemed to be" because it is possible to extract good and bad theology from the section reports based upon what is said or not said. Arne Sovik outlined the process of a section report and the further subtleties of equivocal language:
"... when the record emerges from the drafting committee—where the struggle may have continued even longer than on the floor—the fight is not there. It has been wrapped in the cotton wool of carefully inclusive, if not purposefully ambiguous, phraseology, or disappears in the safety of well-worn theological platitude. Or the two sides of an issue are stated in widely separated contexts, thus avoiding the necessity of direct confrontation but

resulting in a paper that, read carefully, is less than fully consistent. The statement is finally approved not because anyone is completely happy with it but because everyone can find something, sometimes a great deal, that is very good, and for the sake of this will tolerate what may not be quite so palatable like a guest at a potluck supper." *Ibid.*, p. 36.

Add to these complexities the inclusion of a sentence out of harmony with the theology of the meeting by an insistent and influential delegate and one has to speak of a trend.

15. *Ibid.*, pp. 376, 377.
16. *Ibid.*, p. 376.
17. *Ibid.*, p. 377.
18. *Ibid.*, p. 37.
19. On two occasions they threatened to withdraw at Nairobi 1975 as well.
20. *The Uppsala Report 1968*, Goodall, editor, p. 28.
21. *Ibid.*, p. 29.
22. *Ibid.*, p. 28.
23. It has already been pointed out that the International Missionary Council had become far more radical and liberal than had the churches of the WCC. This was the first expression of it since the 1961 integration.
24. *The Ecumenical Advance: A History of the Ecumenical Movement*, Fey, editor, p. 424.
25. *Ibid.*
26. *The Uppsala Report 1968*, Goodall, editor, p. 93.
27. Response of Philip Potter to objections raised in a Section meeting at Nairobi 1975. A bishop's committee of the Church of Norway unanimously criticized "the relationship between the secretarial and the elected bodies." "The Church of Norway and Ecumenical Organizations," *WCC Exchange*, No. 1 (March 1977), p. 9.
28. *The Ecumenical Advance: A History of the Ecumenical Movement*, Fey, editor, p. 425.
29. *Ibid.*
30. *The Uppsala Report 1968*, Goodall, editor, p. 32.
31. *Ibid.*, p. 29.
32. *The Ecumenical Advance: A History of the Ecumenical Movement*, Fey, editor, p. 425.
33. *The Uppsala Report 1968*, Goodall, editor, p. 31.
34. *Ibid.*
35. *Christ Seeks Asia*, Official Reference Volume, Asia-South Pacific Congress on Evangelism, Singapore 1968, W. Stanley Mooneyham, editor (Hong Kong: The Rock House, 1969), p. 8.
36. *Ibid.*, pp. 134, 135.
37. *Ibid.*, p. 135.
38. *Ibid.*, p. 65.
39. *Ibid.*, pp. 66, 67.
40. *Ibid.*, p. 68.
41. *Ibid.*
42. *Ibid.*
43. *Ibid.*, p. 73.
44. *Ibid.*, p. 74.
45. *Ibid.*, pp. 78, 79.

46. *Ibid.*, p. 79.
47. *Ibid.*, p. 143.
48. *Ibid.*, pp. 141, 143.
49. *Ibid.*, p. 81.
50. *Ibid.*, p. 87.
51. *Ibid.*, pp. 109, 111.
52. *Ibid.*, p. 109.
53. *Ibid.*
54. *Ibid.*, p. 112.
55. *Ibid.*, pp. 112, 113.
56. *Ibid.*, p. 117.
57. *Ibid.*, p. 208.
58. *Ibid.*
59. *Ibid.*, p. 9.
60. *Evangelism Now,* U. S. Congress on Evangelism, George M. Wilson, editor (Minneapolis: World Wide Publications, 1965), p. 5.
61. *Ibid.*, p. 7.
62. *Ibid.*, p. 13.
63. *Ibid.*, pp. 15-21.
64. *Ibid.*, pp. 22-28.
65. *Ibid.*, pp. 43, 44.
66. *Ibid.*, p. 48.
67. *Ibid.*, p. 56.
68. *Ibid.*, p. 62.
69. *Ibid.*, p. 147.
70. *Ibid.*, p. 184.
71. *Ibid.*,
72. *Ibid.*, p. 214.
73. C. Peter Wagner, "The Latin American Congress on Evangelism," *Pulse,* Vol. V, No. 1 (February 1970), pp. 3, 4.
74. O. E. Costas, *Theology of the Crossroads in Contemporary Latin America,* Missiology in Mainline Protestantism: 1969-1974 (Amsterdam: Rodopi, 1976), pp. 118, 119. In this doctoral dissertation, Costas points out that the ecumenicity of CLADE was grounded on individual "born again" Christians engaged in common Christian tasks, chief among which was evangelism (p. 119). He noted that both the mainline ecumenical leaders and the more radical Evangelicals like René Padilla and Plutarco Bonilla were barred from the CLADE program. The ecumenical III CELA leadership (among them Emilio Castro, new director of the WCC's Division of World Mission and Evangelism) believed CLADE to have been a North American inspired and directed evangelical gathering because of Clyde Taylor's cochairmanship.
75. Peter Wagner recommended that Escobar's paper be widely circulated throughout the world. According to Wagner, when Escobar had finished reading it at the Congress, "the assembly could not contain their urge to signify their approval by a thunderous standing ovation." Wagner, "The Latin American Congress on Evangelism," p. 5.
76. Samuel Escobar, "The Social Responsibility of the Church," CLADE paper, reproduced, p. 1.
77. Latin America, it may be recalled, was not considered a mission field by Edinburgh 1910, because the missions related to the Church of

England would not participate unless Latin America and Europe were considered Christian lands. Consequently, only evangelical or "fundamentalist" missions initiated work in Latin America during this century.

78. Escobar, "The Social Responsibility of the Church," p. 1.
79. *Ibid.*, p. 3.
80. *Ibid.*
81. *Ibid.*, p. 7.
82. *Ibid.*, p. 9.
83. Ruben Lores, "Upon All Flesh," CLADE paper, reproduced, p. 6.
84. *Ibid.*, p. 8.
85. Wagner noted the "serious thinking as well as differing reactions" Lores' "devotional" message created. One of the side effects was that new tensions arose among conservative Evangelicals. Wagner reported that "almost all the delegates were conservative evangelicals, but new tensions within this camp began to be evident. Whereas none of the evangelicals would agree with the strong group of radical left theologians, now called the 'Isalinos' by Dr. Jóse Míquez Bonino, there is a difference of opinion among evangelicals as to what the attitude of evangelicals should be toward them. One group of evangelicals advocates 'reconciliation' and prefers to stress the similarities between evangelicals and radicals, attempting to pull together with anyone who is articulating theology and who is a native Latin American. The differences are considered secondary and tolerable. On the other hand, another group of evangelicals advocates 'polarization,' claiming that the theology of the radical left is 'syncretism' and 'another gospel' and therefore intolerable to evangelicals. They believe that the differences are essential and should be pointed out clearly." Wagner, "The Latin American Congress on Evangelism," pp. 5, 6.
86. Emilio Antonio Nuñez, "The Position of the Church Toward *Aggiornamento,*" CLADE paper, reproduced, p. 2.
87. *Ibid.*, p. 4.
88. It must be noted that the overwhelming majority of Protestants in Latin America is evangelical and pentecostal, which places the WCC-related movements in a minority relationship, as in many countries of Africa.
89. Nuñez, "The Position of the Church Toward *Aggiornamento,*" p. 4.
90. *Ibid.*
91. *Ibid.*
92. *Ibid.*
93. *Ibid.*, p. 5.
94. "The Church is always reforming but it is always the same one." Lukas Vischer (WCC) is convinced that Tradition now has a place subordinate to Scripture as a result of Vatican II (based on Lukas Vischer-Arthur Johnston interview, August 9, 1976, at Geneva). I believe that the dichotomy has been removed by increasing the meaning of Tradition to include the entire historical sweep of the Church and to place Scripture within this all-comprehensive Tradition. See also the Montreal 1963 Faith and Order meeting on Tradition, tradition, and traditions,
95. Nuñez, "The Position of the Church Toward *Aggiornamento,*" p. 6.
96. *Ibid.*, p. 7.

97. *Ibid.*, p. 9.
98. *Ibid.*
99. English Press Release from CLADE, November 29, 1969; *Pulse,* Vol. V, No. 2 (April 1970), p. 1.
100. *Evangelism Alert,* Official Reference Volume, European Congress on Evangelism, Amsterdam, 1971, Gilbert W. Kirby, editor (London: World Wide Publications, 1972), pp. 275, 276.
101. "Minutes of the Executive Meeting," European Congress on Evangelism, Amsterdam, November 16, 1970 (Minneapolis: BGEA Archives), p. 5.
102. Gilbert W. Kirby, "Postscript," in *Evangelism Alert,* Kirby, editor, pp. 277, 278.
103. *Evangelism Alert,* Kirby, editor, p. 11; "Minutes of the Executive Meeting," p. 5.
104. *Evangelism Alert, Kirby, editor, p. 41.*
105. *Ibid.*, p. 43.
106. *Ibid.*, pp. 46, 47.
107. *Ibid.*, p. 48.
108. *Ibid.*, p. 55.
109. *Ibid.*, pp. 56, 57.
110. *Ibid.*, p. 79.
111. *Ibid.*, p. 80; Latourette records the persistent attempts of the medieval revival efforts of the monastics and popes to purify and christianize the *corpus christi* (the Church) and the *corpus christianum* (society) of the European nations that had been "mass evangelized" by the conversion of a political leader for political or personal reasons (Latourette, *A History of Christianity,* pp. 460, 461). This Constantinian continuity may have done far more harm than good, for the biblical distinction between the Church and the world was diminished in all cases, and all but destroyed in some. Many Europeans, especially, have a false security concerning their eternal destiny.
112. *Evangelism Alert,* Kirby, editor, p. 82.
113. *Ibid.*, p. 78.
114. *Ibid.*, p. 89.
115. *Ibid.*, p. 131.
116. *Ibid.*
117. *Ibid.*, p. 135.
118. *Ibid.*, pp. 142, 152.
119. *Ibid.*, p. 143.
120. *Ibid.*, p. 144.
121. *Ibid.*, p. 152.
122. *Ibid.*, p. 153.
123. *Ibid.*
124. *Ibid.*, p. 155.
125. *Ibid.*
126. *Ibid.*, p. 157.
127. *Ibid.*
128. *Ibid.*
129. *Ibid.*, p. 159.
130. *Ibid.*
131. *Ibid.*, pp. 159, 160.

132. He quotes Augustine: "Let the saints by all means remember that the city of God has in her company during her pilgrimage in the world, joined to her by sharing the sacraments, some who will not be with her to share eternally the lot of the saints. . . ." *(De civitate Dei I. 35) Ibid.,* pp. 155, 156.

133. *The Evangelical Response to Bangkok,* Ralph Winter, editor (South Pasadena, Calif.: William Carey Library, 1973), p. 61.

134. Johnston, *World Evangelism and the Word of God,* pp. 54-90.

135. "Minutes of the Central Committee Meeting," July 30-August 7, 1957, at Yale Divinity School, New Haven (Geneva: WCC Archives). Students of history will recall the predominance of Karl Barth and his theology over that of Emil Brunner in that era of the WCC. See Johnston, *World Evangelism and the Word of God,* pp. 177-187.

136. Jürgen Moltmann, *Religion, Revolution and the Future* (New York: Scribner's, 1969), p. 15.

137. *Ibid.,* p. 163.

138. *Ibid.,* p. 98.

139. *Ibid.,* p. 130. See also Alister Kee, *A Reader in Political Theology* (London: SCM Press, 1974), pp. 42-45, 51-58, for the way in which the *praxis* of the theology of hope became better described as a political theology of revolution. Moltmann was also interpreted by G. C. Berkouwer as a warning against the defeatism of the student revolutionary era and calling the church to service, for the spirit of the Risen Christ works *through us.* See G. C. Berkouwer, "The Theology of Hope," *Christianity Today* (March 15, 1968), p. 16.

140. "Salvation Today," Next Meeting of the Commission on World Mission and Evangelism (1969/70, DWME (Geneva: WCC Archives), p. 2.

141. Consultation on "Salvation Today," August 2-4, 1969, DSME/M 69:24 (Geneva: WCC Archives), p. 1.

142. "The So-called 'Fundamental Crisis' in Mission," interview of Klaus Viehweger with Philip Potter, July 1970, DWME/71/7 (Geneva: WCC Archives); see the Frankfurt Declaration, Appendix 2.

143. Based on author's interview of Philip Potter, at Geneva, March 10, 1969.

144. W. Hollenweger, "A Draft on the Future of Evangelism Desk," to the Divisional Committee, V, September 1971, Document 10 (Geneva: WCC Archives), p. 2.

145. "Minutes of the Committee Meeting," August 8-11, 1972, Program Unit I—Faith and Witness, CWE, 72/112 (Geneva: WCC Archives), p. 4.

146. *Ibid.*

147. *Ibid.,* p. 5.

148. "Minutes of the Central Committee," January 10-21, 1971, at Addis Ababa, Ethiopia (Geneva: WCC Archives), p. 72.

149. Harold Lindsell, "Dateline: Bangkok," *Christianity Today* (March 30, 1973), p. 6.

150. Thomas Wieser (USA) was the CWME staff member responsible for the study on "Salvation Today." "Report on the Salvation Study," *International Review of Missions,* LXII, No. 246 (April 1973), pp. 170-179.

151. *Ibid.,* p. 172.

152. *Ibid.*
153. *Ibid.*
154. *Ibid.*
155. "Minutes of Open Hearing," CWME Third Assembly, January 1, 1973, at Bangkok (Geneva: WCC Archives), p. 2.
156. In 1959, Professor Bratsioti explained this to the Central Committee. He said that "Tradition was connected with the Church, for the Church was the mother of both Scripture and Tradition." "Minutes and Reports of the Twelfth Meeting of the Central Committee," August 19-27, 1959, at Rhodes, Greece (Geneva: WCC Archives), p. 13. This question was further elaborated at Montreal 1963.
157. Wieser, "Report on the Salvation Study," p. 173.
158. *Ibid.*, p. 174.
159. *Ibid.*, p. 175.
160. *Ibid.*
161. *Ibid.*
162. *Ibid.*, pp. 176, 177.
163. *Ibid.*
164. *International Review of Missions* (April 1973), p. 145.
165. *Ibid.*, p. 149.
166. *Ibid.*, p. 150.
167. *Ibid.*
168. *Ibid.*, p. 151.
169. *Ibid.*, p. 155.
170. *Ibid.*
171. *Ibid.*, p. 156.
172. *Ibid.*, pp. 159, 160.
173. *Ibid.*, p. 162.
174. *Ibid.*, p. 168.
175. *Ibid.*, p. 191. See also "Minutes and Report of the Assembly of the Commission on World Mission and Evangelism of the World Council of Churches," in *Bangkok Assembly 1973*, December 31, 1972 and January 9-12, 1973 (Geneva: WCC).
176. *International Review of Missions* (April 1973), p. 192.
177. *Ibid.*, p. 195.
178. *Ibid.*, p. 199.
179. *Ibid.*, p. 200.
180. *Ibid.*, p. 217.
181. *Ibid.*, p. 218.
182. *Bangkok Assembly 1973*, p. 67.
183. *Mexico City to Bangkok 1963-72* (Geneva: WCC, 1972), p. 24.
184. Some of the conciliar-minded Evangelicals reporting the Bangkok controversy have not taken as trenchant a position. Mine is not to be misunderstood as a polemic against Evangelicals within the WCC, but as a recognition of the ultimate hopeless incompatibility between evangelicalism and a theology that begins on a foundation other than that of an infallible Bible and then ends with no biblical Gospel. Kindliness is no virtue when it camouflages the truth and jeopardizes the eternal souls of men. See *The Evangelical Response to Bangkok*, Winter, editor. Decades of history and theology should teach Evangelicals not only charity but perspicacity and discernment.

Chapter Seven **Let the Earth Hear His Voice**
1. It did not categorically remove Evangelicals from the ecumenical dialogue or the contemporary conciliar debate. John Stott, for example, was invited to present an evangelical response in a plenary session at Nairobi 1975. He clearly and succinctly repudiated the universalism, theological relativism, and horizontalism of the new theology of evangelism in the WCC. The omission of a negative statement on Tradition may have been an excusable theological oversight, or it may be interpreted by some as a theological Trojan horse, leading a pluralistic spirit of conciliation into the evangelical fortress.
2. Minutes, International Congress on World Evangelization, March 23-24, 1972, at Vero Beach, Florida, p. 7; John Stott quotes Bishop Jack Dain, *The Lausanne Covenant*, p. 2.
3. Minutes, World Evangelization Strategy Consultation, December 2, 1971, at The Greenbriar, White Sulphur Springs, Georgia, p. 1.
4. *Ibid.*
5. Minutes, International Congress on World Evangelization, p. 3.
6. *Ibid.*, p. 5.
7. *Ibid.*, p. 6.
8. Participant Recommendation Form, ICOWE, 08/24/73 (Minneapolis: BGEA Archives). An obvious question arises over the ambiguity of the definition of "evangelical" given here, but again it must be recognized that evangelical conveners would most certainly understand the intent of the Congress.
9. Minutes, International Congress on World Evangelization, p. 9.
10. *Ibid.*, p. 4.
11. *Let the Earth Hear His Voice*, J. D. Douglas, editor (Minneapolis: World Wide Publications, 1975), p. 5.
12. *Ibid.*, p. 33.
13. Moratorium officially surfaced in the WCC at Bangkok 1973, and has provoked extensive evangelical-ecumenical debates. Some southern hemisphere national Evangelicals have supported aspects of moratorium from northern hemisphere missionaries as well. Graham has focused upon the world needs, while the Covenant conceded some values of moratorium under certain circumstances. *Ibid.*, p. 6.
14. "Minutes of the Planning Committee," August 24-25, 1972, p. 4.
15. "Call to the International Congress on World Evangelization" (Minneapolis: BGEA Archives), p. 3.
16. "Minutes of the Planning Committee," August 24-25, 1972, p. 4.
17. Karl Barth has given a helpful exegesis on some parts of Matthew 28:19 that avoids several theological errors. First, he recognizes the individual and personal nature of discipleship: " 'Go therefore and make disciples. . .' Make them what you yourselves are! Have them learn here, with me, where you yourselves have learned!" Karl Barth, "An Exegetical Study of Matthew 28:16-20," in *The Theology of the Christian Mission*, Anderson, editor, p. 63. Second, Jesus told His disciples not only to "preach," but "make disciples" through Jesus' word and, thereby, found the apostolic Church. In this way the apostolic Church "is constantly renewed as the listeners themselves become 'apostolic' and, as new disciples, begin to proclaim the good news." *Ibid.* Third, the Christian community

exists only where those things commanded by Jesus are "observed."
"All others receive it only from them secondhanded." *Ibid.,* p. 69.
Fourth, Barth avoids the contemporary expression of Tradition as
interdependent with Scripture and the "teaching authority of the
Church"*(The Documents of Vatican II.* Walter M. Abbott, S.J., general
editor, New York: Guild Press, 1966, p. 118) by reaffirming the
self-sufficiency of biblical authority. "For there is no room in the
Church for any other object of Τηρεῖν ('to keep,' 'to preserve') but
the one command by Jesus to the apostles. What they have been
commanded, they must teach without omission, the whole content of
the order of service. This is the New Testament affirmation of the
self-sufficiency of the Scriptures, the crossroad where we must part
from the Roman Catholic Church. Teaching in the Church can only
be repetitive of apostolic teaching." Bart, in *The Theology of the
Christian Mission,* Anderson, editor, p. 69. Thus, on this point Barth
has maintained the necessary balance between the individual who
comes into a discipleship relation with Christ, the Church which
passes on the apostles' teaching, and the Scriptures which alone are
to be observed without omission. Authority for evangelism is not in
the Church, but in the Scripture preserved by the Church.
18. "Minutes of the Planning Committee," p. 3.
19. Stott, *The Lausanne Covenant,* p. 4.
20. *Let the Earth Hear His Voice,* Douglas, editor, pp. 65-87; an expanded
version appeared in *Christian Mission in the Modern World.*
21. *Let the Earth Hear His Voice,* Douglas, editor, p. 66.
22. *Ibid.,* p. 67.
23. Stott, *The Lausanne Covenant,* p. 23.
24. *Ibid.*
25. *Ibid.,* p. 24.
26. *Ibid.,* p. 27.
27. *Ibid.,* p. 35. Stott's exegesis of John 20:21 requires a serious study by
Evangelicals into the Johannine vocabulary and style, for his entire
synthesis of the WCC and evangelical positions seems to be based
primarily upon an interpretation of this passage. Historical and
contemporary exegesis has taught, first, the *historical* acts of both the
Father sending the Son, and the Son sending the apostles. Second,
with this sending, *authority* was understood as conferred upon the
Son only by the Father and upon the disciples by the resurrected
Lord. While explicit passages of the New Testament deal with the
duties and responsibilities of the Church (cf. the Pauline epistles),
this passage does not seem to teach—directly or explicitly—either
that it is the Church that is invested with authority, or that the life of
Christ is a *model* for the mission of the apostle. This latter
interpretation is not upheld either by the vocabulary or the sentence
structure. The words "as . . . so" do not seem to teach a "model"
relationship or servanthood. Emphasis is upon the verbs of
"sending" and upon Jesus as the authoritative sender of the apostles.
   To speak of Jesus as a "model" would seem to require the ministry
of the atonement as well as their incarnation, and miracles of healing
as well as proclamation. One wonders if the "model" view takes into
consideration (1) the purely evangelistic mandate of the other Great
Commission passages, (2) the elements in the New Testament that
are consistently normative for us today, (3) the context of "belief" in

John 17:18 (17:20, 29) and in John 20:21 (20:22, 23, 29-31), (4) the servanthood of Jesus as fulfilled principally in Christ's death as a ransom in Mark 10:45, (5) the apostolic understanding of John 20:21 as obediently experienced in the Acts of the Apostles, and (6) the fervency of the Apostle Paul in asserting the priority of his call to preach (evangelize as even above baptizing and, no doubt, much more above social action.

28. *Let the Earth Hear His Voice,* Douglas, editor, p. 70.
29. *Ibid.,* p. 69.
30. Stott, *The Lausanne Covenant,* pp. 56, 57.
31. *Let the Earth Hear His Voice,* Douglas, editor, p. 69.
32. *Ibid.*
33. Stott, *The Lausanne Covenant,* p. 40.
34. *Let the Earth Hear His Voice,* Douglas, editor, p. 4.
35. *Ibid.,* p. 73.
36. *Ibid.*
37. *Ibid.,* p. 74.
38. *Ibid.*
39. *Ibid.*
40. *Ibid.,* p. 75.
41. *Ibid.,* p. 76.
42. *Ibid.*
43. *Ibid.,* p. 84.
44. *Ibid.,* p. 85.
45. *Ibid.,* p. 86.
46. *Ibid.*
47. *Ibid.,* p. 988.
48. *Ibid.*
49. *Ibid.,* p. 989.
50. *Ibid.*
51. *Ibid.,* pp. 992-997, Appendix III.
52. *Ibid.,* p. 993.
53. Based on author's interview of Don Hoke, June 23, 1976.
54. *Let the Earth Hear His Voice,* Douglas, editor, p. 310.
55. *Ibid.,* pp. 127-132.
56. *Ibid.,* p. 109.
57. *Ibid.*
58. "Our Lord was sent both to preach and to be the servant of all. Each of these two activities has its proper dignity within the wholeness of the mission, and neither should be subordinated to the other." Lesslie Newbigin, *One Body, One Gospel, One World* (London: International Missionary Council, 1958), p. 22. Quoted in *International Review of Missions,* Vol. LIV, No. 216 (October 1965), p. 435.
59. *Ibid., International Review of Missions,* p. 429.
60. *Ibid.,* p. 432.
61. *Ibid.,* p. 435; cf. Stott, in *Let the Earth Hear His Voice,* Douglas, editor, pp. 66-68 and Stott, *Christian Mission in the World,* pp. 22-28.
62. Newbigin, *International Review of Missions,* p. 440.
63. *Ibid.,* p. 439.
64. *Ibid.,* p. 440.
65. *Ibid.,* p. 452.
66. *Ibid.,* p. 454.

67. *Ibid.*
68. *Let the Earth Hear His Voice,* Douglas, editor, p. 99.
69. *Ibid.,* p. 102.
70. *Ibid.,* p. 328.
71. *Ibid.,* p. 380.
72. *Ibid.,* p. 288.
73. *Ibid.*
74. *Ibid.*
75. *Ibid.,* p. 293.
76. *Ibid.,* p. 360.
77. John Stott, *EFAC Bulletin* (January 1975), p. 2.
78. This prohibits making the names public for fifty years. "Minutes of the Planning Committee Meeting," International Congress of World Evangelization, October 16-18, 1974 (Wheaton, Ill.: Graham Center Archives), p. 7.
79. Hans-Lutz Poetsch, "The Theology of the 'Lausanne Covenant,' " an essay delivered October 2, 1974, to the Theological Convention of the Confessing Movements, Frankfurt.
80. Stott, *The Lausanne Covenant,* p. 1.
81. For the entire Lausanne Covenant, see Appendix II.
82. *Let the Earth Hear His Voice,* Douglas, editor, p. 5.
83. *Ibid.*
84. *Ibid.,* p. 6.
85. *Ibid.,* p. 3.
86. Stott, *The Lausanne Covenant,* p. 11.
87. Cf. *Let the Earth Hear His Voice,* Douglas, editor, p. 876.
88. For a contemporary, scholarly, nonevangelical theological review see Carl H. Hallenereutz, *New Approaches to Men of Other Faiths* (Geneva: WCC, 1969).
89. Stott, *The Lausanne Covenant,* p. 4.
90. *Ibid.*
91. *Ibid.,* pp. 30, 31.
92. *Christianity Today,* Vol. XXI, No. 16 (May 20, 1977), p. 44.
93. Stott, however, took a clear position on verbal inspiration.
94. Stott, *The Lausanne Covenant,* p. 38.
95. *Ibid.*
96. Johnston, *World Evangelism and the Word of God,* p. 152ff.
97. James 1:14, 15.
98. *Let the Earth Hear His Voice,* Douglas, editor, pp. 4, 74ff.
99. *Ibid.,* pp. 116ff., 303ff.
100. Cf. *Ibid.,* pp. 86, 994 and Stott, *The Lausanne Covenant,* p. 15.
101. Cf. Montreal 1963.
102. *Let the Earth Hear His Voice,* Douglas, editor, p. 1002.
103. Based on conversations with Lukas Vischer of the WCC, at Nairobi 1975 and at Geneva, August 2, 1976.
104. *Let the Earth Hear His Voice,* Douglas, editor, p. 1002; cf. the Montreal 1963, Bristol 1967, and Louvain 1971 conferences of Faith and Order.

Chapter Eight **The Decisive Decade**
1. "Minutes of the Planning Committee Meeting," International Congress of World Evangelization, October 16-18, 1974, at Honolulu (Wheaton, Ill.: Graham Center Archives), p. 2.

2. "Minutes of the Continuation Committee," January 20-23, 1975, at Mexico City (Wheaton, Ill.: Graham Center Archives), p. 11.
3. *Ibid.*, p. 3.
4. Mildred Dienert, "Worldwide Call to Prayer," Prayer Letter #2, 1976, sent from Philadelphia, Pa., p. 1.
5. "Minutes of the Executive Committee of the Lausanne Committee for World Evangelization," September 6-10, 1976, at West Berlin (Wheaton, Ill.: Graham Center Archives), p. 17.
6. Donald Hoke, "Global Grass Roots Follow-up Keeps Lausanne Goals Alive," A Post-Congress Report, *Evangelical Newsletter*.
7. Margaret Nash, "Confessing Christ Today," *One World* (January/February 1975); "Memorandum to Dr. Leighton Ford from Donald Hoke," April 13, 1976 (Wheaton, Ill.: Graham Center Archives).
8. Billy Graham, "Our Mandate from Lausanne '74," *Christianity Today* (July 4, 1975), p. 3.
9. *Ibid.*
10. *Ibid.*, p. 4.
11. *Ibid.*
12. *Ibid.*
13. *Ibid.*, p. 5.
14. *Ibid.*
15. *Ibid.*
16. *Ibid.*
17. *Ibid.*
18. *Ibid.*
19. *Ibid.*
20. "Minutes of the Continuation Committee," p. 4.
21. In a debate on support of the LCWE, it was decided that the members "should reaffirm their commitment to the Lausanne Covenant each time they met." But the meaning of the reaffirmation would not be taken in the same sense as a creed for a denominational statement of faith. "Minutes of the Meeting of the Lausanne Committee for World Evangelization," January 12-16, 1976, at Atlanta (Wheaton, Ill.: Graham Center Archives), p. 7.
22. *Ibid.*
23. *Ibid.*
24. Hans-Lutz Poetsch, a German theologian, understood the Evangelicals—by the Covenant—to subordinate all church activities to the Great Commission.
The primary theme was the evangelization of the world in the twentieth century. Thus the Great Commission of Christ is the focus of the Covenant. An attempt is made to cover theologically what from the standpoint of Evangelicals is significant in view of this task. This leads to an emphasis that is of far-reaching consequence. For in this way, Christian existence in doctrine and life is immediately coordinated with and subordinated to the Great Commission of the Lord. Poetsch, "The Theology of the 'Lausanne Covenant,' " p. 19.
25. *Ibid.*
26. Peter Wagner believed that those who felt that the social concern element was insufficient signed a separate 2,000-word response to Section 5 of the Covenant.
Partly because he himself agreed with its content but partly also in

order to prevent chaos from breaking loose in the plenary session, the spokesman for the covenant drafting committee, John Stott, asserted in public that he would sign both. C. Peter Wagner, "Lausanne Twelve Months Later," *Christianity Today* (July 4, 1975), p. 7.

27. "Minutes of the Continuation Committee," p. 7.
28. "Forward from Lausanne," from "Minutes of the Continuation Committee," Appendix IX.
29. *Ibid.,* p. 13.
30. Poetsch, "The Theology of the 'Lausanne Covenant,' " p. 23.
31. *Ibid.,* p. 24.
32. "Minutes of the Meeting of the Lausanne Committee for World Evangelization," Appendix I, p. 3. However, the popular presentation of the Committee said that the educational function of the LCWE was to "develop a biblical theology of evangelization concerning current issues." LCWE publicity bulletin (Wheaton, Ill.: Graham Center Archives). In reality, the work of the Lausanne Theological and Education Group is far broader than the biblical theology of evangelism. As will be pointed out later, the WCC Assembly at Nairobi 1975 believed that in this area the WCC and Lausanne theology of *mission* were largely compatible.
33. "Minutes of the Executive Committee of the Lausanne Committee for World Evangelization," p. 19.
34. "Minutes of the Meeting of the Lausanne Committee for World Evangelization," p. 13.
35. Leighton Ford, "Berlin Report" (reproduced message), September 19, 1976 (Minneapolis: BGEA).
36. "A Report from Hong Kong," *Asia Pulse,* Evangelical Missions Information Service, Vol. VII, No. 5 (September 1976), p. 3.
37. "To Members of the Lausanne Committee for World Evangelization," LCWE, Nairobi, June 23, 1976, p. 1.
38. *Ecumenical Press Service,* WCC, Geneva, No. 18 (July 1, 1976), p. 7.
39. *Ibid.*
40. *Mensuel,* WCC, Geneva, No. 18 (July 1976), translated from the French edition, p. 4.
41. "To Members of the Lausanne Committee for World Evangelization," pp. 1, 2.
42. *Ibid.*
43. *Asia Pulse,* Evangelical Missions Information Service, Vol. VIII, No. 1 (March 1977), p. 4.
44. *News,* World Evangelization Information Service (March 24, 1977), p. 1.
45. Based on author's interview of John Stott, January 12-13, 1977, at Deerfield, Illinois.
46. *Ibid.*
47. LCWE subcommittee report, see "Executive Committee of the Lausanne Committee for World Evangelization."
48. Jack Dain, "After Lausanne," *EFAC Bulletin* (January 1975), p. 4.
49. "Minutes of the Meeting of the Lausanne Committee for World Evangelization," pp. 15, 16.
50. "Minutes of the Executive Committee of the Lausanne Committee for World Evangelization," p. 10.

51. Letter of Eric Maillefer to Samuel Odunaike, May 20, 1976 (Nairobi: Association of Evangelicals of Africa and Madagascar Archives).
52. Cf. letter to Eric Maillefer and AEAM Brethren by Gottfried Osei-Mensah (Chairman) and Michael Cassidy (Program Director), PACLA' 1976 (Nairobi: AEAM Archives); letter from S. O. Odunaike to Gottfried Osei-Mensah, June 4, 1976 (Nairobi: AEAM Archives); open letter of Eric Maillefer, Isaac Zokoue, Paul White to PACLA, June 29, 1976.
53. "Minutes of the Executive Committee of the Lausanne Committee for World Evangelization," p. 11.
54. *Ibid.*, p. 18.
55. *Breaking Barriers, Nairobi 1975*, The Official Report of the Fifth Assembly of the World Council of Churches, Nairobi, November 23-December 10, 1975, David M. Patton, editor (Grand Rapids, Mich.: Eerdmans, 1975), pp. 231-236.
56. Mortimer Arias, "That the World May Believe," *International Review of Missions*, Vol. LXV, No. 257 (January 1976), pp. 12-26.
57. *Ibid.*, pp. 30-33.
58. *Breaking Barriers, Nairobi 1975*, Patton, editor, pp. 18, 19.
59. *Ibid.*
60. Hendrikus Benkhof, "Berlin versus Geneva: Our Relationship with the 'Evangelicals,' " *Ecumenical Review*, Vol. XXVIII, No. 1 (January 1976), p. 80.
61. For an ecumenical study on baptism, the eucharist, and the ministry with origins reaching to an apostolic succession of permanence and "continuity of Christ's own mission in which the Church participates," see *One Baptism, One Eucharist and a Mutually Recognized Ministry*, Faith and Order Paper No. 73 (Geneva: WCC, 1975), p. 36.
62. *Ibid.*, p. 39.
63. *What Unity Requires*, Faith and Order Paper No. 77 (Geneva: WCC, 1976), Prepared for 1976 Central Committee Meeting.
64. "Report of the Core Group of World Mission and Evangelism," June 1-5, 1976, at Le Cenacle (Geneva: WCC, CWME), mechanically reproduced, p. 14.
65. *International Review of Missions*, Vol. LXIV, No. 255 (July 1975), p. 311.
66. *Ibid.*, p. 297.
67. Based on author's interview of Lukas Vischer, August 1976 at Geneva.
68. Don Emmanuel Lanne, "Evolution of the *Magisterium* in the Roman Catholic Church," in the March 1976 Faith and Order Study "How Does the Church Teach Authoritatively Today?" (Geneva: WCC, Commission on Faith and Order), mechanically reproduced, p. 34.
69. *Christianity Today* (July 8, 1977), pp. 30, 31.
70. J. E. M. Neale,"Onward from Keele," *Life of Faith* (April 2, 1977), p.3.
71. The "local church" is used both in its historical geographic sense as well as in the newer post-Vatican II "microcosmic sense" where the "fullness of the Church" is expressed in the individual church.
72. "Nottingham '77: Evangelicals Eye Unity," *Christianity Today* (May 20, 1977), n.p.
73. Lindsell, *The Battle for the Bible.*
74. See *Let the Earth Hear His Voice*, Douglas, editor, pp. 985-997.
75. Eugene L. Smith, "Report" (Geneva: WCC Archives), p. 7.

INDEX